HAND BOOK OF BIOFERTILIZERS & VERMICULTURE

LIST OF PUBLICATIONS/BOOKS PUBLISHED BY

ENGINEERS INDIA RESEARCH INSTITUTE 4449, NAI SARAK, MAIN ROAD, DELHI - 6 (INDIA)

Name of Books	Rs.	US$
EXPORT ORIENTED INDUSTRIES/PROCEDURES		
* Hand Book of Export Oriented Industries	1300/-	150
* Start Your Own Export Business (How To Export)	350/-	50
SPICES & COLD STORAGE		
* Hand Book of Spices & Packaging with Formulaes	650/-	90
* Start Your Own Cold Storage Unit	375/-	50
TEXTILE AUXILIARIES & CHEMICALS		
* Textile Auxiliaries and Chemicals with Processes and Formulations	950/-	100
PHARMACEUTICALS & DRUGS		
* Pharmaceuticals and Drugs Technology with Formulations	950/-	100
LEATHER & LEATHER PRODUCTS		
* Hand Book of Leather & Leather Products Technology	850/-	100
BIOTECHNOLOGY		
* Hand Book of Biotechnology	900/	100
AYURVEDIC MEDICINES		
* Ayurvedic & Herbal Medicines with Formulaes	750/-	90
* Hand book of Ayurvedic Medicines with Formulation	900/-	100
RUBBER & RUBBER INDUSTRIES		
* Rubber Chemicals & Processing Industries	400/-	60
* Technology of Rubber & Rubber Goods Industries	900/-	100
FIBRE GLASS MOULDING		
* Hand Book of Fibre Glass Moulding	450/-	60
MINERAL & MINERALS		
* Hand book of Minerals and Minerals based Industries	975/-	100
INDUSTRIAL/TRADE/IMPORTERS DIRECTORIES		
* World Importers Directory of Agro Based & Food Industries	800/-	100
* World Importers Yellow Pages (All Trade Buyer's Directory)	975/-	100
* Garments Export Industry of Delhi & Around Directory	390/-	60
* All India Industrial Directory	600/-	90

Name of Books	Rs.
INDUSTRIAL TRADE DIRECTORIES IN CD ROMS	
* **All India Directory of Food, Bakery, Food Processing, Beverages, Agro Products** Manufacturers, Exporters and Importers with Machineries Suppliers and Foreign Importers Over 40,000 Addresses with Phone, Fax, E-mail and Websites	975/-
* **All India Directory of Plastics and Polymers** Manufacturers, Exporters and Importers with Machineries Suppliers and Foreign Importers Over 26,000 Addresses with Phone, Fax, E-mail and Websites	975/-
* **World Importers Directory (International Buyers) and Indian Exporters** Directory over 1,00,000 Addresses with Phone, Fax, E-mail and Websites	1200/-
* **All India Directory of Textiles, Hosiery, Garments, Fabries, Thread, Yarn, Dyeing, Printing and Other Textile Products** Manufacturers, Exporters and Importers with Machineries Suppliers and Foreign Importers Over 20,000 Addresses with Phone, Fax, E-mail and Websites	975/-
* All India Manufacturers & Traders Directory	1250/-
* Delhi & Around Mfrs. & Exporters Directory	600/-
* All India Directory of Chemicals Industry	600/-
* Punjab Industrial Directory	600/-
* All India Directory of Machinery Manufacturers in India	750/-
PROJECT REPORTS IN CD-ROM	
* Lucrative New 92 Project Reports in Cd	16,500/-
* 44 Infotech/IT, Hospitality, Hospital, College, School & Club	11,000/-
* 23 Profitable Construction Projects	11,000/-
* 56 Agro Based & Food Process Projects	11,000/-
* 52 Food, Dairy, Bakery, Confectionery & Snacks Foods	11,000/-
* Profitable Plastics, Polymers & Allied 100 Projects	16,500/-
* 45 New Chemicals & Allied Project Reports	11,000/-
* 44 Textile, Garments, Hosiery & Allied	11,000/-
* 21 Dairy Farm and Milk Products	11,000/-
* 29 Paper, Pulp & Paper Converting Prod.	11,000/-
* 31 Essential Oils, Perfumes, Flavours & Aromatic Compounds	11,000/-
* 63 Profitable Packaging & Allied Projects	11,000/-
* 36 Profitable Printing & Allied Projects	11,000/-
* 28 Surgical & Disposable Medical Projects	11,000/-
* 99 Profitable Printing & Packaging Projects	16,500/-
* 42 Electroplating, Anodizing & Allied Proj.	11,000/-
* 20 Profitable Plantation & Cultivation Proj.	11,000/-
* Profitable 55 Products (Agro/Ind. Wastes)	12,000/-
* 35 Gums, Adhesives, Sealants & Resins	12,000/-
* 43 Iron, Steel, Casting, Fabrication, Wire Drawing & Rolling Mills Projects	12,000/-
* 54 Paint, Varnish, Solvents, Lacquers, Resins, Enamels, Pigments, Thinner & Powder Coating Projects	12,000/-
* 26 New Educational Projects (School etc.)	11,000/-

Send Draft in favour of "Engineers India Research Institute, Delhi" (Postage Rs. 50/- Extra)

ENGINEERS INDIA RESEARCH INSTITUTE

Regd. Off : 4449, Nai Sarak (B), Main Road, Delhi - 110 006 (India)

* Ph: 9811437895, 91-11-23918117, 23916431, 23840361 * Fax: 91-11- 23916431 * E-Mail : eirisidi@bol.net.in

YOU CAN DEPOSIT THE AMOUNT IN EIRI ACCOUNT WITH UTI BANK LTD. CA - 054010200006248

HAND BOOK OF BIOFERTILIZERS & VERMICULTURE

ENGINEERS INDIA RESEARCH INSTITUTE
4449, Nai Sarak, Main Road, Delhi-110 006 (India)
Ph.: 91-11-23918117, 23916431, 23840361, 9811437895
Fax :91-11-23916431, 23918117
* **E-Mail**: eirisidi@bol.net.in
* **Website**: www.eiriindia.org

Printed and Published by :

ENGINEERS INDIA RESEARCH INSTITUTE

4449, Nai Sarak, Main Road, Delhi-110 006 (India)

Ph.: 91-11-23918117, 23916431, 23840361, 9811437895

Fax :91-11-23916431, 23918117

* **E-Mail**: eirisidi@bol.net.in

* **Website**: www.eiriindia.org

ISBN : 81-89765-01-9

Printed in New Delhi (India)

Rs. 900

Printed and Published by Sudhir Gupta for "Engineers India Research Institute", 4449, Nai Sarak, Main Road, New Delhi-110 006 and Printed at Swastik Offset, Delhi

Preface

The book **'Hand Book of Biofertilizers & Vermiculture'** covers various methods including The Living Soil, Organic Sources and Dynamics, Vermiculture, Application of vermiculture Biotechnology, Composting of Agricultural and Industrial Wastes, Biological Fertilizers, Microbal Inoculants for Nitrogen Fixation, Mechanism and Estimation of Nitrogen Fixation, Biological Mobilization of Phosphorus , The Cyclic System of Nutrient Management, Perspectives, List of Bio-fertilizers Units in India and Abroad, Plant Economics of Agrofertilizer from Leaves, Plant Economics of Biofertilizers from Chicken Refuges, Oil Cakes, Bone Mills, Plant Economics of Biofertilizers from Cowdung & other Wastage, Plant Economics of Biofertilizers (Organic Fertilizers) from Garbage (MSW), Plant Economics of Organic Manure, Plant Economics of Sea Weed Liquid Fertilizer, Plant Economics of Vermi-Composting

The book has been written for the benefit and to prove an asset and a handy reference guide in the hands of new entrepreneurs and well established industrialists.

Director
ENGINEERS INDIA RESEARCH INSTITUTE
4449, Nai Sarak, Main Road, Delhi-110 006 (INDIA)
E-mail : eirisidi@bol.net.in, eiri@eiriindia.org

CONTENT AND SUBJECT INDEX

Chapter	Page No.

5.

COMPOSTING OF AGRICULTURAL AND INDUSTRIAL WASTES .... 74 - 90

6.

BIOLOGICAL FERTILIZERS ..... 91 - 107

7.

MICROBAL INOCULANTS FOR NITROGEN FIXATION ..... 108 - 177

Chapter	Page No.

1

The Living Soil

BIOLOGICAL MANAGEMENT OF SOIL FERTILITY

The practice of biological management of soil fertility is the old concept. It Is the use of biological resources of the ecosystem, particularly those of the soil itself, for the manipulation of soil fertility. It should be clear at the outset that this is not the same as organic farming (NRC, 1989). It does not eschew the use of inorganic inputs, but rather focuses on increasing the efficiency of their use by biological means. Emergence from the circumstances of nutritional deficiency and poverty that characterize the lives of many of the small-scale farmers of the world can only be achieved where there are sufficient resources to raise food productivity. Biological and physicochemical management are essentially based on integrated approach to soil fertility management.

According to Sanchez (1994) "we should rely on biological processes by adapting germplasm to adverse soil conditions, enhancing soil biological activity and optimizing nutrient cycling to minimize external inputs and maximize the efficiency of their use.

It is an ecological approach to soil fertility management, which has favored balanced farming systems. Swift *et al.* Tinsley and Darbyshire Pankhurst *et al.* (1994) and Woomer and Swift (1994) suggested in their review works that increased interest in a biological approach to soil fertility management will help to restore soil fertility and will solve many problems related to soil management.

The biological soil fertility management is an ecological approach for sustainable agriculture and is mainly concerned with the maintenance of yield, closely associated with desires to conserve natural resources, including a greater value accorded to maintenance of biodiversity. An increased efficient use of resource, including the need to utilize all available resources within economic limits will be realized in the long term as well as profitable in the short term too.

Sustainable Agriculture: Needs Of The Hour

There is an urgent need to develop farming techniques, which are sustainable from environmental, production, and socioeconomic points of view. The means to guarantee sufficient food production in the next decades and beyond is critical because modern agriculture production throughout the world does not appear to be sustainable in the long-term. The agricultural community is thus setting it hopes on sustainable agriculture, which will maintain the cycles of input-output and ecosystem balance. Definition form FAO (1988), seems appropriate in this contest.

Sustainable rural development is the management and conservation of the natural resource base, and the orientation of technological and institutional change in such a manner as to assure the attainment and continued satisfaction of human needs for the present and future generations. Such sustainable development, in the agriculture, forestry and fishers sectors, conserves land, water, plant and animal genetic resources, is environmentally non-degrading, technically appropriate, economically viable and socially acceptable.

Evolution of Sustainable Agriculture

In the 1960s and 1970s, a growing environmental agriculture movement evolved in response to increasing soil erosion, pesticide use, and groundwater contamination. Simultaneously, economic conditions for farmers were becoming more stressful and the number of family farms declined.

In 1980s, Wes Jackson of The Land Institute in Salina, K. S., began using the term *sustainable agriculture* to describe an alternative system of agriculture based upon resource conservation and quality of rural life.

While sustainable agriculture has become the umbrella under which, many of the above-mentioned alternatives farming systems fall, it is important to note that sustainable agriculture is really a long-term goal, not a specific set of farming practices. In temperate zones sustainable agriculture was defined as such:

Sustainable agriculture is a philosophy based on human goals and on understanding the long-term impact of our activities on the environment and on other species. Use of this philosophy guides our application of prior experience and the latest scientific advances to create integrated, resource-conserving, equitable farming systems. These systems reduce environmental degradation, maintain agricultural productivity, promote economic viability in both the short and long term and maintain stable rural communities and quality of life.

In this context, sustainable agriculture embraces all agricultural systems, striving to meet these criteria. Many aspects of modern conventional agriculture are included in sustainable agriculture, just as are many aspects of alternative farming systems.

One aspect of modern agriculture receiving a lot of attention in the sustainable agriculture discussion is the use of chemical inputs to supply fertility and pest control. White agriculture chemicals will continue to play an important role in American agriculture. Many farmers are looking at alternatives due to environmental, economical or regulatory reasons. In a transition to farming systems more reliant on biological methods of production, low-input farming serves as in intermediary step.

Sustainable agriculture emphasizes the conservation of its own resources. For a farm to be sustainable, it must produce adequate amounts of high-quality foods, be environmentally safe, and where appropriate, be profitable. Sustainable farms minimize their purchased inputs (fertilizers, energy and equipment) and rely, as much as possible on the renewable resources of the farm itself. This is especially important in the 90 per cent of farms that exist in the third world, where these inputs are often not available or affordable.

Agricultural eco-systems, unlike the natural ecosystems, are human manipulated ecosystems and regular and sometimes intense disturbances are a major part of economically viable agriculture management systems.

Sustainable agriculture is a complex issue associated with producing food while maintaining our biophysical resources including soil, water and biota with no adverse impacts on the wider environment. It should:

1. Maintain or improve the production of 'clean'food
2. Maintain or improve the quality of landscapes, which includes soils, water, biota and aesthetics.
3. Have minimal impact on the wide environment.
4. Be economically viable.
5. Be acceptable to society.

There are different concepts of sustainable agriculture, but none is generally accepted. It embraces several forms of non-conventional agriculture that are often called organic, alternative, ecological or low input. However, from economic and ecological perspectives, two basic criteria must be met if agriculture is to be sustainable in the long term. These are:

Sustainable farming uses some form of integrated pest management for pest control, and this can include the use of chemical pesticides that are not used by organic farmers. Thus, sustainable agriculture does not mean a return to the farming methods of the late 1800's. Rather, it combines traditional techniques that stress conservation with modern technologies, such as improved seed, modern equipment for low-tillage practices, integrated pest management that relies heavily on biological control principles, and weed control that depends on crop rotations. Sustainable farms try to use wind or solar energy instead of purchased energy, and use organic animal manure and nitrogen-fixing legumes as green manure to maintain soil fertility, as much as possible, thereby minimizing the need to purchase inputs from outside the farm. The use of genetically engineered crop strains is certainly not excluded by sustainable farming. The emphasis is on maintaining the environment, not on rules about what can or cannot be done. Profits from sustainable farms can exceed those of conventional farms.

Innovative farmers have developed many alternative farming methods and systems. These systems consist of a wide variety of integrated practices and methods suited to the specific needs, limitations, resource bases and economic conditions of different farms. To make wider adoption possible, however farmers need to receive information and technical assistance in developing new management skills.

Sustainable Livelihood

Scientists, the world over, have developed new technologies for application in the field. Over the years they have come to realize that these technologies must be integrated into existing farming systems, and have been going out into the fields to try to understand the problems and to see how the solutions are working. The large-scale adoption of technology-based agriculture can lead to a loss of knowledge of traditional farming methods, which were developed over many centuries and are adapted to the physical, biological and social environments of the people. The knowledge may be useful in devising strategies for sustaining agriculture in the developing regions. Traditional agricultural methods may be applicable for designing sustainable systems in the developed countries. In other words, the rich and sophisticated can learn a lot from the poor and unsophisticated.

During the past one-decade, there have been important changes in the thinking of agricultural scientists and policy makers concerned with agricultural research in developing countries. It is clear that the type of research that led to the Green Revolution has benefited the resource-rich farmers, whereas resource-poor families have been left behind.

It is increasingly recognized that who produces food and where it is produced may actually be as or more important than how much is produced?

If resource-rich farmers produce food that subsistence farmers cannot purchase, there is no improvement in the food situation. Population projections show that many rural areas with fragile ecologies will have to continue supporting large populations.

Food can be produced in a more sustainable way that protects the resource bases. The techniques are known, available and used by some farmers. Although more researches are still needed, however, these techniques could find more widespread use if given the proper incentives. Currently, the incentives (price supports, tax policies and export subsidies) favour industrial agriculture. Society needs to replace them with an incentive that favours sustainable agriculture. Because sustainable agriculture uses fewer inputs, this may cause some dislocation in the industrial sector and will be strongly resisted. In the

Third World, much research on indigenous farming methods is still needed, and the top-down approach to research needs to be replaced and/or supplemented by on-farm research.

According to Dr. M.S. Swaminathan, *the greening of agriculture requires the greening of both technology and public policy.* Producing more food and agricultural commodities from less land, water and energy is a task that will call for the integration of the best in modern technology, with the ecological strengths of traditional farming practices.

Making Of Sustainable Farming Systems

The shift from chemical to sustainable or ecological agriculture should, however, be gradual. A sudden switchover can spell disaster and discourage farmers from taking to this course. At least two to three seasons will be needed for the transition, and during the interim years the farmers could build up a sufficient organic base to fertilize the fields and improve the productivity of the soil. Once a state of ecological balance has been attained and there are a good number of beneficial organisms to check the explosion of pests and pathogens, crop yields of a high order can be ensured. The cost of cultivation can be brought down substantially as many farm-grown inputs can be integrated efficiently in the farming system.

Sustainable farming can be ecofriendly and profitable too. It is a self-reliant method and has to be an integrated system. Since it is a knowledge-intensive practice, therefore, one has to keep pace with the dynamics of nature to increase the biological productivity of the soil.

Since eco-farming uses several farm grown inputs, and less dependent on market purchased inputs, it is economically attractive to the growers. Case studies show that when a chemical far incurred about Rs. 11,250 towards the cost of cultivation per hectare of rice, an organic farm spent Rs. 10,590. Alternatively, if the biofertilizers and organic nutrient supplements such as neem cake are subsidized to extent the same monetary advantage as chemical fertilizers, the cost of ecological farming will come down significantly.

It has been observed that in chemical farming, fertilizers and plant protection chemicals accounted for nearly 30 per cent of the total cost. The cost of market purchased inputs in ecological farming was far less, and bulk of it went towards the purchase of neem cake.

In both the cases, the yield remained almost the same at 5,625 kg. paddy per hectare. The straw yield was eight tonnes. The net returns from the ecological farming system at the current cost of Rs. 3. 34 per kg. paddy is Rs. 8,197. 50. In chemical farming, the net profit is Rs. 7,500. If one gets a premium price for the poison-free, organically grown rice, the economic returns from the ecological returns from the ecological farming system will be highly encouraging. While the modern system of farming expended nearly 31,000 MJ of energy, the ecological farming method accounted for only 23,400 MJ. High energy inputs such as fertilizer, plant protection chemicals, herbicides and high speed diesel are substituted with biological inputs and low-energy human and cattle power. The output/input ratio in the case of modern farming is 3. 76, while in the case of ecological farming it is more than 4. 95.

Sustainable farming is more labour intensive, and several of its components such as vermicompositing, vermiwash, generation of botanical pesticides and rearing beneficial insects such as *Trichogramma* parasites, ladybird beetles, and spiders for release in the field as bio-control agents offer scope for unemployed and landless youth.

Group and community endeavour holds the key for successful implementation of ecological farming over larger community participation in pest control and rodent eradication will be rewarding. Even in the case of developing biofertilizers such as blue green algae and *Azolla* group action will pay rich dividends.

The above practices are not unique to biological management but common to farming practice through out the world. The use of biological inputs such as nitrogen fixing bacteria, mycorrhiza, or soil fauna as a means of enhancing the endemic biological activities are the means of biological soil management. Direct management is also achieved by the use of organic matter inputs—in effect a means of selectively feeding the heterotrophic biological populations of soil—a practice of very ancient origin but at times eschewed in modern agriculture. Equally direct but usually unintentional effects are also achieved by the use of pesticides, which may kill particular groups of soil organisms that are involved in processes of significance to soil fertility. Management techniques such as tillage and fertilization also influence the activity of the biota indirectly by altering the physical and chemical environment of the soil.

The success of biological management practices depends on following two pre-conditions, which must be satisfied:

1. The availability of a management practice that is practically and economically acceptable to the farmer.
2. The demonstration by the scientist that the practice leads to enhanced soil fertility.

MANAGEMENT OF ORGANIC INPUTS

Regulation of Nutrient Dynamics by Resource Quality Control

Biological management of soil fertility depends on the manipulation of organic inputs to the soil more than on any other practice. The organic matter supplies energy and nutrients to the soil biota to stimulate their activities and therefore promote soil fertility.

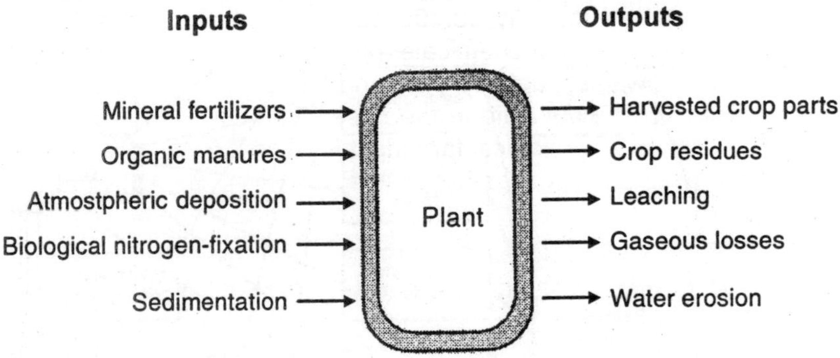

Fig. 1.1: The plant nutrient balance system

Organic inputs are processed by a complex web of soil organisms, however, biological management is based on the assumption that the outcomes are relatively consistent. These outcomes are multiple and include the generation of inorganic nutrients such as NH_4, NO_3, PO_4, and SO_4 from organic compounds of these elements; the synthesis of soil organic matter (SOM) from precursor compounds in the organic inputs; and modification of the physical structure of the soil as a result of stimulation of biological activities. Quantitative variation in these outcomes occurs as result of following variety of potential aspects:—

1. Organic inputs.
2. The diversity of organisms involved in the conversion processes.
3. The complexity of the interactions between them.
4. The biological activities are regulated by the quantity and quality of the organic manure added.
5. The environmental conditions under which the processing takes place (including climate and soil type).
6. The status of the soil community.

Increasing insight into the ways in which these factors regulate soil biological activity constitutes the main progress in achieving a predictive capacity for biological management of soil fertility. Most attention has been given to the use of organic mulches to supply nutrients such as nitrogen and to the possibilities of utilizing *resource quality control* as a tool for managing nutrient availability.

Resource quality refers to the regulatory effect of the chemical composition of an organic resource on its rate and pattern of decomposition and nutrient release.

Early studies of decomposition processes demonstrated the importance of N concentration and C: N ration as determinants of the N-supplying capability of plant residues.

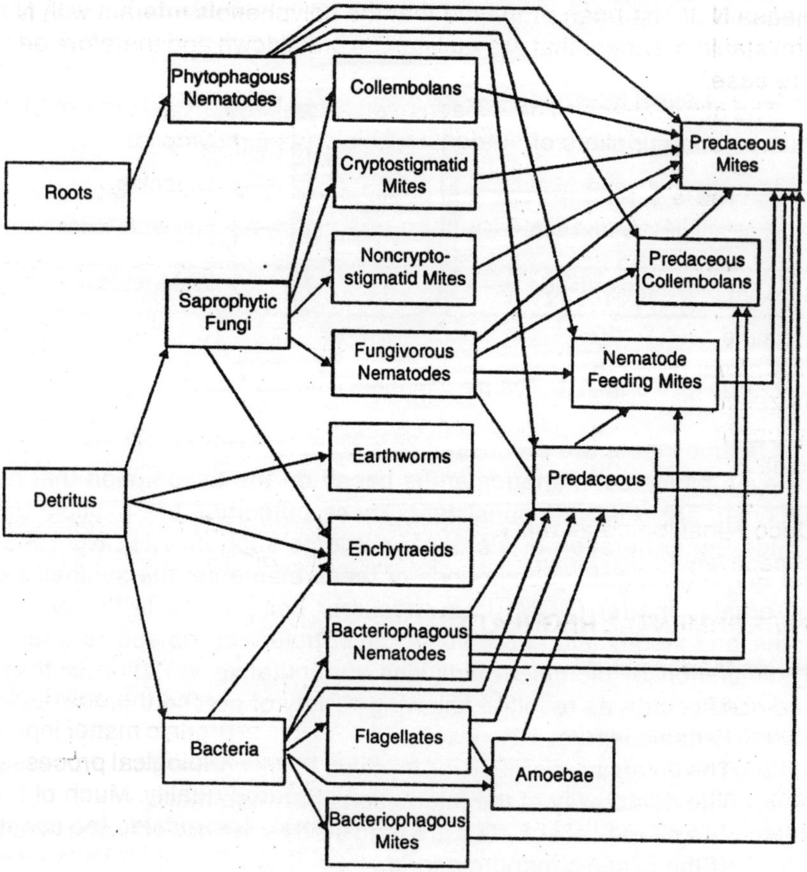

Fig. 1.2: A crop residue (detritus)-based soil food web from a calcareous soil under arable cropping in the Netherlands. Under conventional tillage the bacteria-based food web is dominant; under reduced tillage the fungal and earthworm paths are more prominent

Studies in natural ecosystems subsequently demonstrated that other indices such as the lignin concentration or the lignin: N ratio provided a better predictor of N release patterns.

Berg and McClaugherty (1987) suggested that N is not released from forest litters until decomposition of lignin commences, and others have also stressed the importance of the more recalcitrant components as regulators of decomposition rate and nutrient release.

Polyphenols have also been implicated as regulators of N release in materials that, despite being nutrient-rich and low in lignin, are slow to release N. It has been proposed that the polyphenols interact with N to form stable polymers that are resistant to breakdown and therefore delay N release.

The above theories have been used to evaluate organic residues as sources and suppliers of nutrients within cropping systems.

Table 1.1: Chemical Composition, Decomposition Rate, and N-Release Rate for Various Agricultural Residues

Material	Lignin (%)	Polyphenol (%)	C/N	kDM[a]	kN[a]
Gliricidia	12	1.62	13	0.127	0.152
Rice straw	5	0.55	42	0.106	0.052
Maize stover	7	0.56	43	0.085	0.077
Lecuaena	13	5.02	13	0.062	0.055
Acioa	48	4.09	28	0.010	0.001

[a]Decomposition constant (week^{-1}) for dry matter (DM) and nitrogen (N), respectively. FromTian.G. et al., 1992. *Soil Biol. Biochem.,24:* 1051-1060.

ENVIRONMENTAL REGULATION OF ORGANIC

Matter Management

Organic matter chemistry—resource quality—is not the only factor needed to make reliable predictions of the effects of organic matter inputs. The physicochemical environment has control over biological processes from a higher level in the hierarchy than resource quality. Much of this regulation such as that deriving from the climate lies outside the control of the farmer. There are practices, however, that can be manipulated so as to *environmentally tune* the influence of organic inputs on soil biological processes. These include the location and timing of the application of organic matter. It is well established, for instance, that incorporation of residues in the soil, as opposed to surface mulching, can accelerate decomposition processes significantly and thus alter the dynamics of nutrient availability. The breaking up of the residues during tillage may be a factor in this effect, as well as the transfer of the organic matter into the more favorable environment below the soil surface.

It is well established that cultivation changes the composition, diversity, abundance, activity of the soil community and a variety of farming practices involve the management of organic inputs. For instance, there is now a considerable body of data relating to differences in soil biological populations and processes in minimum-tillage systems as compared with conventional tillage. These effects have been shown to be dramatic in relation to many groups of soil fauna, including such keystone groups as earthworms, with subsequent benefits gained in low-till systems to the physical structure and water regime of the soil. The potential exists to utilize these practices to manipulate the biological community and thence to determine the outcome of decomposition processes. A major challenge is to determine pragmatically the extent to which these "fine-tuning" factors of microenvironment and community structure need to be taken into account when developing management systems.

ORGANIC-INORGANIC INTERACTIONS

Nitrogen

The use of organic inputs of different qualities to improve the efficiency of nutrient transfer to the crop will not be a practice of any significance if the total amount of nutrient available is insufficient to satisfy the needs for production. Significant input of N to replace that removed in harvest may be achieved in farming systems incorporating N-fixing species. The amount of recyclable N can be enhanced in tree-based systems such as traditional fallow rotations, savanna-based mixed farming systems, or modern agroforestry practices. These systems have the additional advantage of mobilizing other nutrients such as P and K by deep capture by tree roots from lower soil layers.

Phosphorus

In a wide range of tropical environments the most critical element limiting production is phosphorus. While mycorrhizal infection can increase the efficiency of P uptake, there is no biological means of increasing the absolute amount of available P in an ecosystem. P in the form of inorganic fertilizer is thus essential for increased productivity in a large range of tropical farming systems. Other nutrients may also need to be supplied in this form as well. One approach advocated for this is management that incorporates both inorganic and organic inputs of nutrients.

Nutrient Mixture

There is a long history of agronomic research on crop response to the application of mixtures as compared with single sources of nutrients. It has been observed that mixtures of organic and inorganic fertilizers result in increased yields beyond those achieved with inorganic fertilizer alone; in others the yields are diminished. High-quality inputs, releasing nutrients early in the process of decomposition, will serve to supplement inorganic fertilizers rather than competing with them. The most effective response of the crop to fertilization, whether from organic or inorganic sources, may come if the maximum demand for nutrients from the plant coincides in time and space with the availability of nutrients in the soil.

NEED FOR ORGANIC INPUTS

Organic farming is the pathway that leads us to live in harmony with nature. Organic agriculture is the key to a sound development and a sustainable environment. It minimizes environmental pollution and the use of non-renewable natural resources. It conserves soil fertility and soil erosion through implementation of appropriate conservation principles.

Several reasons have been emphasized for the need of organic agriculture, like limited land holdings, poor socio-economic conditions of farmers, rise in input cost etc. The broadest view shows two major reasons viz., population and environment, emphasized the ultimate need for ecofriendly technologies. FAO estimates that by the year 2000 the global population will be 25 per cent higher than in the mid 1980s and that 90 per cent of this population increase will be in the developing countries like India. It will be necessary to increase the supply of food and other agricultural products to meet their needs. At the moment, many of the methods being used to increase production are damaging to natural resources and the environment and farmers are supposed to invest heavily into inputs to improve yields and productivity. Further, the produce from organic farming has become inevitable. The food containing pesticides and other chemicals are increasingly made obvious by many research studies revealing the presence of pesticide residues in eatables. About one million people suffered from pesticides poisoning and 20,000 die every year due to the toxic effects of these chemicals world-wide but the crop loss due to pest is still 15,000 crores, apart from killing a portion of the human population by the same pesticide use. This perspective is also one of the needs for organic approach to farming. In order to avoid the deleterious effects of synthetic chemical fertilizers and pesticides, organic agriculture is needed as an alternative to provide ecologically safe methods of farming.

LONG-TERM EFFECTS

Organic matter has long-term effects. The strongest evidence for nutrient transfer from input to plant is obtained in studies using isotopically labeled material. In the few examples available, the N use efficiency of plant residues by a first crop is low, in the order of 15 per cent for legume residues and 5 per cent for cereal straw residues, but there is much variation. This is broadly comparable with, or slightly lower than, the N use efficiency of inorganic fertilizer in the same environment. In the examples given there is, however, a consistently greater partitioning of N from the organic material to SOM than to the plant. This suggests that residual effects are likely to be more important than those in immediate seasons. There is a substantial body of evidence to substantiate this point from long-term experiments in Africa and elsewhere (Swift et al., 1994).

Optimal development of integrated nutrient use systems will be achieved when it is possible to predict the outcome of a given strategy for use and management of nutrient resources (both organic and inorganic) over the long and short term.

Table 1.2: Partitioning of N added in labeled plant residues to the subsequent Crop and to soil organic matter

Authors	Crop (%)	Organic matter (%)
Ladd et al., 1981	11-17	72-78
Janzen et al., 1990	14	21-40
Ng Kee Kwong et al., 1987	11-14	73-84

Source: Myers, R.J.K. et al., 1994. The *Biological Management of Tropical Soil Fertility,* Woomer, P.L. and Swift, M.J., Eds., John Wiley & Sons, London, 81-117.

THE FARMING SYSTEMS CONTEXT

The history of agricultural development over the last several decades contains many examples of failures in adoption or sustenance of technologies that were judged scientifically sound (Lal, 1987). The resource management technology may be failure due to water-management schemes in the inland, minimum tillage practices, poor take-up of improved clearing methods, soil conservation methods, and spread of alley cropping. The other reasons for failure to adopt or persist with technology are social, cultural or economic factors as to technical deficiencies. This necessitates an approach to technology development and transfer than integrates the criteria used by the farmer in deciding the actions, as well as those assumed in the scientist's models.

Soil management is only one small component of a farmer's spectrum of activity. The knowledge and perceptions of soil-based constraints should be combined with a holistic appraisal. Farmer's should have balanced approach between various alternatives based on whole range of available environmental, biological, and economic information.

Technological change is thus more likely to succeed in terms of both adoption and of impact on production when it is adapted to farmers' circumstances rather than merely optimized in terms of scientists' criteria. This is most likely to be achieved when scientists and farmers work together throughout the research and development process.

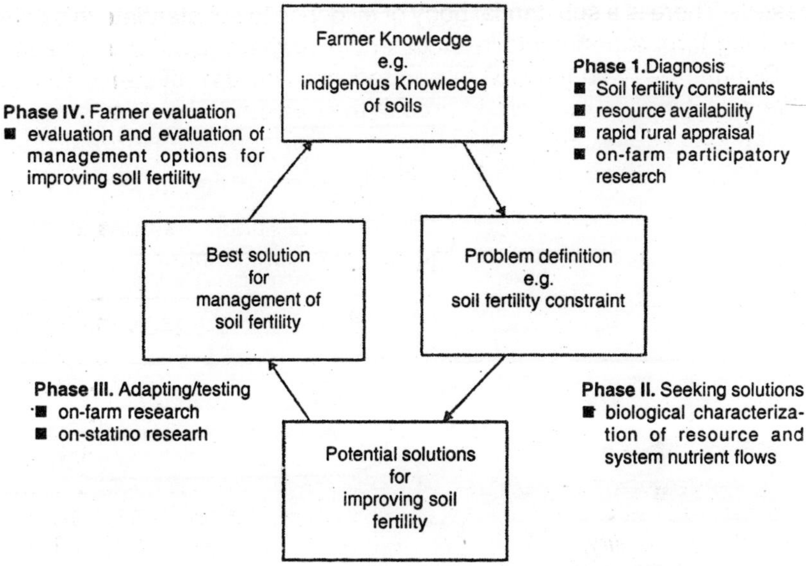

Fig. 1.3 : The *farmer-back-to farmer* approach to agricultural problem identification and solution as applied to soil fertility research.

Above figure illustrates stages in a research processes that is initiated by joint diagnosis of soil fertility problems. This information, based both on farmers' perceptions and on biophysical and socioeconomic characterization of the farming system. It should be used to guide scientific investigation of the opportunities for improvement in soil management practices.

The process-and-system approach places farmer decision making at the center of the technology development process, highlighting the need for detailed characterization of the environmental context that influences those decisions.

The capacity for increasing and sustaining productivity through improved soil fertility management is subject to a variety of limits of physicochemical, biological economic, social, and cultural dimensions. The determination of these limits, the establishment of interactions—including hierarchical relationships, and the opportunities for modifying them is one of the major Purposes of system characterization.

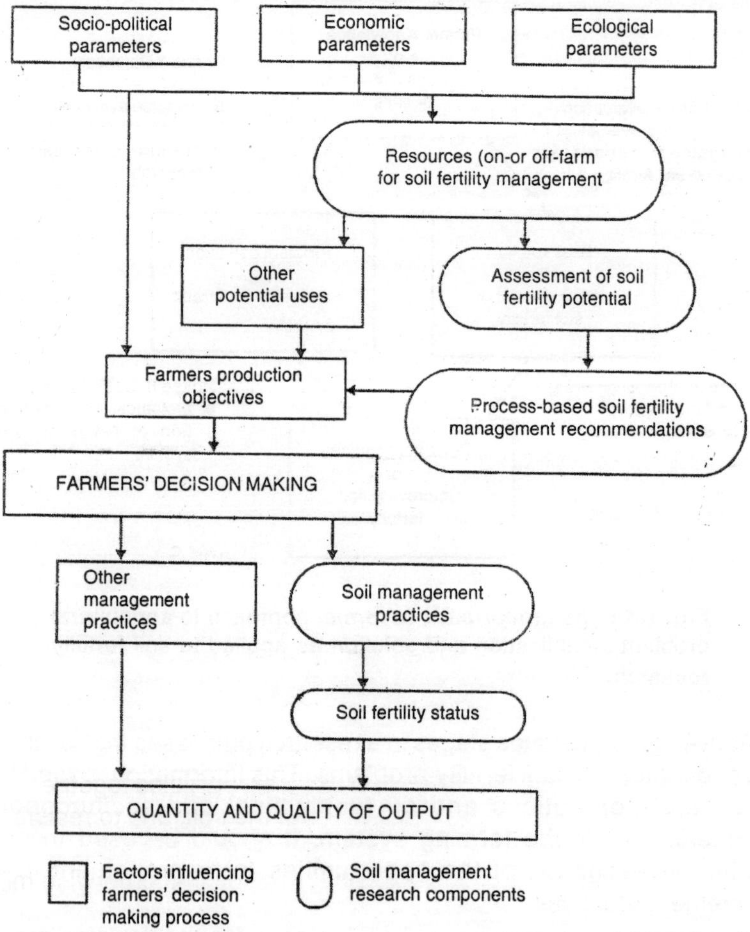

Fig. 1.4: Integration of the research results for biological management of soil fertility with system level information on farmers' decision making.

2

Organic Sources and Dynamics

Organic matter is the food for most of the flora and fauna responsible for soil biological activities. Proper and ensured management of soil organic matter is the prime requirement for an efficient soil biological system.

Farmers since ancient times have recognized significant benefits of soil organic matter to crop productivity. These benefits have been the subject of controversy for centuries and some are still debated today. The following list includes many of the recognized benefits of soil organic matter:—

1. It serves as a slow-release source of N, P, and S for plant nutrition and microbial growth.
2. It possesses considerable water-holding capacity, and thereby helps to maintain the water regime of the soil.
3. It acts as a buffer against changes in pH of the soil.
4. Its dark colour contributes to absorption of energy from the sun and heating of the soil.
5. It acts as *cement* for holding clay and silt particles together, thus contributing to the crumb structure of the soil, and to resistance against soil erosion.
6. It binds micronutrient metal ions in the soil that otherwise might be leached out of surface soils.
7. Organic constituents in the humic substances may act as plant-growth stimulants.

The term **soil organic matter** is generally used to represent the organic constituents in the soil, excluding undecayed plant and animal tissue, their partial decomposition products, and the soil biomass. Thus, this term includes:—

1. Identifiable high-molecular-weight organic materials such as polysaccharides and proteins.
2. Simpler substances such as sugars, amino acids, and other small molecules, and humic substances.

Soil organic "matter is frequently said to consist of humic substances and non-humic substances. Non-humic substances are all those materials that can be placed in one of the categories of discrete compounds such as polysaccharides and sugars, proteins and amino acids, fats, simple organic acids, and so on; humic substances are the other, unidentifiable components.

The term **humic substance** refers to an operationally defined, heterogenous mixture of naturally occurring organic materials. These substances are ubiquitous in nature and arise from the decay of plant and animal residues in the environment. Humic substances are generally classified into humic acid, fulvic acid, and humin on the basis of their solubility in water as a function of pH.

ORGANIC MATERIALS USE

Organic manures, including animal manures, crop residues, green manures, and composts were traditionally and preferentially used in developing countries until the I960's when inorganic chemical fertilisers began to gain popularity.

The shift away from organic recycling practices also served to re-emphasize the value of, and need for, organic amendments for short-term and long-term improvement of cultivated soils and maintenance of soil productivity. Without regular additions of adequate amounts of organic materials to soils, there is often a concomitant increase in nutrient runoff, erosion, and gradual deterioration of soil physical properties.

Environment pollution has also become an international concern. Proper processing and recycling of organic wastes and residues as resources for agriculture can greatly reduce environmental pollution. Additional benefits include improved public health, conservation of resources, and better appearance of both urban and rural communities.

Composting to Enhance the Usefulness and Acceptability of Organic Materials

Composting is one way in which some of the problems associated with the utilization of various organic wastes (e.g., odors, human pathogens, and storage and handling constraints) can be resolved. Composting is an ancient practice whereby farmers have converted organic wastes into resources that provide nutrients to crops and enhance soil tilth, fertility, and productivity. Through composting, organic wastes are decomposed, nutrients are made available to plants, pathogens are destroyed, and malodours are abated. Composts provide a more stabilized form of organic matter than do raw wastes, and can vastly improve the physical properties of soils. For example, addition of sludge compost to sandy soils will increase their ability to retain water and render them less droughty. In heavy-textured clay soils, the added organic matter will increase permeability and water infiltration and clay soils have been shown to reduce soil compaction, lower the bulk density, and increase the rooting depth.

The value of organic materials as fertilisers and soil conditioners is often misunderstood and has been the source of some controversy. The simplest and most common means of estimating the value of organic amendments is by assessing the current market value of the potentially available plant nutrients they contain. Usually this is done in terms of their macronutrient content, i.e., N, P, and K.

Special Management Practices for Utilization of Organic Materials on Land

Special management practices may be needed if we are to obtain the full value of organic wastes as soil amendments and as sources of plant nutrients. For example, the value of organic materials as fertilisers is increased if nutrient release through decomposition and mineralization coincides with the crop's nutrient demand curve. The nutrient release pattern of organic materials can be controlled to some extent by proper timing of application, pretreatment methods such as composting, and by the method of application. For example, certain organic materials may decompose more slowly if left on the soil surface or concentrated as bands in the soil than if mixed thoroughly in the tillage layer.

BULKY ORGANIC MANURES/ANIMAL MANURES/ CROP RESIDUES/COMPOSTS

Agricultural wastes (animal manures and crop residues or mixtures of the two) are now considered quite an important component for horticultural crop production especially that based on organic systems. Agricultural wastes can now be considered to include crop after harvest and primary processing, tree residues organic/plant residues from social forestry, animal excreta and processing left over from the slaughter houses and agro-industrial wastes. Thus, agricultural wastes comprise all organic wastes produced and disposed of or used in primary agricultural production. Of course, these materials are essentially by-products of production rather than wastes in the strict sense of the word. With the advent of abundant and relatively inexpensive chemical fertilizers, agricultural manures became agricultural wastes, and what was formerly an asset is now often regarded as a disposal problem. Traditionally, . cattle, pigs, and poultry were fed on free range or housed in relatively small numbers. Today, in most developed countries, intensive animal production is now being practiced where increasing numbers of livestock are being fed on fewer larger farms.

TYPES OF BULKY ORGANIC MANURES

Farmyard manure (FYM), farm compost, town compost, night soil, sludge and green manures are bulky in nature and supply large quantities of organic matter but small quantities of plant nutrients in comparison to the inorganic fertilisers.

Farmyard Manure

Good-quality farmyard manure is perhaps the most valuable organic matter applied to a soil. It is the most commonly used organic manure in most countries of the world. It consists of a decomposed mixture of cattle dung, the bedding used in the stable and any remnants of straw and plant stalks fed to cattle. It is one of the most important agricultural by-products. Unfortunately more than 50 per cent of the cattle dung produced in India is burnt as fuel and is thus lost to agriculture.

Table 2.1: Average nutrient content of bulky manures

Manure	Percentage content		
	Nltrogen(N)	Phosphoric acid(P_2O_2)	Potash (K_2O)
Animal refuse			
Cattle dung, fresh	0.3-0.4	0.1-0.2	0.1-0.3
Horse dung, fresh	0.4-0.5	0.3-0.4	0.3-0.4
Sheep dung, fresh	0.5-0.7	0.4-0.6	0.3-1.0
Nightsoil, fresh	1.0-1.6	0.8-1.2	0.2-0.6
Poultry manure, fresh	1.0-1.8	1.4-1.8	0.8-0.9
Raw sewage, fresh	2.0-3.0	-	-
Sewage sludge, dry	2.0-3.5	1.0-5.0	0.2-0.5
Sewage sludge, activated dry	4.0-7.0	2.1-4.2	0.5-0.7
Cattle urine	0.9-1.2	tr.	0.5-1.0
Horse urine	1.2-1.5	tr.	1.3-1.5
.Human urine	0.6-1.0	0.1-0.2	0.2-0.3
Sheep urine	1.5-1.7	tr.	1.8-2.0
Wood ashes			
Ash, coal	0.73	0.45	0.53
Ash, household	0.5-1,9	1.6-4.2	2.3-12.0
Ash, wood -	0.1-0.2	0.8-5.9	1.5-36.0
Farm, factory and habitation wastes			
Rural compost, dry	0.5-1.0	0.4-0.8	0.8-1.2
Urban compost, dry	0.7-2.0	0.9-3.0	1.0-2.0
Farmyard manure, dry	0.4-1.5	0.3-0.9	0.3-1.9
Filter-press cake	1.0-1.5	4.0-5.0	2.0-7.0
Plant residues			
Rice hulls	0.3-0.5	0.2-0.5	0.3-0.5
Groundnut husks	1.6-1.8	0.3-0.5	1.1-1.7

Manure	Percentage content		
	Nitrogen(N)	Phosphoric acid(P_2O_2)	Potash (K_2O)
Straw and stalks			
Pearlmillet	0.65	0.75	2.50
Banana, dry	0.61	0.12	1.00
Cotton	0.44	0.10	0.66
Sorghum	0.40	0.23	2.17
Maize	0.42	1.57	1.65
Paddy	0.36	0.08	0.71
Tobacco	1.12	0.84	,0.80
Pigeonpea	1.10	0.58	1.28
Wheat	0.53	0.10	1.10
Sugarcane trash	0.35	0.10	0.60
Tobacco dust	1.10	0.31	0.93
Tree leaves, dry			
Calotropis gigantean	0.35	0.12	0.36
Careya arborea	1.67	0.40	2.20
Cassia auriculata	0.98	0.12	0.67
Dillenia pentagyna ‘	1.34	0.50	3.20
Madhuca indica	1.66	0.50	2.00
Pengamia pinnata	3.69	2.41	2.42
Pterocarpus marsupium	1.97	0.40	2.90
Terimalia chebula	1.46	0.35	1.35
Terminalia paniculata	1.70	0.40	1.60
Terminalia tomentosa	1.39	0.40	1.80
Xylia dolabriformis	1.37	0.30	1.61
Green manures, fresh			
Cowpea *(Vigna catjang)*	0.71	0.15	0.58
Sesbania aculeata	0.62		
Cluster-bean *(Cyamopsis tetragonoloba)*	0.34	-	-
Horse-gram *(Dolichos biflorus)*	0.33		
Mothbean (*Vigna aconitifolia)*	0.80		
Greengram *(Vigna radiata)*	0.72	0.18	0.53
Sunnhemp *(Crotalaria juncea)*	0.75	0.12	0.51
Blackgram *(Vigna mungo)*	0.85	0.18	0.53

COMPOSTED MANURE

Another method of augmenting the supplies of organic matter is the preparation of compost from farmhouse, and cattle-shed wastes of all types. Composting has been advocated and adopted extensively during the past 25 years. Composting is the process of reducing vegetable and animal refuse (rural or urban) to a quickly utilizable condition for improving and maintaining soil fertility. Studies conducted in India and elsewhere have shown that good organic manure similar in appearance and fertilizing value to cattle manure can be produced from waste materials of various kinds, such as cereal straws, crop stubbles, cotton stalks, groundnut husk, farm weeds and grasses, leaves, leaf-mould, house refuse, wood ash, litter, urine-soaked earth from cattle-sheds and other similar substances. These materials are rich in cellulose and other readily decomposable carbohydrates, and have a carbon-nitrogen ratio of 40 or more to 1. The direct application of such undecomposed, low-nitrogen organic matter as manure brings about a temporary deficiency of mineral nutrients (specially nitrates and ammonium compounds) in the soil by stimulating the growth of microorganisms, which in turn, compete with crop plants for available nitrogen, phosphorus and other elements. Hence, before using them as manure, it is necessary.to compost or partially decompose them. This process lowers the carbon-nitrogen ratio to about 10 or 12 to 1.

URBAN COMPOST

In recent years, large-scale composting of town-refuse and night-soil in properly constructed trenches away from human habitations has been taken up successfully by the municipal bodies of many large and small towns. Trenches, 1 to 1.2 m wide, 75 cm deep and of convenient length, are filled with successive layers of night-soil, town refuse and earth, in this order. The compost gets ready in about three months.

BULKY ORGANIC MANURES

Farm Yard Manure (FYM)

The manure is produced in the farm chiefly with animal excreta. It is also called as stable manure, barn manure, dung and cattle manure. The manure consists of a mixture of cow dung, the liquid excreta or urine, the bedding material used in the stable and any remnants of straw and plant stalks fed to cattle. The quantity of dung excreted by an animal depends on several factors such as age, breed and condition of the animal and the nature of food eaten by it. The average excretion of urine per cattle per day is 7-8 litres. Average daily dung excretion pattern is give in Table 2.2. On an average . well rotten FYM contains 0.5 per cent N, 0.2%, P_2O_5 and 0.5 per cent K_2O.

Table 2.2. Daily excretion by animals

Animal	Dung (kg/ha)
Cattle	
Young stock	4.90
Adult female	11.30
Adult male	15.60
Buffalloes	
Young stock	5.70
Adult female	14.80
Adult male	14.90

Manure preparation: Trenches of 6 m long, 2 m wide and 1 m deep are dung. The material consisting of dung and urine soaked in it is collected daily and placed in these trenches. Additions are normally applied in sections of one meter length. When each section is filled upto a height of about 0.5 m above the ground level, the top of the heap is rounded off to the shape of a dome and plastered with slurry of cow dung and earth. Before plastering, it is important to apply 4-5 buckets of water in the pit. Plastering conserves moisture and nitrogen and also prevents housefly nuisance. The manure pit should be protected from sun and rain. The manure becomes ready for use in about 4-5 months after plastering. It is possible to obtain 5-6 tonnes of good quality manure per year per head of cattle. Normally 10-25 cart loads of manure is applied per hectare. A cartload of manure measuring 9 cubic' meters weighs about 0.5 tonnes.

Compost

Decemposed plant residues/farm wastes are known as farm compost. The waste materials that are available in urban areas can be made into compost called urban compost. The processes of composting facilitates narrowing down the C : N ratio of the material to 10 or 12:1 . The nutrient content of compost is 1.01 per cent N, 0.5 per cent P_2O_5 and 0.8-0.9% K_2O. Applications of partially or fully decomposed materials quicken the nutrient release to the crops.

Methods of composting: There are two methods of compost making: aerobic and anaerobic.

Aerobic method

A pit of one m deep, 2 m width and of convenient length is prepared. Organic wastes consisting of a mixture of crop wastes, weeds, leaves etc., that are collected in the farm are spread to a layer of 0.2 to 0.3 m deep. Cow dung solution is uniformly sprinkled to the top of the refuse. If the refuse is too dry, water is sprinkled over the material equal in weight of the refuse. Urine, earth ashes and bone meal may also be spread in a thin layer. This process is continued till the heap rises to about 0.5 m over the ground. After a month, the heap is turned over, mixed well and refilled adding water if necessary. Two more turnings are given, one at the end of the second month and the other after the third month. Sufficient water should be added in each turning over. Decomposition is ordinarily completed within 4-5 months. In places of heavy rainfall or where the water table is high the compost heaps may be prepared above ground level instead of pits.

Anaerobic method

A pit of convenient size (4.5 x 1.5 x 1.0 m) is prepared. Every day collections of mixed farm residues are spread in the pit to a thin layer. A mixture of fresh cow dung, ash and water is sprinkled and compacted. The pit is filled till the raw material stands about 0.5 m above the ground. Later it is plastered to a thickness of 2.5 cm with mud and cow dung. Plastering helps to prevent housefly nuisance. Decomposition is completed within 4-5 months.

ENRICHMENT OF MANURE AND COMPOST

The importance of organic manure is very well established, However, the non-availability of these materials in adequate quantities restricts the farmers to apply the manure at its recommended dose. An alternate method has been developed to reduce the quantity, at the same time maintaining its manurial value. The method is known as enrichment of FYM/compost. By this technique, the nutrient availability of compost can be enhanced by addition of inorganic fertilizers while composting.

Enriched farmyard manure

Well-decomposed and finely sieved FYM is required at 750 kg./ha. Along with this, super phosphate (at the recommended *dose* of P_2O_5 for each crop) is thoroughly mixed. The heap is plastered with red earth-cow dung paste. Adequate care is required to seal the cracks whenever they appear. After about a month, the manure is ready for application. At the time of application, recommended dose of N and K as urea and muriate of potash respectively are added and mixed thoroughly. The enriched manure should be applied in the seed furrow. This is particularly recommended for the dry lands.

Enrichment of compost with microbial inoculants

Compost prepared by traditional method is usually low in nutrients apd there is need to improve its quality. Enrichment of compost using low cost N fixing and phosphate solubilising microbes is one of the possible ways of improving nutrient status of the product. It could be achieved by introducing microbial inoculants, which are more efficient than the native strains associated with substrate materials. Both the nitrogen fixing and phosphate solubilising microbes are more exacting in their physiological and ecological requirements and it is difficult to meet these requirements under natural conditions. The only alternative is to enhance their inoculum potential in the composting mass. Studies conducted at IARI, New Delhi, showed that inoculation with *Azotobacter/Azospirillum* and phosphate solubilizing culture in the presence of 1 per cent rock phosphate is a beneficial input to obtain good quality compost rich in nitrogen (1.8 %). The humus content was also higher in materials treated with microbial inoculants.

Super digested compost

Application of super phosphate at 5 per cent over the raw waste materials during composting improves the manurial value of compost. Application of this compost to acidic, calcareous and heavy soils increases the P availability.

Sheep and goat manure

The droppings of sheep and goat provide a valuable manure. Penning of sheep and goat in the fallow field is the common practice in India. It has been estimated that by stocking 1000 sheep for a night will add about 2 tonnes of droppings. The manure contains 3 per cent N, 1 per cent P_2O_5 and 2 per cent K_2O.

Poultry manure

The excretion of birds contains both solid and liquid parts and hence there is no urine loss. The decomposition rate of the poultry manure is very quick. The manure should not be exposed to sun since there is 50 % N loss within a month. The fresh droppings contain 75 % moisture, 1.5 per cent N, 1.2 per cent P_2O_5 and 0.5 per cent K_2O.

SEWAGE AND SLUDGE

Sewage has two components, the solid portion called sludge and the liquid part called sewage water. Major portion of the suspended solids and effluents (99%) in the sewage is removed by settling. The sludge is latter collected separately, dried and used as manure. Under Indian conditions, the sludge on an average contains 1.5 - 3.5 per cent N, 0.8-4 % P_2O_5 and 0.3 - 0.6 per cent K_2O.

Once the solid portion or sludge is removed, sewage water is known as treated effluent. This can be used for irrigation. Since the sewage water is in concentrated form, therefore, it is important to dilute it with water in the ratio of 1 : 1. It has been reported that irrigation with sewage effluent may result in improved soil structure and water holding capacity by decreasing the bulk density and hydraulic conductivity. Though there are many beneficial effects of sewage effluent, it may also contain harmful bacteria. The municipal sewage, particularly, may contain high amount of heavy metals.

NIGHT SOIL POUDRETTES

Night soil contains appreciable amount of N. It can be profitably converted into useful manure known as Poudrette. Dehydration of night soil can be done as such, or admixture of absorbing materials like soil, ash, charcoal and saw dust. Among the materials, saw dust is the most effective one which can be very well used. Saw dust has high dehydrating capacity as well as the Property of absorbing foul smell. About 40-50 % of saw dust could be added with the night soil. By this way, it is possible to get a dry, acidic poudrette which may contain 2-3 % N. Odourless manure can also be obtained by admixing night soil with equal volume of ash and 10 per cent of powdered charcoal. The poudrette produced by this way contains 1.3 per cent N, 2.8 per cent P_2O_5,4.1 per cent K_2O and 24.2 per cent lime.

CONCENTRATED ORGANIC MANURE

Oil cakes

After extraction of oil from the oilseeds, the residues are called as oil cakes. The edible oil cakes from groundnut and sesame are mainly used as cattle feed. The non-edible oil cakes viz., *neem, karanj, mahua,* etc. are used as organic manures. The powdered oil cakes should be incorporated into the soil before planting for quick decomposition. Effect of oil cake is improved when applied afresh compared to dry form. It has been shown that neem cake application reduces the pest incidence. Oil cakes contain high amount of N and small quantities of P and K they have low C : N ratio (3-15) which helps in releasing the nutrients quickly. Unlike bulky organic manures, they have no residual effect. Oil cakes are sometimes adulterated with earth, sand, hulls or husks and the manurial value is lowered.

Meal group of manures

Bone meal, horn and hoof meal and blood meals are examples for meal group of manures. These are quick acting and can be used in a wide range of soils and crops.

Bone meal is obtained by crushing the bones of animals. When treated with steam, it is known as *steamed bone meal.* This is a good source of phosphorus. It contains about 1-2 per cent N and 25-30 per cent P_2O_5. Bone meal is best suited for acidic soils.

Hoof and horn-meals are obtained by grinding hoof and horns of dead animals. They contain 10-15 % N, 1.0 % P_2O_5 and 2.5 % lime.

Blood meal has high N content (10-12 %) and is obtained from the slaughter-houses. Since the C-N ratio is very narrow (1: 3-4), it decomposes and supplies nutrient rapidly for crops.

Table 2.3: Nutrient content of important oil cakes

Oil Cakes	Nutrient content (%)		
	N	P	K
Karanj(Pongamia glabra)	4.0	1.0	1.3
Mahua(Bassia latifolia)	2.5	0.8	1.8
Neem(Melia azadirachta)	5.2	1.0	1.4

Crop residues

Residues left out after the harvest of the economic portions are called crop residues/straw. In the developing countries like India, they are mostly used as cattle feed. In the developed countries, harvesting is done using combine harvester and hence the straw cannot be used as cattle feed. They are generally burnt in the field itself. Straw has good manurial value since it contains appreciable amount of plant nutrients. On an average, cereal straw and residues contain about 0.5 % N, 0.6 % P_2O_5 and 1.5 % K_2O. The crop residues can be recycled by way of incorporation, compost making or mulch material.

Agro-industrial wastes

Agro-industrial wastes are available in substantial quantities at processing sites and can be effectively utilized as manure.

Rice husk

It is the major by-product of the rice milling industry. Unhulled paddy grain constitutes 20-25 per cent of husk. It is a poor source of manure and the nutrient content is very low (0.3-0.4% N, 0.2-0.3% P_2O_5 and 0.3-0.5% K_2O). Rice . husk should be incorporated into the wet soil and can be used in saline and alkaline soils to improve the physical conditions. li can also be used as a bedding material for animals.

Bagasse

The most important by-product of sugar industry is bagasse. It is mainly used as fuel in boilers of sugar factories. It can be used as manure raw or after composting. It contains 0.25 per cent N and 0.12 per cent P_2O_5.

Pressmud

It is a by-product obtained during the process of sugar manufacturing. It contains about 1.25 per cent N, 2.0 per cent P_2O_5 and 20-25 per cent organic matter. Addition of pressmud is highly useful to acidic soils since it contains high amount of lime (upto 45 %)

Tea wastes

In the tea industry, tea wastes are available during the course of tea production, processing and storage. Tea wastes are used for extraction of caffeine. The decaffeinated tea wastes can be used as manure. Nutrient content of the spent tea waste is 0.3-0.35 % N, 0.4 % P_2O_5 and 1.5 % K_2O.

Coir waste

It is a waste product from the coir industry and mostly dumped near the road sides. Coirpith contains high amount of lignin (30 %), cellulose (26 %) and wide C:N ratio (112:1). To reduce the bulk and C:N ratio, composting is recommended. The composted coirpith contains 1.26 per cent N, 0.06 per cent P, 1.20 per cent K with C/N ratio 24:1 The lignin content is reduced to 4.8 per cent due to composting.

GREEN MANURING

Green manuring can be defined as a practice of ploughing or turning into the soil un-decomposed green plant tissues for the purpose of improving physical structure as well as fertility of the soil. From the time immemorial the turning in a green crop for improvement of the conditions of the soil has been a popular farming practice. Green manuring, wherever feasible, is the principal supplementary means of adding organic matter to the soil. It consists in the growing of a quick-growing crop and ploughing it under to incorporate it into the soil. The green-manure crop supplies organic matter as well as additional nitrogen, particularly if it is a legume crop, which has the ability to fix nitrogen from the air with the help of its root-nodule bacteria. The green-manure crops also exercise a protective action against erosion and leaching.

The adoption of green manuring depends upon the agroclimatic conditions. Broadly the following two types of green manuring can be thought of.

Green Manuring in Situ

In this system, green manure crops are grown and buried in the same field which is to be green-manured, either as a pure crop or as an intercrop with the main crop. In India, various methods of growing green manure crops in situ are followed to suit local conditions. For the proper decomposition of the green manure, it is necessary that the green material should be succulent and there should be adequate moisture in the soil. Plants at the flowering stage, contains the greatest bulk of succulent organic matter with a low carbon/nitrogen ratio. The incorporation of the green-manure crop into the soil at this stage allows a quick liberation of nitrogen in the available form.

Green Leaf Manuring

Green-leaf manuring refers to turning into the soil green leaves and tender green twigs collected from shrubs and trees grown on bunds, wastelands and nearby forest areas. The common shrubs and trees used are Glyricidia *(Glyricidia maculata), Sesbania speciosa, Karanj (Pongamia pinnata),* etc.

Green manuring *in situ* is followed in northern India while green leaf manuring is common in eastern and central India.

POULTRY MANURE : AN EFFICIENT ORGANIC MANURE FOR RICE

Rice crop accounts for nearly 45 per cent of our country's cereal production. It is extensively grown in several States encompassing the zones with varying levels of productivity. The declining growth trends noticed with respect to rice productivity especially in the nineties has made the scientists and farmers to explore new strategies to avert the situation.

Rice is considered to be one of the least fertilizer use efficient crops especially when cultivated in irrigated eco-system. Usually farmers go for application of higher doses of fertilizers in order to meet nutrient requirement of the crop by taking into consideration the inherent losses of nutrients during cultivation. However, in recent years, the ever increasing cost of inorganic fertilizers has become a major prohibitive factor for extensive use of inorganic fertilizers like the contamination of natural resources and deterioration of soil health in rice growing ecosystems have been realized by farming community.

Considering the above factors, integrated approach to mix the right amount of organic manures with inorganic fertilizers has been advocated to rice growers. Among organic manures, farmyard manure (FYM) is the most commonly used. There are also several other sources of organic manures, which could be used in the integrated nutrient management practices. In this context, several organic sources (poultry manure) were evaluated at Agricultural Research Station, Siruguppa, Karnataka. The results of the study suggest that PM was the best among all the other organic manures. In another study different levels of PM (1 to 4 t/ha) in comparison with FYM and without organic manures was evaluated. The results revealed that application of 1 t/ha of PM with 75% NPK (112:75:75 kg/ha) was on par with 100% NPK (150:75:75 kg/ha). The PM has direct as well as residual effect. Permanent plot experiment indicated that 1 t/ha of PM is almost equal to 7 t/ha of FYM in improving the rice yields.

Poultry manure contains 3.03 per cent of nitrogen, 2.60 per cent of phosphorus and 1.4 per cent of potassium, whereas FYM contains only 0.94 per cent nitrogen, 0.56 per cent of phosphorus and 0.72 per cent of potassium. Apart from this, its better nutrient content, PM is also less voluminous than other organic sources thus, helping in transportation from distant places. The cost of nutrients in PM works but to be cheaper when compared to other sources of organic manures, thus helping the farmers to get more monetary returns per unit area.

FORMATION MECHANISMS OF COMPLEX ORGANIC STRUCTURES IN SOIL HABITATS

Soil contains natural reservoir of biotic debris. It consists of plant remains, dead animals, and microorganisms that are subject to continuous turnover. With time, dead biomass is either mineralized or transformed to yield diverse complex organic substances. Transformation proceeds in two stages (Hayes, 1991):

1. The first stage involves degradative processes that lead to the formation of substances. The more recalcitrant lignin components are selectively preserved (Kogel-Knabner, 1993).
2. In the second stage, the substrates and the preserved products are further transformed by synthetic processes to result of humus formation.

Formation of humus is a bio-chemical process. The degradation of biotic debris is catalyzed mainly by microbial enzymes. The subsequent synthesis of the humic material can be mediated by both enzymes and abiotic catalysts that are present in the soil. Soil enzymes originate mostly from microorganisms and to a lesser extent from plants, and clay minerals or metal oxides constitute abiotic catalysts. Polycondensation reactions between reducing sugars and amino acids play a role in humus formation. One of the most important catalytic reactions in soil is oxidative coupling that links phenolic products of the degradative processes into humic polymers through enzymatic reaction and mineral catalysis. Oxidative coupling can also result in the binding of xenobiotics to humus. This reaction is usually accompanied by a detoxification effect and may be catalyzed by either enzymes or minerals. Organic chemicals can be bound to soil through various mechanisms involving either physical sorption or covalent binding. By definition, the adsorption process is reversible; in practice, however, xenobiotics are increasingly difficult to desorb as they become gradually sequestered in inaccessible microsites within the soil matrix. The compounds that are bound through stable covalent linkages are believed to an integral part of humus, thus representing little or no threat to the environment.

ORGANISMS INVOLVED IN ORGANIC MATTER FORMATION

Soil contains various living and non-living components, without this the organic matter would not exhibit such richness. Soil has following components:

Living organisms	less than 1 % of the total volume of the soil
Minerals	about 50%
Organic matter	3-6%
Air the water	up to 50%

Trophic groups of living organisms in soil:

1. Photoautotrophic higher plants, algae and photosynthetic bacteria.
2. Photoheterotrophic bacteria.
3. Chemoautotrohpic bacteria.
4. Chemoheterotrophic organisms.

They include all soil animals, both vertebrates and invertebrates, most bacteria, and most fungi. These organisms are responsible for the biological and biochemical processes of humus formation. Chemoheterotrophs are the only organisms that can perform the two critical functions necessary to the humification process:

1. An active role of transforming raw materials into humus.
2. A passive one of serving as a source of biomass after death.

Chemoheterotrophs (microorganisms) play the most important active role in humification. Plants, however, are most important in passive processes because they serve as the major source of biomass. The tree other groups of organisms play only a passive role in the humification process.

Chemohetertrophic amimals

These include beetle larvae, centipedes, millipedes, and termites in tropical soils. They are primary decomposers and break up plant litter into smaller pieces.

Saprophytic Bacteria, fungi and protozoa

They are also important in the primary decomposition process because these organisms produce extracellular enzymes that catalyze the dissolution of outer protective tissues. Secondary decomposition is performed exclusively by microorganisms, which include most of the soil saprophytic bacteria and fungi. These microorganisms specialize in selectively degrading various large organic molecules such as lignin and cellulose.

The products of microbial degradation can also be linked into humic Polymers by the action of the same microorganisms. The microorganisms involved in humification are those that synthesize the oxidoreductive enzymes required to mediate the processes of synthesis.

Oxidoreductive enzymes

They are designated as either peroxidases or mono-phenol monooxygenases. Peroxidases are found in most higher plants and numberous bacteria and fungi include two distinct classes:

Classes of Mono-phenol monooxygenases	
Laccases	Laccase activity was first detected in the Japanese lacquer tree *Rhus vernicifera.* Microbial laccases were subsequently found in many fungi (e.g., Agaricales, *Aspergillus funigatus, Rhizoctonia pratiocola, Trametes versicolor,* and others) and in actinomycetes like *Actinomyces albocrustosurs, A galbus, and Streptomyces* spp.
Tyrosinases	Tyrosinase activity has been detected in fungi such as *Agaricales (Aspergillus nidulans),* brown-rot fungi, *Psalliota arvense,* and *Russula nigricans* and in various actinomycetes.

Both peroxidase and laccase activity have also been detected in soil extracts, apparently as a result of the production of the extracellular oxidoreductases.

Synthetic Reactions in Soil

The microorganisms responsible for the humification process are ubiquitous, therefore, the synthetic reactions are common in soil. The extent of these reactions is limited only by proliferation of the oxidoreductase producers, and the ability of these microorganisms to proliferate appears to be practically limitless. Various studies have shown that essentially all microbial species can be found in most soils, differing only in numbers and proportions. Even in deep layers of soils (up to 500 m). where only anaerobic conditions are expected to prevail, the composition of the microflora is essentially the same as that observed on the surface. Also, the transformation of organic compounds in both types of environments differs little except in the extent of the reactions.

DEGRADATIVE PROCESSES

Humus formation is a slow decomposition process. It undergoes a constant slow at a rate of about 2-5 per cent a year. Though this process is slow, even than the content of humus in soil remains fairly constant over considerable periods of time due to its systematic replenishment. Plant materials decompose fairly and rapidly, with half-lives varying from days to months. Only a small portion of the total plant input, however, is converted to humic substances. During the first year, about 70 per cent of the plant material is degraded to CO_2, and about 5-10 per cent forms new biomass. Thus, 75-80 per cent of plant substances undergo an initial rapid phase of plant litter decomposition. The material remaining is decomposed more slowly, and only the products of this second phase are incorporated into soil humus.

Types of Plant Material for Decomposition

Alexander (1977) divided these substances into six broad categories:

Table 2.4: Plant materials which decompose in soil. The type of material with their availability

Plant material	Availability in %
Cellulose	15-60% of the dry weight
Hemicelluloses	10-30%
Lignins	5-30%
Water-soluble sugars, amino acids, and aliphatic acids	5-30%
Ether and methanol-soluble fats, oils, waxes, and pigments	
Nitrogen- and sulfur-containing proteins	

The decomposition in the soil may be the *preferential decomposition* (decomposition of easily mineralizable materials) or the *selective preservation* (decomposition of refractory plant components).

Plant components (cellulose, hemicelluloses, and proteins) are easily mineralized while lignins and lipids are refractory to decomposition. During the period of rapid decomposition, the former are quickly mineralized to CO_2 by microorganisms as a source of carbon and energy. Nitrogen contained in proteins is mineralized to ammonium and nitrates.

The pathway of lignin decomposition

Lignin degradation, however, is critical for humification to occur because the process generates phenols and phenolic acids, which are fundamental constituents of the core humus polymers. The pathway of lignin decomposition to soil is not yet fully understood. Lignin has a complicated structure of phenyl propanoid units connected irregularly by C- O-C and C-C side chain and direct ring-to-ring linkages. The CO_2 released during lignin degradation is the product is the product of cometabolism rather than the result of direct microbial mineralization. Compared to cllulose, very little Cess than 1%) lignin carbon is incorporated into new biomass.

Microorganisms for Lignin biodegradation

White-rot fungi are well known of the lignin biodegraders, because they contain peroxidases that remove electrons from lignin aromatic rings with completely etherified hydroxyl groups. This reaction yields cationic radicals that are then stabilized by the cleavage of C-C bonds in the lignin side chains. The radicals then react with O_2 or water and become stabilized by the formation of hydroxy or keto derivatives.

Because lignin is highly resistant to biodegradation, it may stabilize reactive components like cellulose, hemicellulose, or proteins by forming chemical or physical linkages to these molecules. A similar protective effect is produced by soil minerals and humus polymers that anchor unstable plant constituents by various adsorption forces or chemical binding.

Highly degradable proteins, for example, may be protected against rapid biodegradation by their nucleophilic addition to aromatic polymers through free NH_2 or SH groups and/or by adsorption on humus or clay.

Acquired stability

The plant components may not be completely mineralized during the initial rapid decomposition phase. Therefore, many relatively unstable plant constituents, such as polysaccharides, proteins, soluble sugars, and amino acids, can survive in the soil for a sufficient length of time, to participate directly in humus formation.

SYNTHETIC PROCESSES FOR HUMUS FORMATION

The Role of Oxidative Coupling in Humus Formation

Humus (humic acid, fulvic acid, and humin) is a complicated structure. All main fractions of humus have fundamentally similar structures. They have a large aromatic polymer that in nature occurs as micelles. Incorporated into such polymers are various phenols, quinines, nitrogen heterocycles, and benzoic acids having reactive carboxyl, hydroxyl, carbonyl, and thiol groups that can act as binding sites for carbohydrates and amino acids. Humus also contains aliphatic moieties, often hydrophobic in nature, and abounds in stable free radicals that give oxidative properties to humus and enable the attraction of ionized or protonated compounds.

Theories of Humus Formation

One of the oldest theories proposes that humic polymers are lignins or other resistant plant materials that have undergone minor modifications under soil conditions (Waksman and Iyer, 1932).

Plant materials serve exclusively as a source of energy suggests that the role of microorganisms is limited to the production of various amino compounds and phenols that, once discharged into soil, polymerize form humus. It seems possible that each of these processes can, to a certain extent, contribute to humus formation (Bollag and Loll, 1983).

Modern theories of humification

This theory is based on the fact that a central role is played by the process of polymerization. The phenolic compounds derived from lignins (ferulic acid, pyrogallol, orcinol, syringic acid, and catechol) are considered to be the most important substrates for these polymerization reactions. This hypothesis was confirmed by many researchers. They have successfully synthesized humic-like substances by polymerizing one or more phenol-derived compounds. The synthetic polymers produced in this way are quite similar to natural humus, particularly with respect to elemental analysis, exchange capacity, total acidity, resistance to microbial degradation.

Phenolic compounds may be polymerized during the process of humus formation through oxidative coupling reactions that, as with most biological processes, require catalysts. This function is fulfilled by a series of biotic catalysts (the oxidoreductive enzymes) produced by soil microorganisms and abiotic catalysts (clay minerals and metal oxides) present in soils. Humus itself also exhibits catalytic properties due to the presence of free radical components.

The mechanism of coupling requires the oxidation of phenolic compounds involving the loss of a proton and an electron from the hydroxyl group. This loss results in the production of free radicals or reactive quinines that covalently couple to form chains of humic polymers. Such coupling has been shown by Liu *et al.* (1981) who used a simple model involving one of the components of humus, namely syringic acid, to demonstrate the formation of various oligomers, ranging from dimers to hexamers, by a laccase isolated from the fungus *Rhizoctonia praticola.* A similar approach was adopted by Simmons *et al.* (1988). Mass spectroscopy and nuclear magnetic resonance (NMR) techniques were used to identify the products of an enzymatic reaction in which horseradish peroxidase was used to catalyze the oligomerization of guaiacol. Such studies have contributed to an understanding of mechanisms involved in humus formation.

The syringic acid and guaiacol (polymeric forms) are similar to the structure particularly with regard to the oxygen bridges and the direct carbon—carbon linkages between aromatic rings. Liu *et al.* (1985) demonstrated that it is possible to incorporate a per tide unit similar to that depicted in Stevenson's structure into a simplified synthetic model of humic acid. This incorporation could also be mediated by oxidoredus tive enzymes, such as the laccase isolated from *Rhizoctonia proticola*.

3

Vermiculture

Soil fauna play a prominent role in regulating soil processes and among these the termites and the earthworms play a vital role in maintaining soil quality and managing efficient nutrient cycling. In organic farming practices the soil is considered to be a living component with is physical, chemical and biological characteristics.

Various aspects of earthworm activities in nature, and benefits that can be derived with mass culture, *viz.*, for cast production, vermicomposting and commercializing live material, indicate needs of developing mass earthworm culture. This is popularly referred as vermiculture. Vermiculture, as a subject, involve background of various aspects on biology etc. of earthworm. All these are scattered in literature.

Varmicompost is a method of making compost with the use of earthworms, which generally live in soil. They eat biomass and excrete it in digested form. This compost is generally called vermicompost or wormicompost. It is estimated that 1800 worms, which is an ideal population for one sq meter can feed on 80 tonnes of humus per year.

Earthworms form a major component of the soil system and these organisms have been efficiently ploughing the land for millions of years and assisting in the recycling of organic nutrients for the efficient growth of plants. Advent of chemical fertilizers and biocides and their largescale application have changed the structure of soils and have, in most cases, eliminated soil organisms. Thus, human interference in natural ecosystems through modern practices of agriculture, silviculture and horticulture involving largescale application of chemicals in the form of fertilizers and pesticides has been responsible for the destruction of endemic soil fauna. For millions of years before the green revolution, earthworms have been ploughing the soil and fertilizing them.

Earthworms are one of the numerous ranges of burrowing organisms, which improve soils. Fertile soils harbour bacteria, fungi, actinomycetes, protozoans, proturans symphylids, pauropods, spring tails, pseudoscorpions, insects and their larvae, millipedes, centipedes, slugs, snails, snakes, rodents and the earthworms. These fauna along with the flora contribute to soil health. The presence of earthworms in soils is generally indicative of the presence of other faunal representatives contributing to soil fertility.

It would therefore certainly be appropriate to call earthworms as indicators of soil health.

The greatest asset to our country is that we have about 509 species of earthworms and that we need not depend on the exotic spices of earthworms. During the early nineties a New Zealand planarian flatworm *Artioposthia triangulate* had been reported to be eating up earthworms and spreading fast across England, Ireland and Scotland. This parasite had the potential to cause a plague of eliminating earthworms from soils. The chief cause attributed to the arrival of these flatworms into Scotland was by the inadvertent import of potted plants from New Zealand, the soils of which probably might have contained flatworm eggs. Thus transfer of organisms of any kind including the earthworms can directly or indirectly cause irreparable damage to local biodiversity as could be envisaged from this example.

EARTHWORMS AS INDICATORS OF SOIL FERTILITY

Earthworms can generally be called as biological indicators of soil fertility, for soil with earthworms most definitely support healthy populations of bacteria, fungi, actinomycetes, protozoans, insects, spiders, millipedes and a host of others that are essential for sustaining a healthy soil.

Earthworms act on litter and the absence of earthworms is characterized by the presence of litter mats on surface soil. Soils inhabited by earth worms have surface casts to a range of about 98 tons dry weight ha-1 yr-1 in woodlands to about 133 tons dry weight ha-1 yr-1 in grasslands, maximum production however occurring during the wet periods. Soil fertility results from the maintenance of soil conditions such the decomposition processes operate at a level adequate to release plant nutrients from the litter at a rate that will sustain optimum growth. Availability of earthworms in soils have always promoted plant growth. Scientists have eported the production of grass, wheat and clover to increase many fold by the presence of earthworms, while increase in growth of maize, paddy, sugarcane, vegetables and ornamental plants have also been reported.

Soil enrichment

Earthworms that burrow deeply into the mineral strata and return, periodically, to cast faecal material at the soil surface facilitate the transport of certain elements to the surface from deep in the profile. There is abundant evidence that concentrations of exchangeable calcium, sodium, magnesium, potassium and available phosphorus and molybdenum are higher in earthworm casts than in the surrounding soil. The finding is confirmed by similar reports from U.S.A., New Zealand, Europe, Africa, India and elsewhere.

In addition to the physical mixing of the soil by burrowing activities, soil enrichment is achieved by speeding up mineralisation of organic matter 2-5 times by the earthworms:

- Earthworm ingestion causes in increase in surface area of the organic wastes,
- Ingestion removes senescent bacterial colonies and stimulates new bacterial growth,
- Nitrogenous excretions from the worms enrich the soil formed from organic wastes,
- Earthworm burrowing enhances the oxygen penetration,
- Mineral nutrients are released through enhanced microbial mineralisation, and
- Earthworm feeding increases the interaction among microflora, thereby improving the flow and exchange of nutrients.

Earthworms also eliminate pathogens in the waste using two mechanisms:

- their gut microflora outcompete the pathogens; and
- they produce bacteriostatic substances.

Several valuable compounds are also produced through the earthworm microflora interaction. These include vitamins (such as B_{12}) and plant growth hormones (such as gibberellins).

EARTHWORM : THE NATURAL BIOREACTOR

Bhawalkar (1989) designated earthworms as the *Natural Bioreactor.* Earthworms play a key role in soil biology as versatile natural bioreactors. They effectively harness the beneficial soil microflora, destroy soil pathogens, and convert organic wastes into valuable products such as biofertilisers, biopesticides, vitamins, enzymes, antibiotics, growth hormones and proteinous worm biomass:

1. Earthworm's gut is an effective tubular bioreactor, with raw materials (feed) entering from one end (mouth) and the product (castings) coming out through the anus.
2. They maintain a stable temperature through novel temperature regulation mechanisms; thus accelerating the rates of bioprocesses and preventing enzyme inactivation caused by high temperatures.
3. Enzymes are active at a very narrow pH range, and earthworm bioreactors efficiently maintain the highly nonlinear pH parameter. The calciferous glands in them contain carbonic anhydrase, which catalyse the fixation of carbon dioxide as calcium carbonate and prevent any fall in the pH of the body fluid.
4. Earthworm's gizzard is a novel colloidal mill in which the feed is ground in to particles smaller than 2 microns, giving thereby anenhanced surface area for the microbial processing.

5. Earthworm bioreactors have an in-house supply of enzymes such as protease, lipase, amylase, cellulase, lichenase and chitinase. These enzymes biodegrade complex biomolecules into simple compounds utilizable by the symbiotic gut microflora.
6. Earthworms have a built-in oxygen plant, which can separate aerial oxygen by chemical absorption into their blood haemoglobin, which has a strong affinity for oxygen. The haemoglobin is fully oxygenated at an oxygen partial pressure as low as 19 mm Hg, which saturates only 50 per cent of human haemoglobin.
7. Earthworms promote growth of microorganisms in their gut by providing ideal conditions therein. Bacteria and actinomycetes, which are important in waste-degradation increase exponentially along the entire length of the tubular bioreactor, reaching densities, 1,000 times greater than in the surrounding soil. However, *E. coli, Salmonella* and other pathogens are destroyed by competition from the active microflora and the action of intestinal secretions (Satchell, 1983). Most human pathogens are anaerobic and cannot survive in the highly aerobic microenvironment created by the earthworms.
8. Earthworms produce castings containing balanced plant nutrients and immobilized microflora which continue to function in the soil. Vermicastings are also rich in vitamins, enzymes, antibiotics and growth hormones.

Earthworms digest some of their gut microflora (SCP) and build up their biomass. Worm proteins (70 per cent of dry biomass) are balanced with all essential amino acids and have a potential for use in animal nutrition.

INTERACTION OF VERMICOMPOST-EARTHWORM-MULCH - PLANTROOT (VEMP)

VEMP interaction is essential for an effective utilization of the soil ecosystem in agro-practices. Use of green manures in organic farming is also essential. The possibility of interactions of the root hairs with nitrogen fixing organisms may be increased by the VEMP interaction. It is very well known that earthworms prefer lower levels of lignin and tannin, and in case of green manuring younger plants are recommended for ploughing-in for an effective release and uptake of nutrients.

VAM is effective in cases of wheat and other crops. The population of VAM is very well enhanced in the presence of earthworms, as earthworms are reported to be vectors of viable propagules of VAM. The uptake of phosphate, though facilitated by VAM, dispersal of these spores and conservation of such microbes is facilitated by earthworms and other soil dwellers.

RECYCLING OF WASTES THROUGH VERMITECH

Vermitech is useful in recycling the agro-wastes through and the effective utilization of VEMP reduces. Nutrients presenting vermicompost are readily available and the increase in earthworm populations on application of vermicompost and mulching lead to the easy transfer of nutrients to the plants providing synchrony in interfered ecosystems. The availability of microbes in the compost and the nutrients in soil tilled by earthworms are definitely more due to the formation of drilospheres. Vermicompost, therefore, leaves no doubt on its potential for good yields, the yield however depends on the management practices followed by the farmer.

EARTHWORMS AND PLANT GROWTH

The effect by earthworms on plant growth may be due to several reasons apart from the presence of macronutrients and micronutrients in their secretions and in vermicasts in considerable quantities. Certain metabolites produced by earthworms may also be responsible to stimulate plant growth. It is considered that earthworms release into the soil certain vitamins and similar substances. Though the NPK value of the vermicasts is always lower than any standard chemical fertilizer, several experiments have proved that wormcasts can promote lush growth of plants. This probably may be due to plant growth promoters like cytokinins and auxins present in casts.

ADVANTAGES OF ORGANIC MANURE AND THE ROLE OF EARTHWORMS

The green revolution is the result of intensive agriculture. Presently, an extensive use of organic manures may boos agricultural production and can feed to the growing population of under developing countries.

With the intensive use of chemical fertilizers, farmers can harvest three crops in a year with good irrigation facilities, but there was no thought about its adverse effect in the long run on the soil condition in general and on the environment in particular for nearly four decades. To restore the soil composition, farmers are now showing inclination to revert to organic farming. With this changing trend, a comparative picture of the two practices gives better scope for adoption of organic farming to suit to the existing conditions. Along with that it is necessary to produce the organic manure in large quantities from the available sources of organic matter to maintain the high level of produce in the available agricultural land.

Organic manure can be prepared from natural organic matter. These materials are the reservoirs of the nutrients that are required for the plant growth. These nutrients are in the form of complex, bound organic chemicals with strong bonds in most of these plant and animal debris.

The entry of these chemicals in the form of simple organic or inorganic chemical into the plant system is the main basis of biogeochemical cycle. If these chemicals are judiciously made to enter the cycle of events in a regular systematic form in nature, then there will be no dearth for nutrient supply to the plants in a natural way and with this, there will be cleaning of the environment rather than polluting it.

Microbes are the **primary decomposers** while earthworms are the major **secondary** decomposers. Earthworm manure is formed from the dead tissues of plant and animals and thus is naturally the source of macro and micro nutrients in limited quantities. The weather conditions and the soil type in the tropical countries do not favour the restoration of carbon resource in the soils. The application of organic manure replenishes organic carbon to the impoverished soils. The presence of high level of oxidisable organic carbon helps in the slow release of nutrients from the manure and curbs the leaching of nutrients. The beneficial activity is because of the nutrient availability.

What is Vermicompost

Vermicompost is a stable fine granular organic matter, when added to clay soil loosens the soil and provides the passage for the entry of air. The mucus associated with the cast being hygroscopic absorbs water and prevents water logging and improves water holding capacity. Thus, in the sandy soils where there is the problem of water retention, the strong mucus coated aggregates of vermicompost hold water for longer time.

In the vermicompost, some of the secretions of worms and the associated microbes act as growth promoters along with other nutrients. It improves physical, chemical and biological properties of soil in the long run on repeated application. The organic carbon in vermicompost releases the nutrients slowly and steadily into the system and enables the plant to absorb these nutrients. The soil enriched with vermicompost provides additional substances that are not found in the chemicals. The multifarious effects of vermicompost influence the growth and yield of crops.

Vermiculture and Pollution Hazard

Earthworm can minimize the pollution hazards caused by organic waste by enhancing waste degradation. The experiences of the farming community have shown that the exclusive use of chemicals to keep away the famine has turned out be a mirage. It is like giving alms for a day, instead of providing an opportunity to a person to earn for his lifetime to escape from poverty.

The ideal earthworm species of earthworms help to convert waste into wealth. If this operation is made successful by the own efforts of the farming community, one can certainly by hopeful of converting the wasteland into a fertile land. It is this hope of the possibility of producing the needed topsoil or humus by earthworms that has encouraged this effort. This may help in reaching the goal of green revolution from a different angle.

ADVANTAGES OF VERMICOMPOST

1. It enables easy management.
2. Vermicomposting wastes at source or place where one wishes or has facilities, compost can be more profitably utilized and commercialization for economic gains.
3. Management of live population in field too first necessitates development of suitable conditions, which are not easy due to modern agriculture practices. Even if these are made available, a large culture of suitable earthworm species, *viz.*, approximately on tonnage level = about 1 million live individuals per hectare land are required. All such requirements necessitate development of earthworm culture (vermiculture).
4. Huge quantities of domestic, agricultural and rural industrial organic wastes can be recycled for various usages. This also reduces pollution.

The other applications of vermicompost in paddy fields are at the time of tillering, panicle initiation, flowering and drain fillingis essential. Unlike the chemical fertilizers, the loss of nutrients by leaching and other phenomena related to nutrient loss are minimal in case of VEMP interactions. In Azolla applied systems, the decomposition and release of nutrients may be hastened by the application of vermicompost. The effectiveness of blue-green algae with vermicompost is not much understood compared to other biofertilizer. In sugarcane, paddy and other crops, vermicompost can be effectively utilized as a carrier medium for *Azospirillum, Rhizobium* and phosphate solubilisers, which are recommended with FYM (Farm Yard Manure). These also provide very good association for enhancing their interactions with plant roots. Experiments conducted on the effect of earthworms and/or vermicompost and vermiwash through vermitech on the cultivation of vegetables like tomato, brinjal and Okra have yielded very valuable results.

ADVERSE EFFECTS ON CROPS

Earthworm activity can also to a less extent damage crops by either seizing fallen leaves of live plants and pulling them down or by uprooting delicate seedlings. Casts may show up as ugly structures in ornamental lawns or may form an obstruction on golf courses or football pitches. Earthworms have also been occasionally reported to transmit many parasites and diseases of plants and animals.

ECONOMIC VIABILITY

Vermin-technology is popular because it is a simple methodology with low investment. It technology does not need sophisticated infrastructure. All that is required is some pits or containers to initially decompose organic waste and tanks made out of stone slabs or wooden planks, trenches or for any convenient material just to protect earthworms from pests and predators. Therefore, the investment on this is directly related to the choice of the material used to build tanks. Stone slab is subjected to availability while plastic bins would be less durable and expensive. Thus, tanks built using cement and bricks could suit all situations. However, trenches without any cement are popular in low rainfall areas. The cost of bricks and amount spent on construction vary from place

VERMICULTURE PROCESS

It is very simple and easy to method. It needs careful stepwise programme. However, like all live animal or culture of any biological material, first step is to start purely as a test experiment on a small scale. This enables acquire personal experience(s) on various aspects. For beginners, hobbyist and farmers, simple procedure should be first to start on experimental scale and record every detail of steps followed and responses on earthworms. The care should be observed that how these fair in particular medium with increase or decrease in their numbers, waste matter conversion, cast production and composting etc. Following are the important levels of planning:—

1. Site selection.
2. Availability of decomposable organic waste, its daily quantity and quality, alternate organic material, transportation and stocking etc..
3. Marketable outlet and requirement with future scope.
4. Collection and study of know how on earthworms to be cultured.
5. Collection, procurement of suitable species.
6. Testing of suitability of species on performance in available organic waste.
7. Maintenance of seed culture for eventual largescale culture.

Other important considerations should also be kept in mind, like funding, availability of labour, quality of waster and packaging etc. etc. are to be kept in mind. These aspects comprise essential steps in any project formulation. In terms of wider utilization of vermiculture, first step is selection of suitable species for culture and eventual vermicomposting.

SELECTION OF SUITABLE SPECIES

The selection of suitable species for vermiculture is based on the requirement, *viz.,* for composting, poultry and animal feed, marketing for fish or other forms of culture and sale for fish baits. As yet demands in India for fish bait is meagre and lack for wanting development of fresh water sport fisheries, including for selected fish species (like Eel Fish) culture and also large scale culture. For all culture feeds, care has to be taken that earthworm feed does not harbour parasites and pathogens.

The selection for suitable species is based on biological and ecological parameters, like habitat characteristics, distribution in soil or feed media and trophic functions. Usually, following three types of earthworms which can be used in vermiculture:

1. Epiges
2. Endoges
3. Aneciques

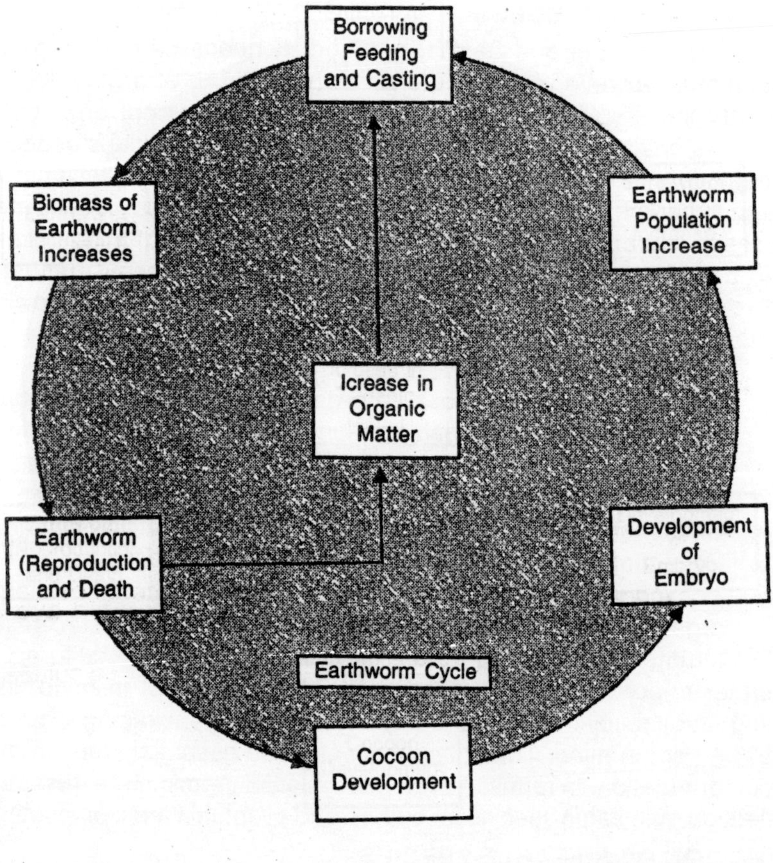

Fig. 3.1: Action of earthworm for production of vermicompost

Epiges

These are small in size. They have uniform body colouration and live on surface litter or dung. These have short life cycle with high reproduction and regeneration rate. They can tolerate disturbance and have active gizzard; but have limited period of activity. These are phytophagous. These species are good bio-degradators and can release good nutrients in the soil. They do not re-dislribute nutrients. Thus have insignificant role in humus formation and are not good for use in field conditions for soil reclamation, unless careful manipulations are done.

Endoges

These are small or large in size. They have weak pigmentation and found in topsoil layer of organic and mineralised matter. Burrow branchings are horizontal and worms moderately tolerate disturbance. They may show some preference in selection of feed substrate (buffered and predictable) conditions. These are **geophagous.** Life cycle is of intermediate duration. They have potential for soil improvements because of high efficiency in energy utilization from poor soils, therefore, can be used in field with some manipulation.

Aneciques

They are large in size. They have pigmentation only at anterior and posterior ends. They are largely nocturnal, deep burrowing and pull leaves or litter matter into soil (burrows) and are **phytogeophagous** and tolerance to disturbance is poor. Their reproduction rate is low. They may have useful role in mixing nutrients as from deep burrow come up to surface for casting.

BASIC CHARACTERISTICS OF SUITABLE SPECIES

Farmers or gardener needs only those species, which can quickly convert organic waste to vermicompost. Therefore, a worm should have following characteristics:—

1. Worm species should be tolerant to disease.
2. The culturing techniques should be simple enough to adopt.
3. Worm should be efficient convenor of plant or animal biomass to body proteins, so that its growth rates are high.
4. It should have high consumption, digestion and assimilation rate (composting qualities).
5. The worm should have wide adaptability (tolerance) to environmental factors (capability to live in varying temperature conditions).
6. The worms should have feeding preference and adaptability for wide range or organic material (high and rich organic matter).

7. The worm should produce large numbers of cocoons that should not have long hatching time, so that multiplication and organic matter conversion is fast.
8. Growth rate, maturity from young one to adult stage should be fast.
9. Worm should have compatibility or tolerance with other worms (as with possibility of mixture of species by ameteurs) as would add to productivity of biomass (worms) and conversion rate at different strata (layers) of organic matter, *i.e.*, faster composting. This feature, *i.e.*, composting with different layer feeders have so far received very little attention.
10. Worms should be disease resistant.
11. Worms on introduction in substrate, should have least inactivity period (= vermistabilization period).
12. The worms should feed near the surface of organic matter.

FIXING EARTHWORMS FOR IDENTIFICATION

1. Paralyse the worms by placing them in water and gradually adding alcohol.
2. When they are narcotized transfer them to a petri plate having 10 per cent formalin solution by holding the worms straight for a few seconds. Worms stiffen.
3. After 24 hours, transfer them into 70 per cent alcohol.

TRANSPORT OF FIXED WORMS TO LABORATORY

1. Dip cotton pads in alcohol (70%) and place fixed worms on these pads.
2. If there are more than one species mark the numbers on small pieces of paper with pencil and stich them posterior end of the worms.
3. Roll the cotton pads and tie with thread.
4. Place the rolled pads in a polythene cover and seal it to prevent drying of cotton pad.
5. Place the polythene cover in paper covers and transport to laboratory.

DESCRIPTION OF SUITABLE SPECIES

In whole world, only 3-4 species are in wide use. In India, only two peregrine species are being extensively used for vermiculture namely *Eisenia foetida* and *Eudrilus eugeniae.* Several species are also available but they have to be tested on various grounds like, their inbuilt-adaptability to climatic conditions, per existing distributional range, local availability and in view of needs for better waste conversion rates etc. The important species for Indian sub-continent are as follows:—

Family: Lumbricidae

Bimastos parvus [= Allolobophora (Bimastos) parvus Eisen]

They are distributed in Kashmir (Gorai, Srinagar); Himachal Pradesh (Kasauli, Barog, Simla, Chail, Narkanda, Kothai); Punjab (Ferozepur and other areas?); Rajasthan (Pratapgarh); and Uttar Pradesh (Nainital and other areas?). They are brownish red body with saddle shaped clitellum, dorsally covering 6 or more segments, from XXIV or XXV to XXX; length 25-40 mm; diameter 1-2 mm; total segments 85-111 usually 90. Other characters morphological and are differentiable by experts only for confirmation. In many temperate countries, allied species, namely, (1) *Allolobophora subrubricunda* and (2) *Allolobophora chloritica,* (3) *Dendrobaena rubida,* (4) *Eisenia honensis* and *Lumbricus rubellus* are used in vermitechnology.

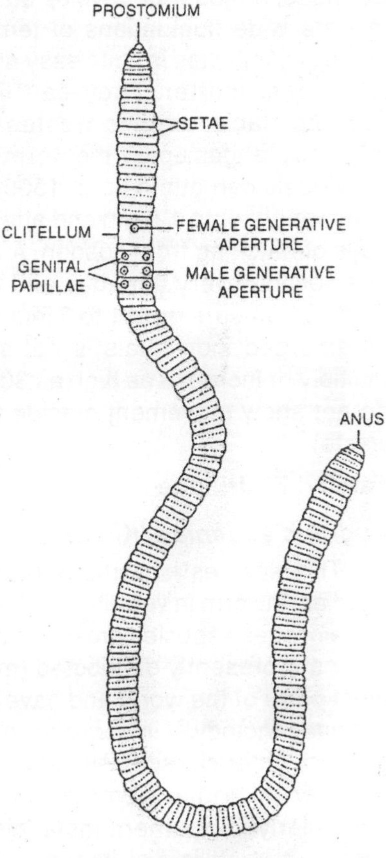

Fig. 3.2: Ventral view of *Metaphire posthuma.*

These species, barring perhaps *E. hortensis* are more or less established in temperate regions of India. In such regions, vermitechnology with these species deserves attention, as live individuals would be more readily available in nature and would be better suited to local conditions. Only one has to search and know local distribution or occurrence in different areas.

***Eisenia foetida* (Sav.)**

Eisenia foetida is perhaps world's most widely used earthworm in vermitechnology for vermicomposting. They are distributed throughout India in nature. They found in sewage dumps (sewage filter mesh grills), sludge, tanks and filters. They are marketed under different names like Red worm, Pink worm or Purple worm, Tiger worm, Brandling worm or even vermiculture or vermicomposting worm. Living worms appears coloured (red, brown or purple or even darker). Careful observation indicates that they have dorsally coloured bands and are often two per segment. Ventrally body is pale. On maturity, clitellum spreads over 7-9 segments in length over XXIV, XXV or XXVI to XXXII body segments. On these, ridges wall-develop on maturity. They are quite hardy and can tolerate wide fluctuations of temperature and humidity. The culturing process of species is quite easy due to feeding adaptability or adjustment to organic matter. They can live on wide variety of degradable/ decomposable organic wastes. On these, the average conversion efficiency ranges upto 7 mg/worm/day. They have fast growth rate. Mature individuals can attain up to 1500 mg body weight. Mature adults attain body weight upto 1.5 gm and attain reproduction capability within 50-55 days of hatching from cocoon. A mature worm on average can produce one cocoon every third day and from each cocoon on hatching (within 23 days) emerge from 1 to 3 individuals. However, generally, survival of all emerged individuals is not seen. Still, on average, numbers can multiply or increase as high as 30 times. Duration of life is 70 days. They do not show movement outside feed substrate (decomposing organic waste).

Family: Eudrilidae

Eudrilus eugeniae (Kinb.)

This species is perhaps fastest growing and second most widely used earthworm in vermitechnology for composting and for use as vermi-protein. These species are originally distributed in Equatorial West Africa. They are presently distributed (may now be naturally occurring also) in most parts of the world and have been introduced for various usages in vermitechnology. It is common in parts of even America and Europe. In parts of America, species is common and is popularly known as *Night Crawler*. In India, common in many vermiculture establishments, particularly in Southern India this species has been recommended for vermiculture. It is distributed in Travancore, Pune and North Konkan. The living worms appear brown and red to dark violet. The general colouration is like animal flesh. Their length ranges from 32-140 mm, diameter is 5-8 mm and total body segments range 145-196. In mature adults, clitellum spreads over 5-6 segments numbering XIII or XIV to XVIII. Spermathecal and female pores are fused commencing after 13/ 14 body segments. Male pores commence before 17/18 body segments. It grows fast (assimilation and conversion to biomass) and is better than other species and ranges upto 12 mg/day. It maximum body weight ranges up to 4.3 mg/individual. They attain maturity within 40 days; and a week later individuals commence cocoon laying, almost 1 cocoon/day or upto 4 cocoons/3 days for 46 days, depending upon appropriate conditions. Total life span in laboratory is estimated to range 1 to 3 years.

Cocoon incubation period that at times, number of individuals per cocoon may range 1-5. They are low temperature tolerant, however, they can tolerate high temperature as well (over 48° F in room conditions, *i.e.*, under indirect sun exposure). Harvesting of the species from culture heaps is little difficult. However, simple solution is to up turn the heap, leave it for 1-3 hours, all worms move to lower layer. From top layers, compost can be collected and worms can be replaced in culture media or harvested for appropriate utilization. Their reproductive activity gradually decreases and so composting activity decreases. In such state is advisable to utilise worm for animal feed or just for burying in fields (a nitrogenous waste).

Family: Megascolecidae

They are available throughout world. So far only six species of this family are in use for vermitechnology work. These are *Amynthas diffrigens, Lampito mauhtii, Metaphire anomala, Metaphire birmanica, Perionyx excavatus* and *Perionyx sansbaricus,* which is endemic to India. It is essential to know about their distribution in of India. For all taxonomic characteristics consultations with specialists is necessary.

Lampito mauritii (Kinb.)

Species is also referred in old documents as *Megascolex mauritii* (Kinb.). They are distributed throughout India (excepting Uttar Pradesh, wherein present distribution is not known). They are reported occurring in Kapurthala (Punjab), many areas of Bengal, Gujarat, Maharashtra, Madhya Pradesh, South Rajasthan, Andhra Pradesh, Tamil Nadu, Goa, Kerala, Andaman Islands, Lakshdweep Island, etc. They are also common in many parts of South and South East Asia. The body colouration is dark yellow except at anterior end, which has purplish tinge. The total body length 80—210 mm with a diameter of 3'/2-5 mm. They have 166—190 total body segments. Clitellum spread over to four body segments, on XIV to XVII and is ring shaped. Male pores on papillae, female pores near each other in pairs on XIV segment and spermathecal pores, in three pairs.

Metaphire anomala Mich. (= Pheretima anomala)

They found in Sibpur (Calcutta). We still need their distributional status. They are expected to be distributed in Orissa, Bihar, South-East Madhya Pradesh, Andhra Pradesh, Tamil Nadu, Karnataka and Kerala, also in parts of Maharashtra. The body colourations have not yet been studied. The total body length 80-90 mm, diameter 5 to 5.5 mm and total body segments 130 (variation range?). Clitellum, ring shaped covering, three body segments, *i.e.* XIII-XVI with XIV ventrally having setae. Spermathecae pores absent but copulatory papillae in pairs present. The details on performance of species in vermiculture work are needed.

Metaphire posthuma (= Pheretima posthuma)

This is common species in India. Unfortunately other details on vermitechnological usages, if any, to-date yet to be studied.

Perionyx excavatus E. Perr.

In India, this genus is spread from eastern or western Himalayas downwards in regions of heavy rainfall. Now perhaps, species are widely distributed and two exotic species, *Perionyx excavatus* and *Perionyx sansbaricus,* believed to introduced from Australia or New Zealand. Only *P. excavator* is in use for vermitechnology in many parts of the world. In India, the species is common in Eastern Himalayas (Dibrugarh, Sadiya and Darjeeling), Western Himalayas (Kumaon Dist., Sahastradhara, Dehradun, Simla) Pilibhit, Bengal (Calcutta, Rajasthan, Sibpur), Maharashtra (Bombay) and Little Andaman Islands. The body colouration on dorsal surface (upper part) deep purple to reddish brown and lower side pale. The total body length ranges from 23 to 120 mm with a diameter of 2.5 mm. They are chitellum ring shaped, covering five or less segments on XIII or part, XIII to XVII. Male pores in a depression (line or area). Spermathecal pores in 7/8 and 8/9, nearly at same distance as male pores. The life cycle duration is of ± 46 days, growth rate is 3.5 mg/day, body weight (max), 600 mg. Reproduction rate is fast. They attain maturity within 21-22 days and reproduction (cocoon laying) commences by 24th day. The average cocoon production is 1.1/worm/day. This is almost double the reproduction rate of most commonly used worms in vermiculture. The incubation period reportedly ranges to ± 18.7 days and mean number of hatchings is 1 to 3 per cocoon.

Perionyx sansbaricus Michaelson

They are widely distributed in many parts of India. The species is found in natural environments of Baroda, Igatpuri, Manmad, Wathur near Mahabaleshwar and Londa near Castle Rock (Maharashtra) Khandwa and Kala Khund near Indore, Coonoor and Kotagiri in Nilgiris, Kodaikanal and New Delhi and vicinity area. The dorsally body colour is purple which is darker at anterior portion. On lower side (ventrally) body is pale. The body length is 32-63 mm with a diameter of 2.5 to 3.5 mm. The total body segments range 84-108. Clitellum is ring shaped, extends on 5 segments, over XIII-XVII body segments. Area of male pores variable (XVIII). Spermathecal pores near the middle line-6/7,6/8 and 8/9.

The other species, which are used for vermicultire are, *Octochaetus (Octochaetoides) surnensis* Mich., *Ramiella bishambari* (Steph.), *Dichogaster bolaui* (Mich.), *Dichogaster affinis* (Mich.), *Dichogaster curgensis* (Micha.), *Dichogaster saliens* (Bedd.), *Ramiella bishambari* (Steph.), *Erythrodraeodrilus suclorius* (Steph.), *Ocnerodrilus (Ocnerodrilus) occidentalis* (Eisen.), *Moniligaster perrieri* (Mich.), *Drawida willsi* (Mich.), etc.

MAINTENANCE OF BASE CULTURE

Base or mother or seed culture is used for large-scale culture. These should be carefully maintained and should be checked for health. The selection of feed of an individual is necessary. It should have any chemical that is lethal to worms. The procurement of organic waste (feed) should also be checked for seepage and contamination. For initial multiplication, the best feed substrate is cow dung manure. It should be at advance stage of decomposition and should be devoid of parasites.

Vermicastings as Inoculant

Earthworm cocoons are invariably associated with vermicastings, which include also beneficial microflora, humus and undigested organic matter.

It is desirable to use vermicastings of burrowing type earthworms, to inoculate new fields. Live, mature worms may not withstand the transport shock and invariably die when introduced into an altered environment.

However, vermicastings containing the beneficial microflora and the worm coccons trigger biological activity in the news soil when covered with organic mulch and properly watered. Earthworms hatched in the newly triggered environment adapt themselves effectively and very soon establish an equilibrium of earthworm population, suitable to thrive there.

VERMICOMPOSTING MATERIALS

The biologically degradable and decomposable organic wastes are used in vermiculture and vermicomposting. Commonly used composting materials are as follows:

Animal dung

Cattle dung, sheep dung, horse dung, goat dung and poultry dropping etc. may be used for this purpose. In use of animal dungs other than cattle dung, various preliminary testing and precautions for pathogens and responses to earthworms are necessary. The uses of horse dung should be done carefully because tetanus virus is common in horse dung and is lethal to human beings.

Agricultural waste

Agricultural waste obtained after harvesting and threshing may be used. They include stem, leaves, husk (excepting paddy husk), peels, vegetable waste, orchard leaf litter, processed food wastes, sugarcane trash and baggase; and processing wastes.

Forestry wastes

These are plant products such as wood shavings, peels, saw dust and pulp. All these besides various types of forest leaf litter can be used. The unutilized forest waste such as leaf litter may also be used for vermicomposting.

City leaf litter

The burnt leaf litter from avenue or residential areas may be used, however, reports are not available. If it is used, this would keep cities clean and would provide useful product. The leaf litter of mango, guava, grasses and certain weeds may be used, but we need more information on this aspect.

Waste paper and cotton cloth etc.

These are decomposable organic waste. These are not being recycled for other useful products, can be recycled with vermicomposting.

City refuge

City refuge or garbage on daily production basis comprises important items of city factors and a considerable portion of city refuge can be sorted and recycled or composted. Most of household as kitchen waste with little manipulation can be used for vermicompose.

Biogas slurry

After recovery of biogas, if not required for agricultural use, *viz.,* in conventional composting can be used for vermicomposting.

Industrial wastes

The industrial wastes like waste from food-processing, distillery etc. can also be used in vermiculture with some manipulations.

PRELIMINARY TREATMENT OF COMPOSTING MATERIAL

Initially, proper collection, sorting or separation of compostable, non-compostable and non-biodegradables like plastics, stone, glass, ceramics and metals should be done. Heavily contaminated wastes (even in kitchen wastes, heavily spicy wastes) with chemicals should be separated. The cleane matter selected for composting should be heaped and large lumps should be broken. The separated matter should be be spreaded in a layer upto 1 foot and to be exposed to sun for a day. This helps in killing several unwanted organisms and removes foul smell. The mixing of daily organic waste produce may be done with somewhat pretreated leaf litter in approximate ratio ranging from 10 to 40 per cent of the waste to be vermicomposted.

Pre-treatment of leaf litter and agricultural waste

They are heaped on ground and exposed to sun. Heaps are then beaten with some stick or bamboo to break into smaller pieces.

Materials like crop plant stems and bagasse etc. are required to be cut into smaller pieces for enhancing decomposition and vermicomposting processes. The non-marketable vegetable produces, which are sometimes infected with insect pests should be chemically treated. The common example to these is insect pest popularly known as brinjal borers, which effect several vegetables.

These insects can be controlled by chopping waste into smaller pieces up to 4" size. They are then spread over ground. This layer is then sprayed with 4 per cent aqueous solution of some Neem insecticidal formulation. This would gradually kill insect pests stages without making waste unfit for vermicomposting. Neem formulation can also be prepared by collecting Neem fruits, drying and taking out seed kernel as we take out almonds by removing hard outer covering. 20-25 gm. Neem seed kernel be wrapped in a cloth over night and squeezed in half liter of water with repeated dipping and squeezing with turning movements. Solution so obtained is insufficient concentration to kill most insect pests stages.

SMALL SCALE OR INDOOR VERMICOMPOSTING

It is done under covered areas (with a shade). It is should be protected from climatic adversaries like high rains, prolonged spells of high or low temperatures (from less than 10° F to more than 45° F) and predators like ants, rodents and large insectivorous birds are abundant. Small scale indoor vermiculture and composting is easy and can be adopted.

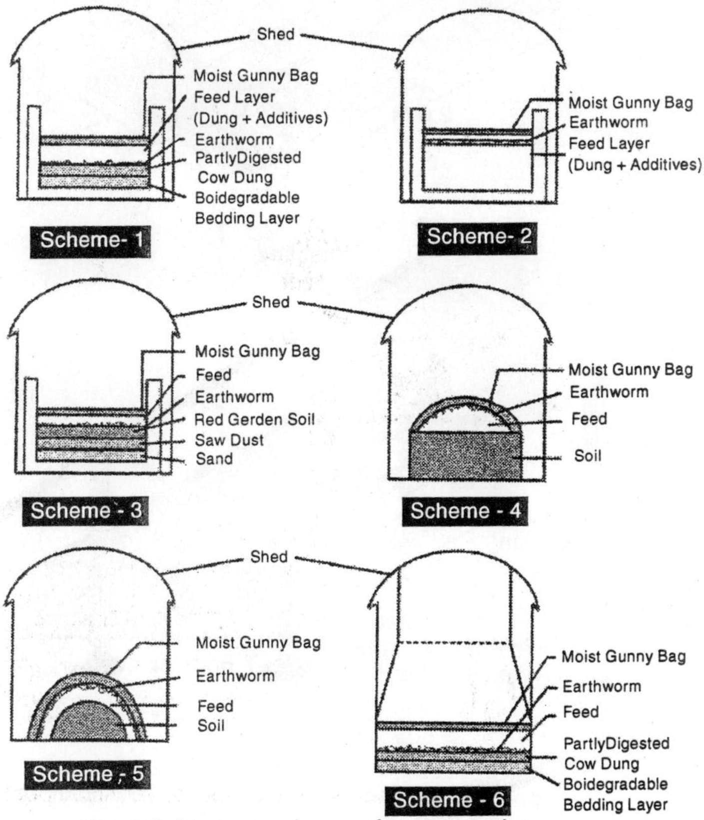

Fig. 3.3: Various schemes for composting.

LARGE SCALE OR OUTDOOR VERMICOMPOSTING

Simple promotion of vermic activity in fallow fields after harvesting crop(s). Large or small quantities of plant wastes to be vermicomposted, after pre-treatment be heaped and mixed with small quantities of mature cow dung manure (FYM). Then add bacterial inoculum for enhancing decomposition process and eventual faster vermicomposting. These heaps be sprinkled with little water (roughly 5 ltrs per 20 kg wastes) and covered with a hesian cloth or left on ground. Whole waste heap be kept

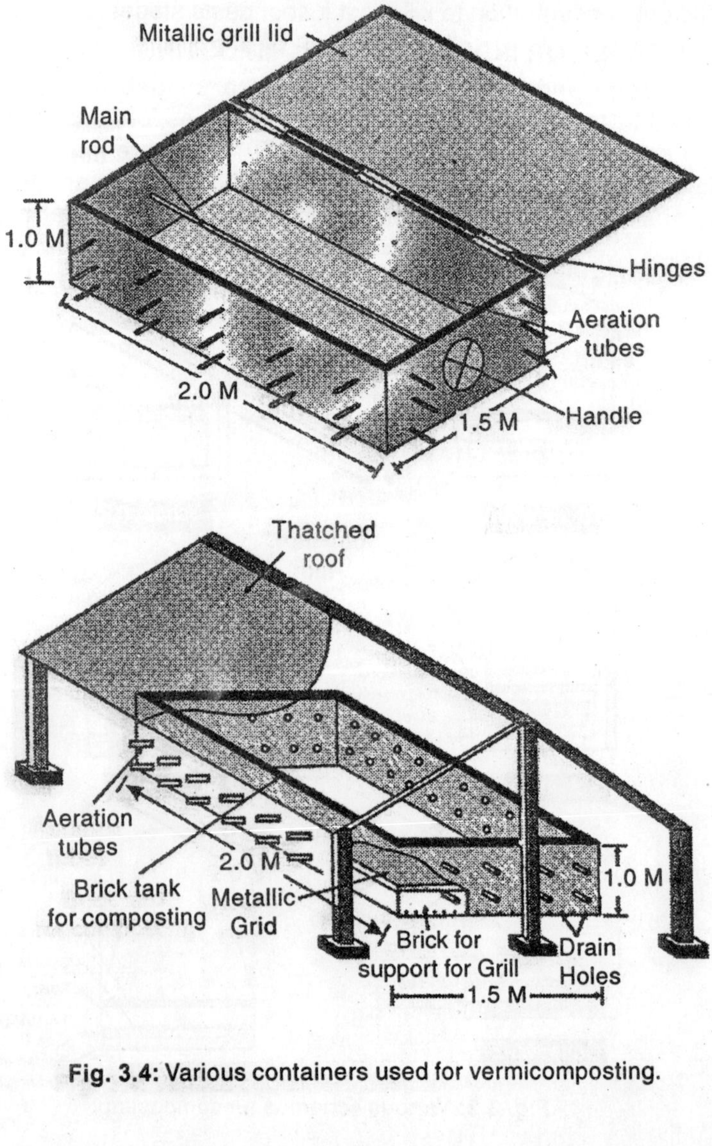

Fig. 3.4: Various containers used for vermicomposting.

moist for 3-7 days and periodically it is upturned and mixed. After 2-7 weeks, heap comes in a stage that verrmicomposting is fast. This waste is now ready for vermicomposting.

REQUIREMENTS FOR VERMICOMPOSTING

Container

The shape and size of the vermicomposting container depend on the requirement, that is quantity of waste to be composted and number of live earthworms we want to culture. On an average, 2000 adult earthworms can be maintained in containers of 1 m^2 dimension. These with appropriate conditioning of composting material would convert approximately 200 kgs. wastes every month. Roughly in a container of 2.23 x 2.23 mt. About 10 kgs. of earthworms can convert approximately 1 ton per month. However, to have optimal conversion normally only upper 9-12" layer is composted. This should be softly scrapped off.

Bedding material

This is the lower most layer of earthworm feed substrate that is required to be vermicomposted. For this any biodegradable matter is used like banana stem peels, coir pith, coconut leaves, sugarcane trash, stems of crops, grasses or husk. Waste or discarded cattle feed can also be used for bedding.

Moisture content

Moisture content during vermicomposting should be maintained between 30—40 per cent. If moisture is high, dry cow dung manure or leaf litter should be mixed with substrate.

Temperature

Requirement for optimal results is 20-30° C. However, survival of earthworms is even at lower temperatures and upto 48° C air temperature. Obviously with little provision of shade, temperature within worm feed substrate (material to be vermicomposted) can be reduced. For this it is desirable that substrate should not be tightly packed in containers.

Successful Adoption of Vermiculture

The potential of earthworms to improve poor and reclaimed soils has prompted attempts to introduce worm populations in farm land. In New Zealand, largescale inoculations of earthworms into pasture land has been practiced for many years. These trials led to significant improvement in soil conditions and grass yields as reported by Stockdill (1982). The reported development of a turf-cutting machine to distribute earthworms from areas with large populations to pastures short of worms is encouraging.

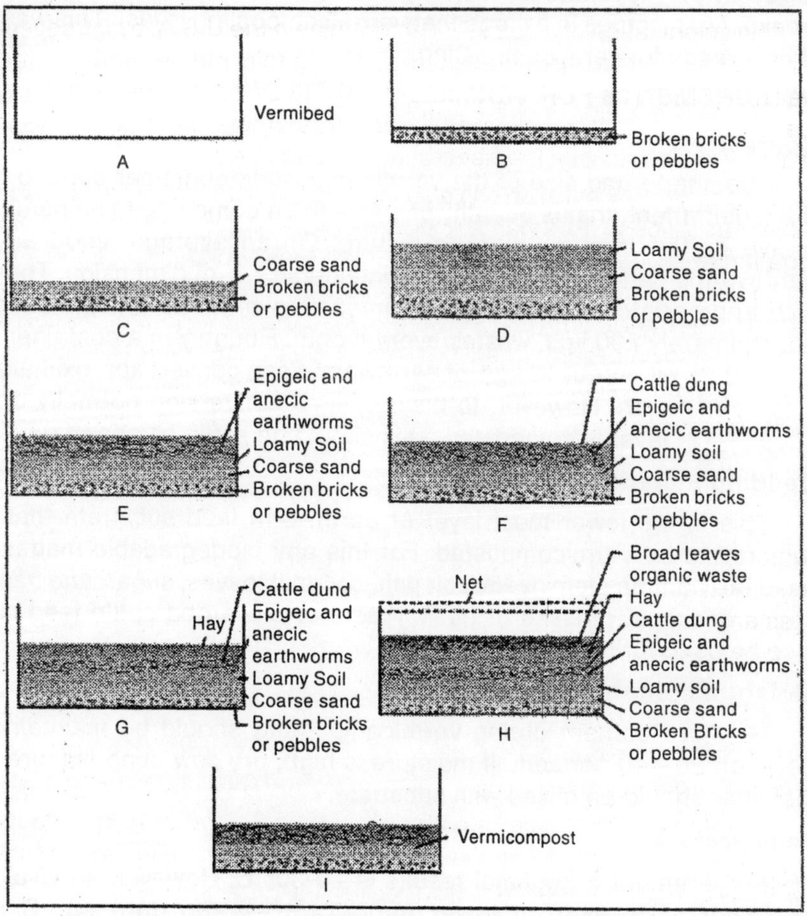

Fig. 3.5: Presentation of various layers for vermicomposting.

Dutch polders reclaimed from the sea suffer from a lack of earthworms. Earthworm inoculations have been done in them to accelerate the process of soil maturation. It was found that without worms, a layer of organic matter is built up on the soil surface, and the tramping of livestock compacted the soil below. Grass roots penetrated only the shallow layer of organic thatch and the ripping action of grazing animals separated the turf from the soil. Earthworms broke down the organic matter on the surface. Infrared photography revealed that the plots with worms were warmer at night and cooler during the day than those without worms. On the polders, earthworms increased grass yield by 10 per cent, enough to pursuade farmers to abandon their traditional practice of regular ploughing and reseeding to maintain production.

The colonization of a calcareousstrip-minein the U.S.A. by introduced earthworms increased incorporation of organic matter and nutrient availability. Curry and Cotton, (1983) found that well-managed, reclaimed peat could be much accelerated through the deliberate introduction of earthworms, especially the deep burrowing species.

The former Soviet Union has also realized the potential of earthworms. In the Republics of Turkmenia and Uzbekistan the desert soils require irrigation to produce high yields of arable crops. Irrigation changes the soil that is inhospitable to earthworms into one where they thrive. Scientists in the Soviet Union have assisted the slow natural spread of earthworms by a programmed inoculation, by transporting sacks of soil from a river-bank richly endowed with worms in convoys of lorries.

Bruce Marshall, a farmer in the uplands of Scotland, improved the yields on his farm by inoculating it with worms. The larger earthworm population has attracted moles, whose criss-cross runs through the soil eliminated the need to install artificial drainage. Marshall's land now supports almost 50 per cent more sheep. He thinks that earthworms are valuable in conservation, providing food for nesting waders, game birds, foxes and badgers.

Researchers at the Field Laboratory of the University 'College of Wales studied the rehabilitation of reclaimed opencast mines. Owing to an improper soil structure, the reclaimed fields were prone to waterlogging and damage by trampling. Inoculation of earthworms and supply of organic matter proved vital to the regeneration of these fields.

Although a variety of earthworm inoculation techniques have been developed, all rely on collecting earthworms from the field. This is very labourious, often requires specialist equipment or expertise and favours the collection of surface dwelling earthworms rather than deep burrowing species. Dependence on field collection has meant that the technique of earthworm inoculation could not be exploited as widely as its potential would warrant. Its future development would depend on advances in the intensive production of appropriate species through proper culture techniques. Much of the research on intensive culturing of earthworms (vermiculture) has focused on *Eisenia foetida*. Little is known about the growth and reproduction of soil dwelling earthworms under intensive conditions.

Scientists at the Open University, U.K. are tackling the problem of producing large quantities of burrowing earthworms under artificial conditions. By defining the optimum needs of worms under culture as well as field conditions these workers expect to keep the worms in high population density.

INITIATION OF VERMICULTURE IN INDIA

The use of *Perionyx excavatus* was the beginning of pioneer attempt in India to employ earthworms for the degradation of solid waste. Later *Eudrilus eugeniae* was brought to the laboratory in University of Agricultural Sciences, Bangalore, India to test the possibility of their establishment in this subcontinent, which has similar climatic conditions as that of its place of origin (Nigeria). Since 1982, *Eudrilus eugeniae* has been promoted for waste degradation. When compared to *Perionyx excavatus,* this species has surpassed both in feeding and reproductive rate. In the beginning of the experiments, it was thought that the response may be short lived, as many organisms show a tendency to perform extremely well in a new environment till they get established. Such a change in their efficiency was not observed in these last 15 years. A series of experiments has shown that it is an ideal species to work on agricultural and agrobased industry waste. Their sensitivity to density pressure and meandering nature demand larger area of space for their establishment. *Eisenia fetida* aiso entered the laboratory from Germany and is preferred species for composting activity in the urban areas (urban waste).

The University of Agricultural Sciences, Bangalore, India initiated vermiculture in India and they propogated the knowledge of vermiculture to farming community. The university released Press Note by the Technology Release Committee in the year, 1984. Till 1990, the technology did not induse much interest in many people. At initial stage, several controversies were developed about the composting and selection of species of earthworms.

Most of the researchers were of opinion that indigenous species of earthworms should be used for composting and not the exotic species like *Eisenia fetida* and *Eudrilus eugeniae.* The group that opposed the use of exotic species in this country lacked the knowledge of their feeding habits, habitat preference, their reproductive potentials and ability to survive in captivity to accept them for vermicomposting. But a detailed and in-depth study of the biology of 15 out of the 60 species of earthworms collected during the survey of Karnataka State helped me to put forward my views that a very few species of earthworms can be used for composting purpose and a few more as co-inhabitants to hasten up the process of decompositing alongwith other soil organisms.

In India, which was under colonialisation for several centuries, exotic species of plants and animals have been transported either intentionally or unintentionally. The northern part of the country has more exotic species of earthworms than the southern peninsula.

Successful Applications in India

Composting of waste

Vermiculture technology is being harnessed to set up units for cost-effective treatment of various non-toxic organic solid and liquid wastes from the cities, dairies, sugar and distillery units, pulp and paper mills, tanneries, fermentation industries and food processing units. Apart from environmental protection through the pollution abatement, these units serve as production centers of vermicastings, which are being used as earthworm culture because of the beneficial microflora and worm cocoons associated with them.

Use in agriculture

Vermicastings produced through the burrowing earthworms are being used by thousands of farmers in diverse agroclimatic conditions of India to change from chemical to sustainable agriculture without a loss of yield. The produce is of better nutritional qualities, without pesticide residues and with better keeping qualities-enhancing expqrtability. The farmers are witnessing soil improvement, as indicated by measurements of soil pH, nutrients availability, electric conductivity and water holding capacity. Eroded as well as saline soils are being developed through vermiculture biotechnology, with noticeable results within a year.

4

Application of Vermiculture Biotechnology

INTRODUCTION

Modern agriculture based on chemicals is not sustainable because of many problems such as loss of soil productivity from excessive erosion and associated plant nutrient losses, surface and ground water pollution from pesticides, fertilisers and sediment, impending shortages of non-renewable resources, and low farm income from high production costs. As a result, there is increasing awareness of the need for alternative agricultural systems. Such a system should integrate traditional practices with modern understanding of life science.

The concept of soil, as a living system, is central to alternative farming systems as opposed to chemical farming. It is essential to establish and maintain an active and abundant soil life in order to produce healthy plants. Therefore, the soil must be "fed" in a way, that the activities of beneficial soil organisms, necessary for recycling nutrients and producing humus, are not inhibited. Use of earthworms for degradation of organic wastes and production of vermicompost is becoming popular and is being commercialised. Darwin (1881) was the first to show that earthworms affect soil formation and development. His conclusion was a clear enunciation of the beneficial effects of earthworms on soil fertility. Thousands of farmers, in the different agroclimatic regions of India, are switching over to sustainable agriculture in field and horticultural crops, by adopting vermiculture biotechnology.

VERMICULTURE BIOTECHNOLOGY

Biotechnology essentially involves a large scale application of bio-systems for economic and effective processing of materials to produce value added products. Vermiculture is culturing of earthworms. Vermiculture biotechnology is, therefore, an aspect of biotechnology involving the use of earthworms as versatile natural bioreactors for effective re-cycling of non-toxic organic wastes to the soil, resulting in soil improvement and sustainable agriculture. Earthworms are invertebrates assigned to phylum *Annelida,* class *Chaetopoda* and order *Oligochaeta. Oligochaeta* includes the major earthworms belonging to

Megascolecidae, Lumbricidae and other families. More than half the earthworm species of the world belong to *Megascolecidae*. The genus *Phretinia* alone has a large number of species. Both *Megascolecidae* and *Lumbricidae* are valuable to agriculture and are, therefore, intimately linked to human welfare, development and progress.

The commonly used species are:

Eisenia fretida, Perionyx excavatus, Lumbrieus rubellus, L. terrestris, Eudrillus spp.

Lampito mauritii, Octochaetona serrata, Drawida Willsi, O. surensis, and *O. thurstoni*

There are four varieties of earthworms available in India, which are called manure worms. These can be cultured on animal dung, poultry droppings and vegetable and others kinds of biodegradable wastes. The worm cast or excretions of worms form the needed organic fertiliser. One worm weights about 0.5-0.6 g and consumes wastes of the same weight as their body weight giving casts of about the same weight in a day. If one million worms exist in one acre the cast they produce in that area is about 500 kg/day/acre *i.e.* about 200 tonnes per year. The worm cast contains all the nutrients in available form and in addition, a great deal of organic matter is provided to the soil which makes it very productive.

Earthworms play a key role in soil biology as versatile natural bioreactors. They effectively harness the beneficial soil microflora, destroy soil pathogens and convert organic wastes into valuable products such as biofertilisers, vitamins, enzymes, antibiotics, growth hormones and proteinous worm biomass. Hence, we can call the earthworms as 'artificial fertilizer factories'.

- Earthworm's gut is an effective tubular bioreactor, with raw materials (feed) entering from one end and the product (castings) coming out through the other end.
- They maintain a stable temperature through novel temperature regulation mechanisms, thus accelerating the rates of bioprocesses and preventing enzyme in activation caused by high temperatures.
- Gizzard is a novel colloidal mill in which the feed is ground into particles smaller than 2 microns, giving thereby an enhanced surface area for microbial processing.
- They have an in-house supply of enzymes such as protease, lipase, amylase, cellulose and chitinase, which bio-degrade complex biomolecules into simple compounds utilizable by the symbiotic gut microflora.
- Earthworms have a built-in oxygen plant which can separate aerial oxygen by chemical absorption into blood haemoglobin.

- They promote growth of micro-organisms in their gut by providing favourable conditions.
- Castings contain nutrients in a balanced proportion and are rich in vitamins, enzymes, antibiotics and growth hormones.

EARTHWORM FOR NUTRIENT MANAGEMENT

Effect on soil fertility

Earthworms modify soil physical, chemical and biological properties and it is believed that they enhance nutrient cycling by ingestion of soil and humus and by production of casts. There is abundant evidence to show that concentrations of exchangeable Ca, Na, Mg, K and available P and Mo are higher in earthworm casts than in the surrounding soil. Also they have a higher base exchange capacity (Table 4.1).

Table 4.1 Comparison of the available mineral elements in the cast of earthworms and in the upper layer of ploughed soil

Particulars	Earthworm cast	Depth of soil layer 0-15 cm	20-40 cm
Loss on ignition (%)	13.1	9.8	4.9
C:N ratio	14.7	13.8	13.8
N©3-nitrogn (ppm)	21.9	4.7	1.7
Available P (ppm)	130.0	20.8	8.3
Available K (ppm)	335.0	32.0	27.0
Exchangeable Ca (ppm)	2.78	1.99	1.81
Total Ca(%)	1.19	0.88	0.81
Total Mg(%)	0.545	0.511	0.548
Exchangeable Mg (ppm)	49.2	162	69
pH	7.0	6.36	6.05

Soil enrichment is achieved by speeding up mineralisation of organic matter 2 to 5 times. Earthworms greatly increase the amount of soluble and available N, P and K.

Nitrogen

Increased availability of N in earthworm casts compared to that in the non-digested soil has been attributed to the higher microbial population and enzyme activities in the casts. Some workers have suggested that earthworm mortality is the probable source of the increase in plant available soil N-pool. However, the contribution of N from this source was relatively small (3-4 per cent) in relation to the total added organic N. Earthworm casts are enriched in N compared to surface horizon. Intimate mixing of plant remains and animal manure with mineral soil also adds to the higher nitrogen content of the casts. An increase in the rate of nitrification in casts relative to the associated soil brings out the potential importance of earthworm in N cycle. Ninety six per cent of the extractable inorganic N in fresh casts is present as NH_4 N and rapid nitrification occurs following cast deposition. Moreover, a portion of the non-plant available N (6 per cent) ingested by *Allolobophora caliquinosa* is excreted in forms readily available to plants.

Phosphorus

Earthworms casts are enriched in water soluble P in comparison to the underlying soil. The plant availability of P in super phosphate (SP) and a phosphate rock (PR) as influenced by earthworms was evaluated in a glass house experiment using perennial rye grass over seven harvests. Increases in the yield of rye grass in the presence of earthworms varied from 2—32 per cent, whereas increase in P uptake ranged from 0—40 per cent over 7 harvests with SP, the initial increases in both rye grass yield and P uptake in presence of earthworm ranged from 20—40 per cent at first harvest to less than 10 per cent by the seventh. In marked contrast, earthworms increased the agronomic performance of pelletized rock phosphate by 15-30 per cent throughout the period. An increase in plant available soil N concentrations due to earthworm activity probably explains the initial difference in performance of super phosphate. The increased agronomic effectiveness of rock phosphate appears to result from the incorporation and intimate mixing of the phosphate rock with the soil by earthworms. It is not clear, however, whether the earthworms directly incorporated RP particles into the soil at lower depths, through their feeding and burrowing activity or the presence of burrows open to the surface simply facilitated the downward movement of surface-applied phosphate rock particles during watering. In addition to the incorporating effect of the earthworm, ingestion of phosphate rock particles during feeding, could lead to an increase in the intimate mixing with soil. Apart from these effects, a biological mechanism, mainly increased microbial activity also occurs. Thus, in the absence of biological mixing, both the form and method of application of phosphate rock materials become an important consideration in evaluating their efficiency. In addition, when earthworms are excluded, the form and method of application of rock phosphate become important in the interpretation and extrapolation of glass house experiment results to the field situation.

The following schematic representation indicates the mechanism of increased availability of P from phosphate rock by worm activity.

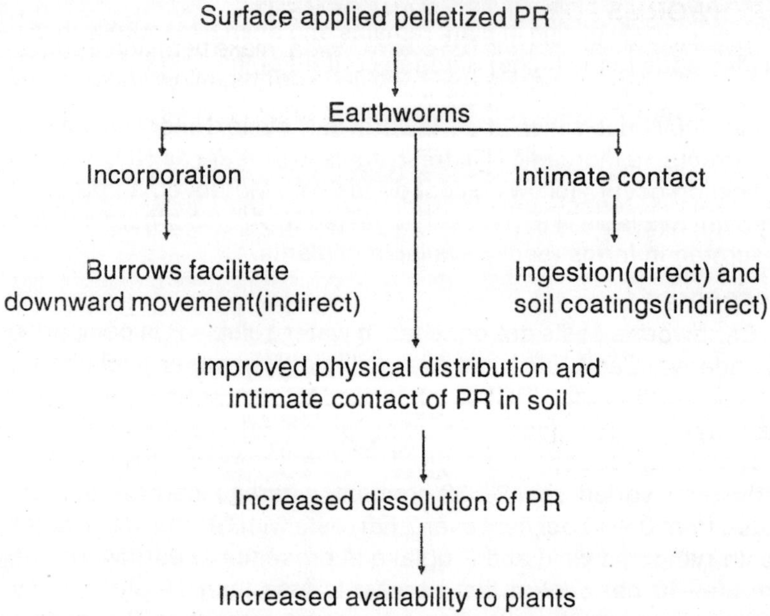

There is no downward movement of phosphate rock(PR) from the site of application in the presence of earthworms and hence, earthworms play no direct role in the incorporation of surface applied PR. Addition of earthworms *(Lumbricus rubellus)* to the soil incubated with PR resulted in a 32 per cent increase in Bray-extractable soil P after 70 days of incubation.

The earthworms increase the short-term plant availability of P from dead herbage 2-3 fold as a result of passage of the herbage through the earthworm and excretion as cast. This is attributed to the physical breakdown of the herbage by worm activity. The plant litter is more easily attacked by other de-composers after the material has been subjected to the grinding action and chemical changes in the earthworm gut. Therefore, the major effect of the surface-casting earthworm with regard to P availability appears to be a result of an increase in the rate of cycling of P (Mackay *et. al.,* 1982).

Potassium

The casts of earthworms contains 2-3 times more available K than the surrounding soil. Under controlled conditions, the availability of K is enhanced significantly following soil ingestion by earthworm. The changes in the K dynamics of soil resulting from ingestion by works must be due, atleast in part, to the changes in the distribution of K between exchangeable and non-exchangeable K forms due to gut processes (Basker *et. al.,* 1992).

EARTHWORMS FOR WATER MANAGEMENT

Earthworms, numbering 0.2-0.5 million/ha, make permanent structurally stable burrows, numbering 0.5-1.0 million per ha, allow water infiltration upto 120 mm per ha. Hence, in spite of heavy spell of rain, there is hardly any runoff and soil erosion, as each burrow acts as a microdam. Earthworms affect the pore space in soils by burrowing and by depositing their casts as loosely packed aggregates on the soil surface (Vanrhee, 1977).

For example, in soils of Dutch orchards lacking earthworms, pore space is determined by the packing of mineral particles and that about 30-40 per cent of the total soil volume consisted of fir filled or water filled spaces (Carter *et. al.*, 1982). Similar soils with earthworms (biomass as high as 200g/m^2) has a total of 60-70 per cent pore space; about 40 per cent water filled and 22-30 per cent air filled. At a depth of 25 cm in orchard soils with high earthworm populations, there are 200 earthworm burrows/m^2 of surface area and most of the air filled spaces in soils of good moisture holding capacity are earthworm burrows. From this we can say that increase of 75-100 per cent in pore space is mainly due to earthworm. Two third of the air filled pore space in soils may be earthworm burrows. The burrows must be regarded as an additional drainage system, a very significant one, within the soil matrix that operates during periods of heavy rain or when soils are irrigated. However, in a permanent pasture with a relatively low population of lumricides, the recognizable earthworm burrows are too wide to conduct water at tensions normal during infiltration and the earthworms have little significance in promoting water movement through soils under Mediterranean climatic regimes.

The total and available moisture content at field capacity and available moisture content for 0-30 cm depth is 17 per cent higher in pasture with lumbricide than in the pasture without lumbricides and macro-porosity decreases markedly from 44.9 to 21.5 per cent at 0-10 cm and from 29.3 to 22.7 per cent over 0-30 cm depth.There was an accompanying increase in bulk density from 0.68 to 0.86 g/cm^2 at 0-10 cm but with no change over 0-30 cm depth where lumbricide has been introduced compared with soils that lacked lumbricides. These changes are mainly due to the observed degradation and incorporation of porous pasture roots by worms (Stockdill, 1966). The rate of infiltration of water, when water is supplied in large quantities, is also greatly affected by earthworms.

Earthworm castings

The castings of earthworm are stable. Earthworms excrete granular, structurally stable castings on the soil surface. These do not disintegrate into micro particles when dry or wet and hence, there is no soil loss due to wind or water. The runoff water, if any, is clear. The activity of earthworms is recognised as beneficial for the improvement of soil physical conditions and plant growth. Also the coarse sand fraction is reduced in castings by selective ingestion by worms. On the one hand this is because of the burrowing activities of earthworms which improve air and water penetration into soil and on the other hand it is because of the earthworm castings which stabilise soil aggregates.

Blanchart *et al.* (1990) assessed the effect of tropical geophagous earthworm, *Millsonia anomala,* on particle aggregation in a tropical soil in the presence of *Panicum maximum* and concluded that in the presence of *M.anomala,* there was substantially increased aggregation. In the absence of earthworms . (with or without plants) a rapid aggregation of soil particles occurred, through the activity of micro-organisms, and/or physical mechanisms although this did not increase consistently across subsequent sampling times. Earthworms do not ingest their own casts and aggregation rapidly increases to a maximum value of 60 per cent when populations are high, and then the earthworm activity declines.

Vermicastings, being granular and with enhanced internal porosity and water absorption capacity, absorb moisture particularly during night and hold it effectively for releasing it to micro-roots of the vegetation.

EARTHWORMS ACT AS BIOPUMP

Earthworms burrow enhances water infiltration and storage over a considerable depth of soil. Earthworms help to bring this moisture to the upper layer by acting as biopump. They produce biological water during the decomposition of organic matter. This 'slow release' water can be effectively utilized by the roots.

EARTHWORMS FOR EFFECTIVE WASTE MANAGEMENT

Vermiculture biotechnology is being harnessed to set up units for cost-effective treatment of various non-toxic organic solid and liquid wastes from the cities, dairies, sugar and distillery units, pulp and paper mills, tanneries, fermentation industries and food processing units. Apart from environmental protection through pollution abatement, these units can serve as production centres of vermicastings because of beneficial microflora and worm cocoons associated with them. Soils with a good population of earthworms could be used to handle various non-toxic organic wastes. Earthworms maintain aerobic conditions in the soil and effect complete waste stabilisation with beneficial soil microflora, which release the plant nutrients and produce valuable products such as vitamins, antibiotics and growth hormones. Pathogens are also destroyed.

Sabine (1983) has summarized the potential benefits of largescale intensive culture of earthworms on organic wastes as follows:

(a) Reduction of noxious qualities of wide variety of organic wastes such as, elimination of smell, reduction of harmful microbes and ease in physical handling.

(b) Production of useful and marketable organic fertilizer, compost or potting media from organic wastes. Protein production for stock feed, or human food from organic wastes.

COMPOSTING OF MUNICIPAL AND INDUSTRIAL WASTES

Hartenstein (1978) described laboratory trials of vermi-composting of aerobic sludge from waste water(sewage) treatment plants with *Eisenia fretida* in the compost. He compared the end-products, comprising worm casts, that have value as a fertilizer and potting soil and earthworm which are high in protein. The latter could be sold as a protein additive for animal feed. The methods of bio-degradation comprise:

(a) Composting with microorganisms, resulting in a material that can be used as a soil amendment but has little value as a fertilizer.

(b) Incineration which is environmentally undesirable, energy demanding and leaves a virtually unusable residue, and,

(c) burial which is energy demanding, expensive and can result in pollution of water supplies/bodies.

Albanell *et al* (1988) analysed the castings of *Eisenia fretida* from sheep manure alone and from that mixed with cotton wastes for their properties and chemical composition and compared with the same manures in the absence of earthworms. The results showed that earthworms accelerated the mineralisation rate and converted the manures into castings with a higher nutritional value and degree of humification. The castings obtained from manure mixed with cotton wastes exhibited good agronomic quality and a low-cost fertilizer suggesting that this kind of industrial residue may be used in vermicomposting.

EARTHWORMS FOR DISEASE AND PEST MANAGEMENT

Healthy soil has a balanced population of beneficial and soil microflora and burrowing earthworms. This reduces the population of soil pathogens, through competition and antibiosis. Almost all insect and pathogenic attacks are targetted to the nutritionally weaker plants. Earthworms produce casts which provide balanced nutrition to plants, thus giving them tolerance to pest attack. Interactions between earthworms, soil microorganisms, and root pathogens have been studied very little. Doube *et al* (1994) evaluated the control of fungal root diseases of cereal crops using earthworms and biocontrol agents, and the influence of earthworms of *Rhizobium* populations. The results indicated that the earthworms dispersed *Pseudomonas coirugata* strain 2140R, a biocontrol agent for 'Take-all' diseases (Ryder and Ravira, 1993) 10-20 cm through tubes of pasteurised soil in the laboratory after 8 days. The larger earthworm, *Aporrectodea trapezoides,* moved the bacteria further and more quickly then did *A.rosea.* Similar densities of *P.corrugata* were present in casts of both the earthworm species and in soil associated with the walls of earthworm tunnels. Further experiments showed that when *P.corrugata* 2140R was mixed with worm food and applied to surface of soils in pots, the worm *A.trapezoides,* dispersed that bacteria and resulted in bacterial colonization of roots of wheat seelings.

Rhizoctonia solani (the casual agent of barepatch disease), the common fungal root pathogen of wheat in Southern Australia, is a saprophytic species which also colonizes living roots. Because earthworms consume microorganisms, decomposing organic matter and possibly living roots have obvious potential to interact directly (as predators) and indirectly (as competitors or facilitators) with soil dwelling saprophytic fungi. Further, the effects of some fungal root pathogens (eg. *Rhizoctonia)* are substantially reduced by mechanical disruption of soil and it is possible that earthworm activity may perform a similar function.

Recent laboratory data have shown that the activity of *A.trapezoides* can substantially decrease the symptoms caused by *Rhizoctonia* in wheat seedlings (Stephen *et al.,* 1993). A decrease in plant parasitic nematodes has been observed in the presence of earthworms, indicating the biological control activity of earthworms although it is yet to be confirmed whether direct feeding or some other mechanism is responsible. Studies are needed to find out whether natural limitation of pest population is associated with the species richness that might be expected in ecological agriculture.

EARTHWORMS FOR NUTRITIONAL CROPS

Increase in crop yields and quality has often been recorded in plants grown in the presence of earthworm casts. Considerable scientific data have been generated to show that organic produce is nutritionally superior, tastes good, has good luster and better keeping qualities. Crops grown organically, with slower growth rates and greater physiological maturity harvest, have been shown, in carefully controlled trials, to have longer storage life. The influence of earthworms/earthworm casts on N metabolism has been indirectly made evident by an increased protein content in young oat plants, barley, rye, wheat and in mushrooms. The earthworm casts could stimulate the activity of nitrate reductase enzymes. It is logical to conclude that the increase in protein content depends on improved protein synthesis although the mechanism involved is still unclear (Galli *et al.*, 1990). But it is evident that microbes and microbial metabolites are involved. In protein synthesis, microbial hormone-like substances could play an important role by regulating ionic absorption and including some enzymatic activities. When used as a component of a casting layer in Agaricus bisporous cultivation, earthworm casts stimulated primordia formation and initiation and enhance the protein content of the carpophore. Microbial metabolites could be responsible for this effect, since they affect fratification of Agaricus.

EARTHWORMS FOR SUSTAINABLE AGRICULTURE AND WASTELAND DEVELOPMENT

Vermicastings produced through the burrowing earthworms are being used by many farmers to change from chemical to sustainable organic agriculture without loss of yields. Eroded as well as saline soils are being developed through vermiculture biotechnology with noticeable results within a year.

The package, particularly suitable for ^crops such as fruits, vegetables, sugarcane, cotton, etc., where a surface layer of organic mulch can be practically maintained, consists of:

- applying a first layer of vermicastings @ 5t/ha.
- watering once in every 15-20 days and
- periodic application of dung and mulches.

Worms hatch out from cocoons in vermicastings within a month. They start processing the dung and organic mulch and produce vermicastings making the system almost a zero external input sustainable agriculture. A transition from- chemical to sustainable organic agriculture takes 3 to 6 years. This is the time required to trigger without excessive reliance on chemical fertilizers and pesticides. This swift change over to sustainable organic agriculture without loss of yield is possible by seeding the soil with vermicastings (with associated microflora and cocoons). This will result in establishing a population of burrowing- type earthworms, about 0.2-1.0 million/ha in 3 months.

EARTHWORMS AS VECTORS OF BENEFICIAL MICROORGANISMS

One of the major constraints for effective root colonization by beneficial soil bacteria is their limited capacity for unaided dispersal though soil. A variety of methods have been used to inoculate beneficial microorganisms into soil (eg. seed inoculation). But these procedures, when used in the field, commonly inoculate only a small portion of soil volume which is available to plant roots. The activity of earthworms has been shown to promote the dispersal through the soil a variety of types of beneficial soil microorganisms including *Pseudomonas, Rhizobia* and *Mycorrhizal* fungi. Reports indicate that earthworms are capable of acting as vector of *Rhizobium trifolii* (Reddell and Spain, 1991). The presence of *L.terrestris* was associated with improved distribution of nodules on the root systems of soybean and this resulted from worm dispersal of *Bradyrhizobium japonicum.* The inoculation of highly effective *rhizobia* into legume seeds does not have always result in the formation of effective nodules and a corresponding high level of N-fixation because seed inoculation tends to result in localization of high cell densities in the vicinity as seed and emerging roots, with considerable lower numbers further away. *Apporrectodea trapezoides* can spread *Rhizobium* through the soil and cause increased root colonization and nodulation of legume roots. Better dispersal is achieved with buried than with surface applied carrier material. *Protozoa* and *fungi* are the major sources of nutrients for earthworms and bacteria are of minor nutritional importance. The distribution of propagates of VAM fungi by earthworms in a number of plant communities indicates that the earthworm cast material contains higher number of spores. It could be due to feeding on senescing roots and earthworms concentrating mycorrhizal propagules in their cast soil. Due to the fact that surface worm casts are more abundant in early succession, the deposition of propagules is comparable to that in older communities (Gange, 1993). Earthworms may, therefore, be important agents in the distribution of VAM fungi thereby influencing plant establishment in early succession.

SUCCESSFUL APPLICATIONS

The potential of earthworms to improve poor and reclaimed soils has resulted in attempts to introduce worm population in farm land. In New Zealand, large scale inoculation of earthworms into pasture land has been practised for many years (Curry and Cotton, 1983). These trials led to significant improvement in soil conditions and grass yields. Development of a turf cutting machine to distribute earthworms from areas with large populations to pastures short of worms has helped in this mechanism. Dutch polders reclaimed from the sea suffer from a lack of earthworms. Earthworm inoculation has been done in these soils to accelerate the process of soil maturation.

The colonization of a calcareous strip-mine in the USA by introduced earthworms increased the organic matter content and nutrient availability and well managed, reclaimed peat could support large populations and the population development could be much accelerated through deliberate introduction of earthworms. The former Soviet Union had also realised the potential of earthworms. In the desert soils, inoculation by transporting sacks of soils from a river-bank richly endowed with worms in convoys of trucks was undertaken (Lee, 1985). Researchers of the Field Laboratory of the University College of Wales studied the rehabilitation of reclaimed open cast mines. Inoculation of earthworms and supply of organic matter proved vital to the regeneration of these soils which had poor structure and were prone to water logging (Curry and Cotton, 1983).

HARNESSING VERMICULTURE BIO-TECHNOLOGY

Selection of proper species

Not all earthworms are active in soil formation. *Eisenia fretida* for example, which is normally found near manure dumps, cannot survive over long period in field soils. Any increase in yield after adding *E. fretida* to soil is short-lived, and is simply due to the decomposition of dead worms rather than to worm activity. Similarly worms such as *Pheyetima elongata, Lumbricus terrestris,* and *Allolobophora caliginosa,* which thrive in soils tend to grow fairly slowly in rich organic culture, or they do not tolerate culture conditions at all.

Use of vermicastings for inoculation

Earthworms cocoons are invariably associated with vermicastings. It is desirable to use vermicastings of burrowing-type earthworms to inoculate the new fields. Live, mature worms may not withstand the transport shock and invariably die when introduced into an altered environment. But earthworms hatched in the newly triggered environment adapt themselves effectively and very soon establish an equilibrium of earthworm population suitable to thrive in the new environment.

Earthworms and land use practices

Effect of organic manure and NPK fertilizers on earthworm activity

Considering the extensive use of organic manures, little is known about their effects on the soil fauna, particularly earthworms. Edwards and Lofty (1982) studied the effect of nitrogenous fertilizers on earthworm populations in agricultural soils, in long term field experiments at the Rothamsted Experimental Station, UK. Various forms of inorganic N, liquid and solid sewage sludge and sewage cake in a wide range of doses were applied. In three arable experiments, all species of earthworms were more numerous in plots. There was a strong positive correlation (r=0.9825) between amounts of inorganic N applied and population of earthworms. Plots which received both inorganic and organic N had the largest population of earthworms. The effects of both inorganic and organic N were much less on earthworms population in grassland than those in arable crops, even in long term experiments, and there was some evidence of adverse effects when an excessive of liquid sludge was applied in a single dose (Brussard and Ridder, 1990). Also, the favourable effects of organic fertilizers were greater on populations of *Lumbricus terrestris* than on those of *Allolobophora longa,*

A.caliginosa and A. *chorotica.*

It is less clear how inorganic N fertilizers favour the build up of earthworm population. However, there was evidence to show that, in terms of amount of N applied/ha, organic matter had a greater effect than inorganic N. Higher concentrations of inorganic N probably influence the amount of plant material and which, in turn, decomposed increasing the soil organic matter content (Tiwari, 1993).Therefore, the use of NPK fertilizers, in addition to organic manure, appears advisable to derive more benefits from nitrogenous, potash and phosphatic fertilizers in acidic soils of sub-tropical regions.

Cultivation

Conventional mechanical tillage practices such as ploughing, rotary-hoeing and harrowing, lead to a reduction in earthworm population, mainly because of:—

1. mechanical damage due to tillage implements, and
2. loss of surface litter.

Minimum tillage in which crop residues are left on the surface and the soil below is sub-tilled has been shown to encourage the build up of earthworm population. Zero cultivation is recommended in perennial crops such as fruit trees, palms, etc. to promote earthworm activity. Drastic tillage methods not only tend to reduce earthworm populations, but also increase their susceptibility to the effects of seasonable differences in soil moisture and so reduce the period during the year when they are able to influence soil conditions and plant growth.

Mulching

The ancient agricultural practice of mulching where animal dung and/or plant residues are spread on soil surface, has the dual purpose of insulating the soil from extremes of temperatures and providing plant nutrients and humic materials for incorporation into the soil. Straw and compost, which provide surface insulation and food for worms, are more effective than plastic mulches.

Irrigation

The deep burrowing earthworm species can be effective even without irrigation. However, a combination of irrigation and mulching is desirable to maintain a high population.

Biocides

Biocides, when applied to soil, are harmful to worms. They should be substituted with safer alternatives which ecologically control insects, diseases and weeds. Earthworms provide balanced nutrition to the plants, thus reducing pest problems. Safer, herbal sprays may be used when the earthworms occasionally attack the epigeal parts of plants. There are a few reports of excessive casting by earthworm leading to poaching of soil by livestock and of worm casts being deposited sufficiently high in cereal stocks to make it difficult to obtain clean grain when thrashing. Earthworms are known to accumulate some heavy metal pollutants. In industrialised countries where these pollutants are present in the environment in hazardous or non-hazardous concentrations, the possibility exists for their further concentration in earthworms fed on composted wastes. If composted municipal and industrial wastes are to be widely used to provide earthworms as a protein source, it would be necessary to monitor the heavy metal content of the wastes and the earthworms.

PROCEDURE TO PREPARE VERMICOMPOST

Culturing technique

A large number of wooden, plastic, card board or cement boxes of various sizes, (the maximum of lm x lm x 0.5m) can be used. This volume can accommodate 1500 worms. Culturing is done indoors avoiding sunlight and rain.

Culture bed

At the bottom of the box, a layer of bedding material is spread to a thickness of 2.5-5.0 cm. This can be any bio-degradable material. On this, a second layer of about 5 cm thick partially digested cowdung is spread. Water is sprinkled on the bed to get a moisture level of 30-40 per cent. Worms or their cocoons are then introduced on to the bed.

Feed composition

Dried dung of cattle, sheep, horse, pigs or droppings of poultry and small shredded pieces of vegetable waste form the ideal food for the worms. Cattle dung can be fed as such if available, but other dung materials or vegetable wastes can be mixed in equal quantity with cattle dung for feed acceptability. Wheat bran, grain bran and vegetable waste, when added to dung in 10:11.1 ratio, will enhance the quality of the compost and biomass production.

Feed application

The feed is to be placed uniformly in a layer on the culture bed and replenished as and when it disappears from surface.

Wormcast production and collection

When compost is ready, watering is stopped for 2-3 days, when all the worms retire to the bed below where some water still exists. The compost is then dry and can be piled in small heaps in ambient conditions for a couple of hours when all the worms will godown the heap to the bed. The heaps then become compost heaps containing worm cocoons.

Fresh feed material should be placed immediately after removing compost. The bedding material will also be eaten by — „ the worms and should be discarded after 6 months and a fresh bed should be laid as done earlier.

APPLICATION OF VERMICOMPOST

In orchards the dose depends on the age of the tree. A deep ring of 15-20 cm is to be formed around the tree. A thin layer of dry cow dung and bone meal with 2-5 kg. of vermicompost is then applied. This is covered with a thin layer of soil. This ring is mulched with organic matter and a light spray of water is given. In pots, a handful of vermicompost should be applied near the rootzone. The application should be repeated after one month and water should be added to keep it moist. For general use in agriculture, vermicompost should be applied at 5 t/ha. Vermicompost is mixed with equal quantity of dried cowdung. This is broadcasted when seedlings are 12-15 cm high and water should be sprinkled.

CONCLUSION

Vermiculture bio-technology can be fruitfully utilised to gain several benefits:-

To Farmers:

- Less reliance on purchased inputs leading to low cost of production.
- Enhancement of soil productivity.
- The produce with better taste, lustre and keeping qualities without toxic residues can be produced, fetching a higher prices.
- Recycling of organic wastes is achieved. To Industries.
- There is a cost-effective pollution abatement technology.

To Environment:

- Wastes create no pollution, as they become valuable raw materials for the soil bio-technological processes.
- There is more groundwater recharge and less ground water depletion.
- Soil salinisation is reduced with low soil erosion and runoff. To

To National Economy:

- Lesser import of agrochemicals, saving valuable foreign exchange.
- Savings on subsidies.
- Boost to rural economy.
- More export of agricultural produces with lower pesticide residues.
- Reduced wasteland formation.

FUTURE RESEARCH NEEDS

If the production of vermicompost is to be undertaken on a large scale, it is more important to determine the long-term effects of its applications rather than the immediate response obtained. No work has been done so far on these lines. The exact dose and time of application of vermicompost is not yet worked out for many crops.

The use of selected species of worms for vermicompost production in a more economical way as well as evolving methods to substantially improve the quality of manure is essential. One such improvement in the quantity of manure lies in enhancing the number of N-fixers in vermicompost. If repeated application of vermicompost improves the soil and provide the base for establishment of beneficial free living and symbiotic microbes, its application becomes more meaningful than introduction of worms into field. Little is known about the effect of NPK fertilisers on earthworm activities in the soil. The possibility that a mixture of earthworm food and beneficial microorganism may provide a basis for a new technology for dispersing and introducing biocontrol bacteria and rhizobia into soil may be looked into.

There is a need for better understanding of the effect of heavy metal contaminated industrial wastes and other chemicals like pesticides, their uptake and accumulation by the earthworm and the subsequent effect on food chain. It has recently been demonstrated that microorganisms in the gut of some tropical earthworm species, may fix atmospheric nitrogen in quantities that are significant for the earthworm's metabolism and as a source of nitrogen for plant growth. It is not known whether this process is common in earthworms, and, if so, which species has this faculty, whether some species are more effective hosts they may be effectively utilised in promoting the availability of nitrogen for plant growth. Hence there is a need for research on the physiology of nitrogen metabolism and possible mutualistic relationships with microorganisms and different species of earthworms for understanding the possibilities of using earthworm to promote the availability of nitrogen to plants.

5

Composting of Agricultural and Industrial Wastes

INTRODUCTION

The organic matter content of cultivated soils of the tropics and sub-tropics is low due to high temperature and intensive microbial activity. Therefore, soil humus has to be replenished through microbial activity and periodic additions of organic manures for maintaining soil productivity as increased cost of fossil fuels, shortages in energy and production of chemical fertilisers are expected to accentuate in the near future. Availability of chemical fertilisers to the farmer at a reasonable cost will be a real problem. There is, thus, a need for utilising organic manures/wastes for supplementing chemical fertilisers. Preparation of organic manures from rural and urban wastes would provide not only plant nutrients and humic materials but also will result in hygienic disposal of the organic wastes which, otherwise, may cause pollution problems.

Farmers in developing countries need adequate resources for augmenting the crop productivity. Proper soil management ensuring continued maintenance and building up of soil fertility is indispensable for greater productivity from agricultural land. There is no need to emphasize that organic manures influence favourably plant growth and yield. Their indirect effects include augmentation of beneficial microbial population and their activities in the soil of organic matter decomposition, biological nitrogen fixation, solubilisation of insoluble phosphates and availability of plant nutrients. The direct effect is through addition of nitrogen, phosphorous, potassium and small amounts of micronutirents such as manganese, zinc, copper and iron. In the use of organic materials as manures for crop production, farmers are faced with the problems of organic materials being bulky, with a low nutrient content in relation to their volume, and being often messy and smelly. Further more, application of fresh organic material may reduce the soil fertility and produce substances harmful to plant growth.

Sewage sludge, biogas slurry, waste water, fish pond effluent, pressmud, coir pith, seaweed residue, arecanut waste, tannery waste and wastes from different industries and mined areas are some of the wastes which can be effectively utilised as organic fertilisers after giving proper treatment. With the mounting disposal problems and widening gap between demand and supply of nutrient sources, the concept of composting of organic (agricultural/industrial) wastes, is getting renewed attention. Composting is a process by which the organic component is biologically decomposed until the material forms a stable, inoffensive organic fertiliser.

DEFINITION

Composting is a process by which organic wastes are converted into organic fertilisers by means of biological activity under controlled conditions(Kiyonori Haga, 1990).

Composting is defined as a method of solid waste management whereby the organic component of the solid waste stream is biologically decomposed under controlled conditions to a state in which it can be handled, stored and/or applied to the land without adversely affecting the environment (Golueke, 1977).

It is an important technique for recycling organic (agricultural/ industrial) wastes and for improving the quality and quantity of organic fertilisers. The objectives in composting are to stabilize the putrescible organic matter in raw agricultural/ industrial wastes to reduce offensive odours, to kill weed seeds and pathogenic organisms and finally to produce a uniform, slow release organic fertiliser which stimulates soil life; improves soil structure; helps plants to tolerate/resist pests and diseases.

PRINCIPLES OF COMPOSTING

Composting is a self heating, thermophilic and aerobic biological process which occurs naturally in heaps of bio-degradable organic matter such as manure, moist hay and straw. This bio-degradation process is carried out by different kinds of heterophytic microorganisms, bacteria, fungi, actinomycytes and protozoa, which derive their energy and carbon requirements from the decomposition of carbonaceous materials. For every 10 parts of carbon, one part of N is required for building up their cell protoplasm. Fungi are most efficient in carbon assimilation than bacteria and actinomycetes. Under aerobic conditions, heterotrophic organisms derive energy from the decomposition of organic matter, resulting in the production of CO_2, humic substances and release of available nutrients. Under aerobic conditions, the following major reactions are likely to occur:

Sugars, cellulose, hemi- $(CH_2O)X + XO_2 \longrightarrow XCO_2 + XH_2O + \text{Energy}$
cellulose, lignins, proteins

Organic N $\longrightarrow NH_3 \longrightarrow NO_2 \longrightarrow NO_3$

Organic S + XO $\longrightarrow SO_4$

Organic Phosphate $\longrightarrow H3PO_4 \longrightarrow Ca(HPO4)_2$
(phytin, Lecithin)

Under anaerobic conditions, microorganisms break down organic materials by a process of reduction in the absence of O_2. First, special group of acid producing bacteria and facultative heterotrophs degrade organic matter into fatty acids, aldehydes and alcohols. Then a group of bacteria convert the intermediate products to methane, NH_3, CO_2, and H_2.

CH_2O+O_2--------->CH_3COOH----------->CH_4+CO_2
Organic N---------> NH_3.

AGRICULTURAL WASTES

India has a vast potential of agricultural and industrial wastes. The major agricultural sources are livestock and human wastes, crop residues, tree wastes and aquatic weeds, green manures, urban and rural wastes, agro-industrial by-products, marine wastes and tank silt. With the introduction of high yielding varieties and adoption of intensive systems of cropping, large quantities of crop residues such as straw, leaves, twigs and stubbles along with huge amounts of grasses and weeds are readily available on farms. Potential hazards related to nutrient management, trace elements, trace organic chemicals, pathogens and soil physical problems may be encountered when the above wastes are applied directly to the soil-plant system for crop production. Moreover, because of their wide C:N ratio, these agricultural wastes are known to reduce the availability of important mineral nutrients to growing plants through immobilisation into organic from and also produce some phytotoxic substances during their decomposition. The traditional method of composting is a slow process and takes more than six months. Also the product thus prepared contains very low quantity of nutrients. In addition, farmers generally prefer burning these waste materials in situ (*eg*. cane trash). This adversely affects the environment and causes deterioration of the biological properties of the soil. All these drawbacks can be only set right by developing a technique for a rapid treatment of these wastes by composting.

Moreover, in India, a major part of residues is used as animal feed, while some find use as fuel and some may make housing materials in the rural areas. Thus, only a small part of the crop residues would be available for direct incorporation into soil for composting. The production of crop residues and their potential of nutrient availability is discussed in detail in the chapter "Crop Residue Management:". Table 5.1 gives the average nutrient status of some common organic manures and composts from agricultural wastes.

Table 5.1. Average nutrient content of some common composts of animal and plant origin

Manures/Composts	Nutrient content (%)		
	N	P_2O_5	K_2O
Farm Yard Manure	0.80	0.41	0.74
Poultry Manure	2.87	2.93	2.35
Rural compost	1.22	1.08	1.47
Urban compost	1.24	1.92	1.07
Mixed farm wastes	0.87	0.59	2.22
Mixed dry residues	0.90	0.45	1.95
Cotton stalks	1.61	0.48	3.38
Water hyacinth compost	2.00	1.00	2.30
Paddy straw	1.59	1.34	3.37
Dry grass/weeds	1.90	0.55	1.09
Cotton wastes and grounnut husk	1.62	1.04	1.26
Lantana stalks and leaves	1.55	0.52	1.07
Wheat straw	2.90	2.05	0.90
Maize stalks	1.99	1.30	1.01
Sugarcane trash	2.73	1.81	1.31
Vermicompost	1.60	2.20	0.67

Source: Misra and Hesse, 1982. Hand book of Manures and Fertilisers ICAR, New Delhi.

Methods for composting of Agricultural wastes

Indore Method

The waste materials such as plant residues, animal wastes, vegetable wastes and weeds can be composted with the Indore method. First the waste materials are chopped into small pieces of 5-10 cm size and are dried to 40-50 per cent moisture before stacking. Then, they are spread in layers of 10-15 cm thickness either in pits or in heaps of one m width, 4-6 m length and one m depth. The heap is properly moistened with dung, using earth or night soil. Sufficient quantity of water is sprinkled over the heap to wet the composting materials to the level of 50 per cent moisture. Periodical turnings, usually three times at 15, 30 and 60 days after filling, are given to aerate and the material is covered with a thin layer of soil of about 2-3 cm thickness. Under the aerobic process of decomposition, losses of organic matter and nitrogen are heavy (40-50 per cent at initial stage). This process, however, involves considerable labour in the preparation of the heap and periodical turnings and so becomes expensive and impracticable when large quantities of materials are to be processed. The site selected must be at a high level to prevent rain water stagnation. It should be nearer to cattle shed and water source for easy transporting. The compost obtained by this Indore method would have a composition 0.8 per cent N, 0.3 per cent P and 1.5 per cent K_2O.

Activated compost

Fowler developed this technique in which fresh materials are incorporated in an already fermenting heap so that quicker decomposition can be obtained with already established microbial population. This method is useful, particularly when offensive materials like night soil are to be quickly and effectively disposed off.

Banglore method

Pioneering work in preparation of manure in pits was carried out by Acharya (1939), particularly on the utilisation of town residues and night soil. This process is otherwise called as hot fermentation method of manure production. In this method, the compost production depot is located on the city outskirts to transport town refuse and night soil to the pits. The depots normally accommodates about 200 trenches with a spacing of l-5m between trenches. First the refuse is to make 15 cm height layer. Then night soil is discharged over this and spread to a layer of 5 cm. After filling the pit with refuse and night soil in alternate layers, the pit is filled to 15 cm above ground level with a final layer of refuse of 15cm on the top. This may be dome-shaped and covered with the thin layer of soil with red earth or mud to prevent moisture loss and breeding of flies. Sullage water, if collected in carts as in some towns, may be emptied over the layer of refuse. This system provides a method of disposal of any kind of waste, including slaughter house waste, carcasses of animals, sewage, etc.

The materials are allowed to remain as such without any turning and pot watering for about three months. The decomposition of dumped materials in pits takes place largely in the absence of sufficient air except in the surface layer. Though the decomposition is comparatively slow, high temperature is not developed in the lower layers. Since the material does not receive any turnings, decomposition into a homogenous mass of manure does not take place. Even then, the C/N ratio is reduced to less than 20:1 in about six months and the manure is ready for use. As there is no watering and turning, it is suitable to areas having low water availability and with scarce labour. When pits or trenches are not available for composting, town refuse and night soils can be composted in above ground heaps of 1 m height, 1 m width and of any convenient length by placing refuse and night soil in alternate layers as in trenches and adding the final refuse on the top (Gaur *et al.*, 1984). In this method, the material decomposes more quickly than in pits and can be used after 3-4 months. The compost obtained by this method would contain 1.5 per cent N, 1.0 per cent P and 1.5 per cent K_2O.

NADEP Compost

In this method, plant wastes, dung slurry and clay soil are used as raw materials for composting. The process is similar to heap method of composting, but is one in bricklined enclosures provided with air holes on all sides. However, this method has the disadvantage of using large proportion of soil which is not desirable or acceptable under all situations.

Coimbatore method

It is anaerobic degradation followed by aerobic process. First, pits of 4m length, 2m width and 1m depth is formed in which crop residues or farm wastes are filled to a thickness of about 15cm. Over this layer, cowdung slurry to enhance the rate of bio-degradation is applied to a thickness of 5cm. Above this layer, 1kg of bone meal, or rock phosphate to minimise the nitrogen loss and to add phosphorous, is applied. Thus, application of crop residue/farm waste, cowdung slurry, bonemeal and rock phosphate in alternate layers is repeated till the height reaches 0.5m above the ground level. Then the above ground portion is covered with red earth or mud to prevent the rain water entry and it becomes an anaerobic process. After 30-35 days, the material is turned and it becomes an aerobic process. The compost will be ready within five months.

Synthetic Compost

The principle behind this procedure is that addition of dung to supply organic nitrogen required by microorganisms, can be completely substituted with fertilizer N compounds like urea and ammonium sulphate which are utilised effectively for decomposition of carbonaceous compounds. The basic principle of C/N ratio in manure preparation can be applied in synthetic composting as well by adding nitrogenous fertilisers in sufficient quantity to reduce the ratio to about 30-40 per cent and then allowed to decompose. This method is highly suitable to the areas where supplies of dung are either short of requirements or not available at all and large quantity of organic waste materials is available in the farm.

Either pit or heap method can be used for composting where the organic waste material is spread out in thin layer and sufficiently moistened. Super phosphate may be added to fortify the phosphorous content of the manure. Sprinkling of fertiliser solution followed by lime application may be done. This process is continued layer-wise until the heap or pit is filled and then, the heap or pit is allowed to decompose for a period of 4-6 months by which time, it is ready for field use. It resembles FYM in its effect on soil and plant growth.

Windrow composting (leaf compost)

Windrows are prepared as they allow efficient material handling, provide good aeration and allow sufficient absorption of water. First, windrows of 2.5-4m width at the base, 2.5-3m height and of any convenient length based on the availability of leafy materials are formed. It is better to use higher windrows for better composition of leaves at the base resulting in aerobic conditions. When the moisture content of incoming leaves is low, it is desirable to add sufficient quantity of water to maintain 40-60 per cent moisture. If the C/N ratio of the leaves is high (30), amending with sewage sludge, urea or grass clippings may be done. Periodical mixing may be given for good aeration. The leaf compost with a neutral pH (6-7) will be ready within 6-9 months under optimum environmental conditions. The use of finished compost (leaf mold) as covering material(10-15cm) in the subsequent preparations of leaf compost is good to supply a heavy inoculam of microorganisms as in the case of activated compost' (Eberhardt and Pipes, 1972).

Accelerated composting and enrichment

For getting better compost, it is necessary to add nutrients, N,P and K which hastens the process of composting. Addition of mesophyllic cellulolytic fungi, or *Coprinus ephemerus,* a cellulose decomposer to compost pit may reduce the composting period by one month with an improvement in compost quality. Inoculation with *Aspergillus niger* or *Pencillium* sp. increases the total N content, available P and humus content of jowar stalk plus wheat straw compost and Jamin leaf compost (Gaur *et al.*, 1982). Further, this may also prove beneficial in the case of *in situ* application of plant residues where thermic rise is unlikely to be more than 40-45°C. Similarly, inoculating the compost previously amended with rock phosphate with cultures of *Azotobacter chrococcum* and the phosphate solubilising strain *Aspergillus arvamori* increases the total nitrogen and humus content.

Vermi-composting

In Asia, vermi-composting is being effectively practised in Philippines. The earthworms, *Lumbricus rubellus* and/or *Perionyx excavator,* are used for composting organic residues where 1000 t of moist organic matter can be converted by earthworms into 300 t of compost, rich in N,P,K, Ca and Mg contents with increased bacterial and actinomycete population. This method of composting can be suggested for sludge management. Method of vermicomposting, its advantages and applicability are discussed in detail in the chapter on "Vermiculture Biotechnology".

Animal waste composting

Animal manures of different kinds are available in huge quantities in India. If they are not used properly, it will lead to water pollution through rains and runoff water, air pollution in the forms of disagreeable odours and human health hazard through multiplication of flies and other insects. Animal waste composting is an effective and environmentally safe method to eliminate odour, to control flies and other insects, to reduce mass and volume, and to handle the material easily with agreeable smell. The type of animal, quantity and quality of feed, housing and waste handling techniques will decide the charectersitics of the manure. In general, beef and poultry manures are rich in nitrogen and undergoes decomposition more effectively with lower moisture level content. Addition of carbonaceous material such as straw, wood bark, saw dust, or corn cobs can often help the composting charecterisitcs of a manure. They can be used to reduce moisture content and to raise the C/N ratio, as it is usually practised in all villages. However, under Indian conditions, conjoint composting of the manure slurries with plant residues is more viable and profitable.

Mutsuzaki (1977) produced animal waste compost witn 30-40 per cent moisture content in about 2 weeks, by regulating the moisture content of raw materials to 55-65 per cent. Using this low moisture compost (seed compost) as a moisture regulator and an inoculam of useful microorganisms, he devised a method of continuous composting of fresh animal wastes in which high quality compost can be obtained every two weeks, regardless of weather conditions and with no use of supplementary energy.

Oil palm waste composting

The palm oil industry plays a major role in the economic development in South East Asia, and is slowly gaining momentum in Southern India. Compost can be prepared by using equal proportion of oil palm waste and wheat straw mixed with small quantity of deep litter chicken manure. Before composting, the waste is anlysed for its physical and chemical characteristics. The ingredients mentioned above are thoroughly mixed and wetted to give a compost mixed with no draining liquid. The prepared compost mixture (800g) is then placed on a perforated stainless steel platform within each flask and the flasks immersed in the water bath such that the water level is above the enclosed substances The thermostat is initially set at 45-50°C, to allow a gradual buildup of the naturally occurring microflora and each flask is independently aerated with humified air at 4 1/hr throughout the composting period. When the compost temperature has attained 50°C the water bath thermostat is raised to 60°C to pasteurise the material within the flasks. After 6 hrs at this temperature, the compost temperature is reduced to 53-55°C where it is held for a further 2-3 days until the concentrations of ammonia fall below 20 ppm which is determined using a Draegar gas detector. The purpose of adding wheat straw is to improve the water holding capability and chicken manure to increase the total N content of the compost. Compost mixture of 500 g wheat straw + 500 g oil palm waste + 250 g chicken manure + 30 g gypsum will have total N 1.1 per cent, 36.6 per cent total C, and a C:N ratio of 33:31. It can be supplemented with carbohydrate sources such as sugarcane baggase or molasses to activate the resident microflora.

Phospho-compost

Phospho-compost can be prepared by mixing farm wastes/crop residues, cattle dung, soil, compost, chopped grasses and tree leaves with mussoorie rock phosphate at the rate of 30 per cent of the compostable material. This mixture is made into slurry so as to provide adequate moisture and after uniform mixing, the slurry is allowed to decompose in a compost pit for about 60 to 90 days (Mishra *et al.*, 1984). Moisture is, maintained at 70 per cent throughout the period of composting and the compost will be ready for use in 60-90 days. Normally, this phospho-compost is prepared by mixing organic wastes and mussourie rock phosphate in the ratio of 7 to 7.5: 2.5 to 3.0.

Re-inforced compost from sugarcane trash and pressmud

First, sugarcane trash is spread to a thickness of 15 cm over an area of 5-7 m x 3 m depending on the area available. Over this, pressmud is spread to a thickness of 5 cm. The fertiliser mixture containing mussourie rock phosphate, gypsum, and urea in the ratio of 5:4:1 is sprinkled over these layers at the rate of 10kg/100kg of trash. Enough water is sprinkled to keep it moist. This has to be repeated till the height of heap rises to a height of 1.0-1.5 m above the ground level according to the convenience. Cowdung slurry may be used instead of water to moisten the layer. This is covered with a layer of soil and pressmud at 1:1 ratio to a thickness of 15 cm or with cowdung paste. Water is sprinkled once in 15 days. A thorough turning is given after 3 months and again heaped. Another turning is given after a month. The trash is composted and is ready in five months. This method increases the material value of trash compost by increasing N, P and Ca contents. It also brings down the C:N ratio by 10 times as compared to raw cane trash.

Enriched FYM (EFYM)

FYM is bulky and low in major plant nutrients such as N,P, and K. Hence there is a need to improve its quality. EFYM is recommended to rainfed crops which require available P for their root proliferation to withstand the initial growth stages under dry land conditions. First, 750 kg. of well decomposed FYM is taken. After sieving, the recommended dose of P and K_2O for the crops to be grown is mixed with the sieved FYM. The mixture is spread in the form of heap and plastering is done with red-earth paste. This anaerobic process is maintained for 30 days. Then, the nitrogenous fertiliser recommended for basal dose of the crop to be grown is mixed and it should be applied immediately before sowing.

Weed composting

Though weeds contain large quantity of nutrients, they affect the farm operations considerably; compete with crop plants for nutrients, space and water; poses health problem to human beings.

This problem can be overcome by bio-converting the weeds using lignolytic and cellulolytic organisms like *Trichoderma viridi, Fusarium* sp., and *Pleurotus sajorcaju* through composting which gives a clean environment in addition to improved moisture conservation, water use efficiency, nutrient use efficiency and soil health. The weeds can be bio-degraded individually or by pooling all the weeds together depending upon the quantity available and necessity. The arable and waste land weeds like Mexican poppy, thorn apple, nut grass, water grass, barnyard grass, crowfoot grass, wild grass, carpet weed Parthenium, Cassia etc and the aquatic weeds like Ipomea, water hyacinth and sea weed can be used for composting. A common bio-conversion technology is suggested for all the weed materials. Composting of parthenium weeds by this bio-conversion technology is given below as an example to other weeds.

Composting of parthenium

Parthenium, a problematic introduced weed prevailing in cultivable and fallow areas, affects crop yield and poses health hazards to human beings by causing skin and eye irritation, asthma, fever, etc. partehnium seeds have long storage life and higher germination percentage and spread quickly by wind. For composting purpose, the parthenium plants are to be cut into small pieces of 10 cm size by using chaff cutter. These chopped material is spread to a thickness of 10 cm. Over this inoculum *viz.*, compost cultures (Trichoderma viridi, Fusarium sp) is spread uniformly. Then, weed material is spread over this to thickness of 10 cm. Over this layer, 0.5 per cent urea is spread (5 kg urea/t of chopped materials). This has to be repeated till about 1m height is obtained. Then plastering with mud is done. Periodical sprinkling of water is done to maintain 50-60 per cent moisture. After 2 weeks, a through mixing is given. In 40-45 days, the parthenium compost is ready for field application. This compost contains 2.49 per cent N, 0.73 per cent P and 1.37 per cent K with a C:N ratio of 21:1. The same method is followed for other weeds also. The Ipomea weed compost contains 2.49 per cent N,

0.32 per centP, and 0.50 per cent K with a C:N ratio of 20:1 whereas the water hyacinth compost will have 2.11 per cent N, 0.3 per cent P and 0.73 per cent K with a C:N ratio of 22:1.

Hints for composting agricultural wastes

From the several composting methods, the following few practical hints are offered for proper composting of agricultural wastes:—

- Collect plant wastes and make the composting mass heterogenous by mixing two or three types of materials.
- Shred the material to 5-7cm size
- Mix the material with cowdung slurry in the ratio of 70:20:10 (agricultural wastes: animal dung:soil)
- Add super phosphate or rock phosphate at 5 per cent(w/w)
- Maintain the medium moisture content at 50-60 per cent by sprinkling water.
- Do plastering with red earth or mud.
- Give periodical turning depending on the method employed.
- Within six months, the compost is ready for field application.
- If needed, retain a part to serve as mother and seed compost for subsequent cycle of composting.

INDUSTRIAL WASTES

Industrial wastes are those which come out as wastes from industries and factories, commonly known as effluents. These wastes contain considerable quantity of organic matter and nutrients in addition to non-compostible materials. The quantity of wastes available depends on the size of industries/factories. In the case of big industries, the quantity of waste available will be large enough even to maintain their own farm. The sources of industrial and factories wastes are given below:—

1 Textile industry
2 Paper factories
3 Cordite and ammunition factories
4 Fertiliser plants
5 Sugar factories and Distilleries
6 Food processing units
7 Coir industry
8 Tanneries
9 Lignite and coal mines
10 Petroleum industry
11 Cosmetic factories
12 Mushroom centres
13 Chemical Plants
14 Electronic Industries
15 Photofilm Industries

16 Tinning plants
17 Foundries
18 Electroplating centres
19 Cement factories
20 Dyeing factories
21 Automobile works
22 Sago industry
23 Heavy metal/lectrical plants

The above list of available industrial wastes gives a good picture but it is not exhaustive. Among the different industrial and factory wastes, tannery effluent causes serious hazards and environmental problems by affecting streams, fresh water bodies, ground water and agricultural lands. This effluent contains sodium, chlorides, sulphate, bio-carbonates and chromium (300-465 ppm). The rice grain produced from tannery polluted soil contains 1.02 to 2.8 ppm chromium while the straw contains 96-200 ppm (Nandakumar and Rajendra Babu, 1984). The milk from cow and buffalo and goat which feed on the fodder grown in the tannery effluent affected lands show a chromium concentration of 0.079 to 0.390 ppm.

The paper factory effluent has pH 8.4, EC 1.6 dsm^{-1}, 2.1 CO_3, 10.8 HCO_3, 8.0 SO_4, 21.0 Cl_2, 10.0 Ca, 5.5 Mg, 25.0 Na mg/litre. Besides it also contains 774 mg/1 of suspended solids and 1044 $mg/^1$ of dissolved solids. The colour of the effluent is brown due to the presence of phenolic compounds. The sago factory effluent is rich in coloured starch and organic material which affect soil drainage leading to pasification of yeasts and causes severe environmental hazards: The cement dust from cement factories from a thick coating over plant canopy and affects the respiration and photosynthesis. It also accumulates continuously with the soil and induces soil crusting. Most of the urban areas are polluted by the excess presence of sewage and sludge wastes. In India, sewage production is 12,500 ML/D. Sewage sludge from highly industrial areas contains heavy metals in the range of 3.5-8.3 mg/kg of sludge which poses toxicity problems. However, sewage sludge can supply 5.1, 2.9 and 2.8 thousand tonnes of N, P and K_2O per annum in India.

Pressmud, an organic waste material from sugar industries, contains about 33 per cent organic carbon, 0.8 per cent N, 2.0 per cent P, 1.1 per cent K, 4.45 per cent Ca, 1.12 per cent Mg, 3100 ppm Fe, 80 ppm Cu, 150 ppm Zn and 80 ppm Zn with a C:N ratio of 41:1 However, it can supply 33.3, 79.4 and 55.4 thousand tonnes of N, P and K_2O respectively every year. It has a manurial value equivalent to 54.4 kg NPK/t besides contributing micronutrients. Slurry from biogas unit provides 44 kg nutrients as composed to 19 kg by FYM and 27 kg by compost. It contains 1.6 per cent N, 1.5 per cent P_2O_5 and 1.2 per cent K_2O in addition to some quantity of micronutrients.

The sea weed residue left in the industries after extracting agar contains nutrients at appreciable level *viz.* 1.596 per cent N, 0.06 per cent P and 0.076 per cent K. Application of sea weed residue at 12.5 t/ha to groundnut resulted in increased soil moisture conservation, shelling percentage and oil content besides higher uptake of N, P and K. Coir pith production potential of India is 0.66 mt. It has 0.2 . per cent N, 0.05 per cent P, 0.8 per cent K, 0.4 per cent Ca, 0.36 per cent Mg, 0.07 per cent Fe, 30 per cent lignin, 25 per cent cellulose, 115:1 C/N ratio and 5.4 pH with a water holding capacity of 500 per cent. The nutrient status of industrial wastes is given in Table 5.2.

Table 5.2: Nutrient status of some industrial wastes

Source	Nutrient content (%)		
	N	P_2O_5	K_2O
Coirpith	0.26	0.05	0.84
Pressmud	1.15	2.40	1.98
Seaweed residue	1.50	0.50	4.20
Cotton mill waste	1.40	0.60	1.20
Sawdust	0.25	0.20	—
Sewage Sludge	1.50	2.00	1.50
Bagasse	0.25	0.12	0.40
Biogas slurry	1.60	1.50	1.20
Mushroom spent waste	1.68	0J50	0.63

Source: Thangavel, P. 1995. Composting of Industrial wastes. In Manual on Bio-conversion of agricultural wastes. Published by TNAU, Coimbatore-3. pp:27.

When these wastes are efficiently processed and utilised, they can serve as good source of nutrients and can replace the inorganic fertilisers to a significant extent. Composting, a better way of disposal of waste rather than incineration or land filling, reduces the bulk volume of materials (solid waste pollution abatement) and at the same time, the nutrients are added to the soil (an efficient recycling process). Composting technique is available for coirpith, pressmud and effluent. To manage other effluents/wastes, the following measures should be adopted for better disposal and to ensure clean environment:

- Using treatment plant (with chemical, physical and bio-organisms treatment), the effluent let out from tannery, textile, sago, sugar, paper and chemical industries could be treated to reduce the intensity of pollution.

- Site evaporation tanks and tagoor with cement lining should be constructed to prevent contamination of ground water resources.
- Spraying water through fine nozzle droplets in chimneys prevents the dust pollution by cement and granite factories.
- The diluted sugar factory and paper factory effluent (to an extent of 40-50 times) could be successfully used for growing tolerant sugarcane varieties.
- The soil affected by tannery effleuts could be reclaimed by organic manure application and growing resistant crops like maize, ragi, NB2 grass, Desmanthus and Korai.

Composting of coir pith

India ranks third in the world in the production of coconuts with an annual production of 100.43 m nuts from an area of 1.5 m.ha. The area under coconut in Tamil Nadu is 2.40 lakhs ha with more than 1.7 lakh t of coirpith production. The coir pith or dust is a waste product in the coir industry after extracting the coir. The coir wastes (dust and bits of fibres of lesser length) accumulate in large quantities near the location of coir industries and its disposal is posing a serious environmental problem. However, this material can be converted into valuable organic manure by composting. The material contains high amount of lignin and carbon compounds with small amount of nutrients like sulphur and phosphorous. First, an area of 5 m length and 3 m width, preferably in a shady place, is selected. Spreading of 100 kg of coir pith is done. One bottle (300g) of *Pleurotus sajorcaju* spawns is spread uniformly on the surface of the coir pith. After applying fungus, sprinkling of water is to be done to maintain 200 per cent moisture content. Above this, another layer; is formed with 100 kg coir pith on the surface of the second layer one kg of urea is uniformly spread and sprinkling of water is done as that of first layer. This process of sandwiching *Pleuertous* and urea in alternate layers of coir pith is repeated till the heap reaches one metre height. The heap is periodically sprinkled with water to maintain 200 per cent moisture content which should be felt with hands. At the end of 30 days, coir pith turns into dark brown mass of compost. The chemical composition of raw and composed coirpith is given in Table 5.3.

The composted coirpith reduces the volume by 42 per cent besides narrowing the C:N ratio. This composted coir pith can effectively be used as manure for both dry land and irrigated crops to increase the crop yield, as an amendment in sodic soils and as an alternative to K fertiliser.

Table 5.3: Composition of raw and composted coir pith

Properties	Raw coirpith	Composed coirpith
Lignin (%)	30.00	4.80
Cellulose (%)	26.52	10.10
Organic carbon (%)	29.00	24.90
N(%)	0.26	1.06
P_2O_5(%)	0.01	0.06
K_2O(%)	0.78	1.20
Ca(%)	0.40	0.50
Mg(%)	0.36	0.48
Fe(%)	0.07	0.09
Mn (ppm)	12.50	25.00
Zn (ppm)	7.50	15.80
Cu(ppm)	3.10	6.20
C : N ratio	112: 1	24: 1

Source: Nagarajan, R., P.P. Ramaswamy, P. P. Savithri and T.S. Manickam, 1989. Coir waste in crop production. Tamil Nadu Agricultural University, Coimbatore.,39 pp.

Composting of Pressmud

Using distillery effluent

It can be done by mixing with distillery effluent which is also a rich nutrient source. First, the moisture content of the pressmud is reduced from 75 per cent to 50 per cent using aerotiller. Then, additives containing materials like composted coir pith 5 per cent, sugarcane trash 2.5 per cent, water hyacinth 2.5 per cent and rock phosphate 2.5 per cent are mixed with pressmud. Then, one tonne of pressmud is inoculated with 1.5 litre of composite culture containing thermophilic microbes *Bacillus* sp. and *Pseudomonas* sp. Above this, distillery effluent is added to bring 60 per cent moisture level. Then, heap is reformed with aerotiller until a temperature of 60-70°C is reached. After 4-5 days, adding of next dose of effluent is done when the moisture content goes below 50 per cent. Again, the heap is reformed with aerotiller. Likewise composting of pressmud and adding effluent are continued. The addition of effluent is about 4000 litres which is added in 1-2 months. For better enrichment of pressmud, super phosphate is added at 2.5 per cent and mixed well. The heap is allowed for curing for about 15 days. Then, $FeSO_4$ at 20 kg and $ZnSO_4$, at 10 kg/t of pressmud is added and allowed for curing for a period of 15 days. To the composted materials, biofertilisers *viz.*

Azotobacter, Azospirillum and phosphobacteria each at 2 kg/ha is added at the time of application, which enables N fixation and solubilization of native and added phosphorous.

Using microbial inoculum

First pressmud is spread to a height of 10 cm over an area of 1 x 1 m. Over this surface, urea and cowdung slurry are sprinkled. Then inoculation of pressmud is done with microbial inoculum *(Aspergillus fumigatus* and *Bacillus* sp.). This process is repeated several times based on the availability of pressmud. Then, plastering is done with sand. Sprinkling of water is done to maintain 50 per cent water holding capacity, as and when required. The compost is ready within 45 days, which is rich in nutrients and microflora.

Using pressmud and Distillery effluent

Distillery effluent-based compost is prepared by using pressmud, a by product obtained from sugar factory. First, pressmud is spread in the compost yard to form a heap of 1.5 m with 3.0 m length and 3.5 m breadth. Ten litres of bacterial culture diluted with water in the ratio of 1:10 is sufficient for a tonne of pressmud. After 3 days, distillery effluent is sprayed on the heaps to a moisture level of 60 per cent and the pressmud heaps are allowed for 4-5 hours to absorb the effluent; then the heaps are thoroughly mixed by aerotiller. When the moisture level drops below 30-40 per cent, again the effluent is sprayed, mixed with pressmud and heaps are formed. Effluent should be sprayed once or twice in a week depending on the moisture content of pressmud heaps. Mixing of effluent and heap formation should be repeated for 8 weeks so that the pressmud and effluent proportion reaches an optimum ratio of 1:3. Then the heaps are allowed for curing for a month. During the process of composting, the temperature of the heaps may raise to 60 to 68°C on 10th day and may reach a maximum of 80° C on the 50th day. The compost obtained from this process is neutral in pH with a EC of 3.12 to 6.40 dS/m. It contains 1.53 per cent N, 1.50 per cent P, 3.10 per cent K, 130 ppm Cu, 180 ppm Mn, and 220 ppm Zn. The organic carbon and C/N ratio are reduced from 36 to 18 per cent and 28.06 to 16.3, respectively.

CONCLUSION

Agricultural and industrial wastes are available in large quantities in India. They contain valuable plant nutrients. Composting of these wastes gives a good solution as a waste disposal method, besides increasing the availability of plant nutrients, destruction of pathogens, elimination of unfavourable odours and easy handling. As a result, pollution problems and bio-magnification of toxic chemicals in the various biological systems can be minimised. They have the potential to raise soil productivity by improving physical, chemical and biological properties of the soil, thereby improving the plant growth. These wastes, after proper treatment, can be used as good amendment in reclaiming the problem soils like sodic soil. In the days of increasing fertiliser price and in view of the necessity to improve the yield of rainfed agriculture, it is imperative to look for these agricultural waste recycling by composting. With these refinements, in the not so distant future, composting may well be as much an artful science as wine making.

FUTURE NEEDS

Methods of combining bio-fertilisers with the composted organics have to be taken up, so that the efficiency of both can be combined:

- Research has to be carried out to hasten and stabilize composting.
- Organics have to be composted and produced in forms that will be easy for transportation.
- Collaborative work with engineering professionals is needed to design various bio-reactors for efficient and large scale composting.
- Recommendation is to be given on the dosage of the composted organic materials for various crops.
- Awareness on the use of composted organic manures is to be created among farmers.

6

Biological Fertilizers

Over the past century, many of the basic scientific principles of plant nutrition and soil fertility have been explained. In developed countries, inorganic chemical fertilizers have been widely accepted as a major source of improving and maintaining soil fertility. Plants need sufficient nutrients in proper balance for normal growth and development. Sixteen chemical elements are known to essential for plants. Except carbon, hydrogen and oxygen, rest of 13 elements are taken up by plants from the soil. There is a continuous removal of nutrient from soil for crop production and yield. Depletion of soil nutrients poses a major threat to sustainability of crop production and underlines the need for maintaining it by tapping other plant nutrient sources.

The term biofertilizers includes selective microorganisms like bacteria, fungi, and algae, which are capable of fixing atmospheric N or convert insoluble phosphate in the soil into forms available to plants. Biofertilizers are cost effective, eco-friendly and renewable sources of plant nutrients to supplement chemical fertilizers. Biofertilizers also play a vital role in maintaining longterm soil fertility and sustainability.

SOIL BIOTA IN SUSTAINABLE AGRICULTURE

Agricultural ecosystems, unlike the natural ecosystems, are human manipulated ecosystems and regular and sometimes intense disturbances are a major part of economically viable agriculture management systems. Sustainable agriculture is a complex issue associated with producing food while maintaining our biophysical resources including soil, water and bitoa with no adverse impacts on the wider environment. It should:—

1. Maintain or improve the production of *clean* food.
2. Maintain or improve the quality of landscapes which includes soils, water, biota and aesthetics.
3. They have minimal impact on the wide environment.
4. It should be economically viable.
5. It shpuld be acceptable to society.

There are different concepts of sustainable agriculture, but none is generally accepted. It embraces several forms of non-conventional agriculture that are often called organic, alternative, ecological or low input. However, from economic and ecological perspectives, two basic criteria must be met if agriculture is to be sustainable in the long term. These are:—

1. A reduction in the use of non-renewable resources;
2. Protection of the environment.

Agricultural practices in developed countries have become highly dependent upon fossil energy inputs in the form of fertilizers, cultivation, herbicides and pesticides. Inputs of man made chemicals could be reduced if agricultural practices were targetted towards capturing the benefits that could be derived from improved management of the biota. Such benefits include:—

1. The enhanced supply of nutrients *via* management practices that encourage nutrient recycling from organic residues,
2. Improvements in soil structure *via* practices that encourage the activity of earthworms and other burrowing soil animals, and
3. Improvements in plant health *via* practices that promote biological control of pests and diseases.

These management practices also promote biological control of pests and diseases, help to reduce the off farm effects resulting from loss of man made nutrients (*e.g.*, losses of N. P. and S through leading), that damage the environment through pollution of ground water supplies.

BIO-DIVERSITY OF SOIL BIOTA

The soil biota contains representatives of all groups of micro-organisms and fungi, green and blue green *algae*, and all but a few entirely marine phyla of animals. In a fertile temperate soil, the biomass may exceed 20 t ha^{-1} and its diversity has been compared with that of coral reefs, although it is probably more complex.

Possible Management Strategies

1. Increase soil organic status by organic matter retention/ incorporation, continual crop cover and decreased cultivation to minimize mineralization.
2. Improve nutrient status of the organic resource by introducing legume crops. Cut and carry of legume residues to ensure mineralization occurs at Peak Plant demand.
3. Avoid applying soluble or readily mineralized nutrient sources at times when they may be lost from the soil profile.
4. Choose rotations that maintain VAM inoculation.
5. Strategic use of fertilizers may be necessary to maintain crop production where organic and soil microbial processes are unable to meet the crop demand.

Root activity and Rhizosphere transformations are intensively investigated to develop plant growth promoting products, induction of defense, release of metabolities, bio-remediating principles *etc.*,

IMPORTANCE OF BIOLOGICAL SOURCES OF NUTRIENTS

When wee say *farming,* we really talk about the growing of plants for our food. To know about plants the way they are, live and grow are thus the things we need to understand.

For that we should first look at the figures on the nutrition of plants in the table below:

I. Elements from the Atmosphere

They represent 95 to 98 per cent of a plant's dry weight. Vital elements all constitutive: *carbon, oxygen, hydrogen, nitrogen.*

II. Elements from the Soil

- They represent 2-5 per cent of a plants' dry weight.
- 12 vital elements:
- 2 non-constitutive
- Potassium and chlorine; and 10 constitutive:
- Phosphorus, boron, calcium, magnesium, sulfur, iron, manganese, molybdenum, copper, zinc.
- 18 trace-elements
- 4 non-constitutive
- Lithium, sodium, rubidium, cesium; and
- 14 constitutive
- Fluorine, silicon, selenium, cobalt, iodine, strontium, barium, aluminum, vanadium, tin, nickel, chromium, beryllium, bromine.

The above table shows as that plants feed themselves in two distinct ways, from the atmosphere and from the soil. Elements taken from the atmosphere are; carbon 44 per cent hydrogen 6 per cent and nitrogen (via the microbial world) 2 or 3 per cent. It thus appears that the bulk of a plants food is taken from the air. It is easily available for plants and there is plenty of it. It also appears that we have a lot to do to control pollution.

The balance, a mere 5 per cent of a plant's diet, comes from the soil. This consists of small quantities of various minerals. It can be concluded that plants feed quantitatively from the atmosphere and qualitatively from the soil. To feed plants quantitatively from the soil, as is being done in conventional agriculture, is thus going against their physiology.

The elements taken from the soil are of two kinds, constitutive and non-constitutive of plant matter. The constitutive elements are absorbed by plants either in an oxidized or chelated way. These transformations are brought about by the microorganisms of the soil.

The non-constitutive elements (e.g., Potassium, Lithium, etc.) are borrowed from the soil, so to say, and simply provide the plants with electric charges needed for their various growth processes. These elements are returned to the soil at the maturity stage. Only green plants and other living parts such as the seeds, contain minute quantities of these elements.

It thus appears that all constitutive elements pass through the biological cycle and are thus entering the plants in an organic way. The only elements to enter plants in an atomic way are not constitutive of plant matter. Plants have thus an organic diet.

For example, a crop of rice at an average of 2 tons per acre consists of 1900 kg. of air (elements from the atmosphere) and of 100 kg. of soil (elements taken from the soil). One of the elements taken from the soil by the rice plant is zinc, at about 8 ppm. However, in conventional farming the prescription is to apply 12 kg. of zinc sulphate to the acre (Plumbers or farmers that is the question). The conclusion is that conventional farming promotes odd practices that go against the nature of the plants or are aimed not at enriching the soil but at enriching others.

Therefore, is clear that plants feed organically from the soil that is *plants have mainly or purely a mineral diet.*

Overcoming Soil Deficiencies Nature's Way

The soil contains most of the nutrients needed by plants. There are exceptional cases wherein soils may be naturally deficient in one mineral or the other but this is a rare phenomenon. Nature usually corrects herself, by growing accumulator plants for instance. Wild thistles seem to thrive in soils deficient in Phosphorus, Potassium and Selenium, through on analysis we find that thistles have a high content of these minerals! Mushrooms accumulate zinc! Thus for zinc in rice fields think of wild mushrooms. By growing accumulator plants as a green manure or associated with the crops, we can assist nature in recreating a balance. Of course a farmer cannot always wait until his soil has regained balance. Hence it might be necessary to add rock powders containing the element in short supply. Another way to overcome deficiencies is to collect leaves of various plants, young leaves, manure leaves and old leaves, compost them and apply in small quantities of plants. Or else simply buy a little of the mineral from a drug store and add it to the compost pile.

The fact however is that the deficiencies are usually, brought about either by wrong fertilization or wrong cultivating methods like mono-cropping or by using hard chemicals that kill the microorganisms. In no way does it mean that this or that element is, as such, lacking in the soil but that there are no soluble forms of it available.

In fact the core of the question of farming is to find out *how to stimulate and enlarge the microbial population in our soils.*

The come back to the elements from the soil, how they are taken up by plants and in what quantities.

Therefore, most of the soils contain enough elements to provide us with bountiful and nourishing food.

Is it not strange that farmers are advised to apply up to 12 kg. of zinc per acre for rice? Agricultural science could study the factor that make for a high quality of agricultural soils. High quality and high productive soils can still be found in the natural state. We need to protect at all cost whatever remains of these natural margins. To study their agricultural methodology and to learn how all problems of agriculture have already found a solution there, is what is truly needed.

Table 6.1: Essential elements and their organic sources

Element	%of dry matter	Manner of uptake	Origin
		I. ATMOSPHERE	
Carbon	44	Photosynthesis	Carbonic gas from air
Oxygen	44	Photosynthesis	Carbonic gas and water
Hydrogen	6	Photodecomposition	Rain water
Nitrogen	1 - 4	Biological fixation by microbes of the soil	Nitrogen gas from the air
		II. SOIL	
Potassium	0.1- 2.5	Element "on loan" from the soil solution and returned to the soil at the end of the plant's life cycle.	From the mother rock reserves 20-80 t/ha. Potassium from micr-oflora reserves up to 60 kg/ha.
Calcium	0.1 - 3	Acid Soils: Decomposition of the mother rock by climate, roots and microbes. Alkaline soils: Decarbonation of mother rock by microbes	Calcium from the mother rock reserves 15-1200 t/ha. Calcium from humus reserves 300 kg -3/ha.
Magnesium	0.1 - 0.9	Chelatino or oxidation of magnesium by microbes	Magnesium of the mother rock reserves 300 kg-3/ha.
Phosphorus	0.1 - 0.9	From the mother rock: oxidation by soil microbes. Liberated from humus by soil microbes. From clay particles by microrhiza filaments which recover retrograde phosphates.	Phosphorus from the mother rock reserves 600 kg-15 t/ha. Phosphorus from humus reserves 150 kg-1.5 t/ha.
Sulfur	0.1 - 0.5	Mother rock: oxidation by soil microbes.	From mother rock reserves 300—900 kg/ha. From humus

		Mineralisation of the humus by soil microbes.	reserves 120 kg. 1.2 kg/ha. From atmospheric pollution possible 10-100 kg/ha. coming through the leaves as SO_2.
Chlorine	0.01 - 0.9	Element "on loan" from the soil solution and returned to the soil at the end of the plant's life cycle.	From mother rock reserves 300-600 kg/ha. Cl from the world of microorganisms reserves 30-60 kg/ha.
Iron	500 ppm	Mother rock chelation by soil microbes Liberation of organic iron from the humus.	From the mother rock reserves 20-300 kg/ha. From humus reserves 3-15 kg/ha.
Boron	500 ppm	Mother rock: chelation by soil microbes. Liberation of organic boron from humus.	From the mother rock reserves 12-300 kg/ha. From humus reserves 3-15 kg/ha.
Manganese	500 ppm	Mother rock: chelation by soil microbes. Liberation of organic Mn from the humus.	From the mother rock reserves 300 kg-15 t/ha. From humus reserves 3-15 kg/ha.
Copper	20 ppm	Mother rock: chelation by soil microbes. Liberation of organic copper by soil microbes from the humus.	From the mother rock reserves 3-300 kg/ha. From humus reserves 1 -5 kg/ha.
Zinc	20 ppm	Mother roci: chelation by soil microbes. Liberation of organic zinc by soil microbes from the humus.	From the mother rock reserves 30-1500 kg/ha, From humus reserves 1-2 kg/ha.
Molybdenum	1ppm	Mother rock: chelation by microbes. Liberation by soil microbes from the humus.	From mother rock reserves 3-30 kg/ha. From humus reserves ± 1 kg/ha.

BIO-FERTILIZERS FOR SUSTAINABLE AGRICULTURE

Biofertilizers have for long witnessed shifting fortunes in agriculture. While the technology of using them has been successfully exploited in many developed countries, competent exploitation in developing countries has been hampered by several factors, including lack of trained personnel, lack of appreciation of the benefits of inoculation and absence of suitable industrial support. A major problem, especially relevant to our bio-fertilizer programme has to do with relations between research institutions and industry. A transfer of technology between the research institutions and industry is essential. It must be promoted as effectively as possible through co-operation between institutional research, which is usually public and industrial research and production, which are either private or public. At the same time, we should not overlook the significance of ensuring and maintaining a high quality standard of the product. The limited shelf-life, particularly of bacterial bio-fertilisers dictates that product streams must be handled with a quick delivery system at low temperatures. A strong extension and training programme, actively supported by research and industry is the need of the hour. We should recognize that in adopting a rational approach to the use and management of natural resources in sustainable agriculture, the microbial fertilisers hold vast potential for the future.

In developing countries, the most important challenge is to produce sufficient food for the growing population from in elastic land area. Products of biological origin can be advantageously blended to replace a part of the energy-intensive inputs. It is in this context, bio-fertilizers can provide to the small and marginal farmers an economically viable lever for realizing the ultimate goal of increasing productivity. These microbial systems siphon out appreciable amounts of nitrogen from the atmospheric reservoir and enrich the soil with this important but scarce nutrient. The crop-microbial-soil ecosystem can, therefore, be energized in sustainable agriculture with considerable ecological stability and environmental quality. Although the potential of bio-fertilizers in crop production systems has been well documented and substantiated, the major reason for the shifting fortunes of these biological inputs lies in the lack of an organised industrial back-up, an effective quality control system, a powerful extension machinery and a broad research base.

Bio-fertilizers are inputs containing microorganisms, which are capable of mobilizing nutritive elements from non-usable form to usable form through biological processes. They are less expensive, eco-friendly and sustainable. The beneficial microbes in the soil, which are the greater significance to horticultural crops are biological nitrogen fixers, phosphate solubilizers and mycorrhizal fungi which are the phosphate scavengers.

Nitrogen is one of the chief and important constituents of protein and nucleic acid molecules that play the basic role in cell metabolism, growth, reproduction and transmission of heritable characters. Therefore, without a constant supply of this unavoidable element, life can not go on.

Biological nitrogen fixation (BNF) is the reduction of atmospheric nitrogen to ammonia by microorganisms in the soil. It involves a highly specialized and intricately evolved interactions between soil microorganisms and higher plants for harnessing the atmospheric nitrogen. It is a fascinating biological phenomenon studied extensively to provide low-cost nitrogen and improve crop productivity. The nitrogen fixing organisms associated with horticultural crops are the *Rhizobium* species, living in symbiotic relationship with the leguminous plants and free living fixers belonging to the *Azotobacter* family and the *Azospirilla* living in association with the root system of crop plants.

Some soil microorganisms play an important role in improving soil fertility and crop productivity due to their capability to fix atmospheric nitrogen, solubilize insoluble phosphate and decompose farm wastes resulting in the release of plant nutrient. The extent of benefit from these microorganisms depends upon their number and efficiency, which however, is governed by a large number of soil and environmental factors. When the number and activity of specific microorganism called microbial inoculant or biofertilizer is used to hasten biological activity to improve availability of plant nutrient. One of the essential plant nutrients on which successful agriculture depends to a great extent is nitrogen. High crop requirement, susceptibility to gaseous and leaching losses have made nitrogen the most in demand fertilizer material followed by phosphorus. Although air has about 80 per cent of nitrogen, plants cannot make use of atmospheric N. The discovery of bacteria which had the ability to reduce non-usable (atmospheric nitrogen) into usable form (ammoniacal) had been a major breakthrough in the field of agricultural research. Of late, increasing attention is being paid to harmness the potential benefits from these renewable sources of plant nutrients because of the following reasons:—

1. Depleting soil fertility due to widening gap between nutrient removal and supplies.
2. Depleting feedstock/fossil fuels and increasing cost of fertilizers.
3. Growing concern about environmental hazards.
4. Increasing threat to sustainable agriculture.

A number of products are now available that are generally referred to as soil and plant additives, of non-traditional nature. These products include:—

1. Microbial fertilizers and soil inoculants contain unique and beneficial strains of soil microorganisms.
2. Microbial activators that supposedly contain special chemical formulations for increasing the numbers and activity of beneficial microorganisms in soil.
3. Soil conditions that claim to create favourable soil physical and chemical conditions, which result in increased growth and yield of crops.
4. Vermincompost helps in improving soil health and fertility.

Nitrogen fixing organisms can be provided to the farmers in the name of microbial inoculants otherwise termed as bio-fertilizers. The bio-fertilizers containing biological nitrogen fixing organisms are of utmost important in agriculture in view of the following advantage:—

1. They help in the establishment and growth of crop plants and trees.

2. They enhance biomass production and grain yields by 10-20 per cent.
3. They are useful in sustainable agriculture.
4. They are suitable in organic farming.
5. They play an important role in agroforestry/silvipastoral systems.

After the advent of the acetylene test for assessing nitrogen fixing potential, rapid progress has been made in identifying nitrogen-fixing organisms. Out of a large number of microorganisms possessing the property of nitrogen fixation, only a few such as *Rhizobium, Azotobacter, Azospirillum,* BGA, Azolla, etc. have been commercially exploited. The reaction in biological nitrogen fixation is essential the same as in production of chemical fertilizers (Haber-Bosch process) i.e. the catalytic reduction of dinitrogen (N_2) to ammonia (NH_3).

HISTORY OF BIO-FERTILIZER RESEARCH

Although the beneficial effect of legumes in improving soil fertility was known since ancient times, the field of biological nitrogen fixation opened up with the discoveries by Boussingault and Hellreigel in 1886. Nobbe and Hiltner produced for the first time a laboratory culture of Rhizobia under the name *Nitragin* in 1885. Starting with Rhizobia, a vigorous search for other N fixing microorganisms began and soon it was found that there were other non-symbiotic bacteria such as *Azotobacter,* which could fix atmospheric nitrogen. It was followed by a third group called blue green algae. Subsequently, microorganisms capable of solublizing phosphate were discovered. In 1970, a new group of bacteria called *Azospirillum* was identified. Vesicular-Arbuscular Micorrhiza (VAM) are the latest introduction in the list of bio-fertilizers which mobilize phosphorus.

In India, systematic research on bio-fertilizers started with the first study of N.V. Joshi in 1920. This was followed by extensive research by Gangulee, Sarkaria and Madhok on the physiology of the nodule bacteria and its inoculation for increasing crop yields. Important milestones in production, development and promotion of bio-fertilizers in India are given in Table 6.2.

Microorganisms induce many biochemical transformations in the soil. These include mineralization of organically bound forms of nutrients, exchange reactions, fixation of atmospheric nitrogen and various other changes leading to better availability of nutrients already present in the soil. The group of microorganisms responsible for nitrogen fixation, phosphorus solubilization and compost decomposition are being put to beneficial use in the form of bio-fertilizer.

Table 6.2: Some milestones in research, production and promotion of Bio-fertilizers in India

Year	Events
1920	First study on Legume-*Rhizobium* symbiosis by N.V. Joshi
1934	Earliest documented production of *Rhizobium* inoculant by M.R. Madhok
1956	First commercial production of Bio-fertilizer
1957	Study on solubilization of phosphorus by micro-organisms by Sen. and Pal
1964	Spurt in demand of Bio-fertilizer for soybean particularly in Madhya Pradesh
1970	Scope for use of charcoal, lignite and FYM as alternate carriers to peat reported by V. Iswaran
1977	Use of ISI mark for *Rhizobium*
1983	Setting up of National Project on Development and Use of Bio-fertilizers by Ministry of Agriculture, Government of India
1986	Setting up of National Facility for BGA Collection at IARI, New Delhi by Department of Biotechnology, Government of India.
1990	Setting up National Facility for *Rhizobium* Germplasm Collection at the Division of Microbiology, IARI, New Delhi by Department of Biotechnology, Government of India.

Among the major part nutrient elements, nitrogen is an example of deficiency in sufficiency considering the presence of 80,000 tonnes of atmospheric nitrogen of hardly 100 kg^1 ha^{-1} . All living beings with the exception of those members endowed with *nif* genes depend on fixed nitrogen to meet their requirement. Chemical fertilizers like urea, ammonium sulphate etc. are examples of industrial nitrogen fixation. There also exist atmospheric fixation (lightning etc.), combustion fixation (industry and automobiles), ozonization and biological fixation. Biological nitrogen [1] fixation contributes maximum (67.5%) towards enriching earth surface with nitrogen.

Microorganisms capable of assimilating nitrogen are marked with *nif* genes. They synthesize nitrogenase enzymes responsible for converting otherwise inert N_2 to plant usable NH_3. Such common useful organisms are *Rhizobium, Azotobacter, Azospirillum* and Blue Green Algae (BGA). There are some microorganisms capable of solubilizing insoluble soil phosphorus while some collect available phosphorus from remote places out of reach of plant root hairs by sending elongated filaments (e.g., vesicular arbuscular mycorrhiza). Few of the heterotrophic organisms decompose cellulose rapidly. Such beneficial organisms are domesticated in suitable carriers, which on application to soil augment crop growth and yield. These carriers are slangishly called bio-fertilizers or appropriately called bioinoculants or microbial inoculants or microbial fertilizers.

Bio-fertilizers do not come under the purview of the definition of the term fertilizers, as they do not contain substantial quantity of plant nutrients as other fertilizers like urea, diammonium phosphate, muriate of potash etc. contain. The term bio-fertilizer is a misnomer but is in wider use. They should be termed as inoculants, after the name of the microorganisms they contain, *viz Rhizobium* inoculant, *Azospirillum* inoculant or blue green algae inoculant.

Bioinoculants or bio-fertilizers are different from chemical fertilizers (Table 6.3). Bio-fertilizers on application remain in soils, multiply and keep benefiting the growing crops. They do not get depleted as in the case of fertilizers and, therefore, if the optimum soil conditions prevail, population of added microorganisms builds up and frequent application of bio-fertilizers can be avoided.

Table 6.3: Various sources of Nitrogen fixation on the earth surface

Nitrogen fixation	10" tonnes year^{-1}	Percent contribution
Industrial fixation (Haber-Bosch)	40	15.3
Atmospheric fixation (Lightning etc.)	10	3.8
Combustion (Industry, automobiles)	20	7.6
Ozonization	15	5.7
Biological fixation	175	67.3

Source: Technical Handbook on Symboitic Nitrogen Fixation, FAO Publication, (1983).

Table. 6.4: Comparative overview of chemical fertilizer and bio-fertilizer*

Factors	Chemical Fertilizers	Bio-fertilizers
Production	Industrial, centralized	Biological, small scale or decentralized
Process	Chemical	Biological
Raw materials and energy	Fossil fuel and others imported, based on	Atmospheric nitrogen for nitrogen fixers, unavailable P

budget	non-renewable energy sources, energy intensive	for PSM and VAM, organic residues for compost decomposing organisms. Indigenous and local, based on renewable energy sources very low energy bill.
Pressure on foreign exchange	Exist	Nil
Global Production	About 40 x 10^6 tonnes	175 x 10^6 tonnes biologically fixed nitrogen annually added to earth surface
Efficiency	40-45 per cent for nitrogenous fertilizer for upland crops and less than 33 per cent for rice, 25-33 per cent for phosphatic fertilizers. Heavy N losses due to leaching, volatilization and denitrifi-caton. P availabilitym decreased due to fixation.	About 90% efficiency. Losses due to leaching, fixation are negligible.
Effect on subsequent crop	For nitrogen - nil or low	Residual effect for nitrogen and phosphorus
Pollution effect	Exists due to indiscriminate use	Pollution free
Cost	high cost input Rs. 6.0 for one kg. N, Rs. 14.0 for one kg. F_2O_5	Low cost input - 20 paise per kg. N through *Rhizobium,* 50 paise through BGA
Targeted	All crops	*Rhizobium-iegumes;* BGA-*Azolla*-Rice; *Azotobacter, Azospirillum-Most* of cereals, cotton, sugarcane.
Shelf life	Long	Short for bacteria, long for BGA
Accessability	Affordable section	Small and marginal farmers
Irrigation	More useful to irrigated field	Useful for both irrigated and dryland farming.
Soil health	Indiscriminate use deteriorates the soil health	Improves the soil health.

**Partly adopted from Venkataraman, G .S. and Shanmugasundaram, S. (1992).*

In India, *Rhizobium* bio-fertilizers specific for different legumes and blue green algae are the most popular among farmers. *Azospirillum* and *Azotobacter* are at an intermediate stage of acceptance while phosphate solubilizing microorganisms (PSM), VAM, *Azolla,* cellulose decomposing organisms etc. are at preliminary stage. The common beneficial organisms which may be used for preparing bio-fertilizers and the crops benefited are presented in Table 6.5.

Table 6.5: Positive response in crops yield by the use of bio-fertilizer

Contributing plant nutrients	Microorganisms	Crops benefited
A. Nitrogen	Symbiotic organisms *Rhizobium* (Symbiosis with legumes)	*Pulse legumes:* chickpea pea, lentil, moong, urad bean, cowpea, pigeonpea *Oil legumes:* soyabean groundnut *Fodder legumes:* berseem lucern
	Azolla (Azolla sp *Anabaena azollae* symbiosis)	Rice
	Associative symbiotic organisms *Azospirillum*	Sorghum, pearl millet, rice, wheat, finger millet, maize, *kodo-kutah*tomato, chilly
	Non-symbiotic organisms Heterotrophs - *Azotobacter*	*Vegetables:* onion, brinjal, tomato, cabbage *Flower:* chrysanthemum marygold *Cereals:* wheat, rice, maize, sorghum, sugarcane
	Photoautotrophs - BGA	Rice
Phosphorus	P. Solubilisers and mineralizers *Fungi-Aspergillus penicillum Bacteria-Bacillus pseudomonas* P absorbers (Root fungus symbiosis) Vesicular Arbuscular Mycorrhiza (VAM) Ectomycorrhizae	For all crops
	Endomycorrhizae-Glomus	Linseed, maize, wheat, soybean
Zinc	Root-fungus symbiosis Linseed, wheat VAM.	

Source: Venna, LN. and Bhattacharyya, P. (1990).

ECONOMICLA AND ENVIRONMENTAL BENEFITS

The production of fertilizers depends on non-renewable energy sources and is energy intensive. The energy requirements for the production of one kg. fertilizer nitrogen 11.2, phosphorus 1.1 and potash

1.0 KWH. The requirement of petroleum based energy source in the production of bio-fertilizer is almost negligible. Organisms like *Rhizobium, Azospirillum* etc. assimilate 20-40 mg. nitrogen g^{-1} of carbon. The bio-fertilizer production cost is very low so is the selling price. It has been estimated that one kg. of fertilizer nitrogen costs more than rupees six while bio-fertilizer nitrogen costs only twenty paise through *Rhizobium* and fifty paise through Blue green algae (BGA). On nutrient basis, one tonne of *Rhizobium* bio-fertilizer is equivalent to 100 tonnes of fertilizer nitrogen (considering 50 kg. N fixed ha^{-1} by application of 500g. *Rhizobium* biofertilizer) and one tonne of soil base BGA is equivalent to two tonnes of fertilizer nitrogen (considering 20 kg. of N fixed ha^{-1}) by application of 10 kg. BGA (Verma and Bhattacharyya 1991).

Table 6.6: Average requirement of energy per metric tonne of product in 10^3BTU's

Energy Sources	Nitrogen Urea 46% N (a)	Phosphate TPS 46% P_2O_5 (b)	Potash KC 60% K?O (c)
Natural gas	30,552	920	1,356
Electricity	2,334	2,600	1,063
Fuel oil	26	730	1
Imported steam	6,152	360	-
Total	**39,064**	**4,610**	**2,420**

(a) Based on ammonia plants using centrifugal compressors, (b) Including rock production and energy recovery from sulphuric acid manufacture, (c) based on shaft mining.

Source: FAO Publications, (1985). Fertilizer 85/4.

Bio-fertilizers are cost effective as well as environment friendly. They have a favourable influence on soil health. Bio-fertilizers are compatible with chemical fertilizers and agrochemicals like pesticides and herbicides without demanding extra or special care in their handling. They are safe to crops and users both.

The use of bio-fertilizer in various cropping systems may save 20-40 kg^1 ha^{-1} of fertilizer nitrogen and 10-20 kg^1 ha^{-1} phosphoric acid per cropping season. The success in the transfer of *nif* operon from nitrogen fixing bacterium *Klebsiellapneumoniae* into non-nitrogen fixing bacterium *Escherichia coli* has shown promising possibilities like achieving nodule formation in non-nodulating plants, industrial preparation of nitrogenase enzymes and their use in nitrogen fixation by-passing the use of non-renewable energy sources.

Bio-fertilizers are available for almost all crops and for three nutrients—nitrogen, phosphorus and zinc—and, therefore, the biofertilizer consumption is expected to increase many folds in coming years.

DEVELOPMENT OF BIO-FERTILIZER INDUSTRY

The prominent role of legumes in soil fertility was first noted by J.B. Boussingault (1834), a French farmer, substantiated by Hellreigel (1886) in Germany by identifying root nodule as advantageous growth and Biejerinck (1888), a Dutch Scientist, who discovered that nodule is formed by bacteria, now called Rhizobia. Beginning of legume inoculation was made by Nobbe and Hiltner' (1895) in Germany by using extracts of crushed root nodules under trade name *Nitrogin*™

The early method of a application of inoculum involved top dressing of new fields with large quantity of soils transported from places where the legume grew well. This cumbersome soil transfer method was probably the reason for the birth of the present day inoculant production industry. Instead of the bulk transfer of soil which involves spreading of soil born pathogens, weed seeds, ineffective rhizobia etc. The present method supplies *Rhizobium* bio-fertilizers in small packets commercially.

The first inoculants were pure cultures of *Rhizobium* growing on solid medium and these were marketed in 8-10 ounces glass bottles. Since then, the methods of producing inoculants commercially have undergone a significant evolution to meet the demands of present day utilization of biological nitrogen fixation technology in agriculture. *Rhizobium* bio-fertilizers are commercially produced in both developed where fertilizer N is affordable and developing countries

The earliest documented evidence of the production of bio-fertilizers from isolated *Rhizobium* strains in India is that Madhok, (1934). India in the largest producer and consumer of bio-fertilizers in the world, Madhya Pradesh, Tamil Nadu and Gujarat being the major producing states.

GROUPS OF BIO-FERTILIZERS

Organisms used for biological fertility management, are either free living or having symbiotic association with plants. They directly or indirectly contribute nutrition to crop plants.

Table 6.7: Types of microorganicms and their associations

Free living	This group includes numerous species of blue algae and certain bacteria such as *Azotobacter.*
Symbiotic association	The bacteria, Rhizobium, live symbiotically on the roots of legumes. *Azolla,* a water fern, fixes atmospheric N in symbiotic association with blue-green algae (BGA), *Anabaena azollae* in rice ecosystem.
Associative symbiotic	One of the species of Azospirillum, *A. lipoferum* has associative symbiosis with higher plant systems.

Based on the type of microorganisms, the biofertilizers can also be classified as follows:

1. Bacterial bio-fertilizers e.g., *Rhizobium, Azospirillum, Azotobacter, Phosphobacteria.*
2. Fungal bio-fertilizers: e.g., Mycorrhiza.
3. Algal bio-fertilizers: e.g., blue green algae (BGA) and Azolla.
4. Actinomycetes bio-fertilizers: e.g., *Frankia.*

Bio-fertilizers are mostly cultured and multiplied in the laboratory. However, blue green algae and azolla can be mass-multiplied in the field.

Table 6.8: Some nutrient equivalent of bio-fertilizers and organic / green manures

Component	input Level	Nutrient Equivalent
I. BIO-FERTILIZERS		
Rhizobium	Inoculant	19-22 kg. N
Azotobacter and Azospirillum	Inoculant	20 kg./ N
Blue Green Algae	10 kg/ha.	20-30 kg. N
Azolla	6-12 t/ha.	3-4 kg./t
II. ORGANIC/GREEN MANURES		
Organic Manure (FYM)	Per tonne	3.6 kg. N + P205 + K2O (2:1:1)
Green Manure (Sesbania)	Per tonne	4 4 kg N*
Green Manure (Sesbania)	45 days crop	50-60 kg N for HYV Rice
Cowpea Intercropped with Castor	Legume Buried after 6 weeks	30 kg. fertilizer N on castor
Leucaenia Loppings Sorghum	88 kg. N in Leucaenia	25 kg. fertilizer N on
Sugarcane Trash	5 t/ha.	12 kg. N/t.
Rice straw + Water Hyacinth	5 t/ha.	20 kq N/t.

* = For tall rice varieties, Effect expected to be higher on HYVs.
Source: H.L.S Tandon (1992).

CONCLUSION

The management of soil fertility through biological fertilizers is a vital component of sustainable agriculture. The hypothesis of sustainable agriculture is of recent origin and denotes the maintenance of crop productivity at levels necessary to meet the requirement of increasing population without deteriorating the environment and depleting the natural resources. Thus, it envisages an integration of traditional techniques with appropriate modern advances. The need for integrated nutrient supply system and its assumed importance towards sustainable agriculture need to be investigated. The great potential of bio-fertilizer can be exploited for this purpose.

CLASSIFICATION OF BIO-FERTILIZERS

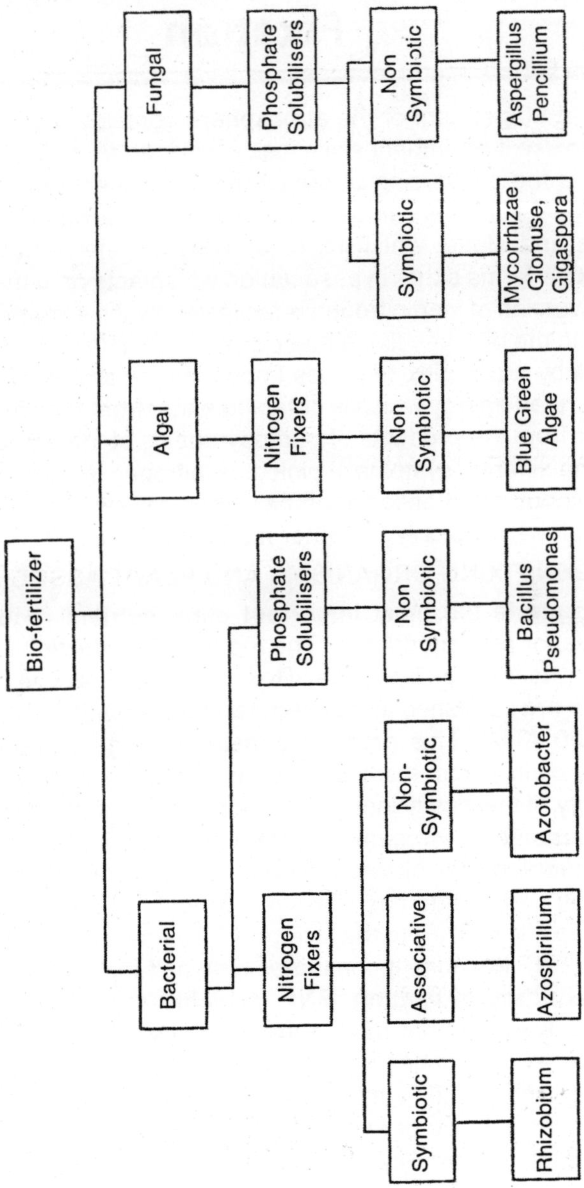

7

Microbal Inoculants for Nitrogen Fixation

About 80 per cent of the atmosphere contains nitrogen, plants are unable to use it as nutrient since it exists in inert form. Biological nitrogen fixation is the conversion of atmospheric nitrogen by living organisms into forms that plants can use. The process is carried out by a group of bacteria and algae, which fix or convert the elemental nitrogen into assimilable forms either in association with plants or in free-living state. The conversion of inert nitrogen is facilitated by the enzyme, nitrogenase, present in the nitrogen fixing microorganisms. The enzyme nitrogenase is coded by a complex of genes known as *'nif* and to fuel the process bacteria need energy which is obtained either from the organic materials in soil or from the products of photosynthesis of the associated plants.

Of the different systems of biological nitrogen fixation, the *Rhizobium* —leguminous plant association has been reviewed in detail. As such, this chapter covers only the other major systems.

NITROGEN FIXING ORGANISMS AND PLANT ASSOCIATIONS

Nitrogen is the most important plant nutrient required in large quantities for crop production. The industrial production of nitrogenous fertilisers is mainly by Haber-Bosch process where nitrogen and hydrogen are combined at high temperature (400-500° C) and pressure (200-1000 ATM). This process consumes large amounts of energy obtained mainly from fossil fuels. The increasing cost and diminishing availability of this costly input is a major concern in many countries. The continuous use of inorganic nitrogen also endangers soil health and causes problems of nitrate pollution. Search for alternative ways of increasing crop yields has obviously brought the subject of biological nitrogen fixation (BNF) to the forefront. The energy economics is also in favour in BNF because it consumes only half the energy consumed by industrial nitrogen fixation. BNF is highly attractive for developing countries, which do not have enough reserves of fossil fuels and are unable to pay high prices for their purchase.

The nitrogen fixing microorganisms form either non-symbiotic, associative symbiotic or symbiotic relationship with plants (Table 7.1). Non-symbiotic or free-living organisms fix nitrogen in soil and their numbers are generally more in rhizosphere of plants. They can be categorised into obligate aerobic, facultative or anaerobic organisms. Although a number of bacteria are reported to be nitrogen fixers in this group, the benefits of inoculation have been proved only with *Azotobacter* and the blue green algae. Associative symbiosis refers to an intracellular relationship between plant roots and a dinitrogen fixing bacterium, *Azospirillum*. They are found in cortical cells ,and protoxylem vessel sin crops such as *Digitaria, Panicum,* maize, sorghum, wheat, barley, pearl millet and a number of others. In case of the symbiotic nitrogen fixers, the bacteria called rhizobia fix nitrogen in nodules on the roots of leguminous plants. In the symbiotic relationship, the bacteria receive the products of photosynthesis as energy source and, in return, they fix nitrogen from the air for their host. The symbiotic association of cyanobacterium, *Anabaena azollae* and the water fern *Azolla* is a potential source of nitrogen for high yielding rice crop. *Frankia,* an actinomycete form nodules called 'actinorhiza' in woody species of 18 genera, including *Casuarina.*

Table 7.1: List of nitrogen-fixing microorganisms in arable soils

Type of association	Microorganisms involved
	Asymbiotic/Associative symbiotic
Bacteria	
Aerobic	*Azotobacter, Beijerinckia, Derxia, Azomonas, Azotococcus, Methanosinus,*
Acetobacter	
Microaerophili	*Azospirillum, Herbaspirillum, Coryne-bacterium, Thiobacillus*
Faculative	*Klebsiella, bacillus, enterobacter, Escherichia, citrobacter, Pseudomonas*
Anaerobic	*Clostridium, Propionibacterium, Desulfovibrio, Rhodospirillum, Rhodospirillum, Rhodopseudomonas*
Blue green algae	*Nostoc, Anabaena, Aulosira, Calothrix, Tolypothrix, Chlorogloea, Aphanothece, Schizothrix, Scytonema, Stigonema, Anabaenopsis, Campylonema*
Symbiotic	
Bacteria	*Rhizobium* with legumes and *Parasponia Azotobacter* with *Paspalum notatum*
Actinomycetes	*Frankis* with woody plants
Algae	*Anabaena azollae* with *Azolla, Anabaena/Nostoc* with *Cycads, Nostoc* with *Gunnera Lichens* (alga + fungus)

AZOTOBACTER

Among the heterotrophic free-living nitrogen fixing bacteria, *Azotobacter* is the most intensively investigated genera. *Azotobacter* are present in neutral or alkaline soils and *A. chroococcum* is the most commonly occurring species in arable soils. *A. vinelandii, a. beijerinckii, A. agilis, A. insignis* and *A. niacrocy to genes* are other reported species. The number of *Azotobacter* rarely exceeds 10^4 to 10^5 g^{-1} of soil. The isolated cultures of *Azotobacter* fix about 10 mg nitrogen g-1 of carbon source under *in vitro* conditions. Apart from its ability to fix atmospheric nitrogen, *Azotobacter* is also known to synthesis biologically active growth promoting substances such as indole-acetic acid (IAA), gibberellins and B-vitamins in culture media. Many strains of *Azotobacter* also exhibited fungistatic properties against plant pathogens such as *Fusarium, Alternaria* and *Helminthosporium.*

The population of *Azotobacter* is generally low in the rhizosphere of crop plants and in uncultivated soils. The occurrence of this organism has been reported from the rhizosphere of a number of crops such as rice, wheat, maize, cotton, sugarcane, bajra, vegetables and plantation crops. A species of *Azotobacter, A. paspali* form specific association with the grass, *Paspalum notatum* which is abundant in many acidic sandy soils of Brazil (Dobereiner and Campelo, 1971).

BEIJERINCKIA

The distribution of *Beijerinckia* is restricted to tropical and sub-tropical regions. They are capable of growing on a wide range of pH from 2.9 to 10.0 and higher population of this organism is reported from soils having a pH 4.9 to 7.4.

Beijerinckia indica is the dominant species in acidic soils. *B. fluminensis, B. mobilis* and *B. derxii* are the other species reported from tropical soils. A survey on the distribution of *Beijerinckia* in several Brazilian states demonstrated the presence of the organisms in 97 per cent of the soil samples under sugarcane and 60 per cent of the soil samples from other vegetation. Rhizosphere occurrence *of Beijerinckia* has been reported in rice, sugarcane, forage grasses such as *Digiteria decumbens, Panicum purpurescens, Cvnodon dactylon* and *Setaria sphacelata,* plantation crops such as coconut, arecanut, cashew, cocoa and pepper and pearl millet.

AZOSPIRILLUM

Though this organism was first described as *Spirillum lipoferum* by Beijerinck in 1925, its potential to fix nitrogen was realized only in 1975 by Doberiener and Day. They isolated the organism from the roots of *Digitaria* and described the plant *Spirillum lipoferum* association (Dobereiner and Day, 1976). Tarrand *el ai,* (1978) renamed the organism as *Azospirillum* and described two species, *A. lipoferum* and *A. brasilense.* Though three more species, *A. amazonense, A. halopraeferens, A. irakense* were added to the genus, the world wide distribution and benefits of inoculation have been proved mainly with the first two species. Of the two physiological types within the genus *Azospirillum,* one group has an oxidative metabolism and the other has the ability to ferment certain sugars, producing acid. In addition to their nitrogen fixing ability, certain strains denitrify under anaerobic conditions and could also assimilate NH_4, NO_3 or No_2.

Azospirillum is a common soil inhabitant of tropics. The organisms form associative symbiosis with many plants particularly with those having the C_4-dicarboxyliac pathway of photosynthesis (Hatch and Slack pathway). They grow and fix nitrogen on salts of organic acids such as malate, succinate, pyruvative or lactate. The development of white, dense and un-dulating fine pellicle on semi-solid malate medium is the characteristic of *Azospirillum.*

OTHER BACTERIA

A number of bacteria capable of fixing nitrogen have been isolated from the rhizosphere and roots of tropical grasses and cereals. They include *Klebisella pneumoniae, Klebsiella oxytoca, Enterobacter cloacae, Enterobacter agglomerans, Citrobacter freundi, Alcaligenes faecalis, Pseudomonas* sp. *Escherichia intermedia, Bacillus polymyxa, Bacillus macerans and Bacillsu circulans.* Wani (1985) isolated *Derxia gummosa, Erwinia herbicola, Enterobacter* sp. and *Bacillus polymyxa* from a survey in 200 sites in the traditional millet growing areas in Northwestern India. Kundu and Tauro (1986) found the association of *Bacillus, Pseudomonas* and *Klebsiella* with the roots of wheat, barley and pearl millet. A new bacterium, *Acetobacter diazotrophicus* was recently isolated from certain sugarcane varieties which were capable of obtaining large quantities of nitrogen through biological fixation. The bacterium behaved as an endophyte and possessed unique physiological properties for a diazotroph such as tolerance to low pH, high salt and sugar concentrations, lack of nitrate reductase activity and nitrogenase activity which tolerates short term exposure 10 ammonia.

Mishustin and Yemtsev (1982) reported variation in the distribution of different species of anaerobic *Clostridium* such as *C. pasteurianum, C. butyricum* and *C. acetobutylicum* in different agroclimatic zones in USSR. Nitrogen fixing ability of different species varied from 2.6 to 9.5 mg nitrogen g^{-1} of glucose. Application of carbon containing compounds, particularly plant residues, stimulated anaerobic nitrogen fixation in flooded soils sown to rice.

ASYMBIOTIC BLUE GREEN ALGAE

The rice fields in India and South East Asia provide a congenial environment for the growth of blue green algae (BGA) comprising of unicellular, colonial and filamentous forms. The nitrogen fixing BGA mainly belong to the orders Nostocales and Stigonematales. Most of the nitrogen fixing BGA possesses heterocysts which are large, thick walled empty cells. Evidences suggest that heterocysts are the sites of nitrogen fixation. There are also reports of nitrogen fixation by non-heterocystous forms. The results of an All India Survey, which covered 2213 soil samples from rice fields revealed the occurrence of nitrogen fixing BGA in 33 per cent samples (Kaushik, 1985). The distribution pattern of algae in different states were: Uttar Pradesh (87%), West Bengal (60%), Orissa (43%), Tamil Nadu (10%), Kerala (9%) and Kashmir (7%).

SYMBIOTIC BLUE GREEN ALGAE

Blue green algae form symbiotic association capable of fixing atmospheric nitrogen with fungi, liverworts, ferns and flowering plants. The association between heterocyst forming nitrogen fixing blue green alga—*Anabaena azollae* and the aquatic fern *Azolla* can be a potential source of organic manure and nitrogen in rice production. The fern forms a green mat over water with a branched stem, deeply bilobed leaves and roots. The dorsall fleshy lobe of the leaf contains the algal symbiont within a central cavity. *Azolla* can be applied as green manure by incorporating in fields prior to rice planting. It can also be grown simultaneously with rice seedling after transplanting and incorporated into soil by hand. *Azolla pinnata* is indigenous in Asia, but recently other species such as *A. caroliniana, A. microphylla, A. fdiculoides* and *A. mexicana* have been introduced for agricultural use because of higher biomass production.

The alga-fungus association, known as lichen occurs on soils, rocks and plant tops. *Nostoc, Calothrix* and some other genera of BGA are involved in the symbiosis. Nitrogen fixation has been proved by ^{15}N technique in genera of lichens such as *Colema, Sterecaulon, Leptogium, Lichina* and *Peltigera.* Some species of mosses and liverworts have the lower surface of the thallus inhabited by species of *Nostoc.* Yet another example of symbiosis is the occurrence of *Anabaena* and *Nostoc* in distinct zones in the cortex of coralloid nodules in roots of higher plants belonging to *Cycadaceae.*

FRANKIA

Angiosperms belonging to the several general such as *Casuarina, Alnus, Myrica, Dryas, Coriaria, Ceanothus, Discaria, Elaeagnus, Hippophae, Shepherdia,* etc. form symbiotic associationwith actinomycete, *Frankia.* Among the nodulated non-legumes, those species, which belong to the genus *Casuarina* have the potential to stabilize eroding land surface and to improve the nitrogen status of improverished soils in addition to providing timber, firewood or charcoal. The nodules first appear as small lateral swellings on the roots but later develop into new lobes at their apices, so that a clustered coralloid structure is formed. In the host cells, the endophyte is seen in the form of hyphae, vesicles and bacteria like cells. Convincing evidence of nitrogen fixation has been obtained in the species of *Alnus, Hippophae, Casuarina, Shepherdia* and *Ceanothus* when studies were conducted with nodulated plants using ^{15}N labeled gas.

RHIZOBIUM

Agrobacterium (A. radiobacter, A. tumefacions) has also been included in the species: *Rhizobium radiobacter,* but this splitting of *Rhizobium* at the generic level into *Agrobacterium* is not accepted by most of the microbiologists.

Rhizobium is relatively more effective and widely used. *Rhizobium,* in association with legumes, fixes atmospheric N. The legumes and their symbiotic association with the rhizobium bacterium result in the formation of root nodules that fix atmospheric N. Successful nodulation of leguminous crop by rhizobium largely depends on the availability of a compatible strain for a particular legume. *Rhizobium* population in the soil depends on the presence of legume crops in the field.

The presence of *Rhizobium* bacteria in the root nodule can be seen under high power microscope by crushing a washed nodule between two glass slider. This kind of bacteria, preferentially, infect legumes as compared to non-legumes. Structurally, *Rhizobium* are rod shaped but great variation can be observed during their life cycle. These are coccoid, very small, highly motile and ellipsoidal forms. The bacteroids are usually irregular with X, Y, star and club-shaped forms. They are 0.5 to 0.9 micron by 1.2 to 3.0 micron in size. All the species are non-sporing and non-acid fast. These symbiotic bacteria *(Rhizobium)* are difficult to cultivate in ordinary culture media but they grow on manitol agar. *Rhizobia* are susceptible to antibiotics (produced by other microorganisms of soil) and also to the action of bacteriophages. Fungicides, herbicides and other plant protectants are also toxic to *Rhizobia.*

The most widely used bio-fertilizer is *Rhizobium,* which colonizes the roots of specific legumes to form tumour like growths called root nodules. It is these nodules that act as factories of ammonia production. Rhizobia have the ability to fix atmospheric nitrogen in symbiotic association with legumes and certain non-legumes like *Parasponia.* A mature nodule consists of a central 'bacterial zone' surrounded by several layers of cortical cells. The process of N-fixation is wholly dependent on the activity of the enzyme nitrogenase which is located within the bacteriods. The volume and number of bacteroids have a direct positive relationship with the amount of nitrogen fixed.

In the absence of legumes, the population of rhizobium in the soil diminishes. Most strains of rhizobia native to the soil are effective in N fixation. Some of them may be ineffective and produce ineffective nodules. These nodules are smaller in size, soft and whitish in colour. Their N fixing capability is much low. The effective strains produce large, pink and firm nodules. Their N fixing capacity is far greater. Artificial seed inoculation is often needed to restore population of effective strains of rhizobium near the root zone to ensure high yields. Each legume requires a specific species of rhizobium to form effective nodules (Table 7.2).

Table 7.2: Cross inoculation group of Rhizobium

Rhizobium species	Cross inoculation group	Legume types
R. leguminosarum	Peas	*Pisum, Vicia*
R. phaseoli	Beans	*Phaseolus*
R. trifolii	Clover	*Trifolium*
R. meliloti	Alfalfa	*Melilotus, Medicago Trigonella*
R. lupini	Lupini	*Lupinus, Orinthopus*
R. japonicum	Soybean	*Glycine*
R. sp.	Cowpea	*Vigna, Arachis*

There are specific *Rhizobium* for every legume and inoculation with efficient strains of *Rhizobia* is essential for the nitrogen gains and better crop yields. Inoculation of pulse crop with appropriate cultures can give yield increases of the order of 15-30 per cent. Thus *Rhizobium-legume* symbiosis can generally meet 80 per cent of the N requirement of the legume crop. A starter does of N as chemical fertilizer is required (equivalent to about 20 per cent requirement of legume crop) for good crop yields.

The *Rhizobium-legume* association can fix upto 100—300 kg N/ha. in one crop season and in certain situations can leave behind substantial nitrogen for the following crop. The range of nitrogen fixed per hectare per year by different legumes is 100-150 kg. for clover, 80-85 kg. for cowpea, 100-300 kg for alfalfa, 240-320 kg. for faba bean, 90-100 kg. for lentil, 150-200 kg. for lupins, 50-60 kg. for groundnut, 60-80 kg for soybean, 50-55 kg. for mungbean and 100-400 kg. for pasture legumes.

Many legumes may be nodulated by diverse strains of rhizobia, but growth is enhanced only when nodules are produced by effective strains of rhizobia. It is thus extremely important to match microsymbionts prudently for maximum nitrogen fixation. A strain of rhizobia that nodulates and fixes a large amount of nitrogen in association with one legume species may also do the same in association with certain other legume species. This must be verified by testing. Leguminous plants that demonstrate this tendency to respond similarly to particular strains of rhizobia are considered "effectiveness" group. The effectiveness grouping of leguminous plants are given in Table 7.3.

Table 7.3: Effectiveness Groupings of Legumes (Legumes that tend to respond similarly when inoculated with the same strain of rhizobia)

Rhizobium species	Effectiveness groupings	Leguminous species
Rhizobium	1.	*Medicago sativa, M. falcate, M. minima, M. meliloti tribuloides, Melilotus denticulate, M. alba, M. officinalis, M. indica.*
	2.	*Medicago arabca, M. hispida, M. lupulina, M. orbicularis, M. praecox, M. truncatula, M. scutellata, M. polymorphi, M. rotata, M. rigidula, Trigonella foenum-graecum.*
	3.	*Medicago lacmata*
	4.	*Medicago rugesa*
Rhizobium trifolii	5.	*Trifolium incarnatum, T. subterraneum, T. alexandrinum, T. hirtum, T. arvense, T. angustifolium.*
	6.	*Trifolium pratense, T. repens, T. zybridum, T. fragiferum, T. procumbens, T. nigtescens, T. glomeratum*
	7.	*Trifolium vesiculosum, T. herytheum, T. bocconei, T. biossieri, T. compactum, T. leacanthum, T. mutabile, T. vernum, T. physodes, T. lasyurum*
	8.	*Trifolium ruepellianum, T. tembense, T. usambarense, T. steudneri, T. burchellianum var. burchellianum, T. burchellianum var. johnstonii, T. africanum, T. pseudostriatum.*
	9.	*Trifolium semipilosum var. kilimanjaricum, T. masaiense, T. cheranganiense, T. ruepellianum var. lanceolatum.*

	10.	*T. medium, T. sarosience, T. alrestre*
	11.	*T. ambiguum*
	12.	*T. heldreichianum*
	13.	*T. masaiense*
	14.	*T. reflexum*
	15.	*T. rubens*
	16.	*T. semipilosum*
Rhizobium leguminosarum	17.	*Pisum sativum, Vicia vilosa, V. hirsute, V. faba Ve. Tenuifolia, V. tetrasperma, Lens esculenta, Lathyrus aphaca, L cicera, L. hirstus. 'L. odoratus, L. sylvestris*
	18.	*Lathyrus ochrus, L. tuberosus, L. szenitzii*
	19.	*Lathyrus sativus, L. clymenum, L. tingitanus*
	20.	*Vicia faba, V. narbonensis*
	21.	*Vicia sativa, V. amphicarpa*
Rhizobium phaseoli	22.	*Phaseolus vulgaris, P. coccineus, P. angustifolius*
Rhizobium lupini	23.	*Lupinus albicaulis, L albifrons, L. albus, L. angustifolium, L. arboreus, L. argenteus, L. benthamii, L. formosus, L luteus, L. micranthus, L. perennis, L. sericeus, Lotus uliginosus, L americanus, L. pedunculatus, L. strictus, L. strigosus.*
	24.	*Lupinus densiflorus, L. Vallicola*
	25.	*L.nanus*
	26.	*L. polyphyllus*
	27.	*L. subarnosus*
	28.	*L. succulentus*
Rhizobium japonicum	29.	*Glycine max*
Rhizobium spp. (cowpea type)	30.	*Vignaunguiculata, V. sesquipedalis, V. luteola, V- cylindrica, V. angularis, V. radiata, V- mungo, Desmodium sp., Alysicarpus vaginatis, Crotalaria sp., Macroptilium lathyroides, M. atropurpureum, Psophocarpus sp., Lespedeza straita, L. stipulacea, Indigofera sp., Cajanus cajan, Cicer arietinum*
	31	*Phaseolus limensis, P. lunatus, P. aconitifolius, Canavalia ensiformis, C. lineata*
	32.	*Arachis hypogaea, A. glabrata, Cyamopsis tetragonoloba, Lespedezsa sericea, L japonica, L. bicolor*
	33.	*Centrosema pubescens, Galactia sp.*

	34.	*Lotononis bainesii*
	35.	*Lotononis angolensis*
Rhizobium spp. (lotus)	36.	*Lotus corniculatus, L. tenuis, L. angustissimus, L. tetragenolobus, L. caucasicus, L. crassifolius, L. creticus, L. edulis, L. frondosus, L. subpinnatus, L weilleri, Dorycnium hirsutum, D. rectum, D. suffrutitosum, Anthyllis vulneraria, A. lotoides.*
	37.	*Lotus uliginosus, L. amercanus, L. scoparius, L. anguttissimus, L. pedunculatus, L. strictus, L. strigosus, Ornithopus sativus, Lupinus angustifolius, L. alous, L. luteus.*
Rhizobium spp. (corozilla, Petalostemon-Onobrychis)	38.	*Corozilla varia, Onobrychis viciifolia, Petalostemon purpureum, P. candidum, P. microphyllum, P. miuiflorus, P. villosum, Leucaena leucocephala, L. reusa.*
Rhizobium spp. (various)	39.	*Daleaulopecuroides*
	40.	*Stroptostyles helvola*
	41.	*Robina pseudoacacia, R. hispida*
	42.	*Amolpha canescens*
	43.	*Caragina arborescens, c. frutescens*
	44.	*Oxytropis sericea*
Rhizobium spp. Astragilus sp.	45	*A. cicer, A. falcatus, A. Canadensis, A. mexicanus, A. oriziculatus.*

Source: Legumes inoculants and their use. FAO (1985).

The amount of nitrogen fixed by legumes through root nodule bacteria exhibits considerable variation. Fixation is influenced by soil factors particularly nutrient status. For efficient performance under field conditions, legumes require adequate availability of soil nutrients such as phosphoric acid, potash, calcium etc. In arable soils, which receive liberal dressings of nitrogenous fertiliser, legumes do not turn to atmospheric nitrogen. Estimates of nitrogen fixation by some legumes are presented in Table 7.4.

General Taxonomic Characteristics of Legumes

The following family and sub-family descriptions for legumes are in the form of botanical descriptions. The glossary contains a brief description of the sub-families and information on the approximate number of species and their genera] distribution.

Table 7.4: Estimates of nitrogen fixed by some legumes

Crop	Nitrogen fixed (kg ha^{-1})
Alfalfa	100-300
Clover	100-150
Chickpea	26-63
Cluster bean	37-196
Cowpea	53-85
Groundnut	112-152
Lentil	35-100
Greengram	50-55
Pigeonpea	68-200
Soybean	49-130
Peas	46
Fenugreek	44

Source: Wani and Lee (1991).

Characteristics of the family Plants, shrubs, woody vines, and annual and perennial herbs

Leaves usually alternative and compound-bipinnate, simply pinnate, or palmate, rarely simple. Inflorescence variously racemose, in simple racemes, panicles, spikes or heads. Flower structure varies to the extent that 3 sub-families are recognized; corolla typically 5-parted; stamens 3 to many, mostly 10, free, or united by their filaments in various ways; pistil single, free, Fruit characteristically a pod (legume), dehiscent or indehiscent.

Characteristics of the sub-families Mimosoideae: Plants, shrubs, woody vines, a few perennial herbs

Leaves pinnate or bipinnate, often with glands on the rachis; leaflet pairs many, some with sleep movements, or touch-sensitive; in certain groups - for example *Acacia* - characteristic broad, modified petioles (phyllodes) simulate leaflets lost after the seedling stage; stipulates in some genera reduced to spines. Flowers regular (actinomorphic), crowded into globose heads, or cylindric spikes, rarely recemose, some inflorescences monoecious; calyx lobes 5, usually valvate; petals 5, equal, valvate in bud, usually united above the base; stamens mostly 10 or multiples thereof, free, jointed at el base, or united forming a tube. Fruit a pod, straight, curved, or spirally twisted, usually 2-valved, dehiscent, some breaking transversely into 1-seeded segments.

Caesalpinloideae: Plants, shrubs, rarely

scandent, rarely herbs

Leaves pinnate or bipinnate, rarely simple; some with translucent dots. Flowers mostly irregular (zygomorphic), usually in showy racemes or panicles; calyx lobes 5, overlapping or separate; petals usually 5, sometimes rudimentary or absent, slightly unequal, the upper petal distinctive and innermost in bud; dehiscing by joined, 10 or fewer, some may be staminodes; anthers indehiscent, some with winged sutures (samara), or fleshy and drupelike.

Papilionoideae: Plants, shrubs, annual or perennial herbs

Leaves mostly palmately 3- or more-foliolate, or odd or evenly pinnate, not bipinnate, or trifoliate, rarely simple; some with tendrils or spines. Flowers very irregular (papilionaceous), in 1 - to many-flowered, terminal or axillary inflorescences; calyx tubular, regularly 5-toothed or lobed; petals 5, unequal, overlapping; standard uppermost and outermost; the 2 wings lateral, intermediate; the 2-keel petals lowermost, inside, usually joined along the lower margin, hiding the ovary and stamens; stamens; stamens 10, rarely fewer, usually united into 2 bundles (dialdelphous) of 9 + 1 or 5 + 5, or in 1 tubular bundle (monadelphous), rarely free (Sophoreae). Fruit a variously shaped pod, straight, curved, winged, or moniliform, usually 2-valved and dehiscent, some transversely jointed (loments), ripe joints separating.

TECHNIQUES TO ENUMERATE RHIZOBIA

Several direct and indirect methods have been found useful in the enumeration of rhizobia both from soil and in broth culture. Many workers have enumerated viable rhizobia in the aliquots directly by the dilution plate count method (Vincent, 1970, Karren and Wollum, 1980 and Hoben and Somasekaran, 1982). Drop plate count technique of Miles and Misra was found to be more convenient in estimating viable rhizobia (Hoben and Somaskaran 1982). Development of fluorescence technique further helped in the precise enumeration of rhizobia directly from the soil (Schmidt *el ai,* 1968; Schmidt, 1974; Bohlool and Schmidt, 1973; Reyes and Schmidt, 1979). Enzyme linked immunosorbant assay (ELISA) was also used to enumerate soil rhizobia (Nambiar and Anjaiah, 1985).

Plate Count Technique

Vincent (1970) demonstrated the plate count technique to enumerate viable rhizobia by spreading an aliquot on the surface of congo red agar medium. The above method gave good results, when the population of other heterotrophic microorganisms was not more than ten times the population of rhizobia. He also suggested a rough grading for natural rhizobia based on their appropriate number in one gram of soil as absent or sparse (<25), few (25 to 1 x 10^3), abundant (I x 10^3 to 1 x 10^5) and very abundant (>1 x 10^5). Further, the difficulty in this method was to distinguish a particular *Rhizobium* sp. in the presence of other rhizobia and similar soil bacteria. Attempts were made to develop a specific medium to isolate *Rhizobium* directly from soil using appropriate antibiotics in the growth medium. A selective medium for *Rhizobium* consisting of six antibiotics was developed by Grahan in 1969. This medium was, however, found not useful when the rhizobial counts were low.

Three methods of dilution plating *viz.*, pour plate, spread plate and Miles and Misra drop plate were compared by Hoben and Somaskaran, (1982). They reported that all the three plating methods gave close estimates, but Miles and Misra drop plate method has advantages over the other methods because of the economy in materials and labour. Usual plating methods are not applicable to the determination of the rhizobia in soil and un-sterile peat cultures because; (1) no medium is sufficiently selective to exclude the possibility of other forms being confused with *Rhizobium,* (2) where the *Rhizobium* is markedly in the minority in the dilutions at which it would need to be counted, it will be out numbered or antagonized by other microorganisms (Data and Vincent, 1962).

Flourescent Antibody Technique (FAT)

Schmid *et al.* (1968) tested the fluorescent antibody technique (FAT) to study soil rhizobia. The effectiveness of FA technique for detection of a particular strain of *R. japonicum* in soil was studied by the examination of contact slides. *Rhizobium* can be seen in soil by contact slides by means of immunoflorescence compound, but the study of their interactions with soil sites is limited by non-specific adsorption of the FA. Similarly, Bohlool and Schmidt, (1973) studied the persistence and competition of *R. japonicum* in soils using FAT. For the study of persistence of rhizobia in soils, microscopic slides were first buried in the appropriate soil overnight to allow the accumulation of soil film on the surface of slides. Slides were rinsed in distilled water and kept submerged in water suspension of 10 days old shaken culture of *Rhizobium* strain USDA 110 to 30 minutes to allow the bacteria to attach to the soil films. Slides were air dried and kept in air tight plastic containers. Slides were removed at different intervals and stained with FA specific for strain USDA 110. Counting efficiency of FA was estimated to be about 30 per cent (Reyes and Schmidt, 1979).

Enzyme linked Immunosorbant Assay (ELISA)

ELISA was also found to be useful in the enumeration of rhizobia. Nambiar and Anjaiah, (1985) reported that the loss of viability in the peat carrier does not interfere with the enumeration of live rhizobia by ELISA. A single ELISA microlitre plate can be used for testing eight samples and results can be known in 2 days. One person can process 20 microlitre plates in a day. However, ELISA requires mainly gamma-globulin conjugation step which limits the use of this technique in ecological studies.

Non-sustainability of ELISA-test when the population is less than 10^{-3} cells g^{-1} of soil is also reported. Under such conditions plant infection technique can be employed (Nambiar and Anjaiah, 1985).

Plant Infection Technique

Most probable number (MPN) by plant infection technique is a frequently used method to enumerate rhizobia in soil and in inoculants when other microorganisms are present. Accuracy of this technique for counting *R. japnonicum, R. meliloti, R. trifoli* and *R. leguminosarum* has been established (Date and Vincent, 1962; Brockwell, 1963; Weaver and Frederick, 1972). But the accuracy of the MPN plant infection method for enumerating cowpea rhizobia has not been well established.

The method consits of inoculating the test plants grown aseptically with aliquots from a dilution series of the sample under examination. The number of rhizobia in the sample can be calculated from the proportion of test plants forming nodules at each dilution. Plant infection test though time consuming was found reliable and accurate to enumerate rhizobia and also to exclude other diverse microorganisms (Brockwell, 1963). Tuzimura and Watanabe, (1961) compared the pour plate method and plant infection method to estimate pure culture population. They reported that the plant infection technique does underestimate the number of organisms in pure culture. Similar observations were made by Date and Vincent, (1962).

Weaver and Frederick, (1972) developed a new effective culturing system for Rhizobia towards determining a most probable number count by using legumes grown in plastic growth pouches. The counts obtained by this method were equal to pour plate counts. However, MPN counts were significantly less than the plate counts in two instances out of 8 samples. But even in these instances, the results were comparable considering the 95 per cent confidence interval on the MPN counts. The differences may be due to slight errors in the dilution sequence or to a soil effect (Weaver and Frederick, 1972). Grassia and Brockwell (1978) stated that the estimation of bacterial numbers using plant infection assay was dependent on the probability of bacteria reaching and infecting the roots of test plant which did not follow a probability distribution.

There are truly no selective media for counting rhizobia directly from the soil except when antibiotic resistant strains are used (Bushby, 1981). But these techniques appear too specialized to offer any prospect of distinguishing reliably between rhizobia from various nodulation groups. Therefore, bacteriologically controlled plant infection test is usually employed (Brockwell, 1982). The progress in the study of *Rhizobium* ecology has been hampered by the lack of suitable methods for quantifying population changes in soil and plant rhizosphere (Bushby, 1981). The plant infection test is suitable not only for counting nodule bacteria in soil but also on inoculated seed, in legume rhizosphere or from any other situation where the rhizobia are out numbered by other microorganisms(Brockwell,1982).

Growth system for MPN methods

Rhizobium of a particular host legume, is commonly counted by plant infection technique. This technique involved growing the small seeded legume plant aseptically on a seedling agar in enclosed tubes (Vincent, 1970; Brockwell *et al,* 1975) or partly enclosed tubes (Gibson, 1963) or in plastic growth pouches (Weaver and Frederick, 1972). Large seeded legumes were grown in many systems such as jar assembly (Leonard, 1944; Vincent, 1970) glazed jar (Vincent, 1970; Weaver *et al.,* 1972), plastic growth pouches (Weaver and Frederick, 1972), vermiculite (Grassia and Brockwell, 1978), perlite medium in Leonard's bottle or plastic pots and partly in sterile condition in sand vermiculite mix (Sand: Vermiculite: Grit, 1:2:2 v/v) (Rao and Dart, 1980). Brockwell *et al.* (1975) reported that the dilution nodulation frequency technique (plant infection test) is suitable where a small seeded species like *Glycine ussuriensis* is grown in plant tubes as a test plant for identification and enumeration of *R. japonicum.* Similarly, growing large seeded legumes like chickpea in seedling agar tubes (25 x 200 mm) was also successful when cotyledons were excised under axenic conditions (Rupela and Dart, 1980; Toomson *et al.,* 1984). Growing redgram cultivar ICP-1 (size 10 g/100 seed) in 25 x 200 mm tubes for MPN technique was also successful (Rao and Dart, 1980).

Suitable test host for MPN technique

High symbiotic promiscuity was observed within greengram, groundnut, redgram and blackgram (Dadarwal *et al.,* 1977). Stowers and Elkan (1980) suggested a test host; siratro *(Macroptilium atropurpureum)* for counting rhizobia nodulating cowpea group of legumes such as redgram, groundnut, cowpea, velvet, bean, punabean, lentil and horsegram. However, there was an indication of specificity in redgram *Rhizobium* strains within the cowpea miscellany. Thus there was a possibility of getting higher estimates of cowpea rhizobia with siratro as the trap host than those infective on redgram (Rao and Dart, 1980).

Boonkerd and Weaver (1982) reported on the accuracy of MPN technique as compared to plate counts using five strains of cowpea rhizobia. The number of rhizobia determined by the MPN method using cowpea, siratro and peanut underestimated the population from 10 to 100 fold. Experiments using soybean as a test host indicated that the MPN method was accurate for *R. Japonicum.* The experimenter using the MPN method should be aware of its accuracy for particular *Rhizobium-legume* symbiosis.

Woomer *et al.* (1988) studied the reliability of MPN technique for enumerating rhizobia in tropical soils. They showed that there is no significant interaction of Range Of Transition (ROT) of the *Rhizobium* legume plant infection count data between species and sites. The acceptability of MPN codes (P> 0.99) was the highest (97 to 99%) with *Vicia sativa, Trifolium repens* and *Glycine max* and lowest (72%) with *Leucaena leucocephala.* The two legumes *Medicago sativa* and *Macroptilium atropurpureum* yielded 87 per cent and 75 per cent acceptable MPN codes respectively. Gino and Brunal (1989) working on the use of MPN to detect soil microorganisms stated that MPN technique has the advantage of requiring small amount of space during incubation period and permitted to be used for any laboratory analysis. One can also analyse greater number of samples with more replications for each sample, making it possible to choose a single step dilution factor most appropriate for the less degree of contamination of the samples.

DISTRIBUTION OF RHIZOBIAL POPULATION

Most of the cultivated soils in India are found to contain native or indigenous rhizobia capable of nodulating cowpea group of legumes in varying numbers

(IARI, 1971). Soils contain different rhizobial populations based on legume coverage. This population consists of a number of species, sub-species and strains showing wide range of symbiotic effectiveness with a legume. Number of indigenous rhizobia are influenced by soil types, conditions and soil depths.

Wilson (1931) observed species variation in abundance from time to time in New York soils. *Rhizobium leguminosarum* counts have been observed to range from <10 to>10^5 per gram of soil, whereas the number of *R. trifolii* ranged from 2500 to 10^6 per gram of soil. Population densities were commonly low in acid soils and submerged soils (Wilson, 1926) and seasonal fluctuations have been observed (Wilson, 1930; Gowda and Rai, 1991), The population of rhizobia even within restricted area was found to be diverse and a few samples could give only a poor idea of its real nature (Purchase and Vincent, 1949).

Native nodulation of tropical legumes was observed in India and many other countries like Australia (Mclead, 1962; Diatloff and Langford, 1975), Africa (Obaton, 1977), U.S.A. (Kremer and Peterson, 1982) and others. Population of *Rhizobium* was greater in soils that supported a rotation with legume for which the *Rhizobium* was a symbiont than in a rotation system in which the legume was not present. Thus more *R. meliloti* cells were observed in a soil recently grown with alfalfa than in a soil in which alfalfa was absent in the previous year (Walker and Brown, 1935). On the other hand, Weaver *et al.* (1972) found no correlation between the abundance of *R. japonicum* and the number of years since soybeans were present in a particular field. Similarly, they observed no correlation between the numbers of *R. japonicum* and soil texture, pH or organic matter levels. Conversely Tuzimura and Watanabe (1961) observed that *R. japonicum* was abundant in the fields which had soybeans the year before, the population declined the following year although it was still significantly higher than in adjacent sites not cropped to soybeans for twenty years. The legume rhizosphere is known to specifically stimulate native rhizobial numbers in many cases (Robinson, 1967; Rao and Dart, 1980).

Tuzimura and Watanabe (1962) have demonstrated that rhizobia of different cross inoculation groups are frequently abundant in the rhizosphere of plants, which they are unable to infect. Not only legumes but also non-legumes will occasionally exert a pronounced stimulatory effect on the root nodule bacteria (Rovira, 1961). Reyes and Schmidt (1979) found that rhizobia are stimulated even in non-legume rhizosphere like wheat equally in comparison to legume rhizosphere.

In the soil regularly cultivated with legumes, the native rhizobia formed effective nodules without inoculation indicating a survival of naturally occurring rhizobia over the seasons in appreciable numbers (Diatloff and Langfor, 1975). Ireland and Vincent (1968) estimated clover-rhizobial population for studying quantitative competition for nodule formation by plant dilution count.

Brockwell and Dudman (1968) surveyed the population and effectiveness of *R. meliloti* associated with pastures of *Trifolium subierraneum* in various localities in Australia. Very high populations of 9.8 x 10^5 per gram of soil was recorded but the mean level of nitrogen fixing ability (effectiveness) was 52 per cent of that of control strain used in the commercial clover inoculants. Escuoler (1972) estimated the numbers of *Rhizobium meliloti, R. trifolii, R. leguminosarum* and *R. lupini* in different locations by plant infection count technique. It was reported that *R. trifolii* was most abundant followed by *R. leguminosarum* while *R. meliloti* and *R. lupini* were less abundant and very wide range of effectiveness was recorded in locations where heavy application of fertiliser nitrogen was practised for cultivating the legumes. Chatel and Parker (1973a), estimated rhizobial populations from the samples of rhizosphere and non-rhizosphere soils at different time intervals and reported higher population of *R. lupini* than that of *R. trifolii.* Similarly, Hamdi *et al.* (1978) enumerated the populations of *R. meliloti* and *R. trifolii* in sixty five soil samples by semiquantitative method. There was no quantitative relationship between size of rhizobial population and soil properties such as pH, EC, lime content etc. and also soil types.

Rao and Dart (1979) enumerated cowpea rhizobial population in alfisols and vertisols by using siratro and redgram as trap hosts. They found that alfisols contain more than 10^4 rhizobia per gram of soil than vertisols. Soil types and depth also affected population. Similarly, population of groundnut rhizobia in cultivated soils of India ranged from 10^2 to 10^6 per gram of soil (Sheth, 1979). Due to inadequate method for identifying indigenous strains in the soil, the dynamics and diversity of *Rhizobium* population in a legume field are poorly understood (Noel and Brill, 1980).

There is a large variability in the *Rhizobium* populations between sites and depths within a field. In one alfisol field the *Rhizobium* population was less affected by soil depth, remaining high (10^4 g^{-1} dry soil) through out the profile with a slight reduction at a depth of 150 to 160 cm (10^3 g^{-1}). In another field, the population declined with depth, the reduction being more pronounced below 100 cm in soil profile. Similar patterns have been observed in vertisol fields (Rao *et al.*, 1981). Generally alfisols contain more rhizobia than vertisols. Some soils of ICRISAT sites had fewer than 100 cowpea rhizobia per gram soil (Rao *et al*, 1982).

The estimation of cowpea rhizobial populations using *Macroptilium atropurpureum* as host plant gave great variations in numbers between sampling sites in the same field. More consistent numbers were obtained in alfisols (10^4 to 30 x 10^5 g^{-1} soil) than in vertisols (0 to 10^6 g^{-1} soil) according to Rao *et al.* (1982).

Hegde (1983) enumerated the redgram rhizobial population in 14 soil samples from different places of Karnataka using siratro and redgram as trap host. The population ranged from 1.8 x 10^1 to 1.2 x 10^5 per gram of dry soil. Population changed with soil depth and seasonal conditions. Similarly, population varied in different soil types with different cropping pattern. In general, loamy soils were found to have good population of mung bean rhizobia as compared to sandy loam soils. Panther *et al.* (1984) reported high population of mung bean rhizobia in rice fields in Punjab.

Singleton and Tavares (1986) determined the rhizobial population in four different Hawaiian soils with six legume hosts *viz.*, *Glycin emax.*, *Vigna unguiculata, Phaseolus lunatus, Leucaena leucocephala, Arachis hypogea* and *Phaseolus vulgaris. Rhizobium* population ranged from less than 6x100 to 10 x 10^4 per gram of soil and all the four soils were devoid of *R. japonicum.*

Rhizobium culture

Rhizobium culture has been used for leguminous vegetable crops is in paractice among farmers. *Rhizobium* forms symbiotic association with roots of leguminous crops forming nitrogen fixing nodules on the root system. Rhizobia enter the roots of legumes either through root hairs or directly at the emergence of lateral roots. They form infection threads through which the bacteria enter the root system. The entry of *Rhizobium* into the roots of plans is a perfect symbiosis. Initial stages is symbiosis is the reciprocal molecular conversation, transmission of a gene inducer from legume host to bacterium and the bacteria in response synthesizing a morphogen that is transmitted to the plant, switching the developmental fate of the legume root, the bacteria and formation of bacterioids in the nodules. It is enzyme nitrogenase that reduces atmospheric nitrogen to ammonia. This enzyme has been studied in a very great detail. (Das, 1991).

There are 2 types of rhizobia:

1. Slow growing *Brady rhizobium* sp.,
2. Fast-growing *Rhizobium* sp.

Soil contains native species of *Rhizobium* but all are not capable of forming nodules. Some of the strains are highly specific to certain species. These are called cross inoculation groups. For example, *Rhizobium leguminosarum* can nodulate peas only, while *R. leguminosarum bv. phasioli* can nodulate. French bean and other beans and *Rhizobium* sps. Nodulate cowpea. Artificial inoculations help increase the native population of a particular species in the soil when that crop is grown.

The efficacy of *Rhizobium* inoculation has been established in India beyond doubt by the results of the co-ordinated trials conducted by the Indian Council of Agricultural Research, New Delhi, in farmers' field (AICRP, 1983). Vegetable legumes—French bean, pea and cowpea - have been extensively studied. Effective nodulating strains have been isolated and developed after field testing. French been strains have been isolated and developed after field testing. French been strains have been modified from time to time to suit salinity, alkalinity and acidity of soil (Bhardwaj, 1975; Suryanarayana and Pramod Kumar, 1985; Tomar *et al,* 1985; Yadav and Sanoria, 1994; Wange *et al,* 1996). In iron mine waste soil also rhizobium inoculation could improve nodulation in cowpea. (Ravtray *et al,* 1996). Mutant strains of *Rhizobium leguminosarum* bv *phaseoli* superior to wild strains in nodulation have been induced in French bean through UV induction, antibiotic resistance, acid and azide resistance at the CCS Haryana Agricultural University, Hissar. For cowpea effective strains of *Rhizobium* sps. have been identified at University of Agricultural Sciences, Bangalore, Tamil Nadu Agricultural University, Coimbatore and CCS Haryana Agricultural University, Hissar.

Mundra and Bhati (1994) studied the role of ion, manganese and *Rhizobium* inoculation on growth, nodulation and iron manganese ratio and protein content in cowpea. They found that 20 kg/ha. of *Rhizobium* inoculum increased the number of nodules 38 per cent. The *Rhizobium* sp. also increased nodulation, nitrogen fixation and biomass yield by slow and fast growing cowpea rhizobia in gaur under different environmental conditions (Mand *et al,* 1992). Wange and Patil (1995) studied the response of pea cultivars of *Rhizobium leguminosarum* inoculation. An increased pod yield of 25-66.7 per cent could be obtained in Bonevillae variety. Singh *et al.* (1992) in a field trial in sandy loam soil in U.P. found that *Rhizobium* inoculation and phosphate application (46 kg/ha.) gave maximum yield in pea Rachna. Singh and Singh (1992) also found that *Rhizobium* inoculation and sulphur application (0-30 ppm) improved seed yield in pea cv T163.

It is estimated that about one third off the electrons made available for reduction of nitrogen in legume nodules are used instead to reduce hydrogen and this gas just escapes into the soil atmosphere carrying away wasted energy. Certain species of *Rhizobium* contain uptake hydrogenase enzyme (Hup+ strains) that oxidizes much of the hydrogen to water before it escapes. During this oxidation ATP is produced from ADP and Pi. This process, therefore, conserves energy and are more efficient N fixers. The *Rhizobium* strains possessing this enzyme yield more than the strains that do not possess them. The Hup+ strains have been identified by Dadarwal (1986) to be more competitive than Hup- strains.

Genetic modifications in Rhizobium strains

Efforts have been made to develop genetically modified strains incorporating traits for better competitiveness; Khanuja and Suman (1993) obtained heat shock tolerant mutants in the process of improving rhizobial strains. Sharma *et al,* (1997) introduced gene markers (Gus) in Rhizobium strains to monitor the release of genetically engineered strains in the environment. However, genetically modified strains have not made any impact on legume production under field conditions.

Rhizobium in Root Nodule

The presence of these bacteria in the root nodule can be seen under high power microscope by crushing a washed nodule between two glass slider. Frank (1877) and Beijernick (1888) discovered *Rhizobium* a free living or symbiotic bacteria of leguminous as well as non-leguminous plants.

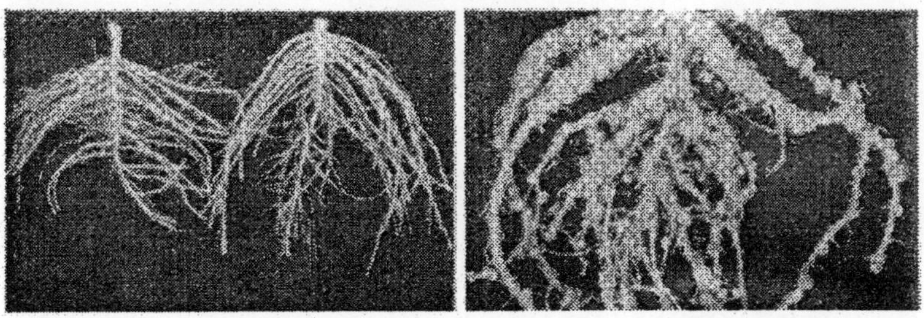

(A) (B)

Fig. 7.1: Bare uninoculated roots of soybean plant (A) and nodulated roots of soybean, (B) inoculated with *Rhizobium*.

This kind of bacteria, preferentially infect legumes as compared to non-legumes. Structurally, *Rhizobium* are rod shaped but great variation can be observed during their life cycle. These are coccoid, very small, highly motile and ellipsoidal forms. The bacteroids are usually irregular with X, Y, star and club-shaped forms. They are 0.5 to 0.9 micron by 1.2 to 3.0 micron in size. All the species are non-sporing and non-acid fast. These symbiotic bacteria *{Rhizobium)* are difficult to cultivate in ordinary culture media but they grow on manitol agar.

Rhizobia are susceptible to antibiotics (produced by other microorganisms of soil) and also to the action of bacteriophages. Fungicides, herbicides and other plant protectants are also toxic to *Rhizobia*. Occurrence of different species of *Rhizobium* in leguminous plants can be enumerated as follows:

Agrobacterium (A. radiobacter, A. tumefacions)

It has also been included in the species: *Rhizobium radiobacter*, but this splitting of *Rhizobium* at the generic level into *Agrobacterium* is not accepted by most of the microbiologists.

One more kind of slow growing asymbiotic bacteria of lupin, soybean, cowpea have been identified and placed under a separate genus *Phytomyxa (P. japonicum)*. In short, the root nodule genera can be delimited into two genera: *Rhizobium* and *Phytomyxa:* the former comprises of three species: R. *leguminosarum, R. meliloti* and *R. radiobacter*, while the latter bears only one species *P. japonicum*.

According to Elken (1969) *Rhizobium* can also be classified on the basis of DNA composition, for example guanine and cytosine composition of *R. leguminosarum* and *R. meliloti* is 56.6 to 63.1 per cent while G+C composition of *P. japonicum* is 62.8 to 65.5 per cent (Delay and Rassel, 1965).

Structure and Function of Nodule

The outermost layer of the nodule constitutes the bacteroid zone which is enclosed by several layers of cortical cells. The rate of nitrogen fixation of nodule is directly proportional to the volume of the effective nodule. Sometimes ineffective strains produce ineffective nodules. These nodules are relatively small and contain poorly developed tissue associated with morphological abnormalities.

Formation of Nodule in Leguminous Plants

Biological nitrogen fixation is the reduction of atmospheric nitrogen to ammonia by microorganisms in the soil. It involves a highly specialised and intricately evolved interactions between soil microorganisms and higher plants for harnessing the atmospheric nitrogen. It is a fascinating biological phenomenon studied extensively to provide low cost nitrogen and improve crop productivity. The nitrogen fixing organisms associated with horticultural crops are the *Rhizobium* species, living in symbiotic relationship with the leguminous plants and free living fixers belonging to the *Azotobacter* family and the *Azospirilla* living in association with the root system of crop plants. Roots of most of the leguminous plants possess circular out-growth or swelling called nodules or tubercules, which are formed after infection of certain types of nitrogen fixing bacteria particularly the different species of *Rhizobium.*

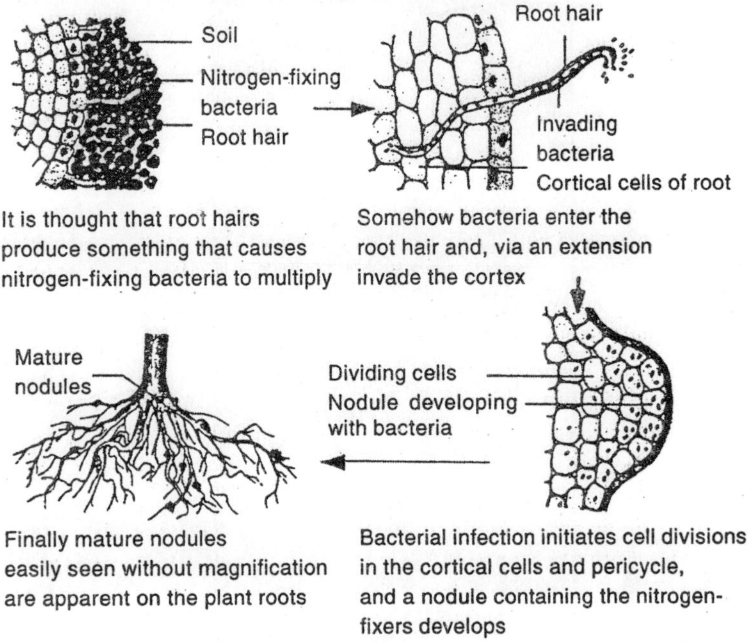

Fig. 7.2: Nodule formation by *Rhizobium* on legume plants. The root hairs are the site of infection. Note the change in the root hair. A characteristic deformation is the curling of the root hair tip to produce a Shepherd's crook. The nodule can be seen on the root.

These bacteria have the capacity to fix free atmospheric nitrogen of soil in nodule.

They infect or get their enterance in root through the soft-hair or other epidermal cells by damaging them. In the first stage of the infection, bacteria grow very profusely at the tip of the root hair and form a long filament in the root hair- called *infection thread.* This thread reaches the endodermis and pericycle area through cortex tissue. Cells of this area (cortex) go on dividing and form a young nodule. The newly formed young nodule pushes the overlying parenchyma and the epidermal tissue towards outside and produces a small swelling on the surface of the root. Anatomically, a nodule is made of thin walled parenchymatous cells which is filled up with the nitrogen fixing organisms. The size and shape of the root nodule varies according to plants in which occur. It is not necessary that all the bacteria, which infect the root, produce nodule.

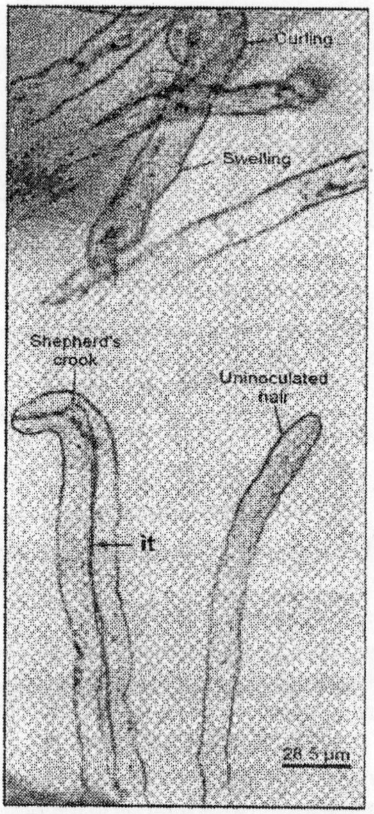

Fig. 7.3: The early host responses to infection leading to the formation of N_2-fixing root nodules. (A) A root hair two hours after inoculation, showing curling and swelling, (B) A root hair (left) tow days after inoculation, showing a shepherd's crook and an infection thread (it). A thin uninoculated root hair is shown on the right.

According to Wipf and Cooper (1939) the root nodule always contains double number of chromosomes as against of normal somatic tissue. If the root lacks such cells (cells with double chromosome number), there will be no formation of root nodule, even after the formation of infection thread. Those plants which do not bear root-nodules will never be able to fix atmospheric nitrogen in the plants. It has been observed by Allen and Allen (1947) that out of 429 genera of family Leguminosae about 179 genera containing 949 species form nodules.

Leghaemoglobin

The effective nodules are usually larger and pink in colour. This is due to the presence of red coloured leghaemoglobin (leg indicating its presence in legume root nodule). This pigment is similar to haemoglobin of blood and is found in nodules between bacteroids and membrane envelops, enclosing them. Chemically, it is haem-protein and it contains a haem meoiety attached to a peptide chain and represents the globin part of the molecule. The molecular weight of leghaemoglobin is 16,000 - 17,000 daltons. The amount of leghaemoglobin in nodules has the direct relationship between amount of atmospheric nitrogen fixed by legumes. The functions of leghaemoglobin are as follows:—

1. It represents an active site of nitrogen absorption and reduction.
2. It acts as a specific electron carrier in nitrogen fixation.
3. It regulates the oxygen-supply in the nodule.
4. It acts as an oxygen-carrier.

According to Scholander (1960), leghaemoglobin acts as a biological-valve in regulating the supply of oxygen to bacteroids in nodules.

Site of Nitrogen Fixation in Nodules

According to Bergersen (1969) the membrane envelops surrounding the groups of bacteroids are the site of nitrogen fixation, but in recent years it has been proved that bacteroids are the seat of nitrogen fixation.

Leguminous Plants/*Rhizobiaceae* Symbiosis

Symbiotic N_2 fixation in agriculture can be attributed mainly to legumes—the plants in the *Leguminosae.* It is estimated that *Leguminosae* contains more than 200 genera, and 20,000 species, which ranges from small plants such as the clover to the large plants such as *Acacia* species. Approximately 90 per cent of them can fix nitrogen from the atmosphere with *Rhizobiaceae,* either with *Azorhizobium, Bradyrhizobium, Rhizobium* or with *Sinorhizobium* in root nodules. The important agricultural legumes can be divided into three groups: crops that grown for their commodities (e.g. grain legumes); forage legumes that may be grazed or harvested for animal fodder; and plants or shrubs in agroforestry systems. Worldwide approximately 1.5 million $km.^2$ of land are cultivated with grain legume plants, mainly in *Glycine max, Phaseolus vulgaris, Pisum sativum, Arachis hypogaea, Cajanus cajan* etc.. The annual harvest of grain legumes are about 200 million tonnes, which provides the plant protein source for human and animal consumption, or vegetable oil and other raw materials. The areas partially covered by the forage legumes mainly in *Trifolium, Lotus, Medicago, Stylosanthes, Macroptilium* and *Mimosa* etc., is even much larger, about 30 million km^2 of grassland in the five continents. The third group consists of the genera *Acacia, Albizia,*

Alnus, Leucaena, Robinia etc., which are mostly used as timber, fuelwood or craftwood, and in the pharmaceutical industry as antibacterial and antifungal agents, or food additives and any other functions.

There are five genera of the *Rhizobiaceae: Azorhizobium, Bradyrhizobium, Rhizobium, Sinorhizobium* and *Photorhizobium.* All members of *Rhizobiaceae* are characterised by a gram-negative cell wall structure. Cells are generally rod-shaped, non spore-forming and motile with differently arranged flagella. All rhizobia are aerobic bacteria that persist saprophytically in the soil until they infect a root hair cell. The enzymes from the bacteria degrade part of the cell wall and allow bacteria entry into the root-hair cell itself, which lead the root hair to produce a threadlike structure called the infection thread. The bacteria multiply extensively inside the thread, which extends inwardly and penetrates through and between the cortex cells. In the inner cortex cells the bacteria are released into the cytoplasm and stimulate some cells (especially tetraploid cells) to divide. Each enlarged, non-motile bacterium is referred to as a bacteroid. These result in a proliferation of tissues, eventually forming a mature root nodule. A typical root nodule cell contains several thousand bacteroids. The nodule contains a protein called leghemoglobin, which gives legume nodules a pink colour due to its prosthetic hem group. Leghemoglobin is thought to help transport O_2 into the bacteroids, which is essential for bacteroid respiration. Nitrogen fixation in root nodules occurs directly within the bacteroids. The host plant provides bacteroids with carbohydrates, which they oxidise and from which they obtain energy. These carbohydrates are first formed in leaves during photosynthesis and then are translocated through phloem to the root nodules. Sucrose is the most abundant carbohydrate translocated, at least in legumes. Some of electrons and ATP obtained during oxidation by the bacteroids are used to reduce N_2 to NH_4+, which is catalysed by nitrogenase.

Isolation and Identification

Leguminous plants are carefully uprooted and their roots are washed in running water to remove soil particles. Healthy intact and pink nodules preferably on tap root are selected and cut out with a portion of the root.

The nodules are surface sterilized by immersion in acidified 0.1 per cent $HgCl_2$ for 5 minutes and repeated washing with sterile water. The nodules are then dipped in 70 per cent ethanol for 30-60 seconds followed by several washings with sterile water. Surface sterilized nodules are individually crushed in sterile water with a sterile glass rod and the resulting suspension is streaked on yeast extract mannitol agar (YEMA) plates containing congo-red poured in 24 hours earlier to ascertain the sterility of plates and culture media. Upon incubation at 28-30°C for 3 to 10 days depending on the nature of *Rhizobium* (slow or fast growing), the colonies of bacteria normally appear as white, translucent, glistening and elevated with entire margin. *Agrobactehum,* the most common contaminant of *Rhizobium* takes up the colour of Congo-red and appears red in colour.

Table 7.5: New system of classification of root nodule bacteria

Genus	Species	Biovars	Host legumes
Rhizobium	Leguminosarum	a. Viceae	Vicia
		b. Trifolli	Trifolium
		c. Phaseoli	Phaseolus
	meliloti	-	Medicago
	loti	-	Lotus
	fredii	-	Glycine
Bradyrhizobium	Japonicum	-	Glycine
Bradyrhizobium	Species	-	Cicer, Cajanus, Vigna, etc.

There are several presumptive tests which are carried out to identify *Rhizobium* isolate. *Rhizobia* grow very poorly on glucose peptone agar medium, does not grow on Hofers alkalie broth (pH 11.0) and does not utilize lactose. But the best way of identifying *rhizobia* is to conduct plant infectivity tests and see if effective nodules are produced. A plant test is done under controlled and sterile conditions with assemblies ranging from small tubes to pots. Small test tubes are used for small seeded legumes like clover, berseem, moong and urd, whereas Leonard jar assembly or small pots are used for testing bold seeded legumes like chickpea, arhar and french bean. Agar-agar, vermiculite or sand can be used as the sub-strate for growing plants. Surface sterilized seeds of specific host are sown in appropriate assembly and inoculated with the bacterial isolate under test. The plants are watered at regular intervals with any N-free nutrient solution. After 5-6 weeks the plants are examined for nodulation, nitrogenase activity and dry biomass. Thus, an efficient strain for a particular crop can be selected. Such strains are then subjected to pot and field trials to assess their potential as inoculants.

After selecting efficient strains, it is necessary to lyophilize them to maintain their efficiency since sub-culturing at monthly intervals on artificial medium may lead to deterioration of the activity of organisms.

MASS PRODUCTION

The *Rhizobial* Inoculant Industry has come a long way since its inception in 1895 when Nobble and Hiltner introduced a laboratory culture of *Rhizobia* under the name 'Nitragin'. The last 100 years have witnessed a number of developments towards the belter exploitation of this technique. Carrier-based *rhizobial* inoculants have almost completely repiaced liquid cultures and agar slope cultures, which were commonly used a few years ago.

For preparation of carrier-based inoculants the *rhizobial* broth culture must attain a minimum population of 10° cells/ml. It is then blended with the finely powdered (100-200 mesh sieves) and sterilized carrier. The sterilization of carrier is carried out in autoclaves at 15 lb psi for 3-4 hrs. continuously or 1 hr each on three successive days. Blending is done by mixing of broth culture with sterilized carrier. In trays either manually (with hands washed and smeared with alcohol) or by using a mechanical mixer. The broth is added equivalent to one-third of water holding capacity of the carrier.

After mixing the carrier with the broth culture, raw-blended carrier is kept for 24 hours for curing. During this time the *rhizobia* get acclimatized with the carrier.

After curing, the inoculant is packed in polyethylene bags. The polyethylene bags are sealed by an electric sealer leaving about two-third vacant space to give proper aeration to the inoculant. Directions for use of inoculant are printed on the packet.

CARRIERS FOR *RHIZOBIUMINOCULANTS*

The medium in which *rhizobia* are allowed to multiply is an important factor in *rhizobial* culture preparation. The carrier is used for this purpose. The carrier is a crucial ingredient in the formulation of inoculant because the shelf life of the products largely depends on it. A variety of carriers are in use at present while some are under testing. Some materials whose usefulness as carrier has been established and used as carriers. Even though typical peat is not available in large quantities in our country, the peat like material available in Nilgiris has been found to be a good carrier. Lignite available from Neyveli Lignite mines in South India is another carrier material widely used. The characteristics of good carrier are:

1. It should be indigenously available and cheap.
2. Should be non-toxic to the Bio-fertilizer bacteria.
3. Should have around neutral pH.
4. Should have an organic matter content around 40 per cent.
5. Should have high water holding capacity and surface area.

METHOD OF INOCULATION

A 10 per cent sugar solution or 10 per cent pharmaceutical grade of gum arabic is prepared to serve as sticker for *Rhizobium* cells seeds. This solution is sprinkled on the seeds required for one hectare and the seeds are spread on a polyethylene sheet and mixed uniformly. The content of the inoculant packet are sprinkled over sticker coated seeds and mixed thoroughly.

Table 7.6: Carriers used for *Rhizobium* inoculation in India (Tilak, 1993).

Carrier	Availability	Location	Water holding capacity (%)	Organic matter (%)
Peat	5.5 million tonnes (total)	Ootacamund (Nilgiri Hills)	52-120	21-56
Lignite	3 million tonnes (annually)	Neyveli	92	28
Farmyard manure	Plenty	Everywhere	40-50	30
Charcoal	Plenty	Everywhere	90	77

If required more water is added but only in sufficient amount to coat the seeds fully with the inoculant. The seeds are spread uniformly for drying on gunny bag or cement floor in shade avoiding direct sunlight. After drying, the sowing is done immediately.

In order to protect the *rhizobi* from adverse situation of soil conditions (acidity, alkalinity, hazard of pesticides, etc.), pelleting method of seed inoculation is recommended. Finely ground calcium carbonate (300 mesh sieve) is added to freshly inoculated wet seeds in a container and mixed rapidly for 2 minutes and until seeds are uniformly coated. Coated seeds are allowed to harden for an hour by spreading on a clean surface. Besides lime, other pelleting agents like gypsum, bentonite, rock phosphate, charcoal etc. have also been recommended.

CROP RESPONSE

The largest contribution of BNF to agriculture is derived from the symbiosis between legumes and species of *Rhizobium*. The *Rhizobium* - legume association can fix upto 50-100 kg N/ha. in one crop season and in certain situations leave substantial N for the following crop. The quantity of N fixed varies with the kind of legumes and agro-climatic conditions. Crops like groundnut, chickpea. Cowpea, green gram and soybean can leave being 20-30 kg N/ha. for succeeding crops, while crops like Lucerne, pasture legumes and green manuring crops like sunnhemp, *dhaincha* add about 50 kg/ha.

The field response to *Rhizobium* inoculation is quite variable. The average response to *Rhizobium* inoculation ranged from 66 kg/ha. at Hisar to 152 kg/ha. at Badanpur in chickpea. In general, most types of legumes are reported to respond to *Rhizobium* inoculation but not at all locations. Studies carried out in All India Co-ordinated Agronomic Research Project taking 5 legumes (moongbean, urdbean, soybean, cowpea, groundnut) indicated significant response at 7 out of 17 locations. Residual effect of *Rhizobium* inoculation on succeeding cereal crop was noticed in 4 cases only. Average response to *Rhizobium* inoculation ranged from 6 per cent in soybean to 18 per cent in cowpea. A residual response of 1 to 3 per cent was noticed on succeeding wheat crop.

FACTOR AFFECTING CROP RESPONSE

Although legume inoculation is a long established practice to maintain soil-health, it has not become popular largely because of its erratic response. Some of the common reasons of poor or no response to inoculation are:—

1. **Failure of seed to germinate**—This is due to the use of poor quality seed and lack of sufficient moisture for germination.
2. **Failure of seedlings to become nodulated**—This may be the result of poor quality inoculant, adverse soil conditions, inoculation with wrong inoculant, compatibility of *rhizobia* with pesticides, etc.
3. **Ineffective nodulation**—This situation may result from the presence of a large native population of *rhizobia* which may compete with *rhizobia* applied for nodule formation and makes it ineffective in fixing N with introduced legume.
4. **Nutritional deficiencies**—Nodule formation is severely affected by nutritional deficiencies particularly phosphorus, calcium and molybdenum because of their role in protein synthesis, cell wall development and in nutrition of *rhizobia*, respectively.
5. **Plant competition**—Failure of the legume plant to promptly nodulate and establish is frequently due to competition for moisture, nutrients, light and space.

Confirming Nodulation

The benefit from the N fixation of Nitrogen fixing species(NFS) plantings, the plants must actually be nodulated and fixing N effectively. These are separately controlled functions. Conflicting reports of nodulation and the influence of environmental factors can result in confusion over whether or not the plants do fix nitrogen. In some woody species, nodules may be large (that is, 5 cm to 7 cm) or black and woody, not resembling nodules of better-known legumes at all (de Faria *et al.*, 1987). Sprent (1986) reports nodulelike structures that are not nodules because they do not contain *rhizobia* and have no nitrogenase activity. Such structures can be confused easily by workers without access to appropriate laboratory facilities. The simple test of opening nodules to look for hemoglobin (as indicated by a pink colour) also can be misleading because this pink colour may be found in outgrowths on roots of plants inhibited by nematodes (Sprent and Sutherland, 1990).

The most certain means of confirming nodulation is to carefully evaluate reports of nodulation using well-established principles. Allen and Allen (1981) list four essential requirements for confirming and reporting nodulation:—

1. The host plant should be correctly identified by a competent botanist.
2. Whole nodule specimens should be accompanied by records of their size, shape, location on the root system, relative abundance, colour, texture, plant habit and habitat, and the date of collection. Rapid transfer of specimens to plastic bags or dry vials is recommended.
3. *Rhizobia* should be isolated from the nodule as much as possible, using Koch's postulates and irreproachable bacteriological procedures.
4. Plant trials with the isolate should be conducted for nodule evaluation, using aseptic plant-growth equipment and seeds that are surface, sterilized.

These steps generally will be taken only by microbiologists with an interest and the facilities to conduct this type of procedure. For non-microbiologists, perhaps the most thorough means of confirming nodulation is to arrange for a microbiologist to assess nodulation. Nodules to be tested should be placed in a small vial over a desiccant such as silica get for transport to the laboratory. For NFS workers who do not have access to a microbiology laboratory, the next best alternative is to evaluate nodulation in the field.

FIELD METHODS FOR IDENTIFICATION OF PLANT ACTUALLY FIXING NITROGEN

Simple surveys of plant roots can provide an estimate of the extent of nodulation, although this can be both difficult and time consuming for large plants. The eastest place to examine roots is in the nursery, where seedlings can begin to nodulate as early as 3 to 4 weeks after sowing. Chen and Rolfe (1988) even found nodules on *L. leucocephala* seedlings 12 days after inoculation. Sprent and Sutherland (1990) suggest that in humid areas young seedlings may be carefully dug up and examined;

but in drier areas, young plants may not be the best subjects. In very dry areas in well-aerated soils, nodules may be at depths of several meters (Jenkins *et al.,* 1988). This also may be true in light soils in humid areas. For example, effective, nodules were observed at a depth o f 1 m on *paraserianthes falcataria* in a very humid site on the island of Oahu in Hawaii. Examination of roots to similar soil depths in the field, particularly in well-acerated soils, will help ensure identification of most nodulation sites.

Examination of roots for the presence of "effective" nodules can be done by carefully noting the colour of nodule tissue. The best time to examine nodules in grain and fodder legumes in the field is at their peak of flowering. Although little is known of the periodicity of noudlation for NFSs, the most reliable time to examine them is likely during periods of least stress (that is, when moisture or temperature are least limiting for growth, such as the beginning of the monsoon or rainy season). Roots should be dug up with a shovel or fork to prevent nodules from being stripped from the roots. The nodules that are found need to be removed from the roots, sliced open and examined for colour. Those with pink, red, orange or brown color are probably actively fixing nitrogen. Green nodules are older and senescent; white to pale green are ineffective and not fixing N. One exception is the green but otherwise normal nodules produced by effective rhizobia on molybdenum-deficient plants (FAO, 1984).

Leaf colour is sometimes used as a rough indicator of nitrogen fixation. In a pot study of *Gliricidia sepium* seedlings, green-leaves seedlings produced higher nodule weights than pale-leaved seedlings (Atta-Krah, 1987a). In the green-leaves group, there also were positive correlations between nodule numbers, shoot and root fresh weights. While chlorosis need not relate to the lack of nitrogen fixation, it can be useful indicator to follow-up with closer examination. Interpreting leaf colour is not a reliable method, however. The need for caution is demonstrated by the non-nitrogen fixing legume *Cassia siamea,* which nearly always produces dark-green leaves but does not nodulate.

Some NFSs such as *Sesbania rostrata* (Dreyfus *et al.,* 1985), *Aeschynomene* spp. (Alzard and Duhoux, 1988) and *Casuarina cunninghamiana* (Dommergues *et al.,* 1990) form stem nodules above ground. While aerial nodules are not common, it is likely that other NFS species also nodulate on the stem or on adventitious roots, particularly in high-rainfall areas. Dommergues *et al.* (1990) note that the aerial nodules of *Casuarina cunninghamiana,* although abundant, are not very conspicuous due to their flat, irregular shape and barklike colour.

THE NEED TO INOCULATE

Nodulation will not occur if appropriate rhizobia of *Frankia* are absent from the soil in which NFSs will be planted. Inoculation, the process of adding inoculant to seed or soil, can introduce enough bacteria to infect the roots. Determining whether or not to inoculate should be based on whether there will be a response to inoculation under specific field conditions.

To determine the response to inoculation, two approaches can be taken. The first is to use crop history as a guide. The second is to conduct a field test. Crop history suggests that if the NFS species has never before been planted on the site, inoculation is probably necessary. An example from two soils in Nigeria demonstrates the importance of inoculating NFSs on "new" planting sites (Table 7.7). Most-probable-number analysis for these and other soils in Nigeria indicated that *leucaena rhizobia* were few or absent in soils without prior *leucaena* cultivation. This same pattern is true for other species, particularly *Robinia pseudoacacia,* which seems to be very specific in its *rhizobial* requirements.

Table 7.7: Effect of inoculation and fertilization of *Leucaena leucocephala* on two soils in Nigeria.

Treatments	Nodule number per plant	Nodules from inoculant strain (%)	Nodule dry weight (mg/plant)	Shoot dry weight (g/plant)	Plant N (kg/ha)	Total P (kg/ha)
	Fashola grassland site, derived savanna					
Uninoculated	36	69	179	26	82	5.1
150kgN/ha.	36	59	87	72	232	15.2
Rhizobium IRC1050	40	78	485	79	228	15.0
Rhizobium IRC1045	15	94	174	68	209	12.8
	IITA transition forest savanna site					
Uninoculated	0	0	0	51	174	14.6
150kgN/ha.	0	0	0	130	445	36.0
Rhizobium IRC1050	17	100	198	103	398	26.9
Rhizobium IRc1045	34	100	277	121	448	35.96
LSD* (5%)						
Fashola	11		23	12	53	1.9
IITA	12		25	22?	66	0.6

Adapted from Sanginga *et al.*, 1987, 'Least significant difference.

Crop history, however, can be a very imprecise means of predicting nodulation and response to nodulation. Akkermans and Houwers (1979) planted uninoculated *Alnus cordata* and *A. glutinosa* in soil with no *Frankia*. Under these conditions, 100 per cent of the *A. cordata* plants nodulated, while nodulation varied from 56 per cent to 100 per cent among the *A. glutinosa* seedlots. The nodules in this case originated from infections by *Frankia* in the nursery soil.

The second and more reliable approach to determining response to inoculation is to conduct a field test to determine the need for inoculation. Three treatments are needed for this experiment (FAO, 1984):

1. inoculated plants from seeds inoculated with the best inoculant available;
2. non-inoculated plants receiving no fertilizer treatment; and
3. non-inoculated plants furnished with fertilizer nitrogen.

The density of indigenous *rhizobia* has been identified as the primary determinant of response to inoculation in grain and forage legumes found a similar relationship with six legume plant species in four soils. High populations of indigenous *rhizobia* can dramatically reduce the response to inoculation. This factor, plus the level of combined soil nitrogen, can greatly influence the economic return to an investment in inoculation.

SELECTING AND HANDLING INOCULANTS

The following suggestions for selecting and storing inoculants largely come from an excellent practical handbook on the use of legume inoculants (FAO, 1984):

1. Different legumes require different inoculants. Be certain to have the right one.
2. Be certain that the inoculant is of the high quality and is still fresh. High-quality inoculant should contain only large numbers of *rhizobia* or *Frankia* capable of producing nodules and fixing large amounts of N on the host (e.g., greater than 1×10^7 per ml). They must be free of other bacteria that may harm the *rhizobia* or host NFS.
3. Keep the inoculant in a cool place, preferably in a refrigerator, until ready to use. High temperatures will harm bacteria, but inoculant stored at temperatures of 4°C or lower will remain effective for several months.
4. Inoculate seeds just before planting because rhizobia die quickly on the seed.
5. When inoculating seeds, avoid ifeaking them too wet. Use only enough water for good adhesion of the inoculant to the seed.

6. Chemicals, fungicides or insecticides applied to seeds or soil may be toxic to the bacteria in the inoculant. If seeds are chemically treated, use a larger amount of inoculant and plant immediately after inoculating.
7. Store inoculated seed in a cool place protected from hot sunshine and excessive drying.
8. Leftover inoculant may be kept safely for short periods if it is in a tightly closed container to prevent drying.
9. Inoculated seed should not be eaten or fed to animals.

INOCULATION

Inoculation—the introduction of appropriate bacteria to the rooting zone of nitrogen-fixing plants—can supply enough *rhizobia* or *Frankia* to meet a plant's requirements. Seed or soil can be inoculated, although inoculation of seed or roots generally is preferred due to grater ease and lower costs. Seedlings, such as those in dibble tubes, can be inoculated with an inoculum/peat mixture suspended in water.

Methods of application

Methods like coating seeds with biofertilizer, drenching biofertilizer suspension on crop rows, if not applied at the time of sowing, are based on the principle to place the nitrogen fixing organisms on seed coat or at closet proximity of roots in rhizosphere. Bio-inoculants are sprinkled on moist seeds so as to load each seed with a minimum of 1000 viable cells. Most of the producers now have stared having adhesives mixed at the time of manufacturing and earlier methods of sprinkling *Rhizobium* treated gur/molasses solution is not required. Soaking the seed in water followed by culture inoculation gives better results because or removal of water soluble seed coat toxic agents.

Quantity of the bio-fertilizer applied in a unit area depends on the number of viable cells present in g^{-1} of bio-fertilizer and size of seeds. Usually 200 g *Rhizobium* bio-fertilizers are used for treating 10-12 kg. of pulse seeds. On an average, 500 g. lignite/charcoal based bio-fertilizer is sufficient to treat the seeds required for sowing one hectare. Under normal conditions 10^3-10^6 when seeds are sown in adverse conditions like drought and acidity caused by fertilizers.

Biofertilizer contains living organisms and all due care and precautions should be taken to save them from extremes of temperature and desiccation. Treated seeds must be sown immediately and should not be mixed with acid forming chemical fertilizers. Recommended pesticides on pulses have no adverse effect on nodulation and yield. Soybean seeds when treated with fungicides followed by *Rhizobium* treatment or *vica versa* did not cause significant yield difference (Gupta *et al*, 1988). Out of four herbicides tested Exadiazona 1.0 kg (active ingredient) hall significantly increased the nodule number and yield of soybean (Khare *et al.*, 1989).

Inoculation methods should be chosen to match both locally available resources and the environment into which the inoculated seed will be planted and the type of seed to be inoculated. A summary of inoculation methods for different soil or planting conditions and seed sizes is found in Table 7.8.

Table 7.8: Recommended methods of inoculation

Soil or planting conditions	Recommended method of inoculation
Small-seeded NFSs	
Normal-good temperature, moisture, pH and seedbed	Slurry using peat-based inoculant, 30 ml. slurry/kg. of seed.
Normal-but with heavy infestation of native ineffective *rhizobia*	Inoculant pellet. Apply 45 g inoculant/kg. seed. Mix 15 g. inoculant with 22 ml of gum arabic solution (45%) and apply to seed. Use the remaining 30 g. inoculant to dry the seed immediately after applying the slurry.
Acid soils, rough, poor seedbed	Lime pellet. Inoculant slurry prepared with gum arabic or synthetic cellulose, 22 ml/kg. seed. Apply double dose of inoculant.
Seeds treated with toxic chemicals, other soil and planting conditions good	Plant without inoculation. Use soil inoculant after seedling emerge.
Large-seeded NFSs	
Normal-good temperature, moisture, pH and seedbed	Slurry using peat-based inoculant, 30 ml slurry/kg. of seed.
Seeds treated with toxic chemicals, other soil and planting conditions good	Use soil inoculant. Apply in seed furrow or nursery soil with seed at sowing time.
Hot, dry soil	Use soil of granular inoculant. Apply inoculant 2.5 cm. to 5 cm. below seed for deeper if moist soil is deeper.
Fragile seeds	Use soil of granular inoculant. Apply in furrow or nursery soil with seed.

Soil or planting conditions	Recommended method of inoculation
Fields of non-nodulated NFSs	
Small seeds sown by broadcasting	Sow granular inoculant at a depth of 5 cm.
Large or small seeds in rows	Sow granular or liquid inoculant in rows beside plants at a depth of 5 cm. to 7 cm.
Seedlings or cuttings	
	Prepare a slurry by mixing the inoculant with water: one volume inoculant to two volumes of water. Dip seedlings of cuttings in slurry and allow to soak for 1 minute or longer. Plant as soon as possible.

Adapted from: FAO, 1984.

BIO-FERTILIZERS AND THEIR USAGE IN FIELD CROPS

Bio-fertilizer are applied in,different ways in the field crop production:—

1. Seed treatment or seed inoculation,
2. seedling dip, and
3. soil application.

Seed treatment

Each packet (200 g.) of inoculant is mixed with 200 ml. of rice gruel or jaggery solution. The seeds required for one ha are mixed in the slurry so as to have uniform coating of the inoculant over the seeds and then shade-dried for 30 minutes. The treated seeds should be used within 24 hours. One packet of inoculant is sufficient to treat 10 kg. seeds. *Rhizobiurn, Azospirillum, Azatobacter* and *Phosphobacteria* are applied as seed treatment.

Seedling root dip

This method is used for transplanted crops. Five packets (1.0 kg.) of the inoculant are required for one ha and mixed with 40 litres of water. The root portion of the seedlings is dipped in the solution for 5 to 10 minutes and then transplanted. *Azospirillum* is used for seedling root dip particularly for rice.

Soil Application

Ten packets (2.0 kg.) of the inoculant are required for one ha. of main field. The inoculant is mixed with 20 kg. of well dried, powdered FYM and broadcast in the field just before transplanting/sowing.

OPTIMIZING NITROGEN FIXATION IN NFS

Although there remain many gaps in our knowledge of how to manage NFSs for optimum N fixation, the best information we have suggests we can improve N fixation through management. The following are site characteristics or management properties that are likely to result in improved N fixation for most, but not all, NFS species:—

1. Well-aerated soils that are not waterlogged or drought-stressed
2. Soil moisture content of 60 per cent to 75 per cent of the soil water-holding capacity
3. Optimum temperatures for plant species growth
4. Mature but not senescent plants
5. Soil pH above 5.5
6. Intermediate spacings
7. Dual inoculation with *Rhizobiwn* or *Frankia* and mycorrhiza
8. Starter N, P and K applied in the nursery
9. Other soil nutrients such as Ca, Mn and Mo above limiting levels

EFFECTIVE AND INEFFECTIVE STRAINS

Soil is the best medium for microorganisms to grow and flourish. It contains effective and ineffective strains. The relative capacity of the symbiotic system, once established to fix molecular nitrogen, is known as it's effectiveness. Many *Rhizobiwn* strains are highly effective while others are largely or completely ineffective. A strain that does not permit fixation at a rate sufficient to meet the demands of the host is either partially effective or totally ineffective. Consequently, mere presence of nodules is not a guarantee that *leguminous* crop is being benefited with fixed nitrogen.

Ineffective *Rhizobium* strains produce a greater number of nodules than effective stains but the nodules are smaller in size and tend to be are widely distributed over the root system. On the other hand, effective *Rhizobium* strains cause larger few nodules congregated on main root. Effective nodules are distinctly red in colour because of the presence of iron containing substance known as leghemoglobin. In contrast, the nodules produced by ineffective strains have neither leghemoglobin. In contrast, the nodules produced by ineffective strains have neither leghemoglobin nor red pigmentation. Consequently, it is possible by visual examination of spiked nodule for its redness to ascertain the relative capacity for active nitrogen fixation. At field level, soybean, chickpea and pigeonpea have shown positive correlation in yield with nodule weight and not with nodule number. Plant nodulated by ineffective strains showed lower dry matter yield, grain yield and nitrogen content, irrespective of the number of nodules than those nodulated by effective *Rhizobium* strains. The yield increase obtained from the sue of bio-fertilizer relates not only to the nitrogen enrichment but also to the antagonistic effect on harmful organisms in *rhizosphere*.

ESTABLISHMENT OF INOCULATED *RHIZOBIUM*

The extent of establishment of inoculated rhizobia in soil through bio-fertilizer is dependent on the type of legumes, effectiveness of strains, inorganic or mineralisable nitrogen content of the soil, level of available soil phosphorus and potassium, pH and presence of suable forms of secondary nutrients. Influence on nitrogen fixation due to unfavourable climatic and seasonal variations is generally more on physiology of host than the symbiotic association.

Nodulation as well as nitrogen fixation are also dependent on the carbohydrate: nitrogen ratio within the host tissues. A widening of the ratio stimulates the resulting from very high light intensities retards the process, retardation of nitrogen fixation in nitrogen rich soil or consequent on the application of fertilizer nitrogen may be associated with narrowing of the carbohydrate: nitrogen ratio status in host. The influence of phosphorus and potassium on nitrogen fixation and nodulation is associated with the vigour and well being of the host rather than the specific stimulation of symbiosis.

Soil pH affects microsymbiont, macrosymbiont and their symbiotic interaction. Infection does not occur much below pH 5.0 as it will be inhibited by the high hydrogen ion concentration as well as the presence of high iron or aluminium and low molybdenum ions. Molybdenum plays an important role in electron transfer. Soils poor in molybdenum, give less response to biofertilizer application.

Rhizobiwn species are susceptible to attack by bacteriophages and, therefore, bacteriophage resistant/tolerant *Rhizobiwn* strains should be used preparing biofertilizer.

PRODUCTION OF *RHIZOBIUM* BIOFERTILIZER

Pulse and oilseed legumes occupy about 30 million hectares in India and to cover the whole area with *Rhizobium* bio-fertilizer, there is a need to produce 15,000 tonnes considering the rate of application at 500 g ha^{-1}, for a realistic coverage of 25 per cent of this area, the annual requirement is 3750 tonnes of bio-fertilizer (Verma and Battacharyya, 1992). The present production level is 1000-1200 tonnes including *Rhizobium, Azotobacter* and *Azospirillum* containing bio-fertilizers, though the total production capacity of the existing 60 production units is 2685 tonnes. There were nearly 30 functional production units with output of 1000 tonnes in 1991.

Bio-fertilizer production technology includes isolation, selection of suitable strains, preparation of mother or seed culture, inoculant production, carrier preparation and their mixing, followed by curing, packaging, storage and dispatch. The requirement of raw materials for the production of one tonne of *Rhizobium* bio-fertilizer has been worked out and presented in following Table 7.9.

Table 7.9: Blue Print of 1 tonne *Rhizobium* production, a general idea (with 40%)

Requirements

(1) Raw Material

(a) 4 litres seed culture containing tested efficient crop specific *Rhizobium* strain providing 10^6-10^7 rhizobia per ml culture.
(b) 396 litres yeast Extract Manitol Broth (Sterilised)
(c) 590 kgs carrier material like charcoal/lignite, passed through 100-200 mesh, sterilized for 4h on first day and for on h on subsequent two days at 121.6°C in 5 cm layers in autoclave. Lime 10-15 per cent added in lignite to bring up the pH to neutral.
(d) 10 kgs gum acacia aqueous solution (sterilized)
(e) 5000 low density polypropylene packets of 50-75 micron, capacity to contain 200 g. inoculant
(f) 125 corrugated 5 ply boxes each having capacity to contain 40 culture packets.

(2) Equipments

(a) Autoclave
(b) Rotary shaker or fermenter
(c) BOD Incubator
(d) Mechanical Mixer
(e) Sealer
(f) Steel trays

(3) Glassware and chemicals

As per requirement.

Production of bio-fertilizer is very technical and complex as it involves microbial lives, though it looks simple like mixing broth and carrier material. This feeling has attracted pseudotechnocrats in business of bio-fertilizer production with the consequence that bio-fertilizer of poor/sub-standard quality are increasingly becoming available in the market. Use of such product has eroded the faith of farmers on the efficiency of this proven low input and important technology. The recently held National Seminar on Organic Farming at Indore, M.P. (Sept., 1992), attended by more than 25X3 delegates took stock of the situation and strongly recommended for the enactment of "Quality Control Act" for products of biological origin and its strict application on similar lines as they exist in the case of fertilizers and insecticides. The Seminar held the view that

'Bio-fertilizer Quality Act' is essential to safeguard the interest of farmers and to instill in them confidence on the efficiency of biological routes of soil fertility management.

Selection of strains

Selection and choice of appropriate strains of *rhizobia* for bio-fertilizer production is as important as the use of quality seed for crop production. Effective strains are isolated from health, characteristic regular shaped pink nodules. More than 70 per cent of the area under pulses and oil seeds in India falls under rainfed/dryland farming zones. Inoculated rhizobia has to face extremes of low moisture regime in soils of such areas and, therefore, the strains for bio-fertilizer production shall be from root nodules of plants growing vigorously with a good stand in soils with low moisture regime. Other characteristics of efficient strains are good competitiveness with native *Rhizobium* strains, capacity of withstand extremes of soil and weather conditions, better host infection ability, nodule forming and nitrogen fixing capacity, bacteriophage resistance and ability to exhibit long shelf life in carrier material and seeds and tolerance to pesticides, fertilizers and other agricultural chemicals. It is equally important to maintain the selected strains without any contamination. The use of 200 ppm actidione to curb fungal and 100 IU/ ml penicilline to avoid bacterial contamination at the time of isolation has been suggested (Bhattacharyya and Singh, 1992).

Both multistrains and monostrain bio-inoculants are produced in the country. But majority of the production units in India prefer to concentrate on monostrain bio-fertilizer production. Bio-fertilizer are produced for individual leguminous species and not for group of legumes included in cross inoculation groups. The use of multistrain inoculants for different hosts or a single is likely to dominate over other strains (Date, 1974). The practice of using wide spectrum strain of cowpea miscellany (most of Indian pulses are indicated) is generally based on results obtained in green house trials where effective cross-infections within a range of pulses have been demonstrated (Subba Rao, 1988). When multistrain bio-fertilizer is produced, individual strains should be grown separately in conical flasks. Adequate care should be taken that all strains have equal growth rates to avoid absence of any strain due to its inability to withstand the competition in carrier material. Many times infection specificity has been observed at variety level which is suggestive of a need for detailed studies on selection of strains for individual pulse species, agroclimate zonewise.

Established effective strains can be also obtained from National Facility of *Rhizobium* Germplasm Collection, Division of Microbiology, IARL, New Delhi 110 012; ICRISAT, Patancheru, Andhra Pradesh 502324; Institute to Microbial Technology, Chandigarh; National Bio-fertilizer

Development Centre, CGO II, Kamala Nehru Nagar, Ghaziabad 201002 and Production Centres of State Agricultural Universities. Some established promising strains are given in Table 5.10. For International strains, one may request to one of the eight Microbiological Resource Centres (MIRCENS). Some of the locations are Bangkok (Thailand) Brisbane (Australia), Cairo (Egypt), NifTal Hawaii (USA), Porto Alegre (Brazil) and Guatemala (Central America).

Table 7.10: Some promising *Rhizobium* strains

Host legumes	Promising *Rhizobium* strains	
Groundnut	NC-92	Niftal 1000
	IGR-6	Niftal 968
	IGR-40	Nitragin 8 All
Pigeonpea	CC-1	P-241
	F-4	Niftal-569
	BDN-A2	Nitragin-21A16
Chickpea	F-6, F-75	Nitragin-27A3
	F-76, H-44, H-45	Nitragin-27A8
Soybean	SB-102	Niftal-102
	SB-103	Nitragin-61A148
		11TA-2127
	SB-119, SB-120	
	UASB-29, Pantnagar	
Lentil	L-6	Niftal-640
	L-1-87	C-4201
Pea	RL(P)114	Nitragin-128A12
Greengram	M-10	UPLB-M6
	GMBSI	THA-301
	MO-5	Nitragin-176A22
Blackgram	DU-2	THA-301
	M-11	Niftal-442
	KU-1	UPLB M-6
	BDN-F	Niftal-174
	DC-28	Niftal-189
	DC-2	Nitragin-176A22
	DC-6	
	FB-77	

Principal Investigator (Microbiology), AICRIP (Except Groundnut and Soybean),

***** USDA Rhizobium Culture Collection Catalogue, Baltsville, MD.***

Carrier materials and their sterilization

Medium matrix on which microbial inoculants grow to a reasonable higher number with long shelf life are called carrier materials. These include peat, lignite, charcoal, bunt rice husk, vermiculite, soil, FYM, coir dust, press niud and polymers. Peat is the most suitable carrier material. Most of the production units of developed countries are using peat. Peat of a good quality (more than 75% carbon) is a rare commodity in India. The available low grade peat retards the keeping quality. Nilgiri peat is of poor quality (below 50% carbon) and does not provide a good medium for the growth of *rhizobia*. According to the availability and cost at production site, choice is only with lignite and charcoal in India. As per the suitability the order is peat >lignite >charcoal >FYM, soil, rice husk, coir dust, oxalic acid industry waste, press mud and others. Lignite can be obtained from Palana (Rajasthan), Neyveli (Tamil Nadu) and Singrauli (M.P.).

Though charcoal is used by production units, quality standards like fineness, extent of pyrolysis, water holding capacity, density, carbon and volatile compounds, ash content and active surface area are not properly adhered to, resulting in the production of inadequate number of *rhizobia* with low shelf life. Few physical properties of common carrier materials are compared in Table 7.11. Good quality carrier material must have good moisture holding capacity, be free from toxic substances, sterilisable, and have readily adjustable pH to 6.5 -7.0. Under Indian conditions where extremes of soil and weather conditions prevail, there is yet no suitable carrier material identified capable of supporting the *Rhizobium* growth even for six months and bio-fertilizer producers feel the urgent need of research for suitable carrier material.

The carrier materials are sundried to five per cent moisture and pulverized to fineness of 100-200 mesh. Coarser materials form balls on mixing with broth and do not adhere on the seeds at the time of inoculation. Lignite powder begin acidic (pH 5.5) in nature, lime is mixed to bring up the pH to 6.7 - 7.0. Using one kg lime is required for nine kg of lignite. Charcoal powder being neutral in pH does not require addition of lime.

Better growth of *Rhizobium* is obtained in sterile carrier. Best method is Gamma irradiation of sterilization for carrier materials. While using autoclave, lime mixed lignite or plain charcoal powder is filled upto two third capacity of steel trays (size depending on the size of horizontal autoclave) and is sterilized at 15 PSI for 3-4 hours continuously or one hour each for three successive days. At the National biofertilizer Development Centre, Ghaziabad, it was experienced that single pass, even for 3-4 hours, often causes temperature tolerant actinomycetes spores to germinate and usually second or third autoclaving for one hour at 121°C on alternate days was essential for achieving desired sterilization, causing time constraint at peak production period. Use of ethylene oxide though is fast, is associated with persistent residual gas and unfavourable growth environment.

Table 7.11: Chemical and physical characteristics of peat, lignite and charcoal

Parameters	Peat (Indian)	Lignite	Charcoal
	A. Chemical*		
Appearance	Dark brown	Brownish black	Black
PH	Acidic, needs	Acidic, needs	Neutral
Odour	Nil	Nil	Nil
Carbon (%)	54.20	72.79	84.00
Hydrogen (%)	5.70	. 4.74	2.30
Oxygen (%)	31.60	19.60	10.70
Nitrogen (%)	1.50	0.98	0.01
Ash(%)	7.00	7.00	3.00
	B. Physica**		
Water hoding Capacity (%)	149.3	198.9	200.00
Moistute (%)	40-50	40-50	20-30
Bulk density (g/cm³)	1.02	1.08	0.43
Particle density (g/cm³)	2.18	1.66	1.62
Porosity (%)	53.16	34.79	73.39
Total surface area	646.60	556.40	870.90
	C. Availability ***		
Quantity	5.5 million tonnes Nilgri valley Tamil Nadu	3 million tonnes a. Neyveli (Tamil Nadu) b. Singrauli (M.P.) c. Palana (Rajasthan)	Plenty Everywhere

*Source: * Arora, B.K. (1984), ** Tilak, K.V.B.R. & Subbarao, N.S. (1978), *** Subba Rao, N.S. (1982).*

Gamma irradiation is capable of penetrating and reaching through out the product under treatment, killing micro-organisms. It is known as one of the perfect and established methods of sterilization. High sterilization efficiency, non/low residual effect on sterilized material, simplicity in operation with control of only one parameter i.e. time of exposure, possibility of sterilizing plastic cans and bags, safety against heat, being cold process and rapidity are additional benefits in favour of

Gamma irradiation over the methods of sterilization. In most of the developed countries like United Kingdom, Australia, France, etc. carrier materials in pouches are sterilized through Gamma irradiation. Sterilization of carrier materials is a very important step in bio-fertilizer production to keep up and improve the standard of quality and shelf life. The recommended dose of Gamma irradiation for sterilization of carrier materials in low density polyethylene (LDPE) packet is 5 mega rads or 50 killoes Grey (Bhattacharyya and Singh, 1992). At present, this facility is available in BARC, Trombay, which may not be able to meet the requirement of existing 60 production units in the country. There is a need of establishing a National Facility for Gamma irradiation, specifically for sterilization of carrier materials.

Suitable nutrient broth

Most commonly accepted suitable medium for *rhizobia* is Yeast Extract Mannitol (K_2HPC_4-0.Sg, $MgSo_4$ $7H_20$-0.2g, NaCl - l0.0g, Mannitol -10.0 g Mannitol - 10.0 g, Yeast Extract -1.0 and distilled water - 1000 ml). Mannitol is the single expensive item, which regulates the production cost of bio-fertilizers. Recently, the use of cheaper carbon and energy source like 5 g molasses or 5 g. sucrose per litre in place of 10 g. mannitol per litre (Bhattacharyya and Singh, 1992) and soybean protein extract in place of yeast extract as organic nitrogen and growth factor source (Wadoux, 1991) has been suggested for commercial production of *Rhizobium* in fermenter. These nutrient substitutes have been reported to support a population of 10^9 - 10^{12} cells ml^{-1}. Distilled water requirement in production unit is enormous and so as the cost and, therefore, ordinary tap water is used for preparation and also as diluent of broth, before mixing with carrier material. Adequate care should be taken that water used is free of excess mineral salts or chloride residues. Demineralised water is used in production units under the Government of India.

Suitable packing material

Three types of polymer bags are used for dispensing required quantity (about 200 g.) of bio-fertilizer. LDPE packets are used universally, as they can be readily sealed, allow high gas exchange with relative low moisture loss (Thompson, 1991). If production technology is based N carrier material sterilization through autoclave, polypropylene or high density polypropylene (HDPE) bags should be used. LDPE bags cannot withstand the temperature of sterilization (121°C). In case sterilization through Gamma irradiation is in practive, LDPE bags should be used as polypropylene is unstable while exposed to irradiation. Small pin holes in bags are both unnecessary and harmful as they cause increased moisture loss and allow easy entry of contaminants. Recommended specifications for LDPE are 50-75 micron thick, flexible sheet pouch type and 15-25 cm in size. Each packet should have information regarding name of product, crop for which intended, name and address of manufacturer, type of carrier, batch or code number, date of manufacture date of expiry, net quantity, the area (0.4 ha.) mutant for instructions for storing as: **STORE IN COOL PLACE AWAY FROM DIRECT SUN AND HEAT.**

Suitable adhesive material

Wall paper glue (5%) gum arabic (4%) carboxy methyl cellulose (4%), honey (10%), powder milk (10%), sugar (10%) etc. are used as sticker and partly as nutrient source until infection process is completed, for *rhizobia* (Rennje, 1991). Inclusion of adhesives within the prepared inoculation is practical, convenient and recommended (Day, 1991). Good quality adhesives do not set, form balls on impregnation, or lose glueing properties during sterilization. In India "gum arabic" also called gum acacia powder, is used as adhesive. Acacia has many species like *A. niotica* (Babul), *A. auriculiformis (Bengal Babul)* etc. Gum arabic is obtained from *Acacia arabica* and some times from *Acacia Senegal.* Unavailability of genuine gum arabic is a major problem. Adulteration is usually with *Azadirachta indica* (Neem) which does not withstand autoclaving.

Fermentation

Starter cultures of selected strains are obtained after ascertaining their performance in green house and at field levels. The tested strain which is kept in tubes is transferred to 250 ml conical flasks placed on rotary shaker and the contents incubated for 3-7 days depending whether they are fast growing or slow growing. The contents of these flasks usually attain a load of 10^5 - 10^6 cells ml^{-1} called seed (500 or 1000 ml) on shaker for charging five litre capacity conical flasks or fermenter. Broth is prepared either by swirling on rotary shaker or in fermenter.

Rotary shaker method

Use of conical flasks on rotary shaker allows visual observations of the contents, which will help in checking the contamination and maintaining the quality. Aeration is dependent on rotation, but increased agitation does not proportionately increase the rate of growth. No contamination should be allowed because even a single contaminant which has a mean generation time of few minutes reduces the *Rhzobium* count considerably during a period of 5 days in the case of slow growing species like *R. japonicum* specific for soybean.

In the National and Regional Bio-fertilizer Development Centres 5 litre conical flasks are being successfully used. Difficulty in operation is experienced while using the rotary shaker of a holding capacity of more than 80 litres broth. Broth, though is being produced by using rotary shaker in most of the State Government Production Units, has limitations like low rate of production (maximum of 500 packets per rotary shaker per day) and as such, large scale demand is not possible to be met considering limited time available for sowing crops. It requires quality control tests of individual unit, which is time consuming and there is continuous irritating sound in the shaker room.

Bioreactor

Commercial bio-fertilizer production through locally fabricated fermenters (bio-reactors) is being successfully carried on by many production units. In these units rotary shaker method has given way to fermenter method of broth preparation. Broth production rate through fermenter is 7-10 times more than that through rotary shaker. Good fermenter has growth vessel with provision of air inlet connected with filter to obtain sterile air, inlet ports for inoculant and antifoaming agents, ample drawing port, product harvest system and a convenient system for *in situ.*sterilization for a fermenter of larger capacity.

In fermenter aeration is regulated by forcing sterile air through spargers. Aeration and pH are the two important factors, which regulate the multiplication rate of *Rhizobium.* Growth is not increased by violent aeration or agitation. Oxygen partial pressure of 0.15 atmosphere is optimum for respiration which can be achieved by introducing 5 litres of air per hour.

For *Rhizobium* broth production, a battery of small fermenters of capacity less than 100 litres in batch fermentation system is considered superior over larger fermenters because of increased chance of contamination accompanied with increased fermentation time in larger units. A chance of contamination can be reduced by decreasing the fermentation period.

Studies on optimization of parameters of production technology are in progress at the National Bio-fertilizer Development Centre, Ghaziabad, with UNDP aid and at the Indian Institute of Technology, New Delhi, with DBT support. Preliminary experiments have shown that by using fermenter, in a medium containing carbon 5 g 1^{-1} through molasses or sucrose, the use of 10 per cent inoculum load (24 hours old culture with 10^{10} *Rhizobium* cells ml^{-1} in 24 hours.

In the United Kingdom, sterilization system of bio-fertilizer production technology is used where carrier in pouch is sterilized by Gamma irradiation. Fermenter is emptied through medium dispenser and sterile rubber pipe fitted with disposable needles. The bag containing sterilized carrier material is quickly wiped with alcohol and the *Rhizobium* broth (80 ml per 200 g carrier material) injected straight from fermenter into the sealed bags. The injection holes are sealed with a piece of adhesive tape. The inoculated packets are blended by using automatic blender and incubated for a week and after labelling, the packets are ready for sale (Day, 1991).

While using rotary shaker, broth prepared in conical flasks are mixed with sterile carrier material 1:3 or 2:1 depending on water holding capacity of carrier material. Verma and Rawat (1991) have suggested that 60 per cent of the water holding capacity of carrier material should be saturated with broth. Thoroughly mixed broth and carrier material is spread in thin layers in trays, covered and incubated for 48-72 hours at 25°C. Aggregates are broken up by intimate mixing and finally pulverized. The homogenous material is passed through 250 mesh sieve and packed in LDPE bags.

Final product must conform with the quality standards set by the Bureau of Indian Standards (earlier ISI) *vide* standard IS: 8268 - 1976. The salient parameters mentioned are that the *Rhizobium* inoculant should be carrier based and pH of the carrier should be between 6.0 - 7.5. It shall contain a minimum of 10^8 viable cells g^{-1} of carrier on dry mass basis within 15 days of manufacture and 10^7 within 15 days before expiry date marked on the packet when stored at 25-30°C. It should have maximum of six months expiry period. *Rhizobium* inoculant should result in 50 per cent or more dry matter production compared to control.

FRANKIACEAE SYMBIOSIS

Some of the actinorrhizal plants like Casuarina and Alnus are found to have nodules infected by *Frankia.* In has been reported that N fixed by *Frankia* in Alnus ranges from 50 to 150 kg/ha/year. The potentiality of these microorganisms has been demonstrated in increasing the biomass yield of *Casuarina* and *Alnus.*

About 200 plant species from 25 genera, 8 families and 7 orders, all non-leguminous angiosperms, have been found to form nodule symbioses with N_2 fixing *actinomycetes* belonging to the genus of *Frankiae.* All of these species are perennial dicots and, with few exceptions, woody shrubs or plants. They are named actinorhizal plants from *actino* in *actinomycete,* and from *rhiza* in the Greek word for root. Actinorhizal plants can be found both on every continent except Antarctica and in most climatic zones. They typically grow on disturbed marginal soils and are pioneer species early in successional plant community development, such as *Dryas* species in arctic tundra; *Casuarina, Hippophae, Myrica* and *Elaeagnus* species in coastal dunes; *Alnus* and *Myrica* species in riparian; *Alnus* and *Dryas* species in glacial till; *Casuarina, Purshia, Ceanothus Cercocarpus, Comptonia* and *Cowania* species in chaparral and xeric; *Alnus* species in alpine; *Alnus, Casuarina, Coriaria* and *Shepherdia* species in forest. Globally, especially in wherever indigenous legumes are absent or rare, actinorhizal plants have potential applications in soil amelioration and reforestation, as fuelwood, timber and pulp, and as windbreak or even for addressing . pyrodenitrification.

The symbiont *Frankia* is a gram-positive, filamentous bacterium belonging to the family *Frankiaceae* within the order *Actinomycetes*. Speciation in *Frankia* is not yet clear and within the genus different isolates are classified. Almost all of *Frankia* are characterised by three structural forms of hyphae, sporangia and vesicles. The hyphae are branched with a diameter of 0.5 to 1.5 *µm* and the mature vesicle is spherical with a diameter of 2 to 4 µm. Both the hyphae and the mature vesicles are septate. When actinorhizal plants, such as *Alnus* and *Casuarina* seedlings are excavated from soil containing *Frankia*, numerous small, multilobed, coralloid-type, amber or whitish nodules are found on their root systems. The oldest and biggest nodules are close to the stem base and the youngest are on the distal parts of the root system. Some *Casuarina* nodules may reach a size of around 5-10 mm in diameter and a weight of about 1 g in dry matter. It has been reported that *Frankia* produced sporangia and vesicles as soon as the microorganism escaped from the mother nodule. This indicates that the formation of *Frankia* structures inside the nodule might be under host control. In general, the nitrogen fixation rates of Frankia-actinorhizal plant symbioses are comparable to that of *Rhizobia-legume* symbioses.

AZOSPIRILLUM BIOFERTILIZER

Azospirillum have been found more effective towards contributing to increased yields in sorghum, pearl millet, *kodo, kutaki,* safflower, maize, mustard and wheat. In general, C_4 plants like corn, sorghum, panicum and setaria showed better response to inoculation than C_3 crops. The optimum temperature for *Azospirillum* growth is 32-35°C. This might be the reason for better performance of inoculated crops in summer under irrigated condition. *Azospirillum* bio-fertilizer consumption in Tamil Nadu ahs increased in the last three years because of consistently good performance of rice crop. Tamil Nadu followed by Gujarat is the largest producer and consumer of *Azospirillum* bio-fertilizer in the country.

Soil nitrogen affects the response to inoculation. In multi-location experiments with pearl millet, maximum of 20 per cent increase in grain yield due to individual inoculation of *Azospirillum* and *Azotobacter* and 27.2 per cent and 18.18 per cent increase in plant nitrogen uptake due to inoculation *of Azospirillum* and *Azotobacter* respectively (Wani, 1992) were observed at zero level of nitrogen application. Increased nitrogen dose retarded the performance of inoculum. The reported nitrogen assimilation of only 5 kg^{-1} in pearl millet seems to be too small a quantity of cause increase in yield on inoculation. It is believed that the increase in yield is due mainly to release of growth promoting agents and protection from diseases than is from the contribution of nitrogen fixation. The presence of *Azospirillum* internally in root system has not been yet conclusively proved.

Tilak and Subba Rao (1987) have reported highest increased grain yield (33.67%) and plant biomass yield (32.71%) by the application of coinoculatns *Azospirillum brasilense* and *Glomus fasiculatum* on sorghum.

Major Species

There are four major species of *Azospirillum viz. A. lipoferum, A. brasilense, A. amazonense* and *A. seropedicae.* Of the four species, first two species are commonly found. The first species *(A. lipoferum)* is commonly found in the roots of C^4 plants while the second one *(A. brasilense)* is found in C^3 plants in tropical and subtropical regions.

Isolation

Half centimeter long root pieces are surface sterilized in 70 per cent alcohol for 3-5 seconds and washed repeatedly in phosphate (buffer pH 7.0). These roots pieces are then placed in semi-soild nitrogen-free sodium malate medium. The tubes are incubated at 35°C for 48 hours. Characteristic growth of *Azospirillum* is indicated by the formation of white pellicle 2-4 mm below the surface of the medium. The isolates thus obtained are purified in two steps. Firstly, the isolates are enriched by repeated transfer into a semi-solid sodium malate medium in small screw cap tubes. These cultures are then subjected to dilution upto 10^{10}. From each dilution 0.1 ml is inoculated into a fresh tube of sodium malate medium. The least dilution which gives good growth is found to be pure and used for further studies.

Mass Multiplication

For mass multiplication of *Azospirillum,* the organism is allowed to grow in flasks containing malic-acid medium augmented with 1 per cent ammonium chloride and incubated at 35°C for 3 days. When there is good growth, the broth culture is mixed with carrier and the carrier-based culture is then packed in small polyethylene packets. Soil and FYM in the ratio of 1:1 sterilized for 3 hours consecutively for 3 days were found to be the best carrier wherein bacterium was able to survive upto 6 months with counts of $1O^6$ cells/g of carrier material.

Method of Inoculation

The most suitable method used for carrier based culture is the seed inoculation. The technique adopted for inoculating the seed with *Azospirillum* culture is same as that described in the case of *Rhizobium.* In case of transplanted rice, the dipping of roots of rice seedlings in the slurry of inoculant is practiced.

Conditions Needed for Successful Inoculation

Seed inoculation with effective strains should be done in shade and subsequently the sowing should be done on the same day. The field should be well saturated during rice transplanting and after transplanting, the flooding should be done only after 5-6 days. For upland crops, moisture at field capacity should be maintained at the time of seeding so that added inoculum may get congenial condition for its growth and development.

Crop Response

The *Azospirillum* inoculation has been found beneficial in a variety of crops including cereals, forage and other crops. The crop response, however, varies greatly types of crop and variety, location, season, soil fertility level, native microorganisms interaction, etc. Crop response to *Azospirillum* inoculation is attributed to its ability to fix atmospheric nitrogen and to produce phytohormones.

A number of field experiment conducted on various crops to find out crop response to *Azospirillum* inoculation observed a wide variation in increase in yield (0-64%) over control. Significant increae in yield was found at about 50 per cent of the locations. On an average, an increase of about 2-3 q/ha in crop yields and an economy of 20-30 kg N/ha equivalent is possible by *Azospirillum* inoculation. Among various field crops, sorghum and millets respond better than others under rainfed conditions. In Tamil Nadu, rice responds very well to *Azospirillum* inoculation.

AZOTOBACTER BIOFERTIUZER

Out of three different typical species of *Azotobacter, A. chroococcum* and *A. beijerinckii* are the most commonly occurring species. The latter is found commonly in acid soils while *A. chroococcum* in neutral and alkaline soils. Aged cells of A. *chroococcum* are characterized by the presence of insoluble black brownpigment (melamin) found as a result of oxidation of tyrosinase, a copper containing enzyme.

Table 7.12: Response of pearlmillet to inoculation with *Azospirillum brasilense* on grain yield (q/ha^{-1})

Treatment	Centers				
	Kanpur	Hyderabad	Parbhani	Delhi	All India
Uninoculated	12.8	12.5	14.5	9.8	12.4
A. brasilense	15.5*	12.8	17.7	11.3	14.3
10 kg N ha^{-1}(urea)	16.3	14.3	19.5	11.8	15.5
10 kg N ha^{-1} + A	19.1*	14.5	22.8*	14.8*	17.8

Treatment	Centers				
	Kanpur	Hyderabad	Parbhani	Delhi	All Incdia
brasilense					
20 kg N ha^{-1} (urea)	17.5	14.8	22.5	12.5	16.4
20 kg N ha^{-1} + A *brasilense*	18.9	17.0	23.2	15.8	18.7
40 kg N ha^{-1} (urea)	20.1	18.5	24.3	18.5	20.4
CD 5%	2.5	1.5	2.9	3.0	2.2

*The figures in brackets represent the soil pH values. * Significant increase over corresponding control. Source: (Tilak and Subba Rao, 1987).*

Isolation

Azotobacter spp. are isolated by soil dilution plating method. Soil sample of 10 g is transferred in 100 ml of sterilized water and serial dilution of thie suspension are prepared by further dilutions using sterile distilled waterr. Petriplates and pipettes are sterilized. Anyone of the nitrogen free agar mediia specific for *Azotobacter* is prepared and poured into petriplates. One mil aliquot of appropriate dilution are spread evenly over cooled and set agar medium in petriplates. The plates are incubated at 30°C in an incubator. After 3-4 days of incubation, soft, milky and mucoid colonies *of Azotobacter* are formed on agar plates. Direct isolation of *Azotobacter* has been practiced by Russian Scientists. Lumps of soils are spread out on a nitrogen free agair medium and the plates are incubated at 28°C. After three days of inoculation *Azotobacter* colonies develop on the agar plates.

Another method is to prepare a paste of soil in nitrogen free liquid medium. This paste is incorporated in a layer of washed charcoal placed in & petriplate. Soil is aerated by burying a glass tube in it. After incubation of the plates at 28°C for 3-4 days, small *Azotobacter* colonies, if present, develop on the soil surface. This method is popularly known as 'soil plate' method.

Mass Production

Mass production of *Azotobacter* for preparing inoculating in India is done either by growing the culture in large flasks on a rotary shaker or in batch fermentors depending on the quantity needed. All precaution and sterilization production in the case of *Rhizobium* are also observed in case of *Azotobacter.*

Method of Application

A slurry of carrier based culture is made with minimum amount of water and the seeds are inoculated by mixing with slurry. The seeds are dried in the shade and then sown. For transplanted crops, seedlings are dipped in the slurry for certain time (20-30 minutes) and planted immediately. For sugarcane, many packets of culture are recommended at regular intervals in the early stages of growth. Second and subsequent inoculation are made by pouring slurry near root zone. The inoculant is also mixed in FYM and broadcasted for the root zone.

Crop Response

The results from a large number of experiments conducted in last four decades, have shown a positive response to *Azotobacter* application on a wide range of crops like cereals, millets, vegetables, cotton, sugarcane etc. *Azotobacter* inoculation increased the crop yields by 0-30 per cent (Table 7.13). The beneficial effect of *Azotobacter* is attributed to its N^2 fixing capacity and also the ability to produce growth promoting substances. The actual contribution under field conditions has been doubled due to its low population in soil. The intensive research efforts are required to develop the *Azotobacter* strains which can multiply in soil and establish high productions.

Table 7.13: Effect of *Azotobacter* inoculation on crop yields

Crop Increase	Fertilizer supplementation (kg/ha)			% yield over control
	N	P	K	
Wheat	120	-	-	11
	-	-	-	10-30
Rice	120	60	60	23
Maize	-	-	-	34
Sorghum	-	-	-	15-20
Pearl millet	-	-	-	o-27
Onion	-	50	100	22
Tomato	-	-	-	2-24
Cotton (fibre) Irrigated	63	30	-	10-20
Non-irrigated	-	-	-	11-16
Sugarcane	-	-	-	24

Source: Venkataraman and Tilak (1990).

Methods of Application of Azospirillum *and* Azotobacter

Application of *Azospirillum* and *Azotobacter* through seed coating is similar to that of *Rhizobium* bio-fertilizer. In Tamil Nadu the use of *Azospirillum* in paddy has gained popularity among farmers. Considering the benefits of *Azospirillum* inoculation, the State Department of Agriculture has recommended the reduction of nitrogen by 25 per cent in those fields receiving *Azospirillum* treatment. *Azospirillum* inoculation has been recommended for paddy, sorghum and sunflower. The methods of application and doses are as follows:

1. *Transplanted paddy and sorghum:* Three packets (600 g) of *Azospirillum* bio-fertilizer are mixed in sufficient water wherein seeds required for one hectare are soaked over night before sowing in the nursery area. Root portion of the seedlings ready for transplanting are dipped for 15-30 minutes in bacterial suspension prepared from 5 packets (1000 g) of *Azospirillum* biofertilizer and transplanted immediately.
2. *Direct seeding paddy:* Ten packet (2kg) of *Azospirillum* are mixed with seed before sowing. Little quantity of rice *Kanji* can be added for sticking the bio-fertilizer to the seeds.
3. *Rainfed sorghum and sunflower:* Seeds required for one ha are treated with 3 packets (600 g) of *Azospirillum* inoculants and in the main field 10 packets (2kg) of *Azospirillum* biofertilizer ha^{-1} mixed with 25 kg. farm yard manure and 25 kg soil are applied.
4. *Sugarcane:* 25 packets (5.0 kg) *of Azospirillum* ha^{-1} are applied in two split doses at 30 and 60 days after planting. For uniform spread, the culture can be mixed with about 500 kg of powdered FYM applied along the base of the clumps.

Table 7.14: Response of sugarcane to *Azospirillum* and *Azotobacter* inoculation (a) with two doses of nitrogen (study conducted on four different soil types at found locations and four seasons during 1982-84)

Treatment	Cane yield t ha^{-1}	Sucrose % juice
120 kg N ha^{-1} + *Azospirillium*	93.2	16.12
120 kg N ha^{-1} + *Azotobacter*	80.8	16.22
180 kg N ha^{-1} + *Azospirillum*	106.4	16.40
180 kg N ha^{-1} + *Azotobacter*	93.8	16.13
240 kg N ha^{-1} Urea alone	99.5	16.24

(b) in various types of soils and varieties through 106 on-farm trials in faemer's fields in Tamil Nadu (1983-'85)

Soils	Treatment	Cane yield		Sucrose	
		t ha-1	Increases over control	% juice	% increase over control
Clay	*Azospirillum*	148.5	13.3	16.50	13.0
(well	*Azotobacter*	112.0	—	14.95	2.3
drained)	*Control*	131.0	—	14.60	—
Clay loam	*Azospirillum*	116.9	9.5	17.10	10.3
	Azotobacter	110.2	31	17.05	10.0
	Control	106.8	—	15.50	—
Loamy	*Azospirillum*	110.9	4.8	16.77	9.3
	Azotobacter	120.6	13.9	17.37	13.2
	Control	105.8	—	15.34	—
Sandy	*Azospirillum*	105.8	—	15.34	—
	Azotobacter	105.2			

Complied from Anonymous (1987).

Table 7.15: Effect of bio-fertilizers on yield and quality of sugarcane (Co 7318)

Treatment	Cane yield (t ha-1)	% increase over control	Sugar (tha-1)	Net return Rs ha-1
300 kg N ha^{-1} (Recommended N)	92.50	38.8	11.52	23,075
*Azospirillum** + 75% N	85.40	28.1	10.30	20,418
*Azospirillum** + 50% N	76.38	14.6	9.63	17,008
*Azospirillum*** + 75% N	87.81	31.7	10.85	21,298
*Azospirillum*** + 50% N	77.26	15.9	9.63	17,304
Azotobacter" + 75% N	94.60	36.8	11.94	23,947
*Azotobacter*** + 50% N	89.07	28.8	11.36	21,910
*Azotobacter*** + No	66.63		8.59	13,455
*Azotobacter*** + No	69.14		8.89	14,377
CD at 5%	13.47		1.84	—

Source: Bangar, *et al.* (1992). *Sett inoculation. ** Soil application.

A detailed study conducted by Sugarcane Breeding Institute, Coimbatore (TN) on four different soil types at four locations four seasons during 1982-1984 has shown that inoculation *of Azospirillum* with 180 kg N ha^{-1} could give an yield of 106.4 t ha^{-1} which compared well with what was obtained at the level at 240 kg ha^{-1} of inorganic nitrogen (Anonymous 1987) indicating a saving of 60 kg N ha^{-1}. In on-farm trials (106), *Azospirillum* performed better in well drained clay soils in increasing the sugarcane yield and improving sucrose per cent in juice. Banger *et at,* (1992) on comparing the application methods through sett inoculation and soil inoculation found *Azotobacter* was performing better than *Azospirillum* under water stress condition. The yield due to *Azotobacter* along with 225 kg N ha" 1 was found equal to that of 300 kg N ha^{-1} alone, thus saved 75 kg N ha^{-1}.

BLUE-GREEN ALGAE INOCULANT

Blue green algae are referred to as paddy organisms because of their abundance in the paddy fields. Many species belonging to the genera, *Tolypothrix, Nostoc, Schizothrix, Calothrix, Anoboenopsis* and *Plectonema* are abundant in tropical conditions. Most of N fixing BGA are filamenters, consisting of chain of vegetative cells including specialized cells called heterocyst which function as a micronodule for synthesis and N fixing machinery. BGA, *Anabaena azollae,* also occurs in symbiotic relation with the aquatic fern, *Azolla.*

In addition to N fixation, BGA also synthesis and liberate growth promoting substances such as auxin and amino compounds which stimulate the growth of rice.

As early as 1939, Dr. P. K. De suggested that fertility of tropical rice fields was largely due to activity of the N-fixing BGA. Blue-green algae are photosynthetic nitrogen fixers *i.e.* they use energy derived from photosynthesis to fix atmospheric nitrogen. They are also called cyanobacteria and are free living organisms. In general BGA show dominance over other classes of algae in India. The utilization of blue-green algae as a bio-fertilizer for rice is very promising. A judicious use of these algae could provide to the country's entire rice acreage as much nitrogen as obtained from 15-17 lakh tonnes of urea. Methods have been developed for mass production of algal bio-fertilizer and rice growers in many parts of the world have already started using these algae. Recent researches have shown that algae also help to reduce soil alkalinity and this opens up possibilities for bioreclamation of such inhospitable environments.

Blue green algae (BGA) when cultured in small pit and used as an inoculum in paddy fields at the rate of 12-15 kg ha^{-1} resulted in nitrogen economy to rice crop of the order of 20-25 kg N ha^{-1} with yield increase of 5-14 per cent.

DISTRIBUTION

The principal genera consisting of maximum number of nitrogen fixing species are *Aulosira, Nostoc, Anabaena, Tolypothrix, Scytonema, Plectonema,* and *Cylindrospermum.* Contrary to general belief that BGA are present invariably in tropical rice soils, the distribution of soils harbouring N fixing BGA varies from as low as 4 per cent to as high as 80%. Species of *Nostoc* and *Anabaena* were ubiquitous in all regions in varying production and formed the major constituent of the algal biotypes in 9 out of 16 states. An all India survey has indicated that out of 2213 soil samples examined, only 33 per cent were found to contain useful N fixing BGA. This indicates the need for inoculation of efficient strain of BGA.

ISOLATION

BGA are generally covered with mucilage and it is easy to locate them as colonies on rice fields. Isolation of BGA involves the transfer of an algae from its natural habitat to medium where it can be grown without any contamination.

MASS PRODUCTION

Currently, the technology for mass production of soil-based algal inoculants is well developed in active use in India. Production involves a simple process with a few modifications to enable the production of algae both at small and large scale. The four common methods of algal production are:

1. Tropical method
2. Pit method
3. Field method
4. Nursery cum algae production method.

Based on the natural ecology of these algae, a simple rural-oriented open-air method of producing them in bulk has been developed at the IARI, New Delhi. The basic principle is to grow them in natural sunlight under conditions simulating those in the rice field. The starter culture - a soil based mixture of *Aulosira, Tolyporthrix, Nostoc, Anabaena* and *Plectonema* is supplied by the Indian Agricultural Research Institute, New Delhi. The details of multiplication from the starter culture are as follows:

Shallow tray (15 cm x 7.5 cm x 22.5 cm) of galvanized iron sheet, or brick and mortar or pits lined with polythene sheets are prepared. The size can be increased if more materials is to be produced. About 10 kg soil is placed and mixed with 200 g superphosphate. The trays are then filled with water (5-15 cm) depending upon the local conditions and rate of evaporation; the pH of the soil should be around neutral. After soil settles down saw-dust and the starter culture are sprinkled on the surface of the standing water. The whole assembly is allowed to expose to sun. In hot summer months, the growth of the algae will be rapid and in about a week a thick algal mat will be formed on the surface of the soil and sometimes even is added intermittently. When the algal growth becomes sufficiently thick, addition of water should be discontinued and the water is allowed to dry up in the sun. The dried algal flakes are collected from the surface and stored in bags for future use in the fields. The trays are again filled with water and a small amount of the dry algal flakes is added, as further inoculum. The process is continued as above. Once the soil in the tray is exhausted (usually 3-4 harvests), fresh soil is put and mixed with superphosphate and process is repeated as before. To prevent the breeding of insects, application of Folidol (0.001 ppm) or Malathion (0.00075 ppm) or Carbofuran (3% granules) is recommended.

METHODS OF FIELD APPLICATION

Algae are applied @ 10 kg/ha over the standing water in the field one week after transplantation. The field is kept water-logged at least for a couple of days immediately after algal application.

Recommended pest control measures and other management practices generally do not interfere with the establishment activity of these algae in the fields.

The sun-dried algal material can be stored for long and used in the field. The algal material should not be stored in direct contact with chemical fertilizers or other agricultural chemicals.

Crop Response

The results of the field trials conducted in India have indicated about 10-15 per cent increase in rice yields with BGA application. The response of BGA application is better in dry season than in wet season and long, duration rice varieties show greater response compared to short duration ones. Use of mixed BGA inoculum is superior to unialgal inoculation. Among different strains, agronomic potentially of *Aulosira* is well established in Indian condition. Grain yield measurements suggest that algalization produces a cumulative residual effect. Comparison of N fertilizer and BGA indicates that BGA inoculation is equivalent to the application of 20-30 kg N/ha. Besides nitrogen, these algae are known to provide growth promoting substances.

Investigations have shown that HYVs of rice respond to BGA inoculation even in presence of moderate level of N application. The observed BGA effect in presence of fertilizer may be due to supply of growth promoting substances to the crop as well as to the N-fixed by the organism.

Table 7.16: Performance of BGA on farmers' fields

Treatments	Vellore (11 trials)	Grain yield (kg/ha) Trichy (8 trials)	Cuddalore (10 trials)
$N_{50}P_{25}K_{25}$	4235	4557	3789
$N_{50}P_{25}K_{2}5$+BGA	4455	4735	3884
$N_{75}P_{37.5}K_{37.5}$	4400	4485	3953
$N_{75}P_{37'5}K_{.37.5}$ 5+BGA	4565	5117	4156

Factors Affecting Crop Response

The factors like the shortage of P in soil, the presence of combined nitrogen in flood-water, presence of predators of BGA and use of herbicides in rice often limit the growth and activity of cyanobacteria. The non-availability of BGA inoculants at large scale due to scarcity of water and high temperature during June in North West India, and cubmber-some method of multiplication are the two major hinderances in their wider adoptability. The development of BGA, which multiply fast and could be inoculated directly in the field may go a long way in the popularization of its use.

Blue Green Algae (BGA) and Azolla

Blue green algae (Cyanobacteria) are photosynthetic nitrogen fixing organisms owing to the presence of nitrogen fixing cells (heterocysts). The algae are congenial to rice ecosystem and are used as biofertilizer in rice crop. The predominant genera in Indian soils are *Anabaena, Nostoc, Aulosoria, Calothrix and Tolypothrix.* The fresh water fern, *Azolla pinnata* contains specialized leaf cavities inhabited by the blue green algae, *Anabaena azollae.* The *Azolla - Anabaena* association in unique because it exists through out the vegetative and reproductive phases of the fern.

The various studies conducted in the country have shown that BGA applied @ 10 kg ha^{-1} a week after transplanting of paddy contributed 20-30 kg N h^{-1} season"' and 5-14 per cent increase in grain yield. In the elaborate on-farm trials conducted by the Indira Gandhi Krishi Vishwa Vidyalaya, Raipur, (M.P.) during 1981-1991, the efficiency of BGA was fond decreasing with increasing dose of nitrogen with maximum increase in yield recorded in combination with 20 kg ha^{-1} (Adil and Katre, 1992). Large scale on-farm trials conducted in Tamil Nadu (118) and Madhya Pradesh (56) had indicated increase in yield at 0 level nitrogen in M.P. and at 100 kg N ha^{-1} T.N. by BGA application (Table 7.17).

Table 7.17: Average paddy yield (q ha^{-1}) due to BGA (10 kg ha-1) inoculation on-farm trials conducted in two major rice growing stats

Treatment	Madhya Pradesh* (56 trials)		Tamil Nadu (118 trials)	
	Gain	% increase	Grain	% increase
ON:40P: 15K	24.1			
ON:40P: 15K + BGA	28.2	17.0		
100N:50P:50K			5.11	
100N:50P:50K + BGA			54.8	7.2

Sources: Anonymous, (1978) **Venkataraman, G.S. and Shanmugasundaram, S. (1992).*

Inoculated BGA on establishment and under good conditions of growth add upto 5 t ha^{-1} organic matter in addition to improvement of rice root respiration, uptake of phosphorus and reduction in sulphide injury. The nitrogen assimilated by BGA, on degradation is utilized by rice plant. During decomposition 10-15 per cent biological nitrogen forms complex with humic acid-type polymers (Verma and Martin, 1976), which is indicative of the residual effect of BGA on the subsequent crops. Positive influences of algal biofertlizers on rice fields have also been observed in Egypt, the Philippines, former U.S.S.R, Sweden, Nepal, Sri Lanka, China and Burma.

MASS PRODUCTION AND APPLICATIONS

Azolla can be conveniently grown round the year. However, the multiplication of *Azolla* is rapid in winter season than in summer. The occurrence of standing water and application of phosphorus are essential requirement for rapid spread of *Azolla.* In India fresh weight of *A. pinnata* increased 2-6 fold in a week.

Two methods of *Azolla* application have been advocated. One is as a green manure by amending it in fields prior to rice cultivation and the other is dual cropping with rice when the fern is grown along with principal crop for sometimes. The rate of inoculation is usually higher for multiplication plots than for dual cropping. The inoculum of 0.1-0.3 kg/square metre is recommended for multiplication plots and 0.5-1.0 kg/square metre (0.5-1.0 t/ha) for dual cropping.

In green manure crop, the fields are prepared for rice cultivation, flooded with water followed by seeding with *Azolla.* After 5 to 10 days, the water of field is drained off and *Azolla* mat is ploughed into the soil. The process may be repeated for two crops of *Azolla.* In dual cropping *Azolla* is grown simultaneously with rice seedlings after transplanting.

Normally, it is inoculated after one or two weeks of transplanting and field is flooded with water. When *Azolla* forms a mat on water surface, water is drained off and *Azolla* mat is incorporated into the soil. The *Azolla* mat required repeated incorporation to avoid chocking of rice plants due to *Azolla* mat.

CROP RESPONSE

Studies carried out in India have shown that *Azolla* green manuring produces 10-12 t/ha of green matter containing 20-40 kg N, whereas its dual cropping provides 20-30 kg N/ha. The supply of N can be further increased by raising more than one crop of *Azolla,* first as green manure and then as a dual crop along with rice. *Azolla* green manuring followed by dual cropping is equivalent to that from 60 kg N/ha. as fertilizer. Combined use of *Azolla* and N fertilizer give better results. Besides other management practices, grain yield response varies greatly with *Azolla* species and strains. On an average, the increase in grain yield due to *Azolla* green manuring ranges from 0.5-2.0 t/ha, whereas dual cropping produces additional yield of 0.5-1.5 t/ha over control.

FACTORS AFFECTING RESPONSE

The growth of *Azolla* and crop yield are significantly influenced by water availability, fertilizer application, rate and time of inoculation, method of rice planting and insects, pests and diseases. Water is prerequisite for multiplication of *Azolla. Azolla* cannot withstand desiccation and cannot be used in upland rice. Water depth of 5-10 cm is maintained during *Azolla* multiplication. *Azolla* requires at least an application of 20-30 kg P_2O_5/ha. Split application of fertilizer P helps in producing higher *Azolla* biomass. Soluble P sources are found to be more effective than rock phosphate.

The amount of inoculum significantly affects the growth rate of *Azolla.* Under poor growing conditions and in areas of excessive algal growth, higher inoculum rate should be used.

Azolla inoculation in early stages of rice growth is preferred because a delay reduces the fern growth due to increased shading of rice. Temperature higher than 34°C + 1°C during day time is detrimental for *Azolla* growth. *Azolla* is often attacked by insects and the entire crop is damaged within a few days, if they are not controlled timely. Pests like *Pyralia* and snails *(limnae acuminata)* and disease particularly black rot caused by *Rhizoctonia solani* are serious ones affecting *Azolla* multiplication. To control pest damage, insecticide application like Carbofuran is usually recommended.

BGA Production Technology

BGA production technology is simple and can be practiced on farmers field incurring negligible cost, although commercially the cost of

10 kg BGA is Rs. 20.00. BGA production and utilization is most popular among the farmers of Tamil Nadu, but is not catching up in other states like Uttar Pradesh, Madhya Pradesh, West Bengal, and Orissa etc. The experience is that growth rate on farmers fields is very low even when sun-shine is ample. Added to it, there is a problem of contamination of green algae and poor competitiveness of inoculated BGA. Farmers also do not get the BGA established in rice fields on inoculation. There is also need for devising appropriate testing kits, which can be easily handled by extension workers and farmers to determine whether the algae growing in the fields are BGA or nitrogen consuming green algae.

Acidic or highly alkaline soil conditions, direct contact with acid fertilizers, poor competitiveness due to slow growth rate, low tolerance to pesticides, predators and cyanophages and low availability of phosphorus and trace elements, are factors responsible for poor establishment of applied BGA in rice fields. Sundried BGA inoculant can be stored for a long time under dry condition and out of direct contact with chemical fertilizers without any quality deterioration. Application of BGA at three consecutive season helps in establishing, if available phosphorus level is not low in the soil.

The methods recommended are simple, rural oriented, open air method and inexpensive. Laboratory or sophisticated equipments are not required as in the case of *Rhizobium* bio-fertilizer.

Trough method

Troughs of 2m x 1 m x 22m capacity each and made up of galvanized iron sheet are filled with 5-10 cm water and placed under sun light. A mixture of 8-10 kg soil and 200 g super phosphate is sprinkled uniformly on the water. Next day BGA mother culture obtained from BGA subcentres (60 BGA subcentres are in operation supported by Govt. of India) is added left under sun. In 7 to 10 days a thick mat of BGA appears. Water is allowed to evaporate and dried algal flakes are collected.

Pit method

Shallow pits of similar dimension as of trough are made, lined with polythelene sheet to prevent drainage. Other procedures are the same as the trough method.

Mass Multiplication of BGA in the Field

Field production of algae is adopted for multiplication of the material on acommercial scale. In the wetland, about 40 m^2 area is demarked and puddled to facilitate water stagnation. The area is encircled with strong earthen bunds of about 15 cm height. Super phosphate is applied at 2 kg for 40 m^2 area. About 5 kg of composite algal culture is required for 40 m^2 area. To control predators like daphnids, snails, and mosquitoes, carbofuran 3 G is applied at 200g. In about 7-10 days period a thick mat of algae develops in clay soils. In loamy soils, about 3-4 weeks are required for full growth of algae. Once the algae have attained full growth with complete coverage, algal flakes are collected and stored in sacks for further use.

During summer months (April - June), the average yield of algae ranges from 20 to 30 kg/40m^2. Continuous harvest of algae may be made from the same area by reflooding the plot and applying super phosphate and pesticides. Addition of further inoculum is not necessary for subsequent production.

DUAL CROPPING OF *AZOLLA* WITH RICE

Out of six species, *Azolla Pinnata* is more common and abundantly found in natural ponds (Verma, 1992). It can double its biomass in 3-5 days and assimilate 60-80 kg ha^{-1}. It can be grown in bunded rice fields and incorporated into the soil while field is puddled for transplanting paddy seedlings. The other method includes growing *Azolla* amidst standing paddy crop as dual crop. The influence of *Azolla* on paddy yields as affected by different methods of application is presented in Table below.

There is no technology available for using *Azolla* as dry inoculum as in the case of *Rhizobium* or other bacterial (including blue green algae) biofertilizers. *Azolla* multiplies through vegetative propagation. Huge quantities of inoculum (10-12 t ha^{-1} as green manuring or 11 t ha^{-1} as dual cropping) are required and difficulty in transport during rainy season is the major constraint experienced in its adoption as biofertilizer.

Table 7.18: Influence of Azolla as affected by methods of application on yield rice (IR-36)

Treatment	Grain yield q ha^{-1}	% increase due to *Azolla*
30 kg N ha^{-1}	33 (28)	17.8
60 kg N ha^{-1}	38(28)	35.7
Azolla dual unincorporated	33(28)	17.8
Azolla dual incorporated	35 (28)	25.0
Azolla basal (green manuring)	32(27)	18.5
Azolla basal + dual cropping (once)	35 (27)	29.6
Azolla basal + dual cropping (twice)	38 (27)	40.7

Figures in parenthesis are grain yield due to no nitrogen. Complied from - Singh P.K. and Singh, D.P. (1992).

AZOLLA-ANABAENA SYMBIOSIS

A small floating water fern, Azolla is commonly seen in low land fields and in shallow fresh water bodies. This fern harbours a blue-green algae, *Anabaena* and Azollae. The *Azolla-Anabaena* association is a live floating nitrogen factory using energy from photosynthesis to fix atmospheric nitrogen amounting to 100-150 kg N/ha/year from about 40-60 tonnes of biomass. The studies carried out under AICARP showed that incorporation of 5 t ha^{-1} *Azolla* gave rice yields equivalent to about 30 kg N ha^{-1} at several locations. Reports of its current use as a biofertilizer for rice China, Vietnam, India, Indonesia, Thailand and other East and South Asian countries are available. An integrated system of rice *Azolla* fish has been developed in China.

Azolla is widely distributed in the rice growing tracts of tropics and temperate zones and grows on the irrigated rice fields. There are six species of *Azolla: A. caroliana, A. nilotica, A. fdiculoides, A mexicana, A. microphylla and A, pinnata.* The common species occurring in India is *A. pinnata.* A heat tolerant species *A. microphylla* is introduced to India from the Latin America. *A. fdiculoides* is a temperate species got from Europe. New crosses between *A. microphylla* and *A. fdiculoides* are also available. Several of hybrids have high nutritive value (4.0 - 4.5 % N on dry weight basis) and grow fast. The hybrids can also withstand both heat and cold.

Azolla mutants with a high degree of tolerance to salinity have been developed at International Energy Agencies, Vienna. Scientists in China and U.S. are now working on introducing a *Bacillus thuringiensis* (Bt) toxin in *Azolla* to fight against insect pests.

Multiplication of Azolla

Propagation

The water fern is mainly propagated by vegetative means. It will yield on an average about 1.5 kg per square meter in a week. Under normal conditions, the fern doubles itself in three days. Multiplying *Azolla* through sporocarp technique has also been developed in many research institutions in the world.

Azolla can be multiplied in small cement cisterns or galvanized iron trays of convenient size. *Azolla* can also be multiplied in the field nursery.

Cement Cisterns

Azolla can be multiplied in cement cisterns of 2 x 1 x 0.3 m. A layer of 7.5-10.0 cm soil is provided at the bottom of the cisterns. About 5.0 - 7.5 cm depth of water is maintained in the cisterns. Super phosphate @ 8-12 g and carbofuran at 2.0 g are applied. About 200 g of fresh *Azolla* is inoculated to each cistern. In about 12-15 days, about 2.0 -2.2 kg of *Azolla* can be harvested. After each harvest, super phosphate is applied to facilitate fast multiplication. Every time, 200g of *Azolla* is inoculated for further multiplication.

Mass multiplication in nursery plots

The field selected for *Azolla* nursery should be nearer to shade, thoroughly ploughed and inoculated. The field is divided into plots of 40 m² area (20 x 2 m) by providing suitable bunds and irrigation channels. Water is maintained to a depth of 10 cm. About 10 kg of fresh cattle dung is mixed with 20 litres of water and sprinkled uniformly throughout the plots. Fresh *Azolla* is inoculated at 8 kg/plot and super phosphate (100g) is applied twice at an interval of 4 days. Carbofuran is added at 100g per plot, 7days after inoculation to control insect pests. About 50-75 kg of fresh *Azolla* can be harvested 15 days after inoculation. *Azolla* can be again inoculated with the addition of cattle dung, super phosphate and carbofuran granules.

Enhanced Crop Production

Nitrogen fixing microorganisms convert about 139-170 million tonnes of nitrogen every year into fertilizer nitrogen for which the energy bill is paid by Nature. It is at least several folds greater than the inputs of nitrogen from chemical fertilizer factories to the tune of 65 million tonnes per year. The fact that the total world biological nitrogen fixation is three times that of industrially produced nitrogen, demonstrates the significance of biological nitrogen fixation in agricultural and natural nitrogen cycles.

Nitrogen fixing systems offer an economically attractive and ecologically sound means of reducing external inputs and improving internal resources. Symbiotic systems such as that of *Azolla* and *Anabaena* complex and that of leguminous green manures with *Rhizobium* and *Azorhizobium* associations can be of particular value to wet land rice crop and renewable biological source supplementing inorganic N for cereals.

In TNAU significant contributions have been made on *Azolla* bio-fertilizer particularly on the selection of new strains of *Azolla microphylla,* which is highly tolerant to high temperature and also tolerant to salinity with higher biomass producing capacity (25t/ha). *Azolla* hybrid has been developed by sexual hybridization. This hybrid is also highly adaptive and has higher N_2 fixing capacity in soil ecosystem. The nitrogen fixation by free-living blue green algae (cyanobacteria) also contributes significantly to the replenishment of soil N. Recently, several attempts have been made to improve the associations between rice and nitrogen fixing soil bacteria and possible nitrogen fixing rice endophytes to achieve a higher contribution of biological nitrogen fixation to rice crop. In these soils, sustainability depends on symbiotic and non-symbiotic BNF system.

Nitrogen fixing free-living cyanobacteria play a vital role in the maintenance of soil fertility and sustainability. The large-scale production of soil based BGA inoculum developed at Tirur by TNAU during 1977 is a crude technology, which is two decades old, and hence has to be updated. Immobilized cyanobacteria inoculum is a recent development in the biofertilizer technology, which was developed in the biofertilizer technology, which was developed by TNAU, Coimbatore with the active collaboration of the Division of Life Sciences, King's College, London, and the Department of Biochemistry and Molecular Biology, University of Seville, Spain, under an EEC project.

Immobilization of nitrogen fixing cyanobacteria under rice field conditions can be done with solid matrices such as polyurethane foam, polyvinyl foam, sugar cane waste, paper waste, and rice husk. The immobilized cyanobacteria could continuously excrete the ammonia extracellularly which could be used for continuous supply of nitrogen to rice crop. The immobilized cyanobacterial system in solid matrix when inoculated in rice field is like a mini *in situ* fertilizer factory, which produces ammonia continuously. The accumulation of ammoniacal N in the flood water as a result of immobilized cyanobacterial inoculation will reflect on the growth and yield of rice.

Table 7.19: Field application methods of bio-fertilizer in different crops

Crops	Recommended bio-fertilizers for nitrogen	Method of application	Quantity required/ha of each bio-fertilizers	Time of application
1. AGRICULTURAL CROPS				
A. FIELD CROPS				
(a) PULSE				
1. Chickpea, Pea G. Nut Soybean, Beans	*Rhizobium*	Seed Treatment	1.0-2.0 kg	Sowing Time
2. Lentil, Lucern, Barseem, Green Gram, Black Gram, Cowpea, Pegion Pea, Guar	*Rhizobium*	Seed Treatment	0.4 - 0.6 kg.	Sowing Time
(b) CEREALS				
1. Wheat, Oat, Barley	*Azotobacter*	Seed Treatment	1.0 - 2.0 kg.	Sowing Time
2. Rice	*Azospirillum*	Seedling Treatment	2.0 - 3.0 kg.	Transplantation Time
	BGA	Broadcasting	10 kg.	After one week of Transplantation
	Azolla	Dual Crops	500 -1000 kg.	- do -

Crops	Recommended bio-fertilizers for nitrogen	Method of application	Quantity required/ha of each bio-fertilizers	Time of application
(c) OIL SEEDS				
1. Mustard, Seasmum, Kusum, Linseeds	*Azotobacter*	Seed Treatment	0.2 kg.	Sowing Time
2. Sunflower, Castor	*Azotobacter*	Seed Treatment	0.5 - 0.8 kg.	Sowing Time
(d) MILLETS				
1. Pearl millets, Finger millets, Kodo millet	*Azospirillum*	Seed Treatment	0.2 kg.	Sowing Time
2. Maize & Sorghum	*Azospirillum/Azotobacter*	Seed Treatment	0.4 - 0.6 kg	Sowing Time
(e) FORAGE CROPS & GRASSES				
1. Baramuda grass, Sudan grass, Napier grass, Guinea grass, Paragrass, Rhodo grass, Star grass etc.	*Azospirillum*	Seed Treatment	0.8-1.0 kg.	Sowing Time
(f) FIBRE CROPS				
1. Cotton	*Azotobacter*	Seed Treatment	0.6-1.0 kg.	Sowing Time
2. Jute	*Azotobacter*	Seed Treatment	0.8-1.0 kg	Sowing Time

Crops	Recommended bio-fertilizers for nitrogen	Method of application	Quantity required/ha of each bio-fertilizers	Time of application
3. Sunhemp etc.	*Rhizobium*	Seed Treatment	0.8 -1.0 kg	Sowing Time
(g) SUGAR CROPS				
1. Sugarcane	*Acetobacter/Azotobacter/ Azospirillum*	Soil/Sets Treatment	4.0 - 5.0 kg.	Sowing Time
2. Sugarbeats	*Azotobacter*	Seed Treatment	2.0-3.0 kg.	Sowing Time
B. HORTICULTURAL CROPS *(a) VEGETABLE CROPS*				
1. Potato	*Azotobacter*	Soil/Tuber Treatment	4.0 - 5.0 kg.	Sowing Time
2. Reddish, Spinach, Ladyfinger	*Azotobacter/Azospirillum*	Seed Treatment	0.4 - 0.6 kg.	Sowing Time \
3. Turnip, Carrot, Perwal Cucerbits Crops	*Azotobacter*	Seed Treatment	0.2 kg.	Sowing Time
4. Onion, Brinjal, Knotknot, Cauliflower, Cabbage, Tomato, Chillies	*Azotobacter/Azospirillum*	Seeding Treatment	1.5 - 2.0 kg.	Transplantation Time

Crops	Recommended bio-fertilizers for nitrogen	Method of application	Quantity required/ha of each bio-fertilizers	Time of application
b) FLOWERS				
1. Merigold and all other seasonal plantation (annuls, perianuals, Herbs/shrubs) flower as well as ornamental plants.	*Azotobacter/Azospirillum*	Seeding Treatment	1.5-2.0 kg.	Transplantation Time
2. Buds (Gladiolus,	*Azotobacter*	Buds/Tuber	3.0-4.0 kg.	Sowing/ Transplan tation Time
Garlic, Zinger, Turmeric, Arbl, banana) Tubers & Sets of Rose Plants etc.		Set Treatment		
C) OTHER MISC. PLANTATION CROPS				
1. Tobacco	*Azotobacter*	Seedling Treatment	2.0-3.0 kg.	Transplantation Time
2. Tea, Coffee	*Azotobacter*	Soil Treatment	3.0 - 4.0 kg	Sowing Time
3. Rubber, Coconuts	*Azotobacter*	Soil Treatment	20 - 30 gm/Plant	Transplantation Time

Crops	Recommended bio-fertilizers for nitrogen	Method of application	Quantity required/ha of each bio-fertilizers	Time of application
II. AGRO FORESTYR/FRUIT PLANTS				
A. FIELD CROPS				
1. All fruit/agro-forestry (herb, shrubs, annuals & as usual perianual) plants grown for fuel wood, fodder, fruits, gum, spices, medicines saps, sugars leaves, flowers, nuts and seeds purpose	*Azotobacter*	Soil Treatment	8-10 gm/Plant	
2. Leguminous plants/Plants	*Rhizobium*	Soil Treatment	20-30 gm/Plant	

Note: **1.** In addition to Nitrogen fixation bio-fertilizers. Same quantity of phosphatic solubilizing biofertilizers (PSB) may also be used to provide phosphorous through soil treatment for all crops as well as by other method of bio-fertilizer application as recommended above.

***2.** @ 1 kg/acre of potash mobilizing bacteria recommended for all crops.*

Source: "Millennium Bio-fertilizer Guide", Complied & Edited by Rajnish Jain, Delhi.

8

Mechanism and Estimation of Nitrogen Fixation

The universal presence of nitrogen in all living matter explains the close relationship that exists between environmental chemistry and biological systems. Although much of the work studying the biological transformation of nitrogen has been conducted on soil ecosystems, it is much the same for those conditions occurring in aquatic ecosystems.

The supply of nitrogen in the atmosphere is vast. However, it exists as an inert gas, a form unusable to life. In order for nature to utilize this immense reservoir of free nitrogen it has to be combined with other elements. The relationship that exists between the various forms of nitrogen compounds and the changes that can occur in nature are illustrated by a schematic diagram of the nitrogen cycle (Fig. 8.1).

This diagram shows how nitrogen in its free form is converted by electrical discharge to nitrates. These nitrates along with nitrogen fixing bacteria and algae form plant protein which in turn provides protein to animals and humans to carry on their life processes. Within the animal body, the protein is used for the growth and repair of tissue and also as a source of energy. Waste products produced by the life processes are formed and excreted as fecal matter and urine. The fecal matter, along with the protein from dead animals and plants, is converted by bacteria to ammonia; the urine is hydrolyzed rapidly to ammonium carbonate. The ammonia produced can be used to produce additional plant protein or be oxidized to form nitrites and nitrates, thus completing the nitrogen cycle.

The form in which nitrogen appears is indicative of the stage of stabilization of the organic matter. Illustrates the various nitrogen forms and how they vary with time. Initially most of the nitrogen will appear in the form of organic nitrogen and ammonia. As time goes on, the organic nitrogen is converted to ammonia. Under aerobic conditions, the ammonia will ultimately be converted to nitrites and nitrates.

Nitrogen in liquid waste can exist in 4 forms, all of which are of interest to the agricultural sanitary engineer. The 4 forms are organic nitrogen, ammonia nitrogen, nitrite nitrogen, and nitrate nitrogen. The total of these 4 forms constitute total nitrogen.

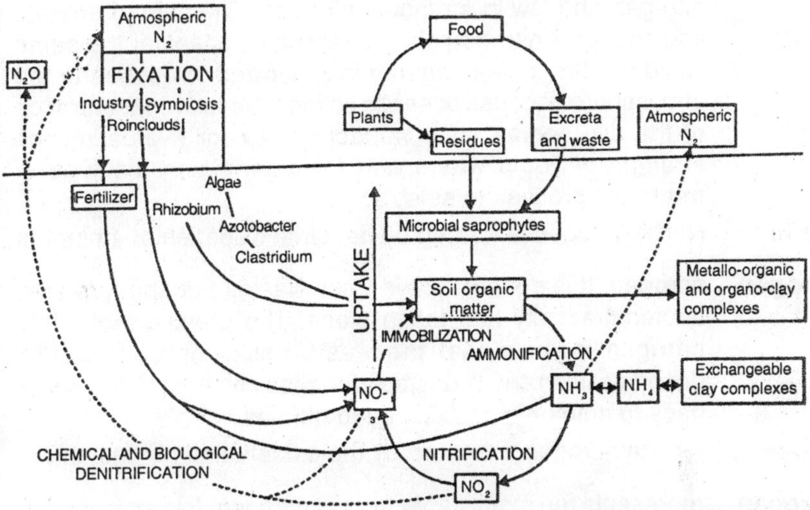

Fig. 8.1. The chemical conversion in the nitrogen cycle. The main activities are indicated together with some of the organisms concerned.

Gaseous nitrogen is the most abundant element of atmosphere (78.08% v/v), and seems to have a highly complex nutrient cycle in the terrestrial and aquatic ecosystems. There is an interrelationship between different elements required for plant growth in environment. These all are affected by microbes. Atmospheric nitrogen is chemically inert. Therefore, it can be used, as such by most of the living organisms. The common source of nitrogen in the nature is the nitrate ions (NO_3). The nitrate ion is often absorbed by the plants as a mineral raw material from the environment. The absorbed nitrate ions are then converted into amino groups ($-NH_2$). The conversion of $-NO_3$ to NH_2 group is only possible by plants and not by animals. Minerals accumulation in soil, dissolution of rock by water, addition of fertilizers in soil are also the sources of NO_3 in the soil.

Table 8.1: Forms of nitrogen

Organic Nitrogen	All nitrogen present in organic compounds is considered to be organic nitrogen. The nitrogen-containing organic compounds are derivations of ammonia, the oxidation of which forms ammonia nitrogen.
Ammonia Nitrogen	The ammonia nitrogen is a result of bacterial decomposition of organic matter. Fresh sewage is generally high in organic

nitrogen and low in ammonia nitrogen. The sum of organic and ammonia nitrogen should remain constant for the same liquid wastes, unless ammonia is allowed to escape to the atmosphere because of septic action. The total concentration of the two serves as a valuable index for evaluating the strength of liquid waste and for determining the type of treatment process to select.

Nitrite Nitrogen Nitrite nitrogen is formed by bacterial oxidation of ammonia nitrogen. It is not present in fresh wastes but appears after bacterial activity has taken place. The presence of nitrite nitrogen indicate that the waste has undergone partial decomposition and is unstable. Nitrites can either be reduced back to ammonia or oxidized to nitrates:

Nitrate Nitrogen Nitrate nitrogen is formed by the oxidation of nitrites and represents the most stable form of nitrogen. It is an indication of stability and is a determination of the completeness of the biological decomposition process.

Apart from these sources, atmospheric nitrogen and oxygen combine together in presence of lightening which come down with the help of rainwater to the ground, and serve as NO_3 source on the earth. Absorbed nitrogen (in the form of NO_3) incorporates into organic structures of plants which remain intact until death. Animals also obtain nitrogen by eating plants. Finally, both plants and animals die or decay. Through gradual decay of all nitrogen of dead plants and animals, it gets concentrated into ammonia (NH_3). The so forming NH_3 is then utiiized as a source of nutrition for nitrifying bacteria. Usually, these bacteria are of two kinds:

- Those bacteria which absorb ammonia and convert it into nitrite ions *i.e.,*

$$NH_3 \rightarrow NO_2$$

- **Those bacteria which** absorb nitrite ions and convert it into nitrate *i.e.,*

$$NO_2 \rightarrow NO_3$$

Thus, the environment again gets NO_3 by the activities of these nitrifying bacteria. The available NO_3 in the environment acts upon denitrifying bacteria which converts it into molecular, atmospheric nitrogen. The free molecular nitrogen is then, utilized by nitrogen fixing organisms in which few species of bacteria and blue green algae have been included. They are often present in soil and water. They absorb nitrogen and incorporate it into ammonia and protein. The process is called **Nitrogen fixation.**

Nitrogen is the mineral nutrient most needed by plants and it often limits plant growth. Some plant species have formed mutualistic symbioses with nitrogen fixing *prokaryotes* and some *eukaryotes*. Those organisms that can directly utilise atmospheric nitrogen as a nitrogen source, are called *"diazotrophs"*, and belong to the kingdoms *eubacteria* and *archaebacteria*. They are able to live independently on soil N for growth. Inside the root nodules, the bacteria on the other hand are supplied with carbon from the host and are sheltered from competition with other organisms. The most important mutualistic symbioses are root nodule symbioses, mainly formed by members of the genera *Rhizobium, Bradyrhizobium* and *Azorhizobium* on legumes, and by the genus *Frankia* on some non-legumes. The reduction of atmospheric dinitrogen (N_2) to ammonium (NH_4+) which occurs in nitrogen fixing organisms is catalysed by an enzyme complex called *nitrogenase*. A minimum 16 ATP and $8e^{-1}$ are needed for a reduction of one molecule of N_2. It is estimated that nitrogen fixation could range from one to a few kg ha^{-1} $year^{-1}$ in lichens and free living bacteria, and up to a hundred or possibly a few hundred kg ha^{-1} $year^{-1}$ in legumes and actinorhizal plants.

Nitrogen fixation has always been a subject of great importance in biology, but since two decades the recent biotechnological development has lent its practical urgency. Nitrogenous fertilizers have become more and more expensive in terms of fossil energy, and hard cash; the population pressure have increased the need for high protein plant food. Biotechnologists are actively engaged in improving the efficiency of microorganisms to fix atmospheric nitrogen in fields. This will improve the functioning of the nitrogen cycle in biosphere which will ultimatly increase plant productivity. The programme of improvement also includes the creation of nitrogen-fixing symbiotic association other than those existing between leguminous plants and bacteria of the genus *Rhizobium*. This will help to improve agricultural production.

DIAZOTROPHIC MICROORGANISMS

The fixation of atmospheric nitrogen by *prokaryotic* organisms is *known as diazoirophy.* The phenomenon has also been observed in *eukaryotic* unicellular green alga, isolated from hot spring, by Yanada and Sakaguchi (1980).

Biological Nitrogen Fixation

This process is brought about by nitrogen-fixing microorganisms. These are soil inhibitants *e.g.*, bacteria, blue green algae, molds, etc. Those microorganisms, which utilize gaseous nitrogen directly and independently in the soil are known as asymbiotic or non-symbiotic nitrogen fixing organisms and the process by which they brought about is referred as non-symbiotic nitrogen fixation. Those microorganisms, which utilize gaseous nitrogen indirectly through the mediation of other living organisms in the soil are called symbiotic nitrogen fixing bacteria and the process brought about by them is referred as symbiotic nitrogen fixation.

Asymbiotic Nitrogen Fixation

Microorganisms

Bacteria: As described earlier, soil contains free-living bacteria that are capable of fixing molecular nitrogen into its compounds. This process was first recognized in bacterium *Clostridium pasturianum* which is a Gram-positive, spore forming rod-shaped bacterium. After seven years of the isolation of *C. pasturianum,* two more important free-living nitrogen-fixing bacteria were isolated by Beijernick (1901). These newly identified bacteria were *Azatobacter chrooccum* and *A. agile.*

Azatobacter chrooccum is usually found in field-soils. They are short, thick, rod-shaped with rounded ends. Some larger void forms are almost yeast-like in appearance. The cells are arranged singly or in end-to-end pairs. They measure 2 to 3 nm by 6 nm in size. They appear-brown in old cultures. They are Gram-negative and non-acid fast. They are motile and the motility is due to the presence of polar flagellum. Physiologically, they are aerobic and remain active in between 25° C. They fix atmospheric nitrogen only after utilizing carbohydrate (dextrose, maltose, lactate, etc.) and give carbon dioxide as a by product. *A. glile* also actively fixes atmospheric nitrogen and produces carbon dioxide.

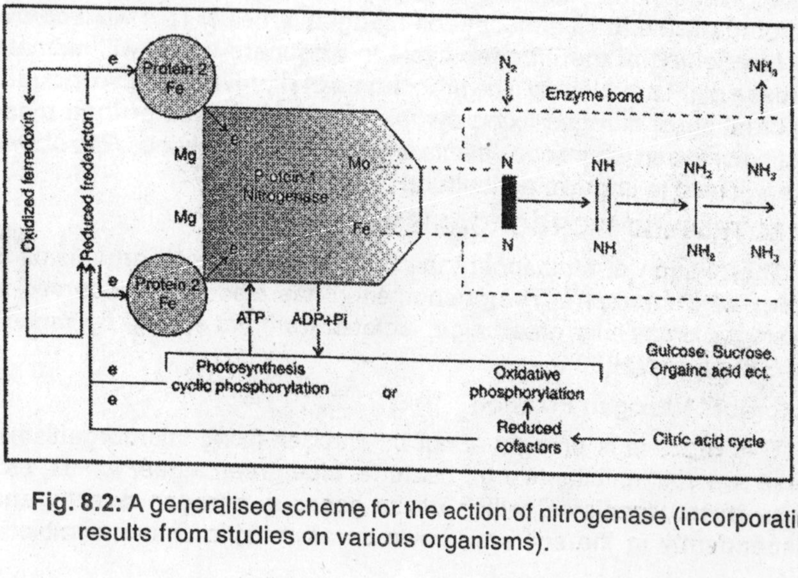

Fig. 8.2: A generalised scheme for the action of nitrogenase (incorporating results from studies on various organisms).

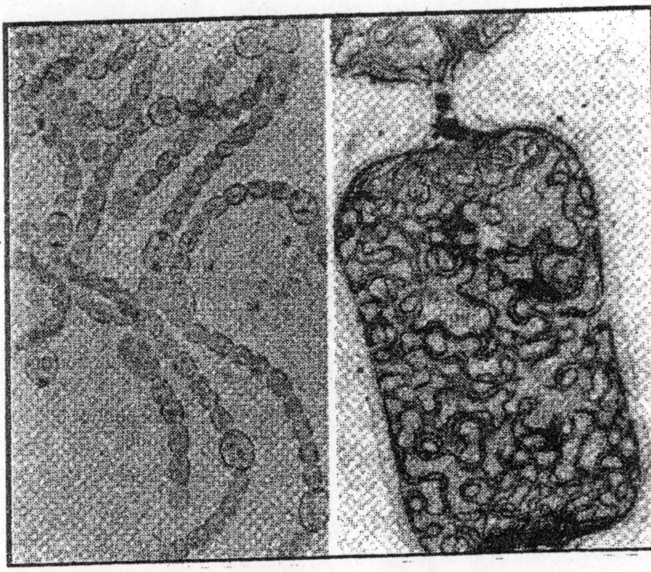

Fig. 8.3. Ultrastructure of the heterocyst of cyanobacteria *Anabaena* (a) filaments of *A. azollae* showing enlarged heterocyst in different stages of development, (b) cross section through a heterocyst of a *A. çylindrica* showing the contorted thylakoid membranes.

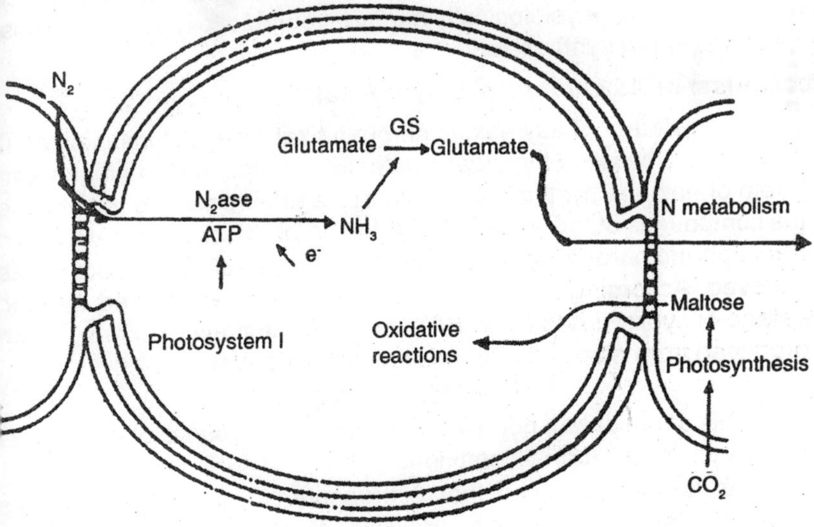

Fig. 8.4: Nitrogen and carbon flow associated with nitrogen fixation in the heterocyst of blue green alga. N_2ase = the nitrogenase enzyme as GS = glutamine synthetase, oxidative reactions including the oxidative pentose phosphate pathway. Polar nodule are not shown.

Apart from *Azatobacter*, other non-symbiotic bacteria lik *Rhodospirillum pneumoiniae*, *Rhodopseudomonas*, *Chlorobium* *Diplococcus pneumoiniae*, *Azatobacter aerogenes*, *Micrococcu sulfurens* have also been known to fix atmospheric nitroge asymbiotically.

The ability to fix nitrogen by microorganisms was confirmed by mean of the technique known as *acetylene reduction* to *ethylene* by diazotrophi microorganisms. The mechanism of this conversion is controlled by a enzymatic complex (or nitrogenous enzyme), which can reduce gaseou nitrogen to ammonia.

The enzyme nitrogenase is sensitive towards oxygen. There ar reports, which reveal that several groups of microorganisms fix nitroge in presence of minute quantities of oxygen. Such microorganisms ar known as **microaerobic fixers.** They oxidize methane. The example are bacteria, Spirilla *(Aquaspirillum and Azosprillium)*, *Xanthobacte autorophicus* and *S. flavus*, *Thiobacillus ferrooxidans and* non heterocystous microaerobic cyanobacteria *(Oscillatoria, Plectonema)* Certain coliform bacteria also fix nitrogen only in aerobic conditions (*e.g. Citrobactor, Enterobacter, Erwinia).* A comprehensive lists o microorganisms have been presented in the book, but in near futur they may need revision in light of findings of bio-chemical and physiologica researches. It is established that oxygen not only inhibits the activity o nitrogenase enzyme but also regulates its bio-synthesis, so that i conditions that are physiologically hardly favourable to nitrogen fixation the enzyme is not synthesized.

Mechanism of Asymbiotic Nitrogen Fixation

The knowledge of asymbiotic nitrogen fixation is still insufficient. I was previously believed that *Azatobacter* fixes atmospheric nitrogen wit the help of enzyme system called azatase and nitrogenase is only on of the compounds of this system. Beijerinck (1901) indicated that fixatio of atmospheric nitrogen took place at the nitrous acid stage, but it wa not proved. According to one more concept, nitrogen is fixed throug the stage of hydrolysis to hydroxylamine or to ammonium nitrate, whic is produced from nitrogen and water as shown below:

$$N_2 + 2H_2O \rightarrow NH_4NO_2$$

But this concept has not been proved. The hydrolysis of nitrogen is very difficult under normal conditions.

It was further proposed that *Azatobacter* fixes nitrogen after its reduction by the active hydrogen. However, this hypothesis was also not proved.

At last the mechanism of nitrogen fixation was described on the physiological basis. It was proved that the protoplasm of *Azatobacter* produces special catalysts, which take part in fixing free nitrogen. The catalysts contain carboxyl and amino group as important parts, which do not take any active part in fixing atmospheric nitrogen. Phenyl hydrogen and hydroxylamine are also present in the composition of the catalysts. It was presumed that molecular nitrogen reacts with catalysts of nitrogen fixation through oxygen of carboxyl group and produces hydrazine as the first product of the reaction. The hydrazine, is then, further reduced by active hydrogen and is transformed into amino acids. They finally enter the proteins of the cell protoplasm. This incorporation of amino acid into protoplasms helps into the growth of a bacterium.

REQUIREMENTS OF NITROGEN FIXATION

1. Oxygen and carboxyl group of the catalysts play an important role in nitrogen fixation.
2. A very small amount of chemical energy (ATP) is used up during nitrogen fixation. About 1 kilo calories fix 2 mg of atmospheric nitrogen. It shows the relationship between respiration and nitrogen fixation.

Some strict anaerobic bacteria are more sensitive to oxygen. *Clostridium pasteurianum* is an obligate anaerobe, therefore, the mechanism of nitrogen fixation of such organism is similar to that *Azatobacter,* because they produce large amount of hydrogen during their metabolic reaction. The various possible pathways of nitrogen fixation have been shown in different 'illustrations.

SYMBIOTIC NITROGEN FIXATION

Agriculturists have noted that a relatively large group of plants- the legumes, are capable of fixing atmospheric nitrogen through a symbiotic association with soil bacteria called *Rhizobium.* These bacteria or nodule bacteria, usually dwell in the roots of various beans, peas, lupines, cloves and other leguminous plants.

Hellriegal and Wilfarth (1888) first of all demonstrated that an increase in nitrogen content in soil is due to the presence of small tumor-like outgrowth on the roots of leguminous plants. It was found that in absence of root nodules, growth of succeding plant-crop was retarded. The results of variousexperiments reveal that root nodule forming plants can feed upon atmospheric nitrogen and this capacity of plants can be obserbed only in those plants, which are growing in non-sterilized or bacteria containing soils. These symbiotic bacteria e.g., *Rhizobium* utilize the free atmospheric nitrogen and synthesize it into new nitrogenous compounds, which are utilized by plants for their growth; and bacteria get their food from these plants. Such a mutual beneficial association of bacteria and plants is referred to symbiosis.

Symbiosis was originally defined by Bary in 1879. Symbiosis ;s the living together of any two organisms. Mutulism is a relationship where both partners benefit, though it greads intó those where the advantage or dis-advantage to one of the partner may not always be obvious. Commensal relationships are usually rather loose association of the benefit of another without any effect on itself.

MECHANISM OF NITROGEN FIXATION IN LEGUMES

The mechanism of nitrogen fixation in legumes has not yet been understood. However, the basic prerequisite for nitrogen fixation in extracts of nodule-bacteriods are similar to those that have been described for asymbiotic bacteria such as *Azatobacter*. It has not been well established that how in both asymbiotic and symbiotic system ^{15}N is converted into NH_3 and then to amino acids, because the intermediate products between ^{15}N to NH_3 have not been determined.

A good number of theories have been proposed by various workers. Two of them are important, which are as follows:

Theory of Virtanen

Nitrogen fixation in root appears immediately after nodule formation. Virtanen (1948) proposed the following scheme of nitrogen fixation in root nodules:

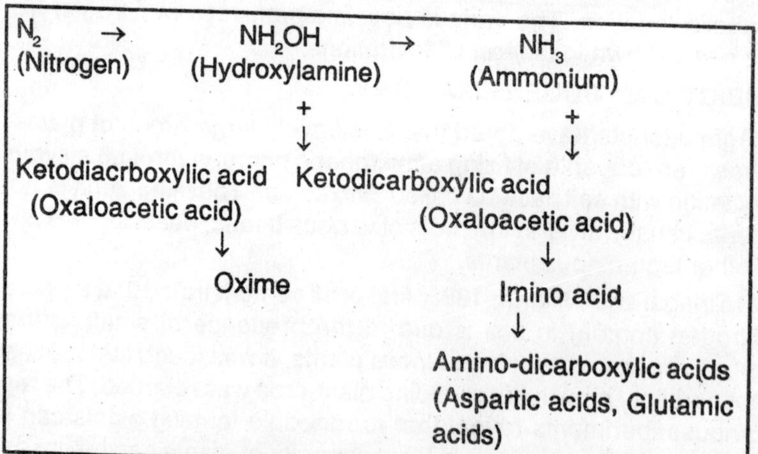

Fig. 8.5: Mechanism of nitrogen fixation

According to him young plants fix more amount of nitrogen than the old plants. A great part of nitrogen is converted into L-aspartic acid and L-glutamic acid. Apart from these, α-alanine is also present in the nodule which is produced from L-aspartic acid by decarboxylation. In addition to this, small amount of Oxime-N and Nitrite-N are also present.

Theory of Burn's and Wilson

According to this theory hydroxylamine is the central compound of nitrogen fixation, from which ammonia is formed through reduction or it can also directly react to the keto acid. The proposed scheme of Burris and Wilson (1945) is as follows:

Both these theories reveal the formation of amino dicarboxylic acid as the primary products in biological nitrogen fixation

NH_2OH		$\longleftrightarrow$	NH_3	
+			+	
Oxaloacetic acid	Ketoglutatric acid		Oxaloacetic acid	Ketoglutatric acid
↑↓	↑↓		↑↓	↑↓
Asparticacid	Glutamic acid		Asparticacid	Glutamicacid

Fig. 8.6: Theory of Burris and Wilson.

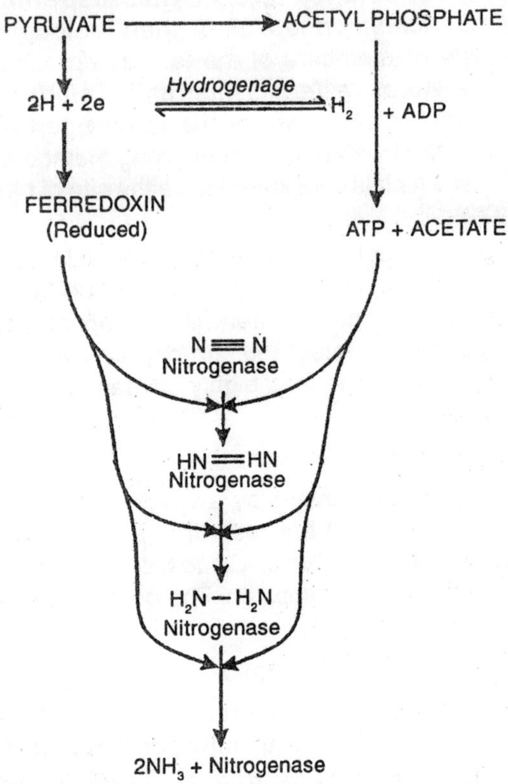

Fig. 8.7: Scheme proposed for mechanism of nitrogen fixation.

NITROGEN CONVERTERS IN THE SOIL

The oxidation of ammonia to nitrate in the soil is one of the important phases in nitrogen cycle. This is brought about by two groups of bacteria- *Nitrosomonas* and *Nitrobacter.* The required energy for the growth of these bacteria is obtained through the oxidation of ammonia or nitrate. Winogradsky (1891) first isolated these autotrophic bacteria and described the conversion of ammonia to nitrite, and nitrite to nitrate. This is called **nitrification.** The conversion of nitrate to nitrous oxide and nitrogen gas by various kinds of soil organisms is called **denitrification.** The process releases nitrogen gas to the atmosphere and completes the complex nitrogen cycle in nature.

CYANOBACTERIA AND NITROGEN FIXATION

Frank (1889) first reported the ability of nitrogen fixation by blue green algae. According to Drewes (1928) *Nostoc punctifonne* and *Anabaena variabilis* have the ability to fix nitrogen in the soil. The principal genera of this group known to fix nitrogen are *Nostoc* spp. *(N. cummune, N. punctifonne, N. muscorum); Anabaena* spp. *(A. ambigua, A. cylindrica, A. fertilissima. A. circularis,* etc.), *Cylindrospermum* spp. *(C. gorakhporense, C. licheniforme)-* all of them belong to the family Nostocaceae. A few of members of the family Microchaetaceae and Rivulariaceae like *Aulosira fertilissima* and *Calothrix brevissima* respectively are known to fix atmospheric nitrogen in rice fields. Significantly most of the free living nitrogen fixing members of this group produce **heterocyst** which is considered to be the site of nitrogen fixation (Kulasooriya, 1972).

The free living diazotrophic cyanobacteria are the largest contributors of the process of biological nitrogen fixation, the second most important biological process on this planet. Their nitrogen fixing ability was first related to the presence of specialized non-oxygen evolving cells called heterocysts in which nitrogenase; a highly oxygen-sensitive enzyme is produced from oxygen.

NITROGEN FIXING FUNGI

The fungi also independently play an important role in fixing free nitrogen in soil. The fungi that are responsible for this function are of species of *Mactosporium commune, Cladosporium herbarum, Phoma, Alternaria tenuiis, Rhodotorula* spp. etc. The occurrence of these fungi has been noted in forest-land.

Bio-chemical Aspects of Diazotrophy

An American company (DuPont) in 1960 started the fundamental research on the bio-chemistry of nitrogen fixation specially on nitrogenase activity in cell free extracts of *Closiridium pasteurianum.*

The experiments were conducted in absence of air because of the very great oxygen sensitivity of nitrogenase. The techniques like chromatography, electrophoresis and fractionation under anaerobic conditions, helped the researchers to isolate nitrogenase from *Clostridium pasteurianum.* Thereafter, nitrogenase was easily isolated from other anaerobic nitrogen fixers while this extraction was more difficult with *Azotobacter vinelandii.* The so isolated enzyme has the property to accept electorn from sodium dithionite and was oxygen-tolerant and evolved hydrogen in the absence of nitrogen. In 1981, nitrogenase in the form of crude preparations was isolated from about 30 microbes and out of which about 6 of them were purified.

Biochemically, nitrogenase is a binary enzyme and consists of two brown metalloproteins, of which the joint activity is essential to reduce nitrogen to ammonia.

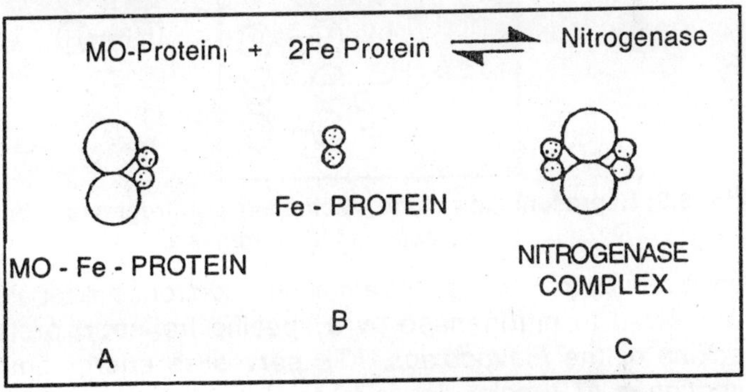

Fig. 8.8: Nitrogenase enzyme.

During nitrogen conversion, nitrogenase binds to molybdoferroprotein (MoFe-protein), which was named disnitrogenase. When nitrogen binds at the molybdenum level in a separable fragment of protein, called FeMoco. The two component proteins of the enzyme nitrogenase are quickly and irreversibly destroyed by exposure to oxygen.

Nitrogenase is also able to reduce other substrates in the place of nitrogen, including hydrogen ions and, in this case it evolves hydrogen.

NITROGENASE PRODUCING *E. COLI*CELLS

Because of the close relationship between *E. coli* and *Klebsiella pneumoniae, E. coli* is specially qualified for the investigation of the nitrogenase system. With *E. coli* C-M74 cells, high nitrogenase activity can be attained in culture medium, supplemented with 50mg/l ammonium sulfate, 1 per cent aspartic acid, and 0.1 per cent yeast extract.

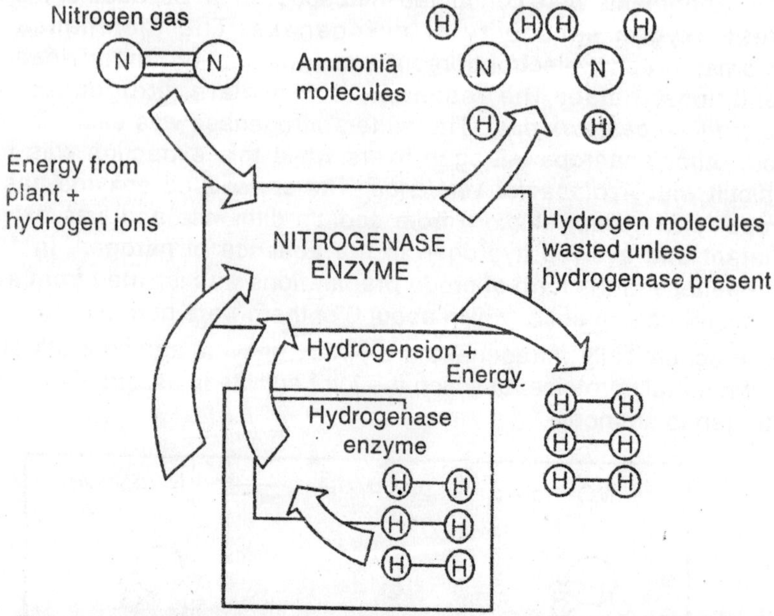

Fig. 8.9: Representation of the mechanism of nitrogen fixation and the action of hydrogenase.

During reduction of nitrogen to ammonia, electrons are required which are transferred to nitrogenase by a specific transport proteins; the *Ferrodoxins* or the *Flavodoxins.* ATP serves as energy source. The consumption of ATP molecules is 12 to 15 per nitrogen molecule. The reason for this high consumption of ATP has not been entirely elucidated.

As evident from the reactions that hydrogen is produced during nitrogen fixation. Certain nitrogen-fixing aerobic bacteria possess hydrogenase enzyme which has the ability to recycle hydrogen produced by nitrogenase in vitro. Therefore, the re-utilization of this hydrogen generates more ATP (by oxidative phosphorylation) and consequently improves the efficiency of nitrogen fixation.

Rhizobium is also associated with soybean plants which contain hydrogen uptake (or *hup)* genes, which have the ability to recycle hydrogen and back into the nitrogenase system and fix nitrogen. Through this mechanism energy is harvested by plants, which is otherwise lost.

The nitrogenase enzyme of bacteria fix nitrogen by converting nitrogen gas into ammonia using hydrogen ions and energy by host plant. During the process there is a production of energy rich hydrogen gas. Some bacteria possess hydrogenase enzyme which can capture hydrogen gas and converts it into hydrogen ions and release energy which can feed back into nitrogenase enzyme.

Genetics of Free-living and Symbiotic Diazotrophs

Organization of Nitrogen-fixation Genes

In molecular terms, very little is known of the means by which the prokaryote specifically recognizes and invades its respective host-plant. However, there has been a growing interest in approaching this problem by identifying and analysing the relevant symbiotic genes and their gene products. Because of the agricultural importance of the *Rhizobium-legume* interaction, the most detailed studies have been conducted on this system. Also, because of bacteria are simpler than plants. Our knowledge of the symbiotic genes of *Rhizobium* is better than that of the plant genes. There have been several recent advances in the analysis of the *Rhizobium* genes that are involved in nodulation, host-range specificity and nitrogen fixation. By dissecting the structure, organization and regulation of these genes, a better understanding of their functions may be forthcoming.

In the fast-growing *Rhizobium* species, which nodulate temperate legumes such as clover, *alfalfa,* peas and field beans, the genes for nodulation and nitrogen fixation are clustered on large symbiotic plasmids. One such plasmid, pRLUI, was isolated from a strain of *R. leguminosarum* (which nodulates peas) and in this case the genes that determined the ability to nodulate peas were located between two groups of genes required for nitrogen fixation: The study of the nitrogen-fixation *(nif)* genes in *Rhizobium* has been greatly facilitated by the fact that at least some of them are very similar to the corresponding *nif* genes in the free-living nitrogen-fixing bacterium - *Klebsiella pneumoniae.*

In *Klebsiella,* 17 *nif* genes have been identified which are variously involved in *nif* gene regulation, the synthesis of the iron-molybdenum cofactor (FeMoCo). Using DNA sequence comparisons, *Rhizobium* species have been shown to contain the *nifHD* and *K* genes (nitrogenase proteins) *nifA* (regulation) and *nifB* (synthesis of FeMoCo). Further studies may well demonstrate similarities between other *Rhizobium* and *Klebsiella nif* genes.

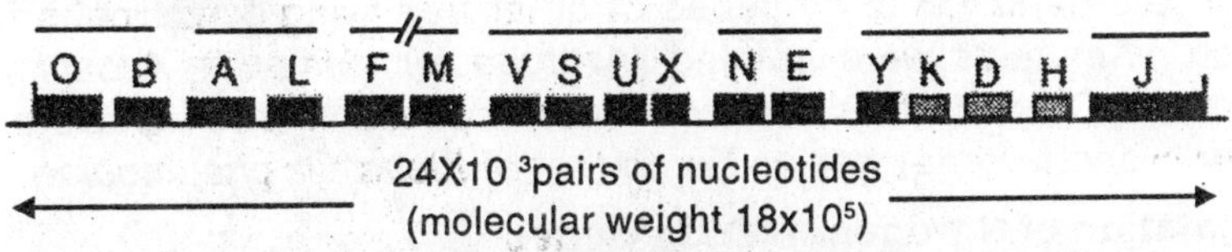

Fig. 8.10: Map of the *nif* gene cluster of the *Klebsiella pneumoniae* chromosome. The capital letters denote the genes (cistrons), the *nif* cluster being located between the genes for bio-synthesis of histidine (his) and those for shikimic acid uptake (shi A). The arrow indicate the separate operations and the direction of their transcription. In 1981 the status of F and M as one or two distinct operons was not clear. The size of most of the genes, however, were known.

The study of nitrogen fixation genes was first carried out in *Klebsiella pneumoniae* (strain M5al); and spectaular progress achieved in 1970s. Although the first report came from the mutants of nitrogen fixing bacteria, which was isolated and bio-chemically characterized as early in 1959. The genetic research by Streicher *et al.* (1971) of U.S.A. and Dixon of Agric. Research Council, Unit of Nitrogen fixation (U.K.) added more knowledge in this field. Dixon and Postgate (1971) successfully transferred the nitrogen fixation genes, called *nif,* to *Klebsiella pneumoniae.* Later on they could able to transfer these genes to *Escherichia coli.* This work encouraged the researchers of this field specially for *Rhizobium* and the presence of *nif* genes in this microorganism. More than a dozen genes, termed the *nif* genes are involved in the assembly of nitrogen-fixation apparatus. The *nif* genes are not found in a free state but are clustered in one region (they are not scattered throughout the bacterial DNA). Therefore, it is much easier to stretch of DNA in a *Rhizobium* chromosome and insert the whole batch into another organism. This has also been done in *Agrobacterium tumefaciens* (Ti plasmids). In 1981, the number of *nif* genes was 17 and they were organized in eight transcription units (or operons), one of which was monocistronic. Brill (1980) also included two other genes: *nif-K* between L and F, and m/-W between F and M.

Nod-Genes for Nodulation

Concerning the genes (called *nod* genes) for nodulation and host-range specificity, an important observation is that, despite the morphological complexity of the infection process, only a few genes on the symbiotic plasmid are required for nodulation. In the *R. leguminosarum* symbiotic plasmid pRLUI, less than 10kb appears to be required for nodulation and for the determination of host-range specificity for peas. The reason has been analysed by DNA sequencing (and thus identifying genes as long open reading frames), isolation and characterization of mutants and by studying the regulation of the *nod* genes.

The organiztion of *nif-genes* of other free-living diazotrophs from which *nif*-mutants were isolated *(Azatobacter vinelandii, Azospirillum lipoferum, Clostridium pasteurianum, Rhodopseudomonas capsulata* and a few cyanobacteria) was as like to that of *Klebsiella pneumoniae.*

Regulation of Nitrogen-fixation Genes

The regulation of *nif* genes is rather complex. Ammonia and nitrogenous compounds (like nitrates and amino acids) inhibit the expression of nitrogenase activity. Excess of aeration in the culture medium also inhibits the expression of *nif-genes.* For induction of *nif-gems,* the presence of nitrogen is not necessary, because these genes can express themselves in cells cultivated in an argon atmosphere. In fact, the *nif-genes* expression is the result of a de-repression rather than that of an induction

Eady *et al.* (1978), Roberts *et al.* (1978) reported that all the products of *nif*-genes are not present in the cultures carried out in the presence of ammonia. When ammonia is added to a completely derepressed cultures, a rapid repression of the mj-phenotype occurs and nitrogenase activity as well as the enzymic proteins disappear within 45 minutes.

The presence of ammonia in the medium plays very important role in the synthesis of various biomolecules, e.g., in presence of ammonia, glutamine synthetase reacts with ATP and seems to lose the enzymic and regulatory functions of m/-genes.

The presence of oxygen in the culture medium represses the bio-syntheis of nitrogenase enzyme in *Klebsiella pneumonia.* Similar results have also been observed in aerobic and anaerobic bacteria. However, the mechanism of oxygen repression seems to be independent from that of ammonia in such microorganisms.

Molybdate does not have any direct effect on the regulation of b-nif-genes, however, molybdoprotein is probably involved in the regulation of at least one of the *Klebsiella nif operons (nif* YKDH). The presence of molybdenum transport and storage proteins is known in *Clostridium pasteurianum* and other diazotrophs.

Step I

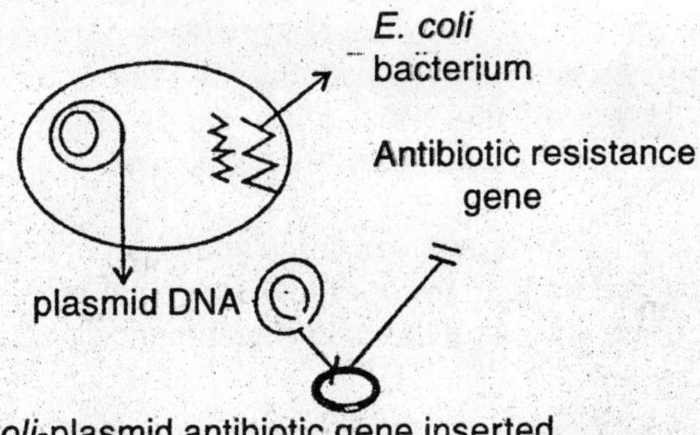

E. Coli-plasmid antibiotic gene inserted

Step II *E. Coli* bacterium ----- Soil bacterium

↓

Engineered *E. coli* plasmid is inserted into soil bacterium where it joins with the soil bacterium's plasmid

---

Step III

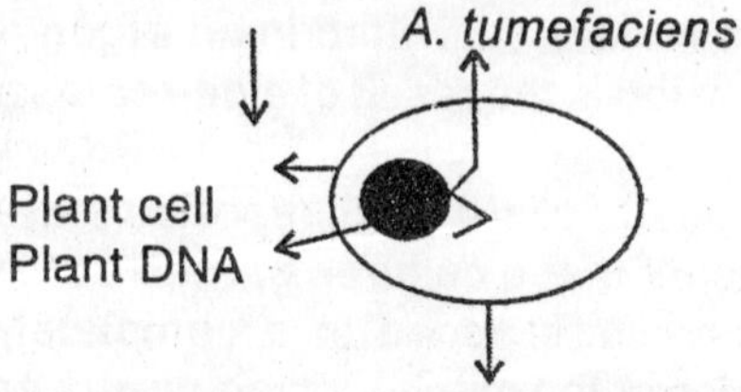

When the *A. tumefaciens* is mixed with plant cells, it inserts the DNA containing the new gene into the plant chromosome

↓

Genetically engineered plant cells with the antibiotic resistancd genes are able to grow on antibiotic medium

↓

Whole planlts are regenerated from the single cell

↓

Regenerated whole plant and its progeny carry the antibotic resistance trait

---

Fig. 8.11: Schematic presentation of plant genetic engineering with Ti plasmids from *Agrobacterium tumefaciens*.

It is now established, after number of current reports that the regulation of the nif-genes of *Klebsiella pneumoniae* is carried out by both *nifA* and *nif L* genes as well as by genes that are remote from the *nif* cluster *(gin* genes). However, there are other genes which are involved in the expression of *nif*-genes , they are as follows:

nar D = which is involved in molybdenum processing.
unc and *a* gene in his operon = which influence ATP supply.
nim gene = gene of the uncertain function near tip.

Genetics of Symbiotic Diazotrophs

Much works has been done on the fast growing nitrogen-fixing bacteria-*Rhizobium*. The genetic map of *Rhizobium* is now established. The studies reveal that *R.leguniosarum, R. phaseoli* and *R. trifolii* have very similar gene organization.

The genes for the component protein subunits of nitrogenase (molybdoferroprotein and ferroprotein) are formed by a single operon in *Rhizobium leguminisarum*. Similar situation has been reported in *Azatobactor vinelandii* and in *Klebsiella pneumoniae*.

TRANSFER OF *NIF-GENES* TO MICROORGANISMS

As mentioned earlier that nif-genes are not found in a free state but are clustered in one region (they are scattered throughout the bacterial DNA). Therefore, it is much easy to cut out the relavent stretch of DNA in a *Rhizobium* chromosome and insert the whole batch into another organism. The construction of self-transmissible plasmids (Ti-plasmids) bearing *nif*-genes made it possible to shift the nitrogen-fixing capacity to non-fixing species or to non-fixing mutant of diazotrophic species like *E. coli (E. coli* C-M74), *Salmonella typhimurium, Serratia marcescens, Pseudomonas flurescence,* and m/-mutant of *Azatobacter vinelandii.*

It is quite easy to transfer *nif-genes* from one species to another, or from one microbial genus to another under laboratory conditions. This may be done by three methods of gene-transfer: conjugation, transduction and transformation. Therefore, the transfer of *nif-genes* between the plasmid and bacterial chromosomes can take place under laboratory as well as under natural conditions.

TRANSFER OF *NIF*-GENES AND DEVELOPMENT OF NEW NITROGEN-FIXING PLANTS

It is easy to transfer grouped genes and the *nif-gene* cluster. Plant viruses could be used as vectors for this purpose. The cauliflower mosaic virus is a deoxyribovirus to which it is possible to join certain *nif-genes* which could become integrated into the plant genome or which could be transcribed into the plant cell at the same time as those of the virus when the latter's replication takes place.

Agrobacterium tumefaciens is a pathogenic bacterium, which contains a large plasmid, Ti and is responsible for the induction of tumours in plant tissues on the site of the infection by the bacterium. These plasmids are of 150 to 230 kilo bases and can able to develop tumours, therefore, they are called Ti or **tumour inducing plasmids.** Ti -plasmids are introduced by either transformation or by conjugation. The DNA of Ti-plasmids have two following regions:

1. The larger region contains information that makes it possible for the bacterium to catabolize derivatives of the basic amino acids, or opines, synthesized by the tumour cells.
2. It corresponds to the T-DNA and is incorporated into the genone of the plant cell. This T-DNA includes the ability of utilization of the latter as well the transformation of its metabolism in order to produce opines. The molecular weight of T-DNA is 15×10^6 daltons.

The development of tumours in plant tissue by Ti -plasmid *of Agrobacterium tumefaciens* is brougnt about by the transfer of a segment of bacterial DNA (from a prokaryotic) and its integration into the genome of eukaryotic cells. This introduction of Ti -plasmid was successfully made by Schell and his coworkers. Out of the seven genes of T-DNA of Ti - plasmid, they found that five of them are responsible for tumorization, that is in blocking cell differentiation. It is of interest to mention that *Agrobacterium tumefaciens* infects only dicotyledonous plants, however, it is not easy to introduce Ti plasmids into the cells of monocotyledonous plants like cereals.

Kemp (1981) used nucleic acid recombination and cloning techniques to transfer genes to plant cells. He has transferred genes for the bean protein-**phaseolin** to sunflower plants. This transfer was followed by the synthesis of mRNA of the storage protein in the sunflower cells, made tumoral by the T-DNA of *Agrobacterium tumefaciens,* which was used as a vector for the gene.

The development of plants, which can able to fix atmospheric nitrogen independently of symbiotic microbes remains a difficult and complex task. However, in the present situation, it is possible to develop and gain better knowledge of the factors that induce nitrogen-fixing symbiosis, with a view of improving their efficiency.

ESTIMATES OF NITROGEN FIXATION

Both direct and indirect methods have been employed to estimate nitrogen fixation associated with various non-legumes in pot culture and field studies. Direct methods include nitrogen balance studies and ^{15}N based techniques such as ^{15}N isotope dilution and ^{15}N incorporation while acetylene reduction assay (ARA) is the widely used indirect techniques.

^{15}N BASED METHODS

^{15}N isotope dilution technique provides the most accurate estimates of the contribution of biologically fixed nitrogen to the nitrogen nutrition of legumes and non-legumes alike. Nitrogen fixation associated with sugarcane, cereals and actinorhizal plants has been estimated by this technique with and without addition of inoculum.

Ventura and Watanabe (1983) reported that a substantial proportion of plant nitrogen (32-35%) was derived from associative fixation in uninoculated rice plants under flooded condition in the Philippines. Yoo *et al.* (1986) observed contribution of 11-19 per cent nitrogen by biological fixation when rice was inoculated with *Klebsiella oxytoca*. de Freitas *et al.* (1984) found that biological fixation contributed 22-26 per cent of plant nitrogen was derived from biological fixation in forage grasses. Biological fixation contributed 53 to 65 percent of plant nitrogen when *Casuarina equisetifolia* was inoculated with *Frankia* (Sougoufura *et al.,* 1990). Boddey *et al.* (1991) reported that certain sugarcane varieties were capable of obtaining upto 80 per cent plant nitrogen from biological fixation.

Nitrogen fixation associated with tropical grasses, sugarcane, rice and sorghum has also been estimated by ^{15}N incorporation technique.

NITROGEN BALANCE STUDIES

Non-symbiotic N_2 fixation to the extent of 18-20 kg N ha^{-1} $year^{-1}$ was reported from long-term nitrogen balance studies at Rothamsted, England (Jenkinson, 1977). Substantial positive balances for nitrogen have been reported in pot experiments with sorghum, pearl millet, finger millet and napier bajra at ICRISAT, Hyderabad (Dart and Wani, 1982). App *et al.* (1980) reported positive N_2 balance for flooded soils in pots planted to rice. There was relatively higher level of nitrogen fixation associated with grasses in the tropics when compared to that in temperate countries. Dobereiner *et al.* (1972) reported fixation of 90 kg N ha^{-1} $year^{-1}$ by *Paspalum notatum.* Substantial nitrogen contribution by *Azolla-Anabaena* associations, blue green algae and photosynthetic bacteria to the total nitrogen input of rice has also been reported (Venkataraman, 1975; Watanabe, 1981).

ACETYLENE REDUCTION ASSAY

This is a simple and sensitive assay for studying the nitrogenase activity of microbial cultures and plants in pot culture and field experiments. Nitrogenase activity has been reported in many grasses by the excised root assay when the roots were exposed to acetylene after pre-incubation for 8-18 h under reduced oxygen tension (Dobereiner and Day, 1975). Soil root cores removed from the field at harvest have also been used for measuring nitrogenase activity of both grasses and grain crops (Day *et al.*, 1975). Wani *et al.* (1984) developed a non-destructive intact plant assay for pot grown plants and it can also be used for screening tube-grown seedlings or bacterial strains in association with plants for their nitrogenase activity. The method has been well adapted for agronomic studies and plant breeding programmes on N_2 fixation in the field. Observations recorded in the IRRI have established that a quantity of nitrogen equal to 50 per cent of the nitrogen removed by the crop was fixed in the standard pot, planted with rice where blue-green algae were spontaneously growing. Alimango and Yoshida (1977) reported nitrogenase activity showing a fixation of 18-33 kg N_2 ha^{-1} in Alby province in the Philippines when assayed by ARA method. The ARA was attributed mostly to blue green algae and *Azolla* and no activity was observed when soil was covered with black cloth.

QUANTIFYING NITROGEN FIXATION IN NFSS

Quantifying nitrogen fixation by NFSs under field conditions is a very difficult and expensive task; a full description of the methods for evaluating biological N fixation is beyond the scope of this book. For such a discussion, readers should see Bergersen (1980) or Sprent and Sprent

Table 8.2: ^{15}N dilution estimates of N_2 fixation associated with various crops

Test Plant Species/cultivar	Test Plant Inoculum	Reference Plant Species/cultivar	Soil treatment	Percentage of plant N derived from fixation	References
Oryza sativa L. IR 42	Nil	*Oryza sativa* L. IR 42	U,C	32-35	Ventura and Watanabe, 1983
Oryza sativa C 5444	*Klebsiella oxytoca*	*Oryza sative* C 5444	H, C	11-19	Yoo *et al.*, 1986
Triticum aestivum L Fielder	*Azospirillum brasilense*	*Triticum aestivum* L Fielder	U	5-11	Kucey, 1988
Saccharum Sp. NA 5679, CB 4176	Nil	*Glycine max* (non-nodulating)	— —	22-26	de Freitas *et al.*, 1984
Sorghum sudanense	Nil	*Triticum aestivum* L. (Ticena 2)	—	16-39	Vose era/., 1982
Panicum maximum (11 ecotypes)	*A. lipoferum* + *A. brasilense* + *A. amazonense*	*Brachiaria radicans* (IRI442)	U	24-39	Miranda and Boddey, 1987

Reference Plants are not inoculated
U-unsterilised, H-heat sterilized, C-Covered with back lid
(Adopted from Chalk, 1991).

(1990). A number of methods are in use, but these methods for quantifying nitrogen fixation do influence the results as demonstrated by Sanginga *et al.* (1990b) in a study using leucaena and *Faidherbia albida*. The isotope dilution methods they used resulted in large negative estimates of nitrogen fixed by *F. albida,* while theymeasured positive values using the A value method.

Table 8.3: Estimated nitrogen fixation from grain and forage legumes

Species	Nitrogen fixation (kg/ha/yr)
Arachis hypogaea	60-80
Desmodium sp., *Lespedeza* sp.	100-400
Medicago sativa	100-300
Trifolium sp.	100-150
Vicia faba	240-325
Vigna unguiculata	85

Source: NAS, 1979

The most common method used for assessing nitrogen fixation is acetylene reduction, although this method actually measures nitrogenase activity, not nitrogen fixation. It has appeal as a tool because it is sensitive, simple and relatively inexpensive, but it has many potential sources of error. The primary limitations are related to the destructive and short-term nature of the method (Weaver and Frederick, 1982) and to the need to calibrate the rates of ethylene production with the actual rates of N_2 fixation (Peoples *et al.*, 1988). Despite the constraints of using acetylene reduction, it is still a useful tool for evaluating the relative effects of short-term treatment on N_2 fixation and for screening purposes.

Table 8.4: Advantages and limitations of methods for estimating N_2 fixation by legumes in the field

Advantage	Limitations
Acetylene reduction method	
Relatively inexpensive Simple Rapid Very sensitive	Indirect (must establish conversion factor for N_2 fixation, which may vary) Nitrogenase activity possibly inhibited by acetylene Short-term estimate Considerable error possible due to incomplete recovery or damage of nodules unless using an in situ assay

N-solute method	
Inexpensive Simple Analyses done by simple colorimetric assays Need not be totally destructive May be done on an individual plant basis Assesses plant dependence on atmospheric N_2 and soil N	Indirect (must establish calibration with plant N_2-fixing status) Cannot be used for interspecific comparisons without calibrating each species Calibrations possibly influenced by development stage of some species Cannot be used on some amide-producers Short-term estimate
N difference method	
Direct Relatively simple Adjusts for soil-derived N	Requires suitable non N_2-fixing reference plant Same amount of soil N must be absorbed by legume and reference plant
Isotope dilution techniques	
Direct Can get time-integrated estimate of percentage N fixed	Requires suitable non-N_2-fixing reference Plant
^{15}N enrichment method	
Potentially accurate	Expensive Requires addition of ^{15}N-labeled compound Critical that legume and reference plant absorb the same relative amounts of soil N and added N Change in ^{15}N level of plant available soil N possible with change in depth and time Reference plant must derive all its N from soil
Natural ^{15}N abundance method	
Additional N not requires Concentration of 15N in plant-available Soil N relatively constant with depth and time	Relatively expensive Insensitive if amount of ^{15}N in soil nears amount of ^{15}N in air Large field variability possible in some cases May have to allow for isotopic fractionation

Adapted from: Ledgard and Peoples, 1987.

N-difference or isotope dilution methods are more costly, but they can provide accurate time-averaged estimates of the proportion of plant N derived from N_2 fixation. It must be noted that while these methods have been successfully used with herbaceous plants or in pot studies with tree seedlings, their application in field studies of NFSs is still limited due to complexity, cost and (or) methodological problems.

It is clear that the choice of methods is restricted by financial, technical and environmental constraints and that methods need to be selected in relation to overall research objectives.

QUANTITIES OF NITROGEN FIXED

Estimates of how much nitrogen NFS species fix vary greatly due to differences in methods used, the conditions under which the trees are growing at the time of the measurement and the degree to which sample data are extrapolated. Thus estimates of the amount of N fixed, such as those included, should be taken with great caution. Some authors have argued that actual N fixation rates can be very low, that is, less than 2 kg N/ha/year (Roughley, 1987), although this estimate was for acacias in arid areas where low rates of N fixation generally are expected. Yet the studies that used the most reliable methods still suggest that annual rates of 50 kg N/ha to 200 kg N/ha are not un-reasonable and are in the same range as values reported for a number of herbaceous legumes.

These values should only be used as a very approximate estimate of the quantities of nitrogen fixed by species. The influences on N fixation noted in previous sections and the differences in assessment methods limit the use of these values for any kind of extrapolation or generalization.

FACTORS INFLUENCING BIOLOGICAL NITROGEN FIXATION

The factors that affect nodulation in the field have been extensively studied for agricultural crops but have been little studied for NFSs. Nevertheless, it appears from a number of studies that there are fundamental similarities between NFSs and herbaceous legumes with respect to rhizobial relations. Since symbiotic biological nitrogen fixation is a product of both the host plant and rhizobia or *Frankia,* factors that influence growth and survival of both the host plant and microbial symbiont are important.

Tree growth is dependent upon interactions between genetic potentials and the environment in which the tree grows. Environmental influences such as radiation, temperature, water, nutrient availability, wind, competition, pollution, fire and allelopathy are compounded by biotic influences such as insects and disease and the influence of man. Each of these factors in turn involves its own set of complex interactions. For example, radiation is an important factor in plant growth, but the extent to which radiation influences growth is dependent upon light intensity and quality plus the shade tolerance of the tree and the management of competition and leaf area. In many cases, experimental results do not provide clear pictures of specific environmental influences on plant vigor or nitrogen fixation.

Simply stated, symbiotic nitrogen fixation probably is limited by any factor that reduces tree vigor and health. Fixation of nitrogen is limited by the biological yield of the host plant even if a suitable symbiont (i.e., *Rhizobium* or *Frankia)* and appropriate soils are present because the host plant is both the source of energy for the symbiont and the sink for the fixed nitrogen (App *et al.*, 1980). Dawson and Gordon (1979) demonstrated the influence of photosynthesis, as reflected by leaf area, on nitrogen fixation in *Alnus glutinosa*. Similar effects of the supply of photosynthate on nitrogen fixation have been found for alder and peas (Wheeler and Lawrie, 1976). Many examples are cited in the next section of how nitrogen fixation can be affected, often by influencing both tree and symbiont. Most of what is known about environmental influences on nodulation comes from research on herbaceous crops. Much of this work has focused on the effects of single factors (*e.g.*, combined nitrogen or temperature); very little has been reported on the effects of multiple factors.

An effective symbiotic association between *Rhizobium* and *legume* can provide most of the nitrogen (N) required for the growth and productivity of the host plant. However, for this to be true, the legume host must be efficiently nodulated by its homologous *Rhizobium.* Inoculant strains/native *Rhizobium* must be capable of survival as saprophytes in soil and be able to compete with other *rhizobia* in soil for nodulation sites. Further, as plants must develop *rhizosphere* to support *rhizobial* growth and also nodules to house the invading *rhizobia,* it is prudent to assume that any factor that adversely affects plant growth will also cause competition for nodulation. Environmental and biological factors that influence biological nitrogen fixation are discussed here.

Biological Factors

Antagonistic interactions exerted by the soil microbial population against *Rhizobium* have much to do with the degree of resistance achieved by different strains *of Rhizobium. Rhizobium japonicum* USDA 123 declined 1000-fold during first five days of incubation in a non-sterile Miamian soil (Vidor and Miller, 1980). The authors established a direct relationship between the population decline of this strain and the simultaneous population increase of lytic organism, probably a bacteriophage. Similarly, Chatel and Parker (1973 b) reported that a number of problems encountered with pasture establishment in Australia could be explained by anatagonistic interactions between *Rhizobium* and other soil micro-organisms. Specifically, they showed that the second year clover mortality problem in western Australia was due to such an interaction (Chatel and Parker, 1973 a).

Schwinghamer and Brockwell (1978) showed that lysogenic strains of *R. trifalii* grown in sterile broth and peat culture strongly suppressed the growth of sensitive strains. In other studies it was found that the addition of virulent bacteriophages to paired strains of *R. thfolii* decreased the numbers of sensitive strains on the roots of clover plans white resistant strains were favoured for nodulation (Evans *et al,* 1979; Barnet, 1980). There are many reports of pleiotrophic effects on symbiotic ability due to phage resistance or sensitivity. This influence may be due to the fact that there is a common site of interaction between phage and bacterium and between bacterium and plant, possibly the lipopolysaccharide.

It is difficult, however, to extrapolate field responses from laboratory studies on antagonistic effects of bacteriophages. In the field, phage *Rhizobium* interactions might be altered by clay particles or organic matter, which could reduce or eliminate antagonistic effects (Roper and Marshall, 1978). Field studies on the role of bacteriophages in persistence and competition of *Rhizobium* in the soil are inconclusive. Bacteriophages that were active against commercial inoculants of *R. trifolii* were isolated from clover fields in New Zealand. Resistant and partially resistant *Rhizobium* strains were isolated from these fields. In other field studies no correlation was found between the number of *R. trifolii* and the number of bacteriophages capable of infecting this species (Lawson and Barnet, 1984). Inoculation of soil with bacteriophages did not affect the total number of *rhizobia* or the number of nodules formed.

Bacteriocinogeny is the ability of a bacterium to produce bacteriocins, with antibacterial action towards other similar bacteria (Schwinghamer, 1971). Bacteriocin producing strains are common among *Rhizobiaceae.* Two groups of bacteriocins are recognised in *Rhizobium:* (a) low-molecular weight non-phage like substances that diffusion readily in agar and (b) less diffusible high molecular weight phage like compound. Two types of bacteriocins, small and medium (according to lysis zone) were found in field isolates of *R. legwninosarum.* The genes encoding medium bacteriocin production were present on large plasmids, one of which also carried *nod* genes. Recently, Brahmaprakash and Hegde (1990) reported bacteriocin nogeny amongst redgram *rhizobia.*

Bacteriocinogenic strains of *R. trifolii* suppress the growth of sensitive strains in liquid culture. Hodgson *et al.* (1985) demonstrated the advantage of using a mixed inoculant of highly effective strains (bacteriocin resistant) and a bacteriocinogenic strain. When a bacteriocin resistant strain and a sensitive strain were used to inoculate *Trifolium* in glass tubes, the bacteriocin resistant strain formed less than 10 per cent of nodules. When a bacteriocin producing strain was added to the mixed inoculant the resistant strains formed 75 per cent of-the nodules. The results were similar when the experiment was repeated in unsterile soil containing a population of bacteriocin sensitive ineffective population of *R. trifolii.* Use of bacteriocinogenic strains in the inoculant increased the proportion of nodules formed by the bacteriocin resistant effective strain. Schwinghamer and Belkengren (1968) described a *R. legwninosarum* bv. *trifolii.* They suggested that the basis for the nodulation competitiveness of T 24 could be its ability to produce anti-rhizobial compounds. Triplett and Barta (1987) have shown by transposon mutagenesis that the symbiotic competitiveness expressed by T 24 includes expression of two phenotypes, nodulation as well as trifolitoxin production. Both nodulation and trifolitoxin production are necessary for nodulation competitiveness because mutants defective in either of the properties could not inhibit nodulation by an effective trifolitoxin sensitive strain in a mixed culture.

Legumes commonly interact with the fungi belonging to the four genera *viz., Acaulospora, Gigaspora, Glomus* and Sclerocytis to produce vesicular-arbuscular mycorrhizal (VAM) associations. VAM are obligate symbionts that provide usable phosphates to the plant in return for fixed carbon. The *legume-Rhizobium VAM;* tripartite association is more efficient than the association of any two of these alone.

Oxygen

An abundant supply of oxygen is necessary for the formation and functioning of nodules, primarily to ensure adequate respiration of the root and nodule tissue, McConnell (1959) determined that nodule formation and nitrogen fixation in *Alnus glutinosa* are considerably reduced at oxygen levels below 0.21 atmospheres. This is consistent with results obtained for soybeans and clover.

The oxygen level in soil usually is less than 20 per cent (in part due to high CO_2 concentrations resulting from respiration) and in heavy clay sols can be much less, presenting an important limitation to nodule formation and N fixation. The failure of plants to nodulate in water or in waterlogged soils can be attributed to the lack of oxygen (Lie, 1974). Periods of excessive water supply also can cause a temporary reduction in nitrogen fixation since even a thin layer of water surrounding the nodule will reduce the supply of oxygen. Poorly aerated soils also cannot nitrify ammonium. Under these conditions, the lack of nitrate from nitrification and nitrogen fixation can cause severe nitrogen stress.

Water stress

Soil moisture can be limiting, both when too low or too high. Experiments with alfalfa, soybean and *Acacia mellifera* have shown that the optimum level of soil moisture for N fixation is approximately 60 per cent to 75 per cent of soil water-holding capacity (Fred et at,-1932; Habish, 1976). Moisture contents above or below this level can adversely affect the number of nodules formed and their longevity. Huang *et al.* (1975) demonstrated that nitrogen fixation can be reduced indirectly by the effects of moisture stress on photosynthesis.

Sprent demonstrated the detrimental effects of water stress on the number of nodules, nodule activity and average nodule weight (Table 6.5) She also showed that acetylene-reducing activity declined by 90 per cent in stressed plants (Sprent, 1976). Under moisture stress conditions, the wilting of lower leaves is usually a good indicator that nodules are operating at suboptimal rates (Sprent, 1972). Under conditions of moisture stress in sandy soils, nodulation in NFSs may occur deeper in the soil (Beadle, 1964).

Table 8.5: Effect of moisture stress on 44-day-old *Phaseolus vulgaris* plants inoculated with two strains of *Rhizobium*.

	Rhizobium strain			
	3601		3605	
	Control	Stressed	Control	Stressed
Pmoles C_2H_4/mg/min	16.45	1.75	37.45	3.15
Nodule number	28.4	8.3	18.50	4.5
Average nodule wt (mg)	1.44	0.95	1.72	1.16
Water content of sand (%DW)	6.54	0.71	6.34	0.81

Source: Sprent, 1976.

Waterlogging also can depress nitrogen fixation, primarily due to oxygen deficiency, although there is large variation among species. The NFS *Alnus glutinosa* growing on permanently waterlogged soils has been found to nodulate primarily in the well-aerated, humid, upper soil horizons, but not on permanently submerged roots (Akkermans and Van Dijk, 1976). In a study of *Sesbania sesban* and *S. rostrata*, Ndoye *et al.* (1990) demonstrated a decrease in the amount of N_2 fixed per plant for *S. sesban*, but not for the stem-nodulated *S. rostrata* when both were grown under waterlogged conditions.

Temperature

The effects of temperature on N fixation in NFSs have not been well studied, but its effects on herbaceous legumes suggest that species differences, plant age and environmental factors influences the degree to which temperature affects N fixation (Gibson, 1976). In the field, temperature effects may be most closely related to development of the host plant. Fyson and Sprent (1982) found that nitrogenase activity began at about the same physiological stage for *Viciafaba* plants grown at two different temperatures.

Different strains of *Rhizobium* also may respond differently to temperature variations. Workign with several tropical grain legumes, Dart *et al.* (1976) reported little difference in nitrogen fixation between strains at 21°C, but found significant differences at air temperatures of 27°C and 33°C.

Perry *et al.* (1979) demonstrate the effect of temperature on two non-legume NFSs, *Alnus rubra* and *Cytisus scoparius.* Optimum temperature for nitrogenase activity for *C. scoparius* was approximately 22°C, while the optimum for *A. rubra* was approximately 35°C. At temperatures of 11°C and 21°C, seedlings of the sub-alpine species *Alnus viridis* fixed significantly more N at the higher temperature (Benecke, 1970). Since growth rates were significantly lower at the lower temperature, however, the total accumulated plant nitrogen as a percentage of total plant growth was greater at the lower temperature. In this case, nitrogen fixation was not the factor limiting plant growth at lower root temperatures.

Age

The age of host NFSs also influences nodulation and nitrogen fixation, but the extent of this influence on NFSs has not been thoroughly studied. Rates of N fixation in *Alnus rubra* from greenhouse and field studies suggest that seedlings can fix as much as 100 kg N/ha during the first year of growth and over 200 kg N/ha/yr in 30-year-old stands (Zavitkovski and Newton, 1968). Sprent (1983) hypothesized a substantial decrease in the amount of N fixed per unit of biomass as trees become older, with an increase in total N fixed per unit area. However, the few studies over time on N fixation in NFSs indicate this may not be entirely correct. In studies of growth and nodulation of *Alnus glutinosa,* Akkermans and van Dijk (1976) concluded that both N fixation and weight of dry nodules per tree increased over time. While this study does not provide biomass data, using reasonable biomass values for 7-and 18-year-old trees (the approximate ages evaluated) and rates on N fixation at those ages, the rates of fixation per unit of biomass do not likely decline.

pH and soil nutrients

Low soil pH generally inhibits nitrogen fixation by reducing the development of *rhizobia*, increasing the numbers of ineffective *rhizobia* or disrupting the infection process (Sprent and Sprent, 1990; Mengel and Shubert, 1988). Low-pH soils canbe low in phosphorus, calcium, magnesium and molybdenum and may have toxic levels of aluminum and manganese, all of which can affect NFS vigor and health. Plants that depend on nitrogen fixation have been found to be more sensitive to pH than plants of the same species supplied with mineral nitrogen

(Andrews, 1976). In general, the critical pH for nodulation of most legumes is above pH 4.5 to 5.5 (Dixon and Wheeler, 1983).

Table 8.6 demonstrated the negative influence of low pH on nodulation, nitrogen fixation and plant growth of several non-leguminous NFSs. Bond (1951b) found that the symbiont of the nonlegume *Myrica gale* was substantially better suited to acid conditions than many legume symbionts, with nodulation occurring at a pH as low as 3.3. In this study, seedlings fertilized with nitrate N showed the best growth at pH 3.3. indicating that poor growth of seedlings at this pH was due to difficulties in nodule formation, not due to the inability of the plant to grow under such strongly acid conditions. Griffiths and McCormick (1984) found nodulation of the non-legume *Alnus glutinosa* was reduced below pH 5.5.

Table 8.6: Influence of age on nitrogen fixed and nodule weight in *Alnus glutinosa*. (Adapted from : Akkermans and van Dijk, 1976)

Species	Nodulation	N fixation and plant growth
Myrica gale	poor at 3.3 good at 5.4-6.3	best at 5.4
Alnus glutinosa	*zero* at 3.3	best at 4.2-5.4
Casuahnas cunninghamiana	zero to poor at 4-5 good at 6-7	best at 6-7
Hippophae rhamnoides	*zero* to poor at 4.2 best at 5.4-7.0	best at 5.4-7.0
Shepherdia Canadensis	zero at 5.0 best at 6.0	
Coriaria myrtifolia	*zero* to poor at 5.0 best at 6-9	best at 7-9

Adapted from: Wheeler and McLaughlin, 1979.

Ahmad and Ng (1981) reported on dramatically reduced leucaena growth with lower pH, total soil nitrogen and concentrations of *Rhizobium*. Given the low concentration of *rhizobia* present in the soil at lower pH levels, it appears that differences in pH had the greatest influence on plant growth by reducing the number of *rhizobia*. Umali-Garcia (1988) found that liming of acid soils to reduce the pH to 6.5 improved the performance of the symbiosis in *Acacia mangium*.

In southern Vietnam, *Acacia auriculiformis* grown in acid sulfate soils of pH less than 4.0 nodulated profusely in the undecomposed litter layer (Oi horizon), but not in the highly acid mineral soil (MacDicken, 1991b). This demonstrates the ability of the symbiosis to adapt to strongly acid soils where effective nodulation would not be possible in the mineral soil.

A similar example is the stem-nodulating green manure species *Sesbania rostrata*. Stem nodules are less affected by flooding and combined nitrogen than root nodules (Rinaudo *et al.*, 1988).

Nitrogen-fixing plants need the same nutrients as other green plants, but they may need additional quantities of cobalt, iron and mylybdenum to produce leghemoglobin and nitrogenase (Sprent and Spreng, 1990; Becking, 1976). The availability of each of these micronutrients is pH-dependent. Molybdenum availability is lowest in acid soil, while the availability of iron and cobalt is lowest in strongly alkaline soils.

In a pot study of inoculated seedlings of *Acacia dealbata,* the omission of P, K or Ca from the nutrient solution reduced specific nitrogenase activity (Chau *et al.*, 1986). Reinsvold and Pope (1987) found that increased P applications increased nodule number, weight, shoot height, above-ground biomass and acetylene reduction activity in inoculated *Robinia pseudoacacia.*

Combined soil N

The inhibitory effects of combined soil nitrogen on the nitrogen fixation process have been recognized for over 100 years (Wilson, 1940). Legumes, for example, do not fix enough N to obtain maximum growth response and therefore require soil nitrogen. Yet high levels of combined soil N may reduce nodulation and nodule activity and accelerate senescence. The levels that inhibit N fixation are not necessarily the same for different rhizobial strains (Murphy, 1988), NFS species (George and Singleton, 1989) or clones of the same species (MacKay *et al.*, 1987).

The inhibitory effects of high levels of combined N reported for herbaceous legumes also have been reported for both legume and nonlegume NFSs. Zhang *et al.* (1990) found a marked decrease in the nodulation rate of *Casuarina cunninghamiana* seedlings as soil N increased. Soil nitrogen in excess of 10 ppm had the greatest effect in reducing the nodulation rate. Zavitkovski and Newton (1968) estimated the relative proportions of fixed and combined soil N at different levels of total soil N with *Alnus rubra*. Reductions of 35 per cent to 45 per cent in number of weight of *Gliricidia sepium* nodules studies (Umali-Garcia, 1990). In the same study, *Acacia auriculiformis* and *Paraserianthes falcataria* showed no negative response to those levels of nitrogen application, but they had virtually no nodulation at 300 kg N/ha.

The response of NFSs, particularly young seedlings, to combined soil N is critical to nursery management of nitrogen fixation. For some species, starter N in nursery soils is detrimental to N fixation and growth. In the case of *Alnus viridis,* seedlings grown under soil N levels of 0, 5, 25, 50 and 100 ppm exhibited maximum growth with no nitrate N added

(Benecke, 1970). Nodulated seedlings with no N performed better than un-nodulated plans at any level of added nitrogen. However, Hill (1970) found that *Leucaena leucocephala* harvested 10 weeks after planting gave a positive response to applications of 33 kg N/ha and 66 kg N/ha. Plants in both the fertilized and unfertilized plots were well nodulated with pink nodules. The response of seedlings to combined soil N is likely dependent on how rapidly the seedlings nodulate - the longer the period before N fixation begins, the greater the response to applied N or higher levels of combined soil nitrogen.

There also may be differences in response to combined N among clones or varieties of the same species. MacKay *et al.* (1987) demonstrated a difference in relative performance of two *Alnus glutinoa* clones propagated through in vitro methods. Nitrogen treatments containing from 0.10 mg N/g to 0.68 mg N/g in dry substrate stimulated N fixation and plantlet growth, but one clone (AG-8) was more dependant upon combined N than the other (AG-4). Varietal or clonal differences may be important in determining the amount of starter N to supply under nursery conditions.

Salinity

Saline conditions can depress N fixation through osmotic withdrawal of moisture from nodules, reductions in bacterial colonization of roots and root hair curling. This depression can be due to a lack of adaptation to saline conditions by either the tree or symbiont. In fact, there is tremendous variation in the response of trees and *Rhizobium* to saline soils. NFS species such as *Prosopis tamarugo* survive and fix nitrogen in extremely saline soils where other NFSs or symbiont strains would not survive.

There are likely to be important interactions between tree and symbiont. For example, Sprent and Zahran (1988) found a host cultivar *x rhizobial* strain interaction in response to salinity in *Vicia faba.* Balla *et al.* (1990) demonstrated the suitability of salt-tolerant *Rhizobium* strains in an experiment using 57 strains of *Rhizobium* and several NFS species. Salt-tolerant strains showed better survival, nodulation and nitrogen fixation than salt-sensitive strains under saline conditions. A strain from each of four NFSs, *Acacia nilotica, Dalbergia sissoo, Leucaena leucocephala* and *Prosopis juliflora,* was tested, and all were found to be highly tolerant to saline conditions (9-12 dS/m).

Lack of suitable bacteria

The presence of suitable *rhizobia* or *Frankia* is essential to nitrogen fixation without them symbiotic biological nitrogen fixation cannot occur. In fields that have not been successfully planted to a given NFS, it is likely that the introduction of suitable bacterial through inoculation will be beneficial. It is important to note that to establish an *effective* symbiosis between NFSs and bacteria, the bacteria must be able to survive in the soil environment of the planting site and be able to fix nitrogen under those conditions. The bacteria must be able to compete with other microbes for nutrients and with other *rhizobia* or *Frankia* for infection sites. Some species of NFSs are very specific in their requirements for *rhizobial* strains, for example, *Acacia mangium;* others are nodulated by several strains of *rhizobia*, for example, *Albizia lebbeck* (Turk and Keyser, 1992).

The genus *Rhizobium* includes fast-growing *rhizobia* that produce acid on yeast mannitol agar and are most often of temperate origin (Wheeler *et al.,* 1991). The three species in this genus are: R *leguminosarum, R. meliloti* and *R. loti.* The genus *Brady rhizobium* contains slow-growing bacteria that do not produce acid on yeast mannitol agar. Bacteria of this genus commonly ? infect tropical legumes, although numerous exceptions make this a loose generalization.

Competition between strains of *rhizobia* can result in reduced or delayed nodulation (Lie *et al,* 1988). The presence of both nodulating and non-nodulating *rhizobial* strains in the rooting zone can result in infection sites being taken by non-nodulating bacteria, preventing or reducing the establishment of an effective symbiosis.

The persistence of introduced *Rhizobium* strains also can affect the amount of nitrogen fixed. In a study of labeled *Rhizobium* and *L. leucocephala,* South (1982) found that at the time of transplanting 46 per cent to 97 per cent of nodules contained the labeled *Rhizobium,* while 10 weeks later 4 per cent or less contained the labeled *Rhizobium.* In this case, the indigenous *Rhizobium* was a better competitor than the inoculated strain for infection sites on the roots.

Sanginga *et al.* (1989) found substantial differences in the amount of N fixed by *L. leucocephala* inoculated with two different strains of *Rhizobium.* Strain IRc 1050 fixed 98 kg/ha in 6 months while strain IRc 1045 fixed 134 kg/ha (estimated by the ^{15}N dilution method). Clearly, the type of bacteria present can directly affect the amount of nitrogen fixed by NFSs. There is also some evidence, however, that ineffective symbiont strains can enhance plant growth when they are present with effective strains. Hahn *et al.* (1990) found that *Alnus gludnosa* seedlings inoculated simultaneously with effective and ineffective *Frankia* strains had greater total dry weight and height than those without the dual inoculation.

RECOVERING FROM STRESS

Symbiotic nitrogen fixation can be affected by a wide range of environmental stressed, but it is clear that many of these effects are both extremely complex and temporary. The direct cause of reduction in N fixation appears to be a reduction in the supply of photosynthate to the nodules. Resumption of higher N fixation levels is dependent upon the ability of the plant to resume production and transport of photosynthate. Gibson (1976) found that the symbiotic system can make a rapid recovery from various stressed such as temperature, light, defoliation and high levels of combined nitrogen. But Wheeler and McLaughlin (1979) found that nitrogen fixation, at least in *Alnus glutinosa,* takes longer to recover from stress than other host plant physiological processes. Numerous examples of N fixation resuming after the removal of stress can be cited for temperature, moisture stress defoliation and salinity (1970).

NITROGEN FIXATION RESEARCH IN INDIA

The word on bio-chemistry of nitrogen fixation has mainly been done at Haryana Agriculture University, Indian Agriculture Research Institute, Punjab Agriculture University and BARC. At HAU, a pathway for ureide biogenesis in nodules of pigeonpea has been proposed. The further metabolism of ureides in aerial parts particularly leaves and developing pods has also been worked out. Detailed bio-chemical and physiological studies explaining nodule senescence have also been carried out at IARI. Attempts have been made to understand the regulation of uptake hydrogenase so as to reduce the energy cost of biological nitrogen fixation. In addition, studies are concentrated on increasing nitrogen fixing efficiency by insertion of uptake hydrogenase genes or by increasing nitrogenase activity in nodules. At BARC, early interactions in legume-*Rhizobium* symbiosis have been investigated, according to which, host-induced alterations of capsular polysaccharides and de novo synthesis of specific proteins by both the partners in response to each other, appear to be among the first steps in the series of signal response interactions. At PAU, the role of extracellular invertase of *Rhizobium* in free sugar metabolism in developing root nodules of legumes has been ascertained.

The activity of nodule is also controlled by nitrogenase enzyme. This enzyme is about 75 per cent efficient. This is because, when soil aeration is poor and nitrogen availability is limited, electrons instead of being used to reduce nitrogen, now combine with protons forming hydrogen. As a result, nodules evolve hydrogen instead of fixing nitrogen. This is a wasteful process. Sufficient progress is being made to identify strains of *Rhizobia* which evolve less hydrogen and fix more nitrogen.

The most ideal situation would be the one in which the higher plant is able to fix nitrogen without the help of the bacteria. Towards this end, attempts' have been made to transfer nitrogen fixing genes (nif-genes) to higher plants from *Rhizobium.* However, it appears to be a long way before it is achieved.

In India, intensive forest cultivation of nitrogen fixing trees, with consequent short rotation is needed. This will require replacement of nitrogen reserves at a greater rate than the present secondary succession leading to old-growth forests. With the increased use of trees, genetically selected, it will be necessary to maximize the potential for biological nitrogen fixation in future forest management, so as to maintain the long term productivity of forest lands without significantly accelerating the rate of nutrient depletion. India is in urgent need of additional professional training and better transfer of technology in this context. Further, improved strains and new species of nitrogen-fixing microorganisms should be investigated/developed in order to reduce the use of chemical fertilizers in the fields.

9

Biological Mobilization of Phosphorus

Phosphorus, the master key element is known to be involved in a plethora of functions in the plant growth and metabolism. The cellular machinery is difficult to be imagined without phosphorus being involved in its metabolic continuity and even perpetuation. Such key functions include cell division and development, photosynthesis, breakdown of sugar, energy transfer, nutrient transfer within the plant and expression. Phosphorus nutrition benefits the plants by producing deeper and abundant roots. So the supply of this element to plant is essential for achieving optimum crop yield. It is supplied through phosphatic fertilizers, animal manures, plant take up their phospho-organic as the primary orthophosphate ion, $H_2PO_4^-$. The secondary orthophosphate ions, HPO_2^{2-} is also believed to be absorbed by plant roots in small quantities.

The P content in average soil is about 0.05 per cent (w/w). The variation being largely due *to* differences in weathering intensity and parent material composition. Relatively high concentrations are often observed in calcareous soils of arid region whereas relatively low P concentrations are often observed in soil subjected to high weathering intensity. But only 0.1 per cent of the total P is available to plants because of its low solubility and its fixation in soil. Thus the soil is rich in phosphorus which needs to be harnessed. Under these circumstances, microorganisms offers of biological system having evolved the mineral phosphate solubilizing trait(s) to acquire sufficient phosphorus.

FORMS OF P AVAILABLE IN SOIL

In soil P exists chiefly as orthophosphate although phosphine and phosphonates have been detected under some conditions. The diverse soil P forms can generally be categorized as soil solution P, insoluble inorganic P or insoluble organic P. Only a very small fraction of soil P exist in soil solution because of its extreme reactivity. Inorganic P in solution exists mainly as primary or secondary orthophosphate depending on soil pH. Organic P may also make up a large fraction of soluble P as much as 50 per cent in soils within higher organic matter content. The main groups of organic compounds in soil include phospholipid, nucleic acids and phytin. It occurs in humified organic matter, organic residues and microbial biomass that accounts for

2-80 per cent of the P content of surface soil. Inorganic P associated with the solid phase is sorbed to the surfaces of soil constituents or occur in calcium, iron, aluminium and silicate minerals. Calcium phosphate tends to accumulate in neutral to alkaline pH whereas FeP and AIP tend to accumulate in acidic soil.

P AVAILABILITY ISSUE

In agricultural systems, P fertilizers are routinely applied to promote crop yields. The P in these fertilizers is initially available to the plant but it rapidly reacts with soil and becomes progressively less available for plant uptake (as often as much as 90%). This is known as *chemical fixation* of phosphorus. Hence the current trend throughout the world is to explore the possibility of using alternate nutrient sources for increasing the efficiency of chemical fertilizers. Since phosphorus availability from the phosphatic reserves i.e. rock phosphate under neutral and alkaline soil condition is very low or negligible, the phosphate solubilizing microorganisms dissolving interlocked phosphates appear to have an important implication in Indian Agriculture.

Table 9.1: List of some important phosphate solubilizing fungi and cyanobacteria

FUNGI	
Alernaria sp..	Humicola inoslens
Aspergillus sp.	*H. lanuginose*
A. awamori	*Mucor meihii*
A. canidus	*Myrothecium roridum*
A. carbonum	*Oidiodendron* sp.
A. flavus	*Paecilomyces fusisporus*
A. foetidus	*Prnivillium* sp.
A. fumigatus	*P- balaji*
A. nidulans	*P. digitatum*
A. niger	*P. funiculosum*
A. terreus	*Rhizoctonia solani*
A. wentii	*Rhizopus* sp.
Cephalosporium sp.	*Sclerotium rolfsii*
Chaetomium sp.	*Trihoderma* sp.
C. globosum	*Trichurus spiralis*
Cladosoprium sp.	*Torula thermophila*
C. sphaerospermum	**CYANOBACTERIA**
Curvularia sp.	*Anabaena* sp.
C. lunata	*Calothrix braunii*
Cyathusafricanus	*Nostoc* sp.
Cylindrocarpon otusisporum	*Scytonema* sp.
Fusarium sp.	*Tolpothrix ceylonica*
Helminthosporium sp.	

Besides fertilization, the availability of P can be achieved by two pathway: (a) the enzymatic decomposition of organic P compound and inorganic P compound, (b) the non-enzymatic solubilization of different rock phosphates and inorganic phosphorus sources.

Many fungi, bacteria, actinomycetes and cyanobacteria are potential solubilizers of bound phosphates in soil. A list of P solubilizers are given in Table 9.1.

Phosphate solubilizing microorganisms are found in all soils but their number vary with soil climate as well as history. The potentially of different PSMs vary with different P-sources. The solubilization is not restricted to calcium salts, Fe, Al, Mg and Mn and other phosphates are also acted upon. However, calcium phosphate dissolving microorganisms are found in large number as compared to other phosphates. PSMs have been isolated from the rhizosphere of various crops, legume root nodules and compos. Fungi are reported to be the efficient P-solubilizers as compared to bacteria, actinomycetes and cyanobacteria.

Mode of Action of PSMs

Primarily there are two schools following of thought interpreting the mechanism of P-solubilization by microorganisms.

1. Solubilization by production of organic acid.
2. Solubilization by action of phosphatase enzymes.

PSM include various bacterial, fungal and actinomycetes forms which help to convert insoluble/phosphate into simple and soluble forms. Species of *Pseudomonas, Micrococcus, Bacillus, Flavobacterium, Penicillum, Fusarium, Sclerotium* and *Aspergillus* are some of the PSM. Among these, soil bacteria belonging to the genera *Pseudomonas* and *Bacillus* and fungi belonging to the genera *Penicillium* and *Aspergillus* are more common. The solubilization effect of PSM is generally due to the production of organic acids by these organisms. They are also known to produce amino acids, vitamins, growth promoting substances like Indole Acetic Acid (IAA) and Gibberalic Acid (GA) which help in better growth of plants.

ORGANIC ACIDS AND P SOLUBILIZATION

The major microbiological means by which insoluble phosphorus compounds are mobilized is by the production of organic acid which is accompanied by the acidification of the medium. The organic and inorganic acids convert tricalcium phosphates to the di- and monobasic phosphates with the net result of an enhanced availability of the element to the plant. The type of organic acid produced and their amounts differ with different microorganism. Tri- and di-carboxylic acids are more effective as compared to mono basic and aromatic acids. Aliphatic acids are also found to be more effective in P solubilization than phenolic acids and citric acid and fumaric acid has highest P-solubilizing ability. The analysis of culture filtrates of PSMs has shown the presence of a number of organic acids including citric fumaric, malic, lactic, 2-ketogluconic, gluconic, glyoxylic and a-ketobutyric.

The extent of P-solubilization also depends on the accessory minerals present in rock phosphate. The solubilized phosphate may react with Ca and Mg present in rock phosphate as soon as pH of the growth medium increases. Presence of free carbonates in rock phosphates also reduces the extent of solubilization as a large part of organic acids is directed towards neutralization of free carbonates.

Enzymes and P-solubilization

The liberation of P from organic phosphate compounds is mainly due to the action of enzymes of esterase type. PSM along with acid production, produces the phosphatase enzyme which cause the solubilization of P in aquatic environment. Besides these two mechanisms the production of chelating substances, H_2S, CO_2, mineral acids, siderophores and cation exchange mechanisms are also involved in P solubilization by PSMs. In addition, the action of PSMs is not only due to the release of plant available phosphorus but also due to the production of biologically active substances like indole acetic acid, gibberellins, cytokinins production is also correlated with P solubilization.

EFFECT OF PSMs ON GROWTH AND P ECONOMY

Efficient and economic use of P-fertilizers could be achieved by using phosphate solubilizing microorganisms in legumes, cereals and other useful crops. P uptake and P content was augmented by the application of PSM in many leguminous plants In wheat an increase in dry matter production and P-uptake from 10-27 per cent and 15-34 per cent respectively observed as a result of inoculation with *P. bilaji*. Superiority of PSM to uninoculation in respect of nodulation, P-uptake, pod yield, oil yield and net realization in respect of nodulation, P-uptake, pod yield, oil yield and net realization in groundnut production was also observed. Seed inoculation with PSM noted the beneficial effect on the yield of crops as was the saving by the use of 75:25 ratio of MRP:SSP. In addition application of P solubilizers causes a replacement of 25 per cent of phosphate fertilizers. Increased yield was observed in cereals, legumes, potatoes and other field crops on the addition of RP and inoculation with PSM. The yield of soybean in sandy loam alluvial soil was significantly increased by 2.4 q/ha due to rock phosphate and *Ps. Striata* whereas as with 80 Kg P_2O_5 of SSP, increase was only 1.0 q/ha. A synergistic effect of PSB was observed at low P rates whereas at higher P rates the effect was antagonistic. Seed inoculation along with 30 kg P_2O_5 gave similar dry matter yield as 60 kg P_2O_5 with and without seed inoculation. Similarly, increased seed yield was observed with 10 kg P_2O_5 and also with seed inoculation. The release of P from rock phosphate by PSM resulted in higher P uptake and dry matter yield of maize.

DUEL INOCULATION OF P-SOLUBILIZERS AND NITROGEN FIXES

Biological nitrogen fixation depends appreciably on the available form of phosphorus. So the combined inoculation of nitrogen fixers and phosphate solubilizing microorganism (PSMs) may benefit the plant better (by providing both nitrogen as well as phosphorus), than either group of organisms alone. Observed beneficial effect of phosphate solubilizers alone or in combination with *A. chroococcum* on cotton in field experiments. A positive responses of combined inoculation with phosphobacteria and *A chroococcum* on the yield and nutrient uptake of different crops was reported. Dually inoculated plants with *Azotobacter* and PSM showed increased nodulation, growth dry weight yield and P and N uptake. In addition, inoculation with bacterial mixers provided a more balanced nutrition and improvement in root uptake N and P.

Stimulatory effect of combined inoculation of *Rhizobium* and PSB with simultaneous application of RP and also indicated a possibility of saving 10 kg and replacing superphosphate entirely by rock phosphate and PSB inoculation. Combined inoculation of *Rhizobium* and PSM showed increased dry matter content, grain yield, nitrogen and phosphorus uptake significantly over uninoculated control in different legume crops. The inoculation effects were more pronounced in the presence of chemical fertilizers.

Isolation

PSM can be isolated from rhizosphere and non-rhizosphere soil and also from other environments such as rock phosphate deposits and marine environments. PSM vary in their efficiency in solubilizing insoluble phosphates. The initial isolation of phosphate solubilizers is made by using a medium suspended with insoluble phosphates such as tri-calcium phosphate. The production of clearing zones around the colonies of the organism is an indication of the presence of P-solubilising organisms. Such cultures are isolated, identified and the extent of solubilization determined quantitatively. It has been observed that the capacity of bacteria isolated to solubilise phosphate depends on the zone of their origin. Those derived from rhizoplane have the highest, the rhizosphere one has intermediate and non-rhizosphere has the least capacity.

Several rock phosphate dissolving bacteria, fungi, yeast and actinomycetes were isolated from soil samples collected from rock phosphate deposits and rhizosphere soils of different leguminous crops. Many isolates solubilize a very high quantity of rock phosphate. The most efficient bacterial isolates were identified as *Pseudomonsa striata*,

Pseudomonas rathonis and *Bacillus polymyxa* and fungal isolates as *Aspergillus awamori, Penicillium digitatum, Aspergillus niger* and *Schwanniomyces occidentalis.* These efficient microorganisms have shown consistently their capability to solubilize chemically-fixed soil phosphorus and rock phosphate from different sources - Mussorie, Udaipur, Matoon, Singhbhum, Morocco, Gafsa and Jordan. In addition, these microorganisms were found to mineralize organic phosphorus to soluble form due to enzymatic activity. By developing improved techniques for isolation of rock phosphate solubilzing micro organisms and by systematic investigations new efficient bacteria such as *Pseudomonas striata, Bacillus polymyxa* and fungi like *Aspergillus awamori* have been selected for preparation of carrier-based inoculant in addition to several basic studies. This preparation is known as 'IARI Microphos Culture', which is now being mass produced and made available to farmers. The first phosphatic bio-fertilizer under the name of *Phosphdbacterin* incorporating *Bacillus megaterium var. phosphaticum* was prepared at the then USSR.

Crop response

Inoculation'of seedlings with phosphate solubilizing organisms resulting in increased uptake of P and crop yields was first shown in 1948 by Gerrtsen. Since then beneficial influence of artificial inoculation with phosphate dissolving organisms has been reported for different crops under diverse agrolcimatic conditions. In India, the microphos culture containing *Pseudomonas striata* and *Bacillus polymyxa* was tested in multilocational field trials with wheat, rice, chick pea, soybean, lentil and potato (9.2). Results showed that inoculation of seed and seedlings increased grain yields of crops. The use of cultures increased the efficiency of rock phosphate and superphosphate applied to neutral to alkaline soils.

Table 9.2: Effect of microphos inoculant (phosphobacteria) on grain yield of crops in multi-location trials

Crop	Number of trials	Percent increase due to inoculant	
		P_0	RP_{60}
Paddy	7	10-20	5-15
Wheat	8	7-42	5-50
Gram	3	10-30	15-25
Lentil	2	-	13-15
Potato	2	30-50	13-15

P_0 - Without phosphorus; RP_{60} = 60 kg P_2O_5/ha as rock phosphate
Source: Gaur (1985).

The role of phosphate solubilizing organisms in increasing crop yield is subjected to controversy due to inconsistent results. Of the total inoculation experiments conducted to far, a significant increase in yield of 5 to 10 per cent has been observed only in about 25 per cent experiments. Several factors such as carbon and nitrogen sources, rock phosphate concentration, particle size of rock phosphate, pH, temperature, aeration, incubation period, etc. affect the efficiency of phosphate solubilizers. In general, the response to phosphobacterins was found to be positive only in soils with high organic matter content and low in available phosphorus.

VESICULAR-ARBUSCULAR MYCORRHIZAE (VAM)

The role of fungi particularly those selectively colonizing the root surface of growing plant roots in increasing the availability of phosphorus has received scanty attention. These organisms are known not only to mobilize phosphates but also perform the function of transferring phosphorus from soil into roots as observed in the case of typical ectorophic mycorrhizae. The term mycorrhizae refers to the association of fungi with rots of higher plants. Mycorrhizae are indeed the chief organisms involved in nutrient uptake of most land plants. VAM occur in most plant species in the two families of major economic importance, the *Leguminoseae* and *Graminae*. They are virtually ubiquitous, being present in tropical, temperate and arctic regions. Their impact in tropical agriculture will be greater because in the tropics phosphate-deficient and phosphate-fixing soils are widespread, phosphatic fertilizers are in short supply and the temperature is more congenial for their activity.

VAM fungi inoculated to crop plants colonize the plant root system and increase the growth and yield of crop plants. The improved plant growth is due to increased nutrient uptake particularly P, Zh and other micronutrients, production of growth promoting substances, tolerance to drought and salinity and resistance to plant pathogens.

Table 9.3: Effect of mycorrhizal (VAM) inoculation on crop yields

Crop	P-fertilizer supplementation (kg P_2O_5/ha)	% yield increae over control
Finger millet	19	18
Soybean	25-50	19
Chilli	37.5	55
Chickpea	40	25
Groundnut	40	10-20

Source: Venkataraman and Tilak (1990).

Trials conducted with the locally isolated *Glomus macrocarpum* on chilli showed the possibility of saving 50 per cent phosphatic fertilizer without affecting the yield levels. Increase in the nutrient uptake and yield of various crops in India and elsewhere has been common with VAM inoculation. Table 9.3 shows the effect of mycorrlizal inoculation on some crop yields. However, it has not been possible to exploit this organism on commercial scale due to difficulties in culturing the organism on laboratory media.

The term *mycorrhizae* comes from the Greek *myco* or fungus and *rhiza* or root and literally means *fungusroot.* Mycorrhizae have been described as perhaps the ultimate in reciprocal parasitism (symbosis) wherein the fungus supplies the higher plant partner with mineral nutrients and plant growth hormones and protects the roots against pathogens, and the higher plant supplies the fungus with energy substrates. Almost all higher plants are dependent upon one of the mycorrhizal associations.

Mycorrhizae are highly evolved, mutualistic symbioses or associations between soil fungi and plant roots. The partners in this association are members of the fungus kingdom *(Basidiomycetes, Ascomycetes* and *Zygomycetes)* and most vascular plants. Mycorrhizal plants have been found in every continent and in every major vegetation type. Depending on the plant and fungal species involved as well as distinct morphological patterns, at least seven different types of mycorrhizal associations have been recognised. They are: vesicular-arbuscular mycorrhiza (VAM); ectomycorrhiza (ECM); orchid mycorrhiza; ericoid mycorrhiza; ectendomycorrhiza; arbutoid mycorrhiza and monotropoid mycorrhiza. In addition, dual associations of both ECM and VAM have been found in some trees and shrubs such as *Acacia, Casuarina, Eucalyptus* etc.

ROOTS AS SINKS AND SOURCES OF NUTRIENTS AND CARBON IN AGRICULTURAL SYSTEMS

Roots are a special category of *soil biota*, being part of organisms that live in two very different types of environment, aboveground and belowground. As they belong to the organisms that form the main target of all agricultural interventions and are directly involved in the efficiency with which nutrients and water are used for crop production, root knowledge should be *at the root* of any discussion on sustainable agriculture. Yet, little direct attention is given to roots, possible because of a lack of:

1. Clear concepts on what to look for.
2. Easy (be it quick and dirty) methods to observe properties in actual root systems.

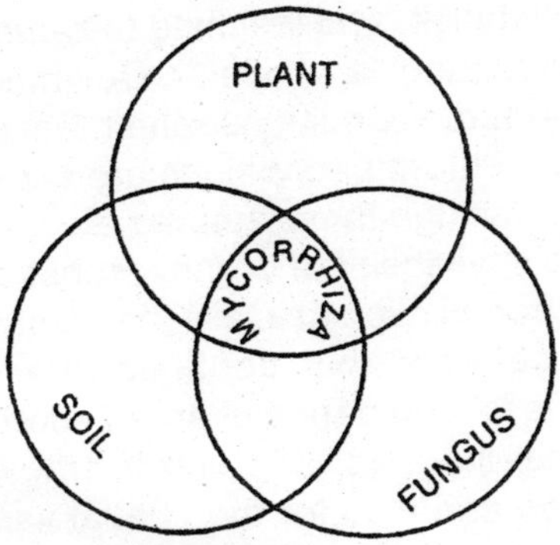

Fig. 9.1: Interrelationship between mycorrhiza, soil and plant.

The need for minimizing resource use efficiency and minimizing environmental pollution has given a new drive for root ecological research.

Within the soil, roots are the main sinks for nutrients during the life of the crop, but may also play a role in immobilizing nutrients during the initial stages of their decomposition: subsequently, they will form a source of nutrients for soil organisms and future plants. The efficiency of roots as sinks for nutrients, both during and after their life, partly determines the conflict between environmental and production aims of agriculture.

For a long time the prevailing concept was *the more extensive the root system, the higher crop production.* We know that this is not true across the full range of agricultural production conditions; maximum plant production can be obtained with relatively small root systems if the daily water and nutrient requirements are met by technical means as in intensive horticultural production systems. Roots are. however, directly involved in the efficiency of plants to use available water and nutrient reserves in the soil, and therefore in reducing negative side effects of agricultural production by leaching and losses to the atmosphere. As a first estimate, we may still expect that *the more extensive the root system, the higher may be the nutrient and water use efficiency.* The possibility of obtaining greater resource use efficiency can only be realized if total supply of nutrients and water is regulated according to the crop demands and the attainable resource use efficiency. On a field scale, both resource supply and possible crop production show spatial variability. Inadequate techniques for dealing with this variation may reduce the resource use efficiency well below what is possible in the normally small experimental units considered for research.

If the long-term organic matter balance is secured, system outputs (harvested products, leaching, and gaseous losses) must be balanced by inputs. In the northern temperate zone the main crop growing season normally has a rainfall deficit, and leaching (beyond the crop root zone) is mostly confined to autumn and winter. Denitrification may occur in summer, but in early autumn conditions winter. Denitrification may occur in summer, but in early autumn conditions are especially conducive for this process as relatively high temperatures are combined with wet soil conditions and ample availability of organic substrates.

Rates of net N mineralization are less than required by crop demand during the growing seasons, but continue after the uptake period. Fertilizer requirements for avoidance of any N shortage in the crop have to allow for the weather-induced variability in crop demand and in rates of net N mineralization and also for the spatial variability within a field treated as a single management unit. Possibilities for *response farming* are limited, however, as late fertilizer applications may not reach the roots under dry conditions.

The relevance of various root parameters for predicting uptake efficiency depends not only on the resource studied but also on the complexity of the agricultural system. In intensive horticulture, with nearly complete technical control over nutrient and water suply, fairly small root systems may allow very high crop production in a situation where resource use efficiency ranges from very low to very high. It depends on the technical control over nutrient and water supply. Fairly small root systems may allow very high crop productions in a situation where resource use efficiency ranges from very low to very high, depending on the technical perfection of the often soil less (hydroponic) production system. In field crops grown as a monoculture, the technicai possibilities are far lower for ensuring a supply of water and nutrients where and when needed by the crop, and it is difficult to achieve maximum crop production rates at high efficiency. The soil has to act as a buffer, temporarily storing these resources. Root systems are important in obtaining these resources as and when available and needed. Adjustment of supply and demand in both time and space (synchrony and synlocation) become critical factors. Critical values of root length density (root length per unit volume of soil) needed to obtain a specified water or nutrient use efficiency can be estimated from existing models. Normally, the rate-limiting step is formed by the transport from the soil matrix to the root surface and therefore by the geometry of the root-soil system and the required transport distances. In mixed cropping systems (including grasslands), the belowground interactions between the various plant species add a level of complexity to the system. On the one hand, mixed cropping system allow complementary in use of the space and thus of the stored resources, hence, improving overall resource efficiency. On the other hand, it means that root length densities that would be sufficient for efficient resource use in a monoculture may not be sufficient in a competitive situation. The plant mixtures found in agro-forestry system increase the complexity by another dimension, as the perennial and annual components have separate time frames on which to evaluate the interactions.

The soil water balance, as affected by climate, irrigation, and drainage, has a major influence on the required root functions in uptake. As the main crop-growing season normally has a rainfall deficit in the northern temperate zone, dry soil conditions hamper diffusive transport and thus increase the root length density required for uptake. A lack of synchrony between N mineralization and N demand, which would lead to a build up to mineral N in the topsoil, is not a real problem under these conditions, as the main leaching risk occurs after the growing season. The main problem for effective use of organic N pools in the temperate zone is that mineralization is too slow in spring: In the humid tropics, by contrast, with a net rainfall surplus during most of the growing season, any accumulation of mineral N will be leached rapidly from the topsoil to deeper layers. Under such conditions synchrony of N mineralization and N demand is essential for obtaining high N use efficiencies and reducing leaching.

Roots are a poorly quantified source of carbon in the soil ecosystem, and widely different estimates are available in the literature, at least partly due to uncertainties and biases caused by the methods used. Fine root residues of annual crops at harvest time tend to be low in nutrient content, as annual crops generally remobilize nutrients toward the end of their growth cycle, redistributing them to the seeds or vegetative storage tissue. For perennial crops with a less pronounced phenology, root decay may be a continuous process during the growing season. During their decomposition by microorganisms, roots may form a temporary sink of N. Little is known on the timing of net N mineralization from root residues and its role in the synchrony between net N mineralization and demand by the following crop.

Importance of Mycorrhiza

In the sand soil ecosystems of India, pioneer plants are subject to deficiency , in major nutrients (N, P, and K) and organic matter, wide fluctuation in soil moisture and temperature. It is widely accepted that arbuscular mycorrhizae are important for the establishment, growth and survival of seedlings, particularly in marginal habitats, where the symbiosis improves stress tolerance as well as conserves soil structures. A lot of work done in the past few decades has enabled these fungi to emerge as a potential bio-fertilizer; a cheap and environment friendly alternative to expensive, petroleum based chemical fertilizers. This aspect especially gains significance for a developing country like India where judicious and large-scale utilization of the technology can prove very useful for getting maximum and long-term gains in various wasteland reclamation, reforestation and aforestation programmes. In addition it gives a much needed thrust in the production of important agricultural crops, on which the economy of the country is dependent.

Mycorrhizal associations are believed to help plants grow. The potential for manipulating mycorrhizal associations to increase productivity in plantation forestry, or plant establishment during ecosystem recovery after severe disturbance, are the focus of major research initiatives. There is also much interest in their potential utilisation in agriculture and horticulture. However, it could be argued that we do not know enough about the role of mycorrhizal associations in natural, disturbed, or managed ecosystems to evaluate their potential for applied use. Suggested roles of mycorrhizal fungi in natural and managed ecosystems.

Benefits to Plants

1. Increased plant nutrient supply by extending the volume of soil accessible to plants.
2. Increased plant nutrient supply by acquiring nutrient forms that would not normally be available to plants.
3. Some ECM and ericoid fungi have the capacity to breakdown phenolic compounds in soils, which can interfere with nutrient uptake.
4. Root colonization by ECM and VAM fungi can provide protection from parasitic fungi and nematodes.
5. Non-nutritional benefits to plants due to changes in water relations, phytohormone levels, carbon assimilation, etc. have been reported, but are difficult to interpret.
6. Mycorrhizal benefits can include grater yield, nutrient accumulation, and/or reproductive success.
7. Mycorrhizas can cause growth form changes to root architecture, vascular tissue, etc.
8. Suppression of competing non-host plans, by mycorrhizal fungi has been observed.
9. Significant amounts of carbon transfer through ECM fungus mycelia connecting different plant species has been measured. This could reduce competition between plants and contribute to the stability and diversity of ecosystems.
10. Networks of hyphae supported by dominant trees may help seedlings become established or contribute to the growth of shaded understorey plants.
11. Nutrient transfer from dead to living plants can occur.

Other Roles in Ecosystems

1. Soil hyphae are likely to have an important role in nutrient cycling by helping to prevent losses from the system, especially at times when roots are inactive.
2. Hyphae are conduits that may transport carbon from plant roots to other soil organisms involved in nutrient cycling processes - co-operating with other members of the decomposition soil food-web.
3. Soil hyphae may have an important role in nutrient cycling by acquiring nutrients from saprophytic fungi.
4. Epigeous and hypogeous sporocarps of ECM and VAM fungi are important food sources for placental and marsupial mammals.
5. Mycorrhizal roots and fungus fruit bodies are important as food sources and habitats for invertebrates.
6. Mycorrhizal fungus hyphae are an important food source for soil invertebrates.
7. Mycorrhizas influence soil microbial populations and exudates in the mycorrhizosphere and hyphosphere
8. Hyphae of VAM fungi are considered to contribute to soil structure. Their role in mechanical aggregation has been questioned, but secretions such as glomalin may be more important. Hyphal mats produced by ECM fungi considerably alter sol structure.
9. Mycorrhizal fungi contribute to carbon storage in soil by altering the quality and quantity of soil organic matter.

Values of People

1. ECM fungi are economically and nutritionally importants human food resources.
2. These mushrooms have also have been used as medicines and natural dyes.
3. Fungi have aesthetic values and are an important part of the as culture, folklore and appreciation of nature by many people.
4. Fungal diversity is a bio-indicator of environmental quality.
5. Fungi, which have adapted to local soil conditions are required for agriculture, horticulture and forestry.

MYCORRHIZAL INTERACTIONS WITH PLANTS AND SOIL ORGANISMS IN SUSTAINABLE AGROECOSYSTEM

Although farming has been affected by technological development, it remains basically an ecological enterprise. It is an activity in which natural ecosystems, open to the influence of climate, substrate, and wild biota, are modified to increase yields of desired food and fiber products. Greater the changes in the basic patterns of structure and function that prevail in the natural system, the greater is the human effort necessary to maintain the agricultural system. Therefore, at the present time, it has been proved that conventional agriculture products ecological disturbance and lack of sustainability, resulting in a reduction of soil fertility and increased damage by pathogens to cultivated plants. In addition, it has been observed that some traditional agricultural systems have higher sustainability and produce less ecological damage. These systems have been called **low external-input agricultural (LEIA)** systems. Studies related with mycorrhizal research in LEIA agro-ecosystems have been scarce. In sustainable agro-ecosystems, mycorrhizal incidence is low and other kinds of microorganisms are abundant and play important role in the sustainability of the systems. So far, there has been insufficient investigation of interactions between AM and soil organisms in LEIA systems.

As opposed to the conventional systems, LEIA agro-ecosystems have high genetic and cultural diversity, multiple uses of resources, and efficient nutrient and material recycling. The search for strategies to improve yields and to maintain these increases is a great challenge to human population at the present time. The role of biological alternatives, because of the intrinsic nature of farming, is of key importance to the search for reduced use of fertilizers, pesticides, and other chemicals. Among these alternatives, mycorrhiza management is particularly important because it strongly influences the plant nutrition processes and the soil stabilization.

It the physiological and ecological importance of mycorrhiza in natural ecosystems and its beneficial effects on cultivated plants have been widely documented. It is well known that the characteristic dominant plants of each major terrestrial community associate mutualistically with soil fungi to form typical kinds of mycorrhiza. Therefore, cricaceous plants, which form the major component of the heathland biome, form with ascomycetous fungi distinctive *ericoid* mycorhiza. In a similar way, the dominant trees of the boreal and temperate forest biomes associate primarily with basidiomycetous fungi to form ectomycorrhiza, and the natural grasslands and most of the tropical rain forest species of the world form arbuscular mycorhiza in association with fungi of zygomycetous affinitie. As natural ecosystem plants, most of the cultivated plants tend to form mycorrhizal associations. AM is the most widely distributed and colonizes most species of agricultural crops. The objective of this contribution is to discuss the importance of the mycorrhizal fungi and their interactions with plant management and other organisms in in LEIA agroecosystems.

SYMBIOSIS

The term *symbiosis* was first used by Frank in, 1877 to describe the regular coexistence of different organisms such as fungi and algae in lichens. It was used as a neutral term that did not imply parasitism. A decade later De Bary (1887) used symbiosis to include parasite as well but, the meaning of the terms *symbiosis* and *parasite* has been changed later on. *Symbiosis* was used more and more for mutually beneficial associations between dissimilar organisms, and parasite and parasitism came to be almost synonymous with pathogen and pathogenesis.

In recent years, *symbiosis* is defined as *the living together of differently named organisms.* This definition includes all associations ranging from *mutualistic,* in which all organisms involved are believed to derive benefit; to *parasitic,* in which one organism benefits to the disadvantage of other member of the association. A more precise definition of mutualism is that associations are *mutualistic* if the fitness (offspring produced) of the associating organisms is greater than they are living apart. In a symbiosis, the organism with the large size is the host and the smaller is the symbiont. The symbiont can either be external to the host (ectosymbiotic) or within it (endosymbiotic). The symbiosis is *obligate* for an organism, which is unable to survive and reproduce in the absence of its living partner, and *facultative* if it is able to do so even if the partner does during the association.

In a dual association, symbiosis is wide-spread especially between higher plants and bacteria in N-fixing symbiosis; between higher plants and fungi in most mycorrhizae; between algae and fungi in lichens; between algae and coelenterate in corals and so on. However, it is not currently known whether symbiosis occurs between higher plants. In addition, the tripartite *symbiosis* of plants, N-fixing bacteria and mycorrhizae (either vesicular-arbuscular mycorrhiza or ectomycorrhiza) has also been found in some *Acacia, Albizia, Casuarina* and *Leucaena* species. Symbiosis are often found in nutrient limiting conditions and nutritional interactions play a key role in most symbiosis. There are two important types of symbiosis: mycorrhizal symbiosis and N-fixing symbiosis.

Mycorrhizae is the symbiotic association of fungi with roots of vascular plants. The main advantage of mycorrhizae to the host plants lies in the extension of the penetration zone of the root fungus system in the soil, facilitating an increased phosphorus uptake. The interconnected network of external hyphae acts as an additional catchment and absorbing surface in the soil beyond the depletion zone that would otherwise be inaccessible to the plant roots. Endotrophic mycorrhizae have been shown to be present in a wide range of horticultural species including apple, walnut, almonds, citrus, avocado, strawberry and grape.

In many cases, the mycorrhizae have been shown to markedly improve the growth of plants.

Some soils are deficit in mineral salts and plants living in them have special means of obtaining nitrogen and other essential elements, for example, the roots of many moorland and woodland plants, particularly coniferous trees, which live in rich humus but deficient in mineral salts possesses a mycorrhizae. Mycorrhizae **(fungus-roots)** are symbiotic associations between fungi and the roots of vascular plants. Two main groups of mycorrhizae are recognized: the **ectomycorrhizae** and **endomycorrhizae,** although the rarer group with intermediate properties, the ectendotrophic mycorrhizae. In the ectomycorhizae. the fungal hyphae form a mantle both outside the root within the root in the intercellular spaces of the epidermis and cortex. No intracellular penetration into epidermal or cortical cells occurs, but an extensive network called the Harting net is formed between these cells. Ectomycorrhizae are common on trees, including members of the families pinaceae (pine, fir, spruce, larch, hemlock), Fagaceae (willow, poplar, chestnut), Betulaceae (birch alder), Salicaceae (willow, poplar, and few other show scaning electron micrographs of two *Pinus contorta* roots, one uninfected and having root hairs and the other infected with an ectomycorrhizae fungus.

Endomycorrhizae consist of three sub-groups, but by far the most common are the vesicular arbuscular mycorrhizae (VAM). The fungi present in VAM are members of the Endogonacae, and they produce an internal network of hyphae between cortical cells that extends out into the soil, where the hyphae absorb mineral salts and water. Although VAM fungi seem to penetrate directly into the cytosol of cortical cells (where they form structures called vesicles and arbuscules, giving them their name), the hyphae are surrounded by an invaginated plasma membrane of the cortex cell. The VAM are present on most species of herbaceous angiosperms, whether monocot or dicot, annual or perennial crops, or native or introduced species; they also occur in the gymnosperm genera *Cupressus, Thuja, Taxodium, Juniperus,* and *Sequoia* and in ferns, lycopods, and bryophytes.

ROOT SYSTEM FORM

The main role of mycorrhizal associations is to acquire nutrients by exploring the soil volume with hyphae that are both more responsive and more extensive than the roots themselves. However, roots of some species of plants are also capable of effectively exploring large soil volumes and responding to temporary soil resources, and these species are likely to have faculative mycorrhizal associations, or be non-mycorrhizal. The production of fine roots or associations with mycorrhizal fungi are the two alternative strategies that both require plants to expend metabolic nergy on their root systems. It is considered likely that mycorrhizal ıngus hyphae should be a more cost effective means of exploring large oil volumes, because of their narrow diameter. Plants generally do not upport both high levels of mycorrhizal colonization and root systems ith fine/active roots, because of the high metabolic cost that would esult.

Considerable variations in root system extensiveness, geometry, epth distribution, and plasticity occur between plant species. In xperiments, total biomass is the parameter most often used to quantify ɔots, but provides much less information than root length or specific ɔot length (length/unit root weight) data. Parameters that could be used) predict nutrient absorption are: total root biomass <fine root biomass root length <root surface area <rhizosphere volume, arranged in ncreasing order of predictive ability. When root parameters of plant pecies are compared, root hairs have been found to be most highly orrelated with their ability to absorb P from soils. Plants with extensive ighly branched, fine, long roots with numerous root hairs) have often een observed to derive little benefit from mycorrhizas in experiments.

In addition to have fine roots with long root hairs, there is a tendency ɔr mycorrhizal plans to have roots, which are less active (grow slowly, ve longer, etc.) than species with little or not mycorrhizal colonization f their roots. The responsiveness, or capacity of plants to exploit small cale or short duration changes in water or nutrient availability by rapidly roducing new roots, is thought to be an important determinant of their uccess during competition for soil resources. Some plants can also hange rhizosphere conditions, such as pH, which may influence nutrient vailability.

Australian non-mycorrhizal plants in the family Proteaceae have uster roots that likely promote nutrient uptake by their large surface rea and production of leachates, which contain organic acids and other ubstances that can increase nutrient solubility. The capacity of plants) influence nutrient availability in soils will also depend on the xtensiveness and activity of their root system, since young roots are e primary source of exudates.

Host and soil factors which can be used to help predict the potential enefit of mycorrhizas are outlined in the Table 9.4 (below Assuming at soil nutrient levels are not unusually high and inoculum of appropriate ycorrhizal fungi is available, root strategy differences will primarily etermine the magnitude of benefits from mycorrhizal associations.

Table 9.4: Generalized relationship between features of root system and the mycorrhizal dependency of plants

Root feature	Mycorrhizal dependency of plant	
	High	Low
ROOT SURFACE AREA	low	high
Root system surface area	low	High
Branching orders of lateral roots	few	many
Branching frequency	sparse	frequent
Root hair abundance and length	few/short	many/long
ROOT ACTIVITY	slow	fast
Root growth rate	slow	fast
Response to soil conditions	slow	fast
Primary root lifespan	long	short
Protective structural features	strong	weak
Root exudation	? less	? more
MYCORRHIZAL FORMATION	efficient	inefficient or inhibited

Notes : *This table is based on differences in root system properties betweer plants of different mycorrhizal status in Canadian forests.*

SOIL AND SITE FACTORS INFLUENCING MYCORRHIZAS

Soil factors that can influence the benefits provided by mycorrhiza fungi to plants are considered below.

Mycorrhizal Inoculum

Plants with mycorrhizal associations predominate in most natura ecosystems, so inoculum of mycorrhizal fungi is present in most soils. The quantity inoculum of mycorrhizal fungi, which are compatible with a host plant in soils can be measured by bioassay experiments. In these experiments, seedlings are grown in intact soil cores or mixed soi samples for sufficient time to allow mycorrhizas to form, then roots are sampled, processed and assessed to measure mycorrhiza formation.

In Australia, there are fewer species of ECM fungi in sites where eucalypt plantations are established than in undisturbed forests. There are also cases where plantations of trees have been introduced to habitats where they do not occur naturally. For example, Australian eucalypts are now grown in exotic habitats in Africa, Europe, Asia and South America, habitats, which are few compatible ECM fungi, because local fungi are specific to other hosts such as conifers.

Soil Disturbance

Propagules of mycorrhizal fungi maybe absent from soils where severe soil disturbance has resulted in topsoil loss, or where host plants are limited by adverse soil or site factors such as salinity, aridity, water-logging, or climatic extremes (Brundrett, 1991). Most studies of mycorrhizal associations in highly disturbed habitats such as mine sites have found reduced levels of mycorrhizal propagules. Less severe forms of soil disturbance, including agricultural tillage, soil animal activities, fire and erosion can also reduce levels of mycorrhizal fungus propagules.

Spores and other propagules of mycorrhizal fungi can introduced to new sites by wind or water erosion or by the activity of animals, which feed on fungi. In a disturbed habitat, the effectiveness of natural vectors will depend on the proximity of un-disturbed habitats containing suitable fungi (and their associated animals) as well as the phenology of fruiting of fungi. Effective colonization of disturbed habitats, such as minesites in Australia, by mycorrhizal fungi has been observed, but there is as yet insufficient information about the time required for this process to occur.

Soil Fertility

A key factor which effects the potential for mycorrhizas to benefit plants in particular sites is the supply of phosphate and nitrogen in soil. Phosphorus is generally considered to be the most important plant-growth limiting factor, which can be supplied by mycorrhizal associations, because of the many abiotic and biotic factors, which can restrict its mobility in soils. Reductions in the benefit is provided by mycorrhizal associations to plants are caused by increasing soil phosphorus levels. High rate of P and N fertilizers suppress ectomycorrhiza development in the field. High concentrations of soil N can influence the relative abundance of different ECM types.

Adverse Soil Conditions

Land degradation due to salinity, water-logging, erosion, etc., are serious and growing, problems in Australia and other countries. Excessive NaCl levels in soil inhibit mycorrhizal formation and restrict the activity of most mycorrhizal fungi, but some can tolerant these conditions. Observations in natural ecosystems have shown that plants with mycorrhizal associations are often less common than non-mycorrhizal species in soils which are waterlogged or saline, but that some mycorrhizal plants are normally present in even the worst sols. ECM fungi can be highly sensitive to water logging of sols, while VAM fungi may be less sensitive.

CHARACTERISTICS OF FUNGAL ISOLATES

Populations of mycorrhizal fungi are thought to have occupied the same soil habitats for millions of years, slowly adapting to changes in site conditions. Some mycorrhizal fungi appear to have worldwide distribution patterns and have apparently adapted to a wide range of habitats, but it is known that soil factors such as pH restrict the distribution of many taxa. Unfortunately, information about the soil and climatic conditions where isolates used in experiments were originally obtained is often not provided. These data are urgently needed to allow isolates to be selected for use in inoculation programmes and to establish correlations between their taxonomy and physiology.

The fact that most mycorrhizal research has been concerned with plant growth responses with little consideration of the fungi involved has also helped to create the false impression that most of these fungi are functionally equivalent. Properties of individual mycorrhizal fungi result from their adaptations to soil/environmental/host factors. Some Properties of fungi considered to be important are:

1. The amount of soil hyphae produced relative to root colonization
2. The rates of hyphal growth and root colonization.
3. Physiological characteristics, which regulate nutrient absorption or nutrient translocation by hyphae and exchange with the host

MANIPULATING MYCORRHIZAL FUNGI

Methodologies have been developed for the inoculation of plants with mycorrhizal fungi. However, there has been less consideration about how we should determine where and when, if ever, it is necessary to do this. The diagram provided below, outlines the steps in a decision making processes that can be used to determine if mycorrhizal fungi that are compatible with host plants are present in soils, or are likely to be introduced by natural mechanisms. This information is required to evaluate the potential benefits of mycorrhizal inoculation in a specific situation. There would only be a need to manipulate mycorrhizal fungi by inoculating plant seedlings of changing site management practices it substantial benefits from these manipulations are expected. Methods for the production of mycorrhizal plants in the glasshouse and nursery to allow experimentation or for use in the field are described in the accompanying manual.

TYPES OF ASSOCIATIONS

At least seven different types of mycorrhizal associations have been recognized, involving different groups of fungi and host plants and distinct morphology patterns.

1. **Vesicular arbuscular mycorrhizas** (= arbuscular mycorrhizas. VAM or AM) are associations where Zygomycete fungi in the Glomales produce arbuscules, hyphae and vesicles within roots. Spores are formed in soil or roots. These associations are defined by the presence of arbuscules. Fungi within roots spread by linear hyphae or coiled hyphae.

2. **Ectomycorrhizas (ECM)** are associations where asidiomycetes and other fungi form short swollen lateral roots covered by mantle hyphae. These roots have Harting net hyphae around cells in the epidermis or cortex.
3. **Ectendo-, arbutoid- and monotropoid mycorrhizal associations** are similar to ectomycorrhizas. These associations have not been found in Australia.
4. **Orchid mycorrhizas** consist of coils of hyphae within roots or stems of plants in the family Orchidaceae. Young orchid seedlings and some adult plants which lack chlorophyll are entirely dependant on mycorrhizal fungi for their survival.
5. **Ericoid mycorrhizas** have hyphal coils in outer cells of the narrow "hair roots" of plants in the plant order Ericales. These associations also occur in thicker roots of Australian members of the Epacridaceae.
6. The Australian lily ***Thysanotus*** has a unique mycorrhizal association where fungus hyphae only grow under epidermal cells.

Table 9.5: Kinds of mycorrhizal associations

<table>
<tr><td rowspan="3">Endomycorrnizae</td><td>1 Vesicular Arbuscular (Va)</td><td>Higher Plants-Great Majority Of The Vasicular Plants Including Ferns, Monocots, Dicots, Fungi-Endogonaceae (Phycomycetes)</td></tr>
<tr><td>2 Ericaceous</td><td>Higher Plants: Ericales. Fungi-Generally Unknown Although A Basidimycete Has Been Found In Association With Azalea.</td></tr>
<tr><td>3. Orchidaceous</td><td>Higher Plants: Orchids.
Fungi: Agaricales and Aphyllophorales (Basidiomycetes).</td></tr>
<tr><td>Ectomycorrhizae

Ectendomy corrhizae</td><td colspan="2">Higher Plants: Great Majority Of The Vasicular Plants Including Ferns, Monocots, Dicots, Fungi-Endoqonaceae (Phycomycetes)
Fungi: Many thousands Of Species In Basidiomycetes, Ascomycetes, And Endogenaceae (Phycomycetes).</td></tr>
</table>

The distinction between ecto-and endomycorrhizae is based upon the morphology of the structure formed by fungus and higher plants. Ectomycorrhizal forming fungi are able to penetrate between, but not into, the cortical cell'of the host root, thus forming a network of fungal strands within the cortex commonly called a "Hartig net". The fungus also normally makes a mantle which completely encloses the infected root tip and from which fungal hyphae extend into the soil. This network of hyphae greatly increase the ability of the root to take up nutrients in three ways:

1. The surface area in contact with soil particles is much greater, and the much smaller hyphae can penetrate fissures in soil particles too small for roots;
2. The fungus excretes enzymes which allow it to dissolve soil nutrients otherwise unavailable to the roots; and
3. The fungus extends the life of an absorbing root from a few days to a year or more.

Inoculation of tree seedlings with appropriate fungus species to stimulate development of mycorrhiza has been shown to be critical to reforestation, especially, in a diverse range of sites and climates from timberline in the Alps to sub-tropical islands like Puerto Rico. The last fiften years have seen great interest in mycorrhiza in the southern states where fungi such as Pisolithus tinctorius are believed to be responsible for increased growth and survival of loblolly pine, especially on harsh sites such as the spoils of mining operations.

Endomycorrhizae differ from the above primarly in that the fungus hyphae penetrate directly into the cortical cells of the root. Neither endo- nor ectomycorrhizal forming fungi are, however, able to penetrate beyond the cortical region - the vascular tissues of the root are not infected.

TYPES OF MYCORRHIZA

Mycorrhizae are classified on the basis of the extent of root penetration, production of external mantle or sheath and the inter- and intracellular structures they form once inside the plant root. Since enormous amount of literature exists on classification and types of mycorrhizas only salient features of different types are mentioned here. So far seven types of mycorrhizae are recognized.

Ectomycorrhiza

Here the fungal members belong to 25 families of Basidiomycotina 7 families of Ascomycotina or 1 genus of Zygomycotina i.e. *Endogone.* The plant symbionts include both Gymnosperms and Angiosperms. A fungal sheath or mantle is present. There is no hyphal penetration of cells. Fungal hypha is generally septate. A distinct Hartig's net is present between the cells. Hartig's net is plexus of fungal hyphae between epidermal and cortical cells. It provides a large surface area for the interchange of nutrients between host and the fungi.

Ectendomycorrhiza

The fungi belong to Basidiomycotina, which covers both Gymnosperms and Angiosperms plants. The fungal sheath if present is very thin. Septate fungal hyphae penetrate the root cells and coil inside it. The fine network of fungal hyphae (Hartig's net) is present in the intercellular spaces and thereis intracellular penetration of living hyphae in cells.

Endomycorrhiza/Arbuscular Mycorrhizal Fungi (AMF)

Fungi are confined to the order Glomales of Zygomycotina. The plant symbionts range from Bryophytes to Angiosperms. There is no fungal sheath. Aseptate hyphae enter the root cortical cells and form characteristic arbuscules and/or vesicles hence the name. The plasmalemma of the host cell invaginates and encloses the arbuscules.

Arbutoid mycorrhiza

Here the funal partner is Basidiomycetous and colonises members of order Ericales (Arbutoidae). Fungal sheath present. Septate hyphae penetrate only the epidermal cells and coil inside it. Hartig's net is present in the intercullular spaces.

Monotropoid mycorrhiza

The fungi belong to Basidiomycotina colonising achlorophyllous member of Angiosperms belonging to family Monotropaceae. Fungal sheath present. Branches from septate hyphae penetrate in the epidermal cells forming haustorial pegs inside. Hartig's net not seen in mature roots.

Ericoid mycorrhiza

Fungal members are usually Basidiomycetous and one, *Hymenoschyphus,* belongs to Ascomycotina. This is found in roots of plants belonging to order Ericales. Rootlets are covered by a loosely woven mesh of dark brown septate hyphae from which branches penetrate the cortical cells, forming intracellular coils invaginating and enclosed by the host's plasmalemma. Hartig's net formed in the intercellular spaces.

Orchidoid mycorrhiza

Fungi belong to Basidiomycotina and mycelia sterlia. These colonise only members of family Orchidaceae (Angiosperm). Septate hyphae enter the cells and develop into coils often called "peltrons". This association is probably pseudomycorrhizal but plays an important role in the establishment of orchid seedlings.

Host Plants

The relative importance of different mycorrhizal associations for plant species is graphically summarized below using data for Angiosperms from the mycorrhizal literature. Many Pteridophytes are also known to have VAM associations, while Gymnosperms may have ECM or VAM associations.

Place of Availability of Mycorrhizal Plants

Field surveys have found that plans with mycorrhizal associations predomniate in most natural ecosystem sin Australia and throughout the world.

Table 9.6: Briefly summarises the importance of mycorrhizal associations throughout the world

Association	Occurrence
Vesicular Arbuscular Mycorrhizal (VAM) Plants	Plants with VAM are common in most habitats. It is easier to say where they are not found Trees with ECM are dominent in coniferous forests, especially in cold boreal or alpine regions
Ectomycorrhizal (ECM) Plants	ECM trees and shrubs common in many broad-leaved forests in temperate or Medite-rranean regions ECM trees also occur in some tropical or subtropical savanna or rain forests habitats NM plants are most common in disturbed habitats, or sites with extreme environmental
Non-mycorrhizal (NM) Plants	or soil conditions
	NM plants appear to be more common in Australia than in other continents.

Mycorrhizal Fungi

Members of the fungus kingdom obtain nutrition from many sources, including decomposition of organic substrates, predation and parasitism, and involvement in mutualistic associations (Christensen, 1989, Kendrick, 1992). Many soil fungi are saprobes with the enzymatic ability to digest organic substrates of varying degrees of complexity, but some subsist on very low levels of organic or inorganic substrates (Wainwright, 1988). Mycorrhizal fungi are a major component of the soil microflora in many ecosystems, but usually have limited saprophytic abilities (Harley & Smith, 1983). Mycorrhizal fungi are considered to have many important roles in natural and managed ecosystems.

Very little is known about the taxonomic or functional diversity of mycorrhizal fungi. Indeed, there is a paucity of knowledge about all Australian fungi, with only about 10 per cent of these organisms having been named, while an estimated 80 per cent of them remain undiscovered. Laboratory and glasshouse experiments have shown that different fungal taxa vary in their capacity to utilize resources, withstand adverse conditions etc. For this reason, mycorrhizal fungus diversity is thought to contribute to the resilience of ecosystems, but there is very, little comparative data that can be used to test this hypothesis. More information about fungi forming ECM and VAM associations is provided in the relevant sections.

Arbuscular Mycorrhizal Fungi (AMF)

AMF are the most widespread in their distribution both among plant species and geographically. They are believed to be disseminated inter-continentally prior to continental drift as supported by fossil record of earlier plants. They occur more frequently in cultivated soils usually in top 15-30 cms. Because most economically important plants form this type of mycorrhiza, this area of research has attracted much attention. Commercial use of AMF may be an alternative to the rising agricultural and fertiliser costs, because of their potential in increasing the crop yields.

Establishment of Symbiosis

These associations do not usually cause observable external changes in the morphology of plant roots, and cannot be detected without appropriate staining. They colonise a wide range of host plants that include most agricultural and horticultural plants both annual and perennial, fruit trees and a large number of forest tree species. AMF do generally not colonise plants that enter into other types of mycorrhiza. They lack host specificity from the host point of view as shown by their wide host range. However from fungal view point the specificity does exist. Of the 150 species that have been described in *Glomales* only a small proportions are presumed to be mycorrhizal. Since these fungi lack sexual reproduction recognition, characterization and classification is based upon their chlamydospores, which show variation in size, shape, cooler and wall characteristics depending upon the species.

These fungi are able to colonise the epidermal and cortical cells of the root, but do not enter the vascular system or the root meristems. The morphological stages of development are variable, depending mainly on the plant species involved.

In general, fungal hyphae growing from spores in the soil or from adjacent plants roots contact the root surface, where they differentiate to form an appressorium. This is the first indication of recognition between the fungus and the plant, and appressoria are not formed in the roots of non-host plants or on synthetic media or membranes. Penetration of the root occurs via the appressoria and the fungus may produce intracellular colls in the sub-epidermal cell layers, followed by intercellular growth into the inner cortex in the sub-epidermal cell layers, followed by intercellular growth into the inner cortex of the root (although sometimes only intercellular hyphae are observed). On reaching the inner cortex, hyphal branches penetrate the cortical cell walls and differentiate within the cells to form highly branched, terminal structures known as arbuscules. Here the symbionts are in intimate contact, separated only by the their membranes. This interfare is assumed to be the site of carbon and phosphate exchange between the symbionts, and the arbuscule generally regarded as a key structure in the symbiosis. Following the formation of arbuscules, some species of fungi also form vesicles in the root. Vesicles are small darkly staining globular or spherical structures formed later. They store oil and Polyphosphate granules, which are utilized by the plant under phosphorus deficiency conditions.

Classification of AMF

There are only six genera of fungi that contain species, which are known to produce AMF with plants. Two of these genera, *Glomus* and *Sclerocystis,* produce chlamydospores only. Four genera form spores that are similar to azygospores: *Glgaspora, Scutellospora, Acaulospora* and *Entrophospora.* Their spore characteristics and the relationship of the spore to the associated hyphal attachments distinguish the genera. The existent genera were establishment to reflect the manner in which the spores were produced, except for the genus *Sutellospora.* Species in this genus are distinguished from species in the closely allied genus *Gigaspora* by wall characteristics, method of germ tube formation, and auxiliary cell characteristics.

The fungi forming AM are are placed in the class Zygomycetes, order Endogonales, family Endogonaceae. The type genus for Endogonaceae is *Endogone,* a genus in which species form zygospores and azygospores but do not produce arbuscular mycorrhizae.

Over the years, numerous attempts have been made to monoculture AMF on artificial media. These attempts, however, have met with little success. Thus, AMF must still be collected from field soils, increased in the greenhouse on living host plants (nurse crops) and collected once again from these "pot culture" soils, where the TERI is specialized. Clearly, the production and collection of propagules from soil remains an important, time-consuming and fundamental part of AMF research, both for inoculum preparation and population estimation. On the other hand, all AMF are not morphologically and physiologically the same, so it is

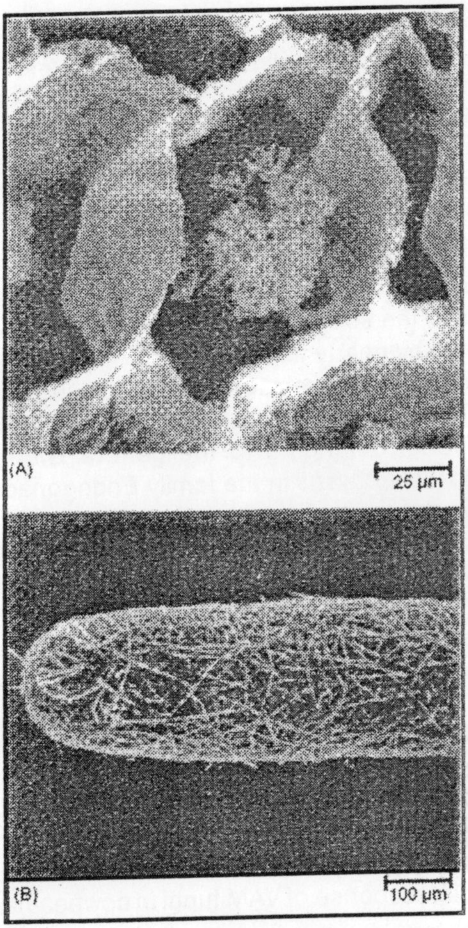

Fig. 9.2: Scanning electron micrographs of mycorrhize. (A) A fully developed arbuscule of an endomycorrhiza in a plant cell. (The term arbuscule means little bush). As the arbuscule decomposes, it releases accumulated nutrients from plant, (B) The mycelial mantel of a typical ectomycorrhizal fungus surrounding a eucalyptus tree root.

important to know the identity of the fungus with which one is working. Although these fungi have extremely wide host ranges, they are very specific in a single plant species and they can differ also in their effect on plants in different ecosystems, soil types, and in similar soils with differeing biological, chemical, and physical components.

ECTOMYCORRHIZAE (ECM)

They are characterised by dense mycelial sheaths around the roots and a Hartig net between root cells, are limited to mostly temperate forest trees and *Basidiomycetes* and some other fungi. Mycorrhizae involve an intimate association of the host plant's root tissue and the fungus, but there is also fungal tissue that extends into the soil as individual hyphae and in some species as more complex strands. The external hyphae can take up mineral nutrients from the soil and transport them into the host root. Mycorrhizal associations can therefore be of great potential benefit to the host plant in nutrient limited systems.

VESICULAR-ARBUSCULAR MYCORRHIZA (VAM)

Zygomycete fungi form arbuscules and/or vesicles and external hyphal networks in the soil and grow extensively within the cells of the cortex, are formed by nearly all vascular plants. The endomycorrhizae, a fungus, (arbuscular mycorhizae) found in close association among angiosperms. The VA mycorrhizae are formed by the non-septate phycomycetes fungi belonging to the genera *Glomus, Gigaspora, Acaulospora* and *Sclerocystis* in the family Endogonaceae of the order Mucorales. They produce vesicles and arbuscules inside the root system. Arbuscules are highly branched fungal hyphae while vesicles are the bullous swellings of these hypae. These VAM fungi are beneficial to the plant, which they colonise. They make more nutrients available to the plant, improve soil texture, disease resistance and help in better plant growth. Besides, mycorrhizae also help in the biological control of root pathogen.

An extensive research on VA mycorrhizal association in horticultural crops have been done at the Unviersity of Agricultural Sciences, Bangalore and Indian Institute of Horticultural Research (IIHR), Bangalore. Tomato, brinjal, okra, bell pepper, chilli and onions have been studied for their response to VAM inoculation (Sukhada, 1993). He also reported beneficial response of VAM fungi in cowpea has been reported (Sukhada, 1993).

In India the beneficial effects of vasicular-arbuscular mycorrhizae (VAM) have been observed in fruit crops like citrus, papaya and *litchi.* Inoculation with *Glomus fasciculatum* fungus was found to increase the dry matter content and the uptake of Fe, Zn, Mn by different rootstocks of citrus (Manjunath *et al.,* 1983).

In litchi, positive correlations of VAM population in the rhizosphere of soil and mycorrhizal infection in the roots with leaf area and fruit have been noticed (Rana and Srivastava, 1984). In papaya, inoculation with *Glomus fasciculatum* and *Glomus mossae* was found to increase the plant height, dry matter content and nutrient uptake with lower doses of applied phosphorus.

Recent studies have shown the possibility of domesticating *Mycorrhizae* in agricultural systems is not in doubt. Lack of a suitable inoculum production technology is the major limitation for commercial exploitation of this system.

Table 9.7: Effect of mycorrhizal (VAM) inoculation on crop yields

Crop	P-fertiliser supplementation (kg P_2O_5/ha)	% yield increase over control
Finger millet	19	18
Soybean	25-50	19
Chillies	37.5	55
Chickpea	40	25
Groundnut	-	10-20

Source: Venkatraman and Tilak (1990).

HOW MYCORRHIZAS WORK

Mycorrhizal associations are defined in the introduction section. Mineral nutrient acquisition from soil is considered to be the primary function of mycorrhizas, but other roles for these fungi have been suggested. These roles are listed below, but many have not been quantified in natural ecosystems. Only the uptake of nutrients is discussed further here.

Nutrient Depletion Zones

The demand for a particular mineral nutrient depends on plant internal requirements, while the supply of that nutrient primarily depends on its availability and mobility in soils. Mineral nutrients such as phosphorus have very limited mobility in soils so that depletion zones - where all the . available nutrient has been utilized, quickly from around roots. Thus to obtain more phosphorus, plants must bypass these depletion zones by further root activity elsewhere in the soil. The outcome of this quest for phosphorus (and other relatively immobile soil resources) should largely be determined by the surface area of a plant's root system. The most important role of mycorrhizal fungus hyphae is to extend the surface area of roots.

Hyphal Activity

Mycorrhizal fungus hyphae are considered to function primarily by increasing the soil volume from which available forms of phosphorus are absorbed and provided to roots. Hyphae of VAM fungi can respond to localized sources of soil nutrients more rapidly than roots and to produce tine highly-branched *absorptive* hyphae in decomposting organic substrates. ECM fungus hyphae also proliferation in decomposing soil organic matter.

It was considered that hyphae of VAM fungi utilized the same forms of nutrients as roots. However, there now is evidence that these associations have a greater benefit when phosphorus is present in less-soluble forms. Hyphae of ECM fungi can utilize both inorganic and simple organic sources of nitrogen and phosphorus. There are some ECM fungi which specialize in growth is soils enrichment with ammonium. Soil mineralisation by organic acids produced by hyphae has been measured within E cm fungus mats. ECM fungus hyphae can also grow within rocks where they contribute to mineral weathering. Thus, mycorrhizal fungi often have access to forms of nutrients which are not directly available to plants, as well as acquiring nutrients which are spatially or chronologically separatd from roots.

Mycorrhizal Dependency

Mycorrhizal dependency is A measure of the benefit provided by mycorrhizas and will depend no relative contribution of root and mycorrhizal mediated nutrient uptake to plants (Janos, 1980). Mycorrhizal dependency has often been quantified by calculating the yield ratio between mycorrhizal plants and un-inoculated control plants grown in a particular soil at a single soil P level. However, it is better to analyse mycorrhizal benefits across a range of soil P levels, by producing nutrient response curves.

The concept that plants have varying degrees of dependence on mycorrhizal associations is gaining acceptance. Detailed examinations of plants in natural ecosystems often show consistent differences between host plant species in the intensity and consistency of mycorrhiza formation (proportion of root system involved). These observations have shown that species generally either have:

1. consistently high levels of mycorrhizas,
2. intermediate, or variable levels of mycorrhizas
3. or are not mycorrhizal.

Plants belonging to these categories can be called obligatorily mycorrhizal, facultatively mycorrhizal, or non-mycorrhizal, as are defined below.

In natural ecosystems, plant with facultatively mycorrhizal associations or non-mycorrhizal roots are more common in very dry, wet or cold habitats where plant productivity is limited by soil/environmental conditions, or in disturbed habitats where mycorrhizal fungus inoculum is limited. Nonmycorrhizal trees are rare (members of the Australian family Proteaceae are one exception). There are a number of non-ycorrhizal genera which are important in agriculture and horticulture including members of the families Chenopodiaceae, Amaranthaceae, caryophyllaceae, Polygonaceae, Brassicaceae, Scrophulariaceae, Commelinaceae, Juncaceae and Cyperaceae.

Obligatorily Mycorrhizal Plants

Obligatorily mycorrhizal plants are those plants, which will not survive to reproductive maturity without being associated with mycorrhizal fungi in the soils (or at the fertility levels) of their natural habitats. These species consistently support mycorrhizal colonization throughout most of their young roots.

Facultatively Mycorrhizal Plants

Plants that benefit from mycorrhizal associations only in some of the least fertile sols in which they naturally occur. In ecosystem surveys, inconsistent mycorrhizas or low levels of mycorrhizal colonization have been used to designate facultatively mycorrhizal species when soil fertility levels could not be manipulated.

Non-mycorrhizal plants

Plants with roots that consistently resist colonization by mycorrhizal fungi, at least when they are young and healthy. Nutrient levels and other soil properties and mycorrhizal propagules dynamics can also reduce mycorrhizal formation, but usually do not prevent it completely.

MYCORRHIZAL FUNGI AND PATHOGEN INTERACTION

Tomato plants inoculated with VAM fungi were highly resistant to *Phythium aphanidermatum* causing damping off Control of nematodes was also reported due to VAM inoculations. Accumulation of phytoalexin in cowpea root during the infection of *G. fasciculatum* and *G. aggregatum* which could be correlated with the degree of infection. Nematode infection had reduced significantly in mycorrhizal plants. The root extract of mycorrhizal plants caused mortality of nematode larval compared to non-mycorrhizal root extracts. Tomato seedlings inoculated with VAM fungi were more resistant to *Meloidogynae javanica.* A similar control of nematode infestation in tomato and brinjal by inoculation with *G. mosseae* and neem cake.

Table 9.8: Crop typs and responses of inoculation

Crop	Inoculation and Response	Reference
Banana	Responds excellently to VAM inoculation. The *G. mosseae* and *G. fasciculatum* inoculationin combination with phosphate solubilizers and *Azospirillum* improved bunch weight in bale Elakki	Sukhada (1997)

Crop	Inoculation and Response	Reference
Banana Dwarf Cavendish	Treated with *G. fasciculatum* 7 days prior to nematode treatment was able to offset the ill effects of the latter and had more vigorous root nematode population reduced.	Umesh *et al.* (1988)
papaya, Citrus, Mango and Pomegranate	plans could be inoculated effectively with VAM fungi in the nursery and transplanted to the field. The inoculation improves the plant establishment, improves of phosphorus in soil and their uptake (Sukhada, 1992). Due to the increased availability of phosphate in soil a saving in the addition of inorganic phosphate in the soil can be brought about.	(Sukhada, 1997). work conducted at IIHR, Bangalore
papaya, Citrus, Mango and Pomegranate	plans could be inoculated effectively with VAM fungi in the nursery and transplanted to the field. The inoculation improves the plant establishment, improves of phosphorus in soil and their uptake (Sukhada, 1992). Due to the increased availability of phosphate in soil a saving in the addition of inorganic phosphate in the soil can be brought about.	(Sukhada, 1997). work conducted at IIHR, Bangalore
Litchi *(Litchi chinensis* Son)	Distribution of endomycorrhizal spores in the rhizosphere.	Rana and Srivastava, (1984)
Papaya (Coorg Honey Dew)	Studied the uptake of ^2P labeled super phosphate by endomycorrhizal and derived that mycorrhizal fungi besides acting as scavengers of phosphate also increased the availability of phosphates in the soil.	Sukhada *et al.* (1995)
	Standardized PCR amplification technique to identify different genera of VAM fungi.	Sukhada *et al.* (199V)

NITROGEN TRANSFER IN MYCORRHIZAL PLANTS

The idea of nitrogen fixed by a legume component may be available to its associated non-legume plant originated from earlier studies in the late of. In several of their experiments they found that as much as 10 to 30 per cent of the total N fixed in field pea was deposited in the growth media of sand, pre-dominantly as amino acids, and a major part was taken up by an associated cereal. In general, the process of N deposition and uptake in a neighbouring plant is often termed N transfer. Since then substantial N transfer have been observed in several legume/crop intercropping systems such as soybean or cowpea/maize or sorghum, owpea/rice, gram clover/wheat, barley or oat/vetch or lupin etc., although ome experiments showed little or no N transfer between them.

Compared to pure stand cultivation, possible benefits obtained by on-legumes or trees may partly be due to transfer of the symbiotically xed N by legumes, either through directly release from nodulated roots r through decomposition of dead nodule and root tissue in the soil or rough a common mycorrhizal network or even enhanced by mycorrhizal yphae. However, the mechanism of N transfer and the role of mycorrhizal yphae in the direct transfer of nitrogen are not well established. herefore, studies in identifying the pathways of N transfer and whether ycorrhizal hyphae play a direct role in facilitating N transfer are needed.

ITROGEN NUTRITION IN MYCORRHIZAL PLANTS

orms of Nitrogen Used by Mycorrhizal Associations

The two most available forms of inorganic N for plants and both VA ycorrhizal and ectomycorrhizal fungi, are NO_3^- and NH_4^+. Originally, H_4^+ is mainly derived from the reduction of atmospheric dinitrogen ymbiotically fixed by nitrogen fixing plants, either by *Rhizobia* in legumes r by *Frankia* in actinorhizal plants. In general, NO_3 is the dominant orm of nitrogen available to plants and fungi in almost all agricultural oils due to the rapid nitrification of NH_4^+. In contrast, NH_4^+, which is eleased from soil humus and other organic N sources by ammonifying rganisms, predominates and NO_3^- may be almost entirely absent in any undisturbed or very acidic soils. NO_3^- is highly mobile and is readily ansported towards the plant roots by mass flow and diffusion. NH_4^+ is bsorbed to negatively charged soil particles and transported towards e plant roots mainly by diffusion.

lycorrhizal Effects on Nodulation and Nitrogen Fixation

The possibility of a direct involvement of ectomycorrhizal fungi in N cquisition by plants was first suggested by Frank in 1894, Then after 0 years of Frank's work, the probably first observation of growth, odulation and mycorrhizal status of a large number of legumes was ade by Asai in 1944. In most cases, improved nodulation and N fixation mycorrhizal plants appears to be the result of relief from P stress and ossibly uptake of some other essential micronutrients, which result in oth a general improvement in growth and yield and indirect effects upon e N fixing system. The differences between mycorrhizal and non-ycorrhizal plants usually disappear if the latter are supplied with a eadily available P source.

It was known that cereals intercropped with grain legumes generally enefit from the association in terms of increased grain and nitrogen ields per unit area compared with monocropped cereals. This indicates that N transfer from the nitrogen fixing plants (donor) to an associate non-nitrogen fixing plant (receiver) is most likely to happen in natur either *via* the interception and uptake of released fixed nitrogen fron donor plant by the roots of receiver plant or through the root mycorrhiza between donor and receiver plants, or even enhanced by mycorrhiza hyphae. Therefore, in agricultural and/or natural ecological communities mycorrhizal associations may be important factors influencing the performance of both donor and receiver plants through the acquisitior and translocation of nitrogen by the mycorrhizal fungus, particularly wher the relatively immobile NH_4^+-N rather than the mobile N_{O3} -N is the majo source of plant available N.

It is therefore, concluded that Nitrogen fixing and non-nitrogen fixing plants can provide a good example for investigating the N transfe between the plants where neighbouring plants may have differing nitroger status. In general, with or without a split root system, combined with the fine nylon mesh to allow the direct mycorrhizal link but not root contact together with ^{15}N-isotope labelling technique to enrich the N in the dono plant, some experiments have demonstrated a below-ground N-transfer whereas others found no evidence for transfer of nitrogen between donor and receiver plants *via* mycorrhizal hyphae (*see* Smith and Read, 1997). Furthermore, there is controversy about the extent to which direc N-transfer is actually being facilitated by mycorrhizal hyphae or by some other indirect means, and whether it is of agricultural or ecologica significance if N transfer do occur between these plants through mycorrhizal hypha.

The following questions still remain to be answered:

1. Does N transfer occurs between mycorrhizal plants at all? If so, how much N is transferred and how much N transferred is enhanced by mycorrhizal hyphae?.
2. How much net N transfer is from nitrogen fixing to non-nitrogen fixing mycorrhizal plants and *vice versa?*

P Response Curves

Using the most efficient fungus for inoculating a particular crop, the amount the P fertilizer that can be saved may be worked out. Found very large grain yield responses to VA mycorrhizal inoculation in unfertilized soil, but no responses in plots give P fertilizer. In this and several other trials, mycorrhizal responses have been recorded in unfertilized plots, but not in highly fertilized plots. These results highlight the need to describe the mycorrhizal growth response against a growth response curve obtained from a range of P fertilizer rates. It should then be possible to select the fertilizer level at which the responses to inoculation can be optimized. These kinds of experiments suggest the amount of P fertilizer that could be saved with mycorrhizal inoculation to produce the same amount of growth or yield. Mycorrhizal inoculation will only be useful in agriculture if it enables the farmer to achieve optimum yield level with a significantly lower level of P fertilizer. The savings from the reduced fertilizer use will be dependent on the shape of the P response curves, and the same could be compared with the costs of supply and introduction of the mycorrhizal inoculant.

INOCULATION METHODS

Various methods have been tried for introducing VA mycorrhizal inoculum into a field crop.

A. Trasplanted crops

Seedlings are raised in sterilized or un-sterilized soil supplied with selected VA mycorrhizal fungi in small nursery beds or containers and planted out when mycorrhizal colonization is well established. This method has been successfully used to produce worthwhile and economic growth response in agronomically important crops like chilli, finger millet, tomato and tobacco horticultural crops like citrus, mango, asters and marigold, and forest tree species like leucaena, *Tamarindus indica, Acacia nilotica* and *Calliandra calothyrsus.*

It can thus be used in many other transplanted crops of importance in agriculture, horticulture and forestry. The possibility of introducing efficieng VA mycorrhizal fungi to cereals through forest tree species in alley cropping needs investigation.

B. Plant directly sown in the field

Coating seeds with VA mycorrhizal inoculum

Coating seeds with mycorrhizal inoculum similar to that which is produced with *Rhizobium,* would be the easiest method of inoculating plants with VA mycorrhizal fungi if it would provide consistently good infection. Seeds are coated with an adhesive, ex. Methyl cellulose, to which inoculum is expected to stick and subsequently infect the emerging radicals. Unfortunately, because of their large size it is much more difficult to attach VA mycorrhizal propagules than bacteria in this way. However, it has been proved satisfactory for large-seeded crops such as citrus in field nurseries.

Mycorrhizal pellets

Rather than coating seeds with VA mycorrhizal inoculum, it seerns technically more feasible to incorporate seeds into the inoculum to form multiseeded pellets. These pellets, about 1 cm in diameter, consist of soil inoculum from pot cultures stabilized with clay, or peat inoculum. Good infection has been achieved by this means. Hall and Kelson have described a system for producing some 5000 VA mycorhizal infected soil pellets per man-day with seeds attached by gum arabic.

Fluid drilling

Incorporation of seeds and inoculum into a uniform suspension in various fluid, ex 4 per cent (w/v) methyle cellulose, and applycing i furrows as a slurry is another means of placing seeds and inoculum i proximity. This has proved successful under field conditions, bu germination of the seeds must be rigorously controlled to prevent damag to the emerging radicle. The advantage of this technique is that th inoculum is less bulky and does not increase appreciably the volume c material drilled and can be combined with *rhizobia* for legumes.

Inoculation in furrows

Placing inoculum under or beside seeds sown in a furrow is probabl an effective method of inoculating field sown crops. For field experiments research workers have placed mycorrhizal inoculum below the seedlin point. The rates of inoculum they used varied from 0.8 to 167 tonnes pe ha, with rates of 20 to 30 tonnes per ha commonly used. Most of thes rates would be unacceptable in practical agriculture.

Used a tractor drawn drill (Model Nodet) to handle fresh or granulate VAM inoculum for onion and maize crops. Mycorrhizal inoculum place 3 cm below the seed at the rate of 1.9 tonnes per ha increased onio bulb yield by 17 present. With modification in the drill the amount c inoculum used could be reduced and it was found that inoculum at th rate of 400 kg per ha and placed along with the seed, increased th yield of maize by 15 present. These field trials show that the existin farm machinery can be modified to accept mycorrhizal inoculum an give biologically and statistically significant increase in crop yield in th field. The least amount of inoculum (400 kg/ha) used in this field trial i also too high to be used in practical agriculture.

Pre-cropping

Populations of VA mycorrhizal propagules can be raised *in situ* b growing strongly mycorrhizal host plants and leaving the infected root and associated spores in the soil to infect the next crop. Hence, wher mycorrhizal benefits look possible, judicious crop rotations might b considered as a means of manipulating the native mycorrhizal fung These can be increased in bulk if they are effective, otherwise efficien introduced endophytes can be built up on the pre-crop. The top soil coul be used as crude inoculum elsewhere. Suggested to partially sterilize microplots by burning straw in furrows (2 kg straw for a plot of 1m x 1n with 5 furrows, each 15 cm deep) and then raise sorghum or Rhode grass inoculated with a desired VA mycorrhizal fungus. After 75 days the top 15 cm soil along with roots (chopped) can be used as mycorrhiza inoculum. In this way farmers can raise their own inoculum in their fiel from a starter culture obtained from an authentic source.

Appropriate VA mycorrhizal Technology

A. Transplanted crops

As pointed out earlier, there is an immediate potential for farmer use of VA mycorrhizal inoculation for transplanted crops. VA mycorrhizal inoculum of suitably selected strains can be used for inoculation in the nursery bed. Growers only need to incorporate inoculum in the nursery bed or seedlings trays or polythene bags at the appropriate rate by hand. Seedlings thus raised will be colonized by the introduced fungus and can then be planted out in the field.- In developed countries seedlings are usually raised in fumigated soil or potting mix.

Inoculation of such substrate, with selected VA mycorrhizal fungi for the crop, is an easy and appropriate technology. Commercial use of VA mycorrhizal inoculation, by this method, in the nursery production of citrus is done in USA. Inoculation of the nursery with efficient VA mycorrhizal fungi has been successful in the large scale production of white ash seedlings for reforestation in and many horticultural plants in France.

In many developing countries and sometimes in developed countries, seedlings are raised in unsterile soil or substrate. Inoculation with appropriate fungi in seedling trays containing un-sterilised potting mix was found to give vigorously growing seedlings of *Asparagus,* which performed well when planted out in the field. In trails in India it was found that inoculation of un-sterile nursery beds with efficient VA mycorrhizal fungi enhanced the growth rate of slow growing tropical tree species and rootstocks of citrus and mango. This technology, which can easily be adopted by farmers is now being tried on a large scale.

B. Field sown crops

Development of appropriate technology for mycorrhizal inoculations is more difficult for crops sown from seed in the field. Work of showed that farm machinery can be modified to accept mycorrhizal inoculum and to give significantly increased yield to directly field sown crops like maize. So technology for applying VA mycorrhizal inoculum using farm machinery for directly field sown crops is already available should be developed further. The main limiting factor would be production of large quantities of inoculum. VA mycorrhizal inoculation by hand, in developing countries, may be feasible for crops with low field densities (because of larger spacing between plants) such as fruit trees and root crops like yam, cassava etc.

10

The Cyclic System of Nutrient Management

Plants require 13 essential nutrient elements (6 major and 7 micronutrients) and can profit from some beneficial nutrients. The amount of nutrients required by crops depends largely on the target yield level. Only under rare circumstances the nutrients required for high yields are "automatically" supplied from the soil nutrient reserves.

The response of crop growth and yield to the nutrient supply can be expressed in growth or yield curves and described by "yield laws". In practical cropping, nutritive minimum factors are often responsible for un-satisfactory yields and thus present growth problems. Therefore, a proper nutrient management (of the nutrients added to the soil as well as in order to keep many nutrients, especially microelements, on a sufficient natural supply level) is of fundamental importance for effective, successful and sustainable agriculture.

The non-compensated use of soil nutrients is usually regarded as exploitation or "mining" of nutrients leading to degraded soil fertility. However, two different concepts should be distinguished: exploitation *vs.* utilization. Their difference can be compared with pumping water from wells. If a water level is slightly or considerably lowered, water is exploited and the system is not sustainable. If the water level is not noticeably lowered even after long period, water *is jusr* utilized, the system could be called sustainable.

Exploitation of soil nutrients is frequently applied which decreases the level of available nutrients quickly or slowly and is therefore non-sustainable.

Utilization of soil nutrients consists in partly removing nutrients without (significant) impoverishment of the nutrient supply or reduction of soil fertility. This can continue on fertile soils for a long time (centuries for some microelements) and creates the impression of permanence of natural nutrient supply.

GEOGRAPHICAL NUTRIENT TRANSFER

In smaller or greater region there are natural nutrient flows and nutrient transfers by trade, *e.g.*, into cities or even export into other countries. These mainly unilateral transfers are of environmental concern since they are not only the cause of nutrient losses from a farming area (and partly completely lost for production), but also unwanted from water eutrophication point of view.

Natural transfers (nutrient flows in landscapes)

A steady flow occurs naturally with surface or ground water movement in hilly or mountainous areas as part of the slow natural erosion process even under natural vegetation cover. The annual losses from the hilly pat of the landscape are relatively small, and so re the gains for the low-lying land. In geological periods, however, this transfer has produced many fertile alluvial sols in river basins that now belong to the best agricultural lands. If this process is accelerated by recent man-made strong soil erosion, it can lead to serious soil fertility decrease in the hilly area and to an excessive input on nutrient (especially N and P) into water.

The extent of nutrient transfers in small watershed areas or whole river basins is difficult to determine because of many factors involved (sources not only from agriculture, but also from towns, industry, *etc.*). Anyhow, several studies of this kind are conducted in Europe in order to estimate those amount of nutrients transferred into rives or lakes for which the agricultural production of this area is held responsible (*e.g.*, as a basis for restrictive regulations on fertilization).

Nutrient transfer into cities

With food and other farm products plant nutrients are transferred from farm areas to villages, towns, big cities and mega-cities. The rate of recycling usually decreases with increasing size of the settlement and depends on the disposal system for sewage and garbage. Many cities are proud of their perfect sewage disposal system (leading biologically treated sewage water into rivers or the sea and filling garbage into deposits). This system of just getting rid of the waste materials, however, means an enormous loss of plant nutrients with the unwanted secondary effect of eutrophication (by N and P).

Very few cities have a direct recycling of treated sewage onto fields, because recycling of sewage sludges compost seems to be more adequate. But even so, farmers are increasingly reluctant to apply composted sewage or garbage as nutrient source (even if offered free of charge) because of the well-known problem of toxic heavy metals (and possibly even toxic organic substances), not only in view of decreasing food quality, but as a potential danger for soil fertility. With the past experience of environmental laws getting ever stricter, farmers suspect, that the critical limits for soil contamination might be decreased for political reasons and thus putting otherwise fertile land out of production by law. In addition, farmers dislike being accused by city people of "poisoning" the soil and thus decreasing food quality while helping them to dispose their waste products.

Theoretically, the measures required for an adequate recycling, are well . known and feasible, namely to provide (almost) uncontaminated organic materials via separating the different waste materials and excluding toxic ones. Although this poses many problems in detail, a more or less quantitative recycling will be essential from the big cities in the future.

Export into other countries

The nutrient export with feedstuff and food into other countries can reach substantial amounts that are lost from the national nutrient budget (although not from the global one). Many developed countries with high animal production, even those, which could produce sufficient feedstuff by their own agriculture, import substantial amounts of feedstuff and corresponding plant nutrients because of the cheaper price. For the Netherlands this import is outstandingly high, namely about 2/3 of P and K of the total fertilizer import.

On the other hand, as long as this unilateral transfer with agricultural products can be compensated by re-import of mineral fertilizer, the nutrient loss of the developing countries will not really be a serious problem since there seems to be no urgent need for self-sufficiency of countries in plant nutrients.

THE CONCERN

First, there are the scientists concerned with agriculture chemistry who produce research data and present theories. The validity of their information is usually taken for granted, however, some conclusions from field experiments and regional studies are not as reliable as claimed by the authors. Some yield increases attributed to better N supply correspond in fact to secondary effects (problem of wrong x-axis), the result being an overestimation of the required N amounts and higher avoidable Josses. As another example, there seems to be a tendency to over-estimate the part of river pollution that must be attributed to the agriculture of the region (whereas other sources tend to be under-estimated). Consequently, the scientific information on fertilization, nutrient flows and losses should be critically examined and evaluated.

Second, advisors are supposed to "translate" the theoretical suggestions into a practical *know-how.* Unfortunately, the information obtained from experts is not always very precise (especially as for the conditions under which the results are valid) or not really prepared for this purpose. Anyhow, advisors have to combine the information available with their own experience, express it in terms of farmer's knowledge and formulate it for practical use.

Third, there are the farmers, eager to produce as high crop yields as possible and who, if they care for their land as owner or tenant, want to maintain its production potential for crops and animals for a long time. In addition to their own experience, they want intelligible and definite guidelines rather than sophisticated models with plenty of vague factors. They know about the difficulties, uncertainties and dis-appointments of primary production on the field and do their best to get along with the information available for sustainable crop production. On the other hand, farmers are also entrepreneurs, living in a world where economical considerations have priority over correct farming practice. It would be a long list describing the deviations from what farmers might want to do and what they are forced to do for economical reasons (in order to maintain their income and their farm).

Least, but not last, there is the general public that is more and more represented by city people. Most of them live rather far away from agriculture and are hardly aware of biological and chemical crop production principles. These consumers demand a lot of good and cheap food, pure drinking water, etc. They try to impose on the farmers their ideas of nature, landscape and farming, as well as their demands for town waste recycling. There should be limits to these demands, however, because many deplorable developments in agriculture are the result of the consumer's pressure. Consumers should realize, that farming has its own rules and that high soil productivity is a man-made valuable property that must be sustained, especially by proper plant nutrient management for generations to come. The world population can be fed in much higher numbers than today, but the pollution problems will set stricter limits.

Future nutrient shortages

The customary approach of agronomists is to adapt the essentials of food production (especially nutrient use) to the requirements of the population being determined by prevailing socio-economic conditions. In many areas, an increasing number of people must be fed according to their nutritional habits, their location, mainly in cities and their desire for cheap food.

If this finally happens on a global scale, there will be shortages of at least some plant nutrients in the not so far future. However, long time before nutrient shortages become really acute (which may first be the case of P, the bottle-neck of world hunger) within a few hundred years, the remaining reserves should rather be used more to replace unavoidable losses than to comply with wasteful nutrient use and to serve an over-extending food demand.

In the long run, instead of adapting the plant nutrient consumption to food demand, the food demand may have to be adapted to the amount of nutrients that can be annually used for the remaining reserves. Sustainable agriculture is not a matter of decades or centuries, but should go on indefinitely. The future agricultural production must not only be sustainable, but its extent and form should also be adapted to the limited resources. With increasing awareness of limited global plant nutrient resources, some conflicts of interest are unavoidable in different respects.

First, the necessity for farmers to produce as much and cheap in order to be competitive on the market may lead to a certain disregard of many well-proven agronomic principles, and even more of good animal husbandry (a list of society-induced "sins" of agriculture would be rather long).

Second, due to the high demand of animal protein, much more grain and other crops must be produced for vegetative food (*e.g.,* the production of 1 kg of meat requires 3 to 4 kg of grain). This is a well-known fact, of course, but rarely regarded from the nutrient supply point of view.

In this context it may be quoted, that promoting long-term sustainable nutrient management will ultimately require radical changes in the way agriculture and society are organized. These include reintegration of livestock and crop farms and the encouragement of closer physical association of people with farmland. Establishing and implementing performance expectations for contemporary patterns of nutrient flow is especially difficult because the scale of transactions is broad and control of most aspects is far removed from the farm level (Magdoff *et al.,* 1997).

Finally, in a distant future, the old *Chinese village* principle may have to be applied to the whole world. If food production (even on all available land and by using all possible means) is limited and there is no population outlet neither to east nor to west nor to other planets, to eating habits may have to shift to predominantly vegetarian food - and even the population number may have to be adapted to the remaining resources.

FROM NUTRIENT FLOWS TO CYCLES

A main objective is converting unwanted flowers into useful cycles. Recycling of nutrients within the farm area tends to be not uniform. For example, slurry is preferably deposited on fields near a farm because of transport costs. On grassland with cows, the manure excreted in distributed very unevenly. Another example is the spotty distribution of ashes after the burning of straw or of the natural vegetation.

None of the cycles is closed, most of them are leaking. Some losses are unavoidable (and may be considered as natural load, a minimum tribute for primary production), whereas, others are avoidable by adequate nutrient management. There is a widespread opinion that decreasing N fertilization is the best preventive measure for reducing leaching losses of nitrate. This holds only true, however, for fertilization systems where N is overemphasized (unfortunately not a rare practice in intensive fertilization cropping), whereas, even high application of N together with a sufficient supply of other nutrients (*i.e.,* with no yield limiting minimum factor) may result only in still tolerable losses.

Cycling is a very complex system. Although it is not so difficult to design a complex model of nutrient flows, their quantitative assessment will partly have to be based on some more or less uncertain estimates. Therefore, the result can only be approximate. For practical use, cycling models should be restricted to the important nutrient fluxes.

In the case of big cities (especially megalopolis) the recycling of imported nutrients to the farm area is rather limited. Many waste products are rather deposited into landfills or led into rivers or the sea (after "biological" treatment, but mostly without extracting phosphate).

Organic Farming and Waste Recycling

Organic farming is the backbone of sustainable agriculture. Organic farming mainly depends on organic recycling. Industrial agricultural chemicals like fertilizers, pesticides, herbicides, etc. are not used or used to the minimum extent necessary in this kind of farming. According to the definition of FAO, organic farming should involve successful management of resources for agriculture to satisfy changing human needs while maintaining or enhancing the quality of the environment and consuming natural resources. Organic farming may result in comparable performance as conventional agriculture and crops grown with high organic manure application could tolerate the pest and disease attack better. It is an ecologically sound and sustainable way of growing more food.

Harnessing the nutrient energy from biological and industrial wastes is of prime importance for maximizing production. When these wastes are recycled as manure for crop production and are subjected to the degradation and assimilative capacity of soil, pollution of streams and/ or rivers receiving these wastes is reduced to a large extent as compared to their direct disposal in water bodies. Organic recyclable wastes include crop residues, animal wastes, farm/industrial wastes, municipal and sewage wastes. They are valuable sources of plant nutrients and humus. In tropical and sub-tropical soils found in India, there is a general deficiency of organic carbon and plant nutrients due to rapid loss of these components by bio-degradation. To make up for these losses, extensive utilization of organic residues in agriculture is essential. In addition, they also protect the soil from erosion. The manurial value and quality of these wastes could be improved by composting and enriching these organic sources along with inexpensive materials such as rock phosphate.

In India, there is a great potential for utilization of crop residues/ straw of some of the major cereals and pulses. Approximate availability of straw is to the tune of 141.2 mt, which contribute about 0.7, 0.84 and 2.1 mt. of N, P_2O_5 and K_2O respectively. Considering that about 50 per cent of these residues are utilized as animal feed, the rest could be very well utilized for recycling of nutrients. Crop residues have wide C:N ratio and when applied directly, nutrients may get immobilized leading to initial adverse effect on crop growth. Hence, adequate care is required to use the residues after proper composting with efficient microbial inoculants. Inoculation of these wastes with efficient cellulotic microorganisms produces enough simple sugars for growth and multiplication of beneficial microflora like free living N fixers and phosphate solubilizers in the soil which ultimately increases crop yields.

While the incorporation of crop residues *e.g.,* wheat and rice straw, as such or inoculated with fungal species had beneficial effects on crop yields and improvement in physico-chemical properties of soils. Incorporation of legume residues *viz,,* green gram or soybean stalks in rice, cowpea stalks in pearl millet or wheat saves energy input besides improving the soil physical and chemical properties.

THE CYCLIC SYSTEM FOR NUTRIENT MANAGEMENT

With a system approach *i.e.* synergistic integration of more than one component, the management of nutrient is to be done in such away so that there is minimum loss along with addition (in organic form) of the nutrient in the soil, taken out in terms of yield. This makes a cyclic system of nutrient management, which has major role in long-term sustainable production.

MINIMIZING NUTRIENT LOSSES

Important loses of nutrients occur through removal of the harvested products, soil erosion, gaseous losses and leaching. In the following chapter we will especially deal with losses through soil erosion, because this is the major form of undesired nutrient loss in Sub-Sahara Africa .

Factors affecting soil erosion are rainfall intensity and quantity of rainfall, erodability of the soil, length and steepness of slopes and soil cover (Young, 1991). Traditional soil conservation projects have been emphasizing the use of physical structures (terraces, etc.), which mainly reduce soil erosion by changing the steepness and length of slopes. Current approaches to soil conservation, however, give more attention to reducing soil erosion by improving soil cover rather tha construction of physical structures.

Ongoing researches explore technologies to modify slopes and improve soil cover. The following section gives an overview of the current approaches.

Changes in soil slope

Reducing soil slope by terracing has been the traditional approach to control soil erosion in many soil conservation projects. Terracing is a very effective way of reducing soil erosion if properly constructed. The major disadvantage is the high labour requirement (Douglas, 1994). The current approach is to give less emphasis to complete terracing and instead promote the use of progressive terracing. Progressive terracing implies that terraces are formed gradually as sediments are deposited in front of a contour barrier. This will often also tend to increase the fertility of the soil in front of the barriers because the deposited sediments are often rich in nutrients. The barriers can be made out of stones, earth, crop residues, vegetation strips, trash etc. In the case where *the* barriers are made out of stones or vegetation, the barriers are semi-permeable allowing water to filter through. They will, therefore, to some extent take care of excess water and thereby avoid complete inundation of the field.

The best choice of barriers depends on the circumstances. It stones are easily available they can be used as building material. Success stories with the use of stone barriers have been reported from Niger (Pretty. 1995). The height of the stone barriers will have to be increased as sediments are deposited and the structures will also need to be repaired.

Vegetation strips can also be used as an effective barrier especially on low to moderately sloping land. The most simple way to establish vegetation strips is to leave some strips of the land unploughed (Osunade and Reij, 1996). Vegetation strips can also be establishing by planting. However, vegetation strips are difficult to establish in areas where there is a high grazing pressure. Under such circumstances non-palatable grasses or herbs should be used as strips. In order arise an interest among the farmers to plant vegetation belts, the plans should have some economic value by, for example, providing thatching material. Farmers should be encouraged to identify local plants, which can be used in barriers. Species used as vegetation strips should not be too aggressive as they can then easily turn into weeds. If grazing can be controlled, use of palatable species can be used in the vegetation strips. This will offer a much greater range of species to choose from. The barriers should contain species, which have a high economic value.

Another simple way to form barriers is to crop residues, weeds or any other material, which is readily available (trashline). Such barriers are not very suitable on steep slopes as they easily break. The major advantage is, however, that they are easy to make and repair.

It is also possible to combine different materials, either using them in alternative barriers or combining them within the barrier. Trashlines can for example be strengthened by using stones at weak points.

No universal answer exists with regards to which material should be used in physical structures. Farmers and project staff need to continuously test and screen technologies.

Soil cover

Improving soil cover can be just as effective in controlling soil erosion as changing the slope (Young, 1989). The initial process in water erosion is detachment of soil particles by the force of raindrops. Improving soil cover will reduce the velocity of the raindrops, thereby halting soil erosion in its initial phase. Soil cover can be altered by changing the crop, increasing the yield by use of soil fertility enhancing methods and use of surface mulch.

Controlling soil erosion by changing species composition from annual to perennial crops is an important way of controlling soil erosion. Annual crops are especially inefficient in controlling soil erosion early in the growing season before they become well established. Perennial plants will cover the ground for a longer period of time and have a more dense cover. It has been reported from Rwanda that coffee is in the order of 18 times as effective as maize in controlling soil erosion (Lewis, 1987). Farmers should therefore be stimulated to use perennials such as coffee, tea and fruit trees. It has, however, not been very easy to convince farmers to plant trees in their farm land. Alley cropping, a technology to which great expectations were attached in 1980s has not been successful among farmers.

The main reason for using soil fertility enhancing methods is to increase yield. However, IPNM technology will reduce soil erosion because plans in vigorous grown give a good soil cover. Erosion can be reduced to less than half under a well managed maize crop as compared to a maize crop grown under poor management (Roose, 1977).

Another way of improving soil cover by increasing yield is to undertake appropriate and timely tillage. In Ethiopia, oxen are used for ploughing. However, there is often a shortage of oxen and the individual farmer does not always have access to the two oxen considered necessary for tillage (Aune and Aragay, 1998). This causes delayed sowing leaving the land unprotected early in the growing season. Research by the International Livestock Research Institute (ILRI) has shown, however, that one ox in good shape can perform the task just as efficiently as two oxen in bad shape. Reduced tillage can be a method for reducing soil erosion because soil left undisturbed is more resistant to the erosive forces of the rain.

HARNESSING UNTAPPED NUTRIENT SOURCES

If used appropriately, the recycling of organic waste from urban to rural areas is a potential, largely untapped, source of nutrients for farm and crop needs, especially on agricultural lands near urban centers. For example, environmentally undesirable wastewater has been used to irrigate fields and return nutrients and organic matter to the soil (Tandon, 1992). Like organic manure, urban waste sludge is a source of primary nutrients, albeit a relatively poor source in comparison with commercial fertilizers. Stabilized municipal waste sludge typically contains about 3.3 per cent nitrogen, 2.3 per cent phosphorus, and 0.3 per cent potassium, although some concentrations can reach as high as 10 per cent nitrogen and 8 per cent phosphorus on a dry weight basis (EPA 1984). Actual nutrient content, however, varies widely and depends on the source of the waste. Urban waste also has a number of other benefits. Like other organic manures, it helps improve soil structure by adding organic matter to the soil. It is also a source of the secondary nutrients and micronutrients that are necessary in small quantities for proper plant growth. In addition, urban waste transforms material that would otherwise be slated for costly disposal into a useful farm product.

Urban waste also contains organic compounds such as dyes, inks, pesticides, and solvents that are often found in commercial and industrial sludge. These pathogens have been shown to cause genetic damage, while others, such as bacteria, protozoa, and viruses can cause salmonellosis, amoebic dysentery, and infectious hepatitis (Conway and Pretty, 1991). Untreated urban waste can put these pathogens in contact with fruits and vegetables. One option is to compost the sludge. Composting concentrates nutrients and helps to kill disease-causing organisms, slow the release of nitrogen that might otherwise percolate into groundwater, and eliminate aesthetically objectionable odors (Kurihara, 1984). Another option is to use ionizing radiation to kill pathogens in and on food without affecting taste. Despite some public concern about the safety of food irradiation, the technique is likely to be adopted more fully in the future in order to protect public health, improve the shelf-life of food, and make it more feasible to apply treated, nutrient-rich urban waste to farmland.

Currently, effective use of urban waste is hampered by its high water content, bulkiness, distance from rural areas, contamination with non-decomposable household items and high handling, storage, transport, and application costs. However, given the cost and the lack of availability of inorganic fertilizers in some areas, the relative abundance and benefit of urban waste as a soil amendment, and the rising cost of environmentally safe waste disposal, economies may make urban waste an appropriate fertilizer choice in areas where agricultural lands are near urban centers.

Alternative sources of inorganic fertilizers will also be required in the future, particularly in those parts of Africa where the fertility of the soil needs to be rebuilt and high costs and supply constraints limit the application of fertilizer. Soil infertility (particularly phosphorus deficiency) in parts of semi-arid West Africa, for example, limits crop productions more than the lack of moisture. Phosphorus application of 15-20 kilograms per hectare can substantially improve crop yields. Medium-reactive and partially acidulated, less-reactive phosphate rock found in Mali, Niger, and Senegal are as agronomically effective as commercial superphosphate fertilizers (Bationo and Mikwunye, 1991). Low-cost technology needs to be developed so that phosphate fertilizer can be locally produced from these and other untouched or currently uneconomical phosphate rock reserves. Where phosphate deficiency is sever in Sub-Sahara Africa, government assistance in developing low-cost technology and in applying phosphate fertilizer should be evaluated. Because phosphorus and phosphorus rock bind to the soil and thereby reduce the opportunity for leaching, and because these fertilizers release nutrients slowly over time, their use to preserve the long-term productive capacity of the land should be considered more of a capital investment than a subsidy or an environmentally undesirable government intervention (Mokwunye, 1995; Gerner and Baanante, 1995; Teboh, 1995).

EXPLORING INTERNAL NUTRIENT SOURCES

Although new sources of nutrients can be developed, genetic engineering offers the potential for plants themselves to generate some of the nutrients they require through nitrogen fixation. In this process, *rhizobium* bacteria infect, invade, and draw energy from leguminous plants, and in return the bacteria convert and store atmospheric nitrogen in a form that the plant can use for growth (Rao, 1993). Besides helping the plants themselves, cereals grown in rotation with leguminous plants can absorb the nitrates released from the decaying roots and nodules of the leguminous plants. Experiments have shown that rice-legume rotations can result in a 30 per cent reduction in chemical fertilizer use (Pingali and Rosegrant, 1994).

Genetic research has begun to identify the genes responsible for such nitrogen fixation and assimilation. Further research offers the opportunity of altering or developing microorganisms that can fix nitrogen in non-leguminous plants, such as cereals. As with leguminous plants, plant nitrogen needs could be partially met by the plant itself, such that farmers would then simply need to top-up crops with inorganic nitrogen fertilizers (Rao, 1993). The task is considerable. Some 17 genes code the enzymes involved in nitrogen fixation. Since these genes, as well as the genes necessary for nodule formation, need to be transferred, the process is complex and its realization will be costly. Furthermore, because the amount of energy required to fix 150 kilograms of nitrogen per hectare could reduce wheat yields by 20-30 per cent, an appropriate balance needs to be found between the nutrient-supply-enhancing benefits of nitrogen fixation and the potential reduction in yields (Greenley and Farrington, 1989; Lipton and Longhurst 1989).

BETTER USE OF NUTRIENT SOURCES

Soil nutrient and soil fertility aspects

Soil nutrients are the basic source of the farm nutrient supply. The part of them are utilized by crops, *i.e.,* the easily available portion (water-soluble, exchangeable) as well as the easily mobilizable fraction. The mobilization of nutrients from (mineral and organic) slowly available sources can be enhanced to a certain extent by activating soil life (in general by organic matter of by special bio-fertilizers), by crop varieties with strongly mobilizing capacity, by better accessibility of nutrients after structure improvement, by deepening of the plow layer or by fallow periods.

The best use of nutrients for crop growth can be obtained on the basis of a high soil fertility level. Soil fertility is a complex term (not very precise, but very useful even in its vague form) which includes many components: soil depth, texture and structure (pore space for supply of oxygen and water), soil reaction, organic matter content and composition, activity of soil organisms, nutrient content, storage capacity for nutrients, content, respectively, absence of detrimental or toxic substances. The result of an Optimum combination of these factors is a high soil fertility that means a high crop production potential.

For the practical use of soil nutrients, the basic problem is the estimation of the amount that will be available during the growing season (in order to fill the remaining gap with additional nutrients). The main diagnostic method is soil testing for available nutrients, and most countries have their soil testing system calibrated for special areas. Whereas, the analytical methods are rather precise, due to the heterogeneity of most soils, the diagnosis can only provide an approximate estimate. Nevertheless, it is possible to draw useful conclusions on the necessity of additional nutrients. For more precise information, systems of plant analysis have been developed.

Very fertile (and thus productive) soils are rarely found in nature. Unfortunately, most soils are far from being ideally fertility and should therefore be improved, not only by adding nutrients, but also by other soil amendments, *e.g.,* lime for correcting strong soil acidity, organic matter for maintaining the activity of "soil life", etc.

Soil fertility may be rather uniform in a field, but it sometimes varies within a short range (in some fields visible by considerable differences in plant height). In such cases, soil productivity studies (by soil and plant analysis) are suitable to determine the cause of such differentiated growth and offer the possibility of eliminating the limiting factor.

Optimum soil reaction

Many soils, due to a continuous acidification caused by several factors, are a little or much too acidic for high productivity. Therefore liming is required and the soil should have its optimum soil reaction which varies with soil texture, cropping intensity, etc. The usual (local) recommendations for optimum pH are generally higher with higher clay content and yield level.

Optimum pH values or ranges are often a compromise between two different goal: first a good soil (crumb) structure which requires rather natural pH range on heavy soils and second a better rate of mobilization of most nutrients, especially micronutrients like Fe, Mn and Zn, which requires a somewhat lower pH range.

In rare cases of over-limed soil in intensive cropping areas, the pH can be temporarily lowered by application of acidifying N-fertilizers (mobilizing nutrients like Mn of Zn on tiny spots).

Soil organic matter

The qualitative importance of organic matter for soil fertility is rather well known, but many quantitative aspects are still to be solved. The main functions of soil organic matter are physical soil improvement (increase in water and air capacity, protection against erosion, etc.) and several chemical functions (increase of sorption capacity, mobilization of nutrients by mineralization of organic matter and from minerals, short term immobilization into soil organisms (which thus compete with crop for N) and long term fixation into stable humid substances (*e.g.* improvement of quality *via* C/N ratio), supply of beneficial organic substances (growth promoters, antibiotics, etc.)

The importance of soil organic matter differs in climatic regions, the role of nutrient source often being a dominant one. It should not be decreased, but maintained at an acceptable level, above critical values corresponding to structural stability and biological activity. In rainfed tropical agriculture, soil organic matter is the corner stone for the building of any sustainable annual cropping system, but there is not yet a definite answer to the critical level that should be maintained (Pieri, 1995).

In areas of intensive cropping, an increased level and better quality of soil organic matter has significantly contributed to the high productivity level.

ORGANIC MATERIALS

There is a large variety of materials produced on the farm as well as *imported* from outside, especially communal and food processing waste materials.

Crop residues and farm manures

Crop residues vary considerably in their nutrient contents (*e.g.*, grain straw *vs.* green leaves). Residues and manures should be returned to the fields with only little nutrient losses. As for animal manures, the change from the old-type animal manure/straw mixture to slurry (induced by the labour-savings but otherwise somewhat doubtful progress due to straw-less stubbles) has substantially contributed to N losses. Main losses of animal sludge distribution occur from ammonia volatilization (sometimes more than half), but losses can be reduced substantially by application of the sludge into the soil instead of spreading it on the surface, the latter procedure being unfortunately still widely used in practice.

A general question of nutrient management is the alternative to using waste materials directly or improving them by special treatments, especially by effective composting.

In many regions, there is a competitive use of organic matter that could be used as feedstuff, fertilizer, fuel for direct burning or for biogas. As a rule, organic matter fit for soil application should not be burned, although in some situations, there may be little choice for a farmer.

Organic materials should be applied to crops which make the best use of them, *e.g.*, the immediately available ammonia of slurry given to crops before the period of rapid growth, or slowly acting N sources to crops with a long growing season and with extra profit from the structural improvement for root growth.

Under humid conditions, crop residues are generally mixed into the topsoil as a nutrient source and also for soil improvement. Input of organic material should not only increase, but also improve (higher C/N ratio, etc.) soil organic matter (Burgos, 1995). In arid regions (although an increase in soil humus would even be more important), crop residues are often left on or near the surface for soil erosion control and for water conservation.

Under high yield conditions it may be difficult to get the straw of the previous crop decomposed in a short time and there can be negative effects like temporary fixing of available N (due to the large requirements of the decomposting bacteria). The practice of burning a surplus of straw and just using the ash as a mineral fertilizer is now forbidden in some countries for environmental reasons (smog).

Commercial and industrial waste products

The waste products that can be used as nutrient sources are materials produced by composting from sewage sludge or (organic) garbage.

It is in the interest of towns and food processing industries to return their waste products to farmers' fields. These waste materials may even be offered as cheap nutrient sources, which can save mineral fertilizer input. The advantage for a farmer can be estimated by taking into account the nutrient content and some additional organic matter effect.

There is a growing concern, however, about some toxic elements and even toxic organic substances that might decrease soil fertility and quality of food and fodder products. Especially in the case of some heavy metals farmers should be very conscious of not enriching their soils above the toxic limit in an irreversible way since amelioration will prove to be very difficult. Some protection against this danger is given by keeping the contents of toxic substances below tolerable limits and by using these materials only on soils which still are rather uncontaminated.

Other organic fertilizers

It is well known, that with some bio-fertilizers the fixing of atmosphere N can be increased by organisms such as *Rhizobium. Azoiobacter,* blue green algae, *Azolla/Anabaena* (Gaur and Singh, 1995). They are described in detail in the previous chapters.

BETTER NUTRIENT MANAGEMENT FOR CROPS AND CROP ROTATIONS

Adaptation of crops and crop rotations to nutrient supply

For cropping conditions of low natural nutrient supply and restricted input special emphasis must be placed on the nutrient efficiency of crops, mainly uptake efficiency, but possibly also internal use efficiency.

Crop species and even varieties differ to a certain extent in their ability for mobilization and uptake of soil nutrients, especially under conditions of low natural supply. Since under low input conditions the contribution of soil nutrient reserves (especially P and K) is of eminent importance (Syers, 1995), varieties should be chosen that provide special mechanisms like root excretions for their mobilization and for improved uptake. The same holds true for cases of rather immobile single micronutrients (*e.g.,* Fe, Mn, Zn, Cu deficiency).

In intensive agriculture more emphasis is placed on high yield performance and disease resistance than on nutrient efficiency since it is more economical to supply extra nutrients (for micronutrients even by leaf spray).

The uptake from only slowly available soil reserves can be further improved by choice of crops with an extra potential of nutrient mobilization *via* mycorrhiza or rhizosphere associated organisms. Symbiotic mycorrhiza fungi (VAM = Vesicular-Arbuscular Mycorrhiza) are widely present in fertile soils (or may be inoculated for special crops). The effect of this symbiosis is an improved nutrient uptake in general, mainly a better P uptake of the roots due to better mobilization of soil P reserves and also to more efficient use of added P fertilizers, furthermore an improved uptake to other nutrients with low mobility like some micronutrient metals. VAM improves the productivity by reducing the input, whereas relying more on soil nutrient reserves, but also by enhancing plant survival under nutritional stress conditions (Barea, 1991).

The most striking example of crop adaptation to nutrient deficiency is the cropping of legumes with *rhizobia* for fixing nitrogen. An example typical for paddy rice is the *Azolla-Anabaena* symbiosis.

Not only a crop has to be adapted to nutrient supply, but also general agronomic measures like proper weed control (saving nutrients for crops) and efficient crop protection (for obtaining and protecting high yields) are required to make the best use of nutrient sources.

Adaptation of crop rotations to nutrient supply

Although monocultures (like tree plantations or sugar cane) offer the easiest way of production on arable land, many crops are not self-compatible and a farmer usually has to consider the nutrient supply of crop rotations (cropping systems).

Rotations are planned for several (an partly competing) reasons: for special products wanted due to economical reasons, for maintenance of soil fertility, for plant disease and pest control, for nutrient supply, etc.

From the crop nutrition point of view, different aspects have to be considered. Rotations can consists of crops with high or low nutrient requirements or of crops known either to improve or decrease soil structure and activity of soil life.

The well-known example of legumes alternating with non N fixing crops should also be mentioned. Rotations may be chosen which do not leave the soil without green cover (intermediate crops, green manure or even weeds) in order to prevent nutrient losses form bare fallow in the period with pronounced leaching.

The soil nutrient supply may also be improved by not using one crop, but crop combinations like intercropping or mixed cropping (Francis, 1989). A widely applied practice is the simultaneous growth of grasses with legumes in fodder production.

NUTRIENT MANAGEMENT FOR QUALITY PRODUCTS AND STRESS RESISTANCE

Higher quality of food and fodder products

Nutrient management, beyond the yield aspect, includes also aspects of quality since food or fodder should contain sufficient minerals elements for healthy growth of men and animals, especially since some critical values for quality are higher than those for high yields. As a general rule, better nutrient supply of crops improves food quality, *i.e.*, increase the mineral and organic components required by men. On the other hand, an unwanted surplus of some nutrients (especially N) may decrease quality parameters. Food quality also includes aspects of undesirable toxic elements like cadmium, the uptake of which should be kept as low as possible.

Nutrient management of grassland for fodder quality

The nutrient cycling in grazed pasture ecosystems has been reviewed by Haynes and Williams (1993). A prominent feature is the recycling with a very uneven distribution because of the spotted deposition of excretions by grazing animals.

As for the quality aspect, an adequate nutrient supply of grassland must take into account not only the yield (of milk, meat, etc.), but also the health and fertility, *e.g.*, of cows. The nutrient requirements of grassland plants and animals are more or less similar, but they can also differ in part. For example, for highly productive milking cows a higher content of P, Mg, Mn, Zn, Cu in the fodder is required than for a high grass yield. In addition, the special requirement of cobalt, selenium or even chromium for animals should be considered, especially in deficient are as (unless mineral supplements are given).

If grassland is included in crop rotations, there should not be too much carryover of such nutrients, which may disturb the nutrient balance of fodder, *e.g.*, surplus of K may induce Mg deficiency.

Higher stress resistance of crops due to better nutrition

The usual concept of nutrient supply is based on "normal" growth conditions. In fact, however, there are frequently constraints for crop growth under stress conditions, which require special nutrient management.

The stress situation is often aggravated by combination of several factors, *e.g.*, low temperature at the time of crop protection spraying.

Resistance of crops against cold stress can be increased by optimizing the supply of some of the nutrients (K, P, Mn, Cu).

For arid conditions, it is important to realize that with better crop nutrition less water is required and that especially with good K supply the transpiration of crops is reduced. Saline soils need a special nutrient management for reducing the uptake of unwanted Na, etc. The water-use efficiency depending on plant nutrient supply is reviewed by Davis (1994).

Soil acidity, problems are wide spread in humid areas, the most striking example being the acid sulfate soils. Soil below about pH 4.5

mostly produce low yields (if at all) and the plants are more susceptible to diseases due to the soil acidity syndrome (lack of some nutrients, especially P, and surplus of toxic substances like Al).

Soil-borne stress can be eliminated or at least decreased by soil amelioration. On soils polluted with toxic heavy metals their negative effect on crops can be decreased by special amendments (stronger fixation of the mobile portion by liming and metal fixing agents).

A balanced nutrient supply (instead of a relative N surplus) generally increased the resistance against certain bacteria and fungi (resulting in a lower requirement of pesticides).

NUTRIENT MANAGEMENT IN FARMING SYSTEMS

All farming systems have their qualifications under special natural or economical conditions. Of the determining factors nutrient management may not have priority, but it nevertheless plays an important (an increasing) role, namely to make the best use of soil and fertilizer nutrients within the framework of the dominating factors for a special farming system.

For the present purpose, various types of farming systems and agricultural land utilization are shortly listed in alternative groups with some corresponding problems of nutrient management added.

Efficient Nutrient-Recycling with Agroforestry

Agroforestry systems can lead to more nearer to the nutrient cycling than agriculture, and hence to more efficient use of nutrients. Under natural woodland and forest ecosystems, a large quantity of nutrients circulate annually between plants and the soil; in a mature (climax) community the plant-soil system as a whole is in equilibrium and the inputs and outputs of nutrients are small. A high-input agricultural system, in contrast, has inputs processes (leaching, gaseous loser and erosion) and removal in harvest. The element of recycling, through decomposition of root and, perhaps, crop residues is relatively small. By the inclusion of trees, agroforesiry systems can achieve a condition intermediate between these extremes, by reducing losses and increasing plant uptake.

This can be expressed quantitatively as the nutrient-recycling raiio. treating the plant-soil complex as a system. Gains and losses are external to the system, uptake and return are internal transfers, respectively soil to plant and plant to soil. Treating the organic and mineral parts of the soil together and indicating where processes affect certain nutrients only, flows in the plant-soil nutrient cycle.

Gain	Atrnospheric: rain and dust Fertilizer Organic additions fixations (nitrogen)

	Symbiotic fixation (nitrogen)
	Deep capture (uptake by roots of trees from below the rooting depth of crops)
	Rock weathering (excluding nitrogen)
Losses	Erosion
	Leaching
	Harvest (including for fodder)
	Removals not treated as harvest
	Gaseous losses: deintrification and volatilization (nitrogen) Burning (nitrogen, sulphur)
	Net fixation on to clay minerals (phosphorus)
Internal flows	
Uptake	Uptake by plants from soil
Return	Mineralization of liter
	Humification of liter
	Throughfall and stenflow
	Ash from burning

For any specified nutrient

Nutrient balance (kg ha-1 year-1) = Gains - Losses

$$\text{Nutrient recycling ratio (\%)} = \frac{\text{Uptake + Return}}{\text{Gains + Losses + Uptake + Return}} \times 100$$

The nutrient balance of the system is the gains minus losses, as kg ha^{-1} year- 1 of the nutrient, and may be positive or negative. The recycling ratio is the average of the internal flows (uptake and return) as a proportion of the external plus internal flows, expressed as a percentage. The recycling ratio would be 100 per cent in a closed system, with neither gains nor losses, and 0 per cent if there were no internal recycling. In rotational systems, both these indices can be averaged over a cycle of land use.

Mature natural forest and woodland have nutrient balances close to zero and can attain recycling rates as high as 90 per cent. For example, for the phosphorus cycle of a rain forest in Panama, the flows (kg phosphorus ha^{-1} $year^{-1}$) were measured as gains = 1.0, losses = 0.9, uptake = 11.0, return = 11.9, a phosphorus recycling ratio of 92 per cent. In savannahs, the trees act as a stabilizing influence, having a slower nutrient cycle than the grasses. In natural ecosystems, the capacity of trees roots to scavenge nutrients and concentrate these beneath their canopies results, over time, in a mosaic of islands of higher fertility, which influence community structure and ecosystem junction.

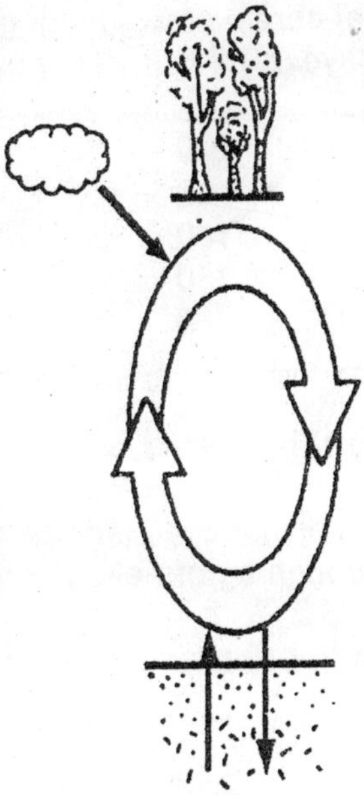

Natural Forest

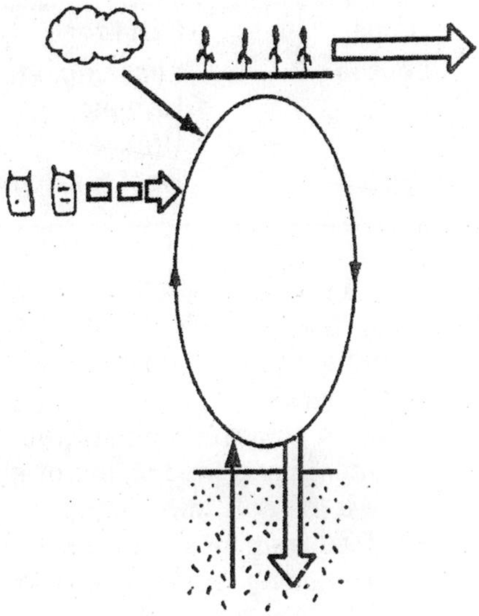

Agriculture

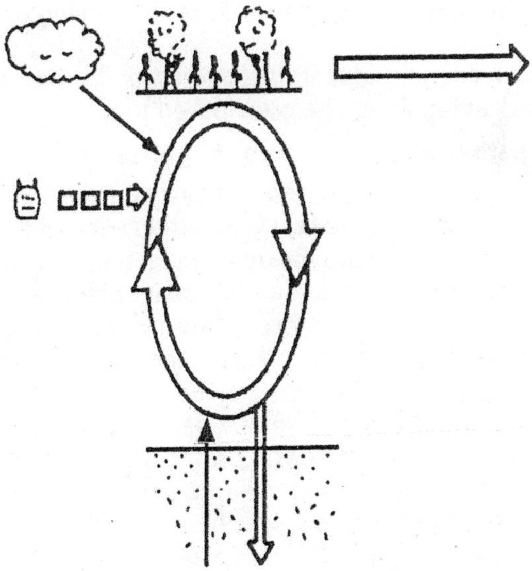

Agroforestry

In contrast, the nitrogen budget for a fertilizer cereal crop, ignoring smaller flows, might be of the order of (kg N ha^{-1} $year^{-1}$).

Gains	Fertilizer	100
Losses	Leaching, etc.	50
	Harvest	100
	Uptake	150
Return	Root residues	50

The nitrogen balance is 100 - 150 = -50 kg N ha^{-1} $year^{-1}$, and the recycling ratio (200/450) x 100 = 44 per cent.

To reduce harvest conflicts with the objective of managed land-use systems. Increases in nutrient-use efficiency through agroforestry can therefore be achieved primarily by:

- Increasing the cycling of nutrients from tree liter and pruning, *via* the soil, into crops;
- Reducing losses by leaching;
- Reducing losses by erosion.

On sloping land without erosion control, the nutrient budget is dominated by losses in eroded soil. Where erosion is moderate to serve, these may amount to an order of 10-100 kg ha^{-1} of nutrients. The large savings in nutrients that can be made by controlling erosion have been noted above.

Since leaching is a loss in the course of the tree-to-crop pathway, recycling and leaching can be considered together.

Recycling paths: short-term and longer-term

There are two paths for nutrient recycling from plant to soil and back into plants: the short-term path, *via* mineralization of plant residues, and the longer-term path, *via* humification and storage as soil organic matter. The short-term or mineralization path takes place within the time span of the growth of an annual crop, in the tropics largely within the first 3 months. In the longer-term or humification path, nutrients stored as organic molecules are released slowly, with a half-life of the order of 10 years in the tropics and up to 50 years in the temperate zone.

In agroforestry, the short-term path concerns nutrient transfer from tree residues to crop grown in the same year. This involves questions of plant-residues decomposition, leaching loss and synchrony between nutrient release and uptake. This aspect has tended to dominate recent agroforestry research. The longer-term path, in which nutrients recycled by trees may reach crops in subsequent years, should not be ignored. It is one of the two major roles played by soil organic matter, along with that of maintaining soil physical properties. Work is in progress to compare the short-term and longer-terms paths with respect to their effects on soil fertility.

AGROFORESTRY SYSTEMS

Numerous agroforestry systems have been developed in different areas. One system differs others in respect of structure, composition, age, intensity, technology etc. Classified agroforestry systems on the basis of structure, function, socio-economic and ecological factors. Suggested classification based on structure, function, physiognomy, floristic characters, ecology, socio-economic scales and history. Each of these criteria has merits and demerits and no single classification method can be accepted as universally, applicable. Therefore, classification schemes will have to be purpose oriented. Since there are three basic sets of components *viz.* trees, agricultural crops and animals therefore, agroforestry classification based on nature of components is a logical one. Suggested following common agroforestry systems in India on the basis of nature of components.

1. Agrisilviculture (Tree + crops)
2. Boundary plantation (Trees on boundary + crops)
3. Block plantation (Trees + crops)
4. Energy plantation (Trees + crops during initial years)
5. Alley cropping (Shrubs + crops)
6. Agrihorticulture (fruit trees + crops)
7. Agrihortisilviculture (Trees + fruits trees + crops)
8. Agrisilvipasture (Trees + crops + pasture/animals)
9. Hortipasture (Fruit trees + pasture/animals)
10. Silvipasture (Trees + pasture/animals)
11. Forage forestry (Forage trees + pasture)
12. Shelter belts (Trees+/-crops)
13. Wind breaks (Trees+/-crops)
14. Live fence (Shrubs/ under trees on boundary)
15. Homestead (Multiple combination of trees, fruit trees, vegetable etc.)
16. Entomoforestry (Trees + sericulture)
17. Aquaforestry (Trees + fishes)

Besides the aforesaid important common systems of agroforestry, there are many more component combinations.

Role of Agroforestry

Agroforestry fulfill both production and service roles. Agroforestry can provide a more diverse farm economy and stimulate the whole rural economy, leading to more stable farms and communities. It increases the income of farm family by providing various products like food, fodder, fruit, nuts, fuel wood, fibres, timber, moles, mulch, medicines, cosmetics, oils reigns, lac, honey, silk etc.

Agroforestry can play a very efficient role in the utilization of all the natural resources in a most effective manner for sustainable crop production. It provides services such as food security, conservation of soils, improvement of soil fertility, moderate microclimate, provide, living fences for crops and fruit trees, demarcation of boundaries, reclamation of degraded lands, stabilization of watersheds and protection of biodiversity.

Agroforestry for soil enrichment

Agroforestry system has the potential to improve the fertility of soil. Agroforestry trees enrich the soil by adding organic matter through litter fall in the form of dead and falling leaves, twigs, branches, and dead roots. The tree helps in recycling of nutrients in the soil. The nitrogen fixing trees species enrich the soil through biological nitrogen fixation. Some trees species have found to fix 100-500 kg N per ha. *Leucaena leucocephala* has been reported to fix as much as 400-500 kg N per ha. The important contribution of trees under agroforestry can be to furnish sufficient quantity of fuel wood thereby diverting 300-400 million tonnes of cowdung for use as manure in the agricultural fields rather than burning it as fuel.

Ecological balance

Our ecological balance is under threat as a result of reducing area under forest. Once forests covered more than half of the Earth's land. Now less than one-third of our planet is forested. Every year more than 15 million ha (37 million ac) of World's forest area are converted to other uses, mostly for in urbanization and large-scale agricultural enterprises but some times by poor, small-scale farmers searching for agricultural lands. In India, forests are confined mostly to hilly soil and poor soils, which are not suitable for agriculture. Marginal lands, environmentally fragile areas, more suitable to forests than agricultural has been brought under cultivation, which has further aggravated the problems of ecological imbalance. The forests now cover only 19.47 per cent of the geographical area of country whereas National Policy provides that the forest in hilly region should be 66 per cent and for the country as a whole 33 per cent. Agroforestry offers considerable scope of harnessing advantages of forest by growing trees on marginal/sub-marginal lands with crops on agricultural lands. Agroforestry therefore, can restore ecological balance without reducing the area under agriculture as such. Non-arable marginal and degraded lands, which are about 43 million ha in India, can be brought under agroforestry systems.

Organic matter and nutrient addition to soil

In agroforestry system, major recognized avenue for addition of organic matter and nutrients to the soil is through aboveground biomass like literfall/pruning, twigs, branches, fruits etc. and belowground biomass such as roots.

Agroforestry systems have the potential to maintain organic matter of soil. Estimated the amounts of plant residues (both above and below-ground) that are needed to maintain the soil organic matter in the three major climatic zones of the tropics. This general of estimates gives a required annual addition of above ground plant biomass, in round figures of 8000 kgs, 4000 kgs and 2000 kgs DM/ha/yr for humid (forest), sub-humid (savanna) and semi-arid environment, respectively. These data may be compared with the potential of agroforestry trees to produce such amounts of biomass. The biomass production potential of multipurpose trees indicates that agroforestry systems can provide required amount of plant biomass for maintaining soil organic matter.

The literfall/purning add nutrition to the soil under agroforestry systems. Reviews indicate that leguminous trees in alley cropping system produced up to 20 t/ha/yr dry matter or pruning, can supply as much as 358 kgs N, 28 kgs, P, 232 kgs K, 144 kgs Ca and 60 kgs Mg. The nutrient contents of plant biomass vary widely. It depends mainly on tree species, relative proportions of leaves and stems in the pruning and their respective nutrient concentrations. In leguminous trees the N concentration of leaves varies from 1.5 to 3.4 per cent or more.

Biological Nitrogen fixation

The nitrogen fixation by the trees represents a clear gain to the nutrient economy in agroforestry systems. The nitrogen fixing trees are introduced in agroforestry system to provide nitrogen to the companion crops. In a green house experiment under N-limiting nutrient medium. Estimated 40 per cent increase in N content over a period of 185 days in sorghum intercropped with nodulated *Leucaena leucocephala.* The increase in N content in sorghum suggested that fixed N was transferred from *Leucaena* to sorghum roots *via* soil. Two possible sources of N from legume are root/nodule turnover and root/nodule exudes.

About 650 trees and large shrub species belonging to 9 plant families are known to fix nitrogen. The legume *(Luguminosae)* dominates this list with about 320 mimosoids, 170 papilionoids and 25 eaesalpinoids. Non-leguminous families include Betulaceae, Casuarinaceae, Coriariaceae, Elaeagnaceae, Myricaceae, Rhamnaceae, Rosaceae and Ulmaceae. The Infixing potential of trees varies widely. The reported amount of N-fixed by most trees suitable for agroforestry is ranging from 20 to 300 kgs N/ha/yr. Some of tree could fix as high as 600 kgs N/ha/yr.

The estimate of N-fixed per hectare per year is 13 kgs for *Gliricidia spium* 20 kgs for *Acacia albida*, 35-40 kgs for *Inga jinicwil*, 60 kgs for *Erythrina poeppigiana*, 60-100 kgs for *Casuarina equiselofolia*, 83-109 kgs for *Sesbania rostata*, 200 kgs for *Acacia mearnsii*, 350 kgs for *Sesbania sesban*, 100-500 kgs for *Leucaena leucocephala*. In general, the fixed nitrogen is 20-65 per cent of the total plant nitrogen.

Nutrient cycling

The combined production of agricultural and tree crops in agroforestry is more efficient in nutrient cycling than monoculture cropping systems. The trees have more deeper and spreading root systems than herbaceous plants of monoculture cropping systems and thus have more potential to capture and recycle nutrients from deeper soil layers. The deep roots of trees may serve as safety net for capturing nutrients that leaches below the rooting zone.

The primary inputs of nutrients for soil plant systems in agroforestry are pruning/literfall, root biomass and biologically fixed nitrogen. The nutrient additions through these inputs are discussed in previous section. The trees are also involved-with inputs of nutrients from the atmosphere and from weathering of primary rock as wet deposition (dissolved in rainfall) and dry deposition (in dust). The trees augment dry deposition of nutrients by reducing near-surface wind velocity. The nutrients also enter into the agroforestry system from the weathering of primary rock minerals. The deep-root systems of trees uptake newly released nutrients from weathering of rocks.

Studies on *Erythrina poeppigiana* as shade trees over *Coffea arabica* in *Coasta Rice* have proved the nutrient cycling potential of agroforestry system.

Some trees and shrubs can accumulate certain nutrients even in soil that contain very low levels of these nutrients. Palms accumulate potassium, tree ferns accumulate nitrogen, *Gmelina arborea* accumulates calcium, and *Cecropia* species appear to accumulate calcium and phosphorus in acid soils. Introduction of these nutrient conserving tree/shrub species in agroforestry may help to enrich nutrient status of the system.

CONCLUSION

Keeping in view the potential of agroforestry systems to meet the increasing demand for food, fodder, fuel and other useful products from shrinking per capita availability of land resources, more emphasis should be given on efficient nutrient management for higher farm productivity on sustainable basis. The nutrient management is more difficult in agroforestry systems than in annual agricultural crops or forest systems as these are structurally and functionally more complex. Some efforts have already been made toward nutrient management in agroforestry by various means *e.g* introduction of nitrogen fixing tree species, nutrient inputs in organic forms through litterfall/prunings, application of mineral fertilizers, improved designed systems which maintain and improve soil productivity by protecting soil from erosion. However, these efforts are not sufficient for efficient nutrient management in various agroforestry systems. Therefore, more research works should be carried out for better management of nutrients.

Studies have shown that nutrients, which are recycled through tree roots and their mycorrhiza in forest stands can be higher than above-ground biomass, but similar information is lacking in agroforestry system. There is little information regarding nutrient contribution through tree roots in agroforestry. Thus, further researches are needed on the role of roots in carbon and nutrient cycling in agroforestry.

In agroforestry, woody legumes, are used as nitrogen source for the systems. In comparison to nitrogen, phosphorus role is limited in agroforestry as recycle of phosphorus through litterfall/pruning is low and removal by the produce is relatively high. The responses of phosphorus application in agroforestry systems have infrequently studies. Therefore, further study should be undertaken in the direction. The emphasis should also be given to study on response of other nutrients including micronutrients its information on these are lacking in agroforestry systems.

The nutrient release patterns of organic inputs are mainly dependent on quality of plant biomass. The synchronization of nutrient release patter with crop demands is most important to achieve higher productivity from agroforestry systems. Some management strategies have already been developed on nutrient synchrony. However, more information is needed on nutrient synchrony for better utilization of plant biomass and recycling of nutrients to increase productivity.

EXPLOITATION CROPPING VS SUSTAINABLE AGRICULTURE AT DIFFERENT YIELD LEVELS

In this section some examples will be given of farming systems with nutrient exploitation and of sustainable systems at low, medium or high yield levels.

Exploitation cropping

Exploitation of soil nutrient basically means cultivating crops until available soil nutrients are exhausted and the yields are so strongly declining after some years that the field must be abandoned and left again to natural vegetation.

A typical example of exploitation and thus non-sustainable cropping is the (standard-type) shifting cultivation used by subsistence farming in tropical forest areas (*e.g.*, described in Africa by Nye and Green-land, 1960, in South America by Sanchez, 1976). After clearing of the land (usually by burning the forest trees) a short rotation of annual crops is grown which uses the available nutrients from soil organic matter. The cropping period is generally short due to nutrient removal and especially to losses by leaching below the root zone of annual crops. This nutrient depletion (together with other causes) results in substantial successive yield decrease. If after 3 to 5 years cropping yield levels of only half or one-third of the first year are obtained, the field is left to natural vegetation again. The "forest fallow" usually restores the soil nutrient status (also by recovering nutrients from the subsoil) and the humus content within a period of 15 to 20 years.

This system of alternating short cropping and long (forest) fallow period is not very efficient, producers only low yields (except for the first few years) and is exploiting because losses are not compensated. Nevertheless, to a certain extent, it is stable as long as there is sufficient land available for long re-generative phases under natural vegetation provided that no serious soil deterioration takes place during the cropping period (the population needs at lest seven times more land than actually used).

The poor reputation of shifting cultivation as a misuse of soil resources is mainly due to deviation from the original concept by shortening the forest fallow period and thus soil re-generation, mostly as a result of an increased population pressure.

Exploitation cropping is still widely used due to economical and other constraints, but at least the systems with insufficient re-generation should be replaced as far as possible by a sustainable type of agriculture.

Sustainable agriculture at low to medium yield level

The concept of sustainable agriculture is getting a high priority. It involves the successful management of resources for agriculture to satisfy human needs while maintaining or enhancing the quality of the environment and conserving natural resources (Plucknett, 1990). Obviously, systems of this kind involve complex interactions and require integration (Edwards, 1990).

A prominent concept is called by the acronym LISA (Low-Input Sustainable Agriculture). LISA is supposed to optimize the management and use of internal production inputs (mainly on-farm nutrient resources) in order to obtain a satisfactory level of sustainable crop yields and profitable returns (Parr, 1993). It is in fact a production at a somewhat lower end of the crop response curve.

Low input agriculture may be required for compelling natural and economical reasons (extensive sustainable agriculture in vast areas of developing countries) or deliberately used because of ideological reasons (bio-or ecofarming in developed countries).

Extensive sustainable farming

In areas with strong yield limiting factors, *e.g.*, in dryland farming, extensive farming with low input and low to medium yields holds still its lace.

The main emphasis lies on the use of mobilized soil nutrients and internal nutrient cycling *via* organic substances, although a complete cycling is difficult to achieve because of some unavoidable losses. Some exceptions may occur on small subsistence farms. The input of mineral fertilizer is kept low since their efficiency is know to be low under stress conditions induced by dryness, etc. Some information on yield limiting factors can be drawn from soil productivity studies on farmer's fields.

Many marginal ecosystems are not precisely sustainable because of low input (Miller and Larsen, 1990). Whereas at least in some years, they could profit from an improvement of the yield limiting factor by fertilization, in general, a fertilizer input is risky because the V/C (value/cost-ratio) of 2 required for economic reasons may not be reached.

Bio-or-ecofarming (deliberate extensive farming)

In developed countries the term bio-farming (organic farming, eco-farming indicates special farming systems without application of chemicals such as factory-made fertilizers or pesticides, but with animal manures, compost, legumes ad nutrient sources and with great care for nutrient cycling in order to produce better, *i.e.*, allegedly non-contaminated food and to protect the environment against unwanted pollution from agricultural chemicals. Somewhat lower yield (30 to 50%) are compensated by corresponding higher product prices.

Although the claims for superior quality food by avoiding chemical fertilizers are not substantiated (Finck, 1992) nor those by avoiding chemical crop protection (Goring, 1990), a limited number of consumers maintain this production of so-called *natural* food.

The further claim that these types of bio-or-ecofarming are less (water polluting because of no chemical fertilizer input also needs correction. Although a lower amount of N leaching often is achieved per unit of land, it rarely holds true per unit of crop product (because almost twice an area of land is required for cropping than with conventional farming).

Sustainable agriculture at high yield level

Sustainability is not confined to low-input conditions. The input, however, should be adequate to the goal that may be even a very high yield level. Such systems could be called AISA (Adequate Input

Sustainable Agriculture), as demonstrated in Western Europe and elsewhere, a high but adequate use of fertilizers results in sustainable production with high yields and yet without significant adverse effects on soil fertility or environment (Finck, 1992). Farming systems of this kind are rather diverse (*e.g.,* rainfed or irrigated), but have many similarities of nutrient management.

The goal is the same as of maximum yield experiments, *i.e.,* obtaining as far as possible the yield potential of high-yielding crops by eliminating all nutritional minimum factors (*via* fertilization and maintaining a high soil fertility) while simultaneously protecting the crop against all kinds of diseases and insect damage.

The details need not be described here since they are available in modern text books to the readers, however, a certain negative aspect of practical nutrient management should be mentioned, namely the tendency for neglecting the soil nutrient reserves and those available in farm waste materials (*e.g.,* slurry), especially if cheap chemical fertilizers are available. This has led to the misleading public opinion in the past that intensive cropping essentially is a *nutrient-easting* system.

Sustaining crop productivity at a high yield level has proved to be possible in many progressive agricultural areas, *e.g.,* in India by integration of chemical, organic and biological nutrient sources and their effective management, partly while even saving mineral fertilizer input (Hedge and Dwivedi, 1993.

Food production can certainly be increased by better nutrient cycling and prevention of losses; but for the food supply of an increasing population, demands cannot be met with the farm nutrient sources nor with the present. use of mineral fertilizers, but require an increasing nutrient input (Angc, 1995).

In fact, the principles of modern comprehensive fertilization concepts and the basic principles of sustainability will have to be combined. Integrated plant nutrition systems, as part of integrated crop production, will be a decisive factor for the final goal: a sustainable high yielding and profitable crop production without avoidable negative effects on environment.

NUTRIENT MANAGEMENT ON ARID LANDS

In rainfed dryland farming, the yield level is limited by shortage of water (rainfall being not only scarce but also variable and thus unreliable). Since better nutrition of crops reduces their water requirement, a proper management of farm nutrients is of farm greater importance than in humid areas.

The main nutritional problem is the *ubiquitous* shortage of total and available N due to the rather low soil humus content. In order to make the best use of the scarce soil N-source, the crop N-requirement should be adapted (*via* sowing time) as far as possible to the nitrate flash occurring from rapid mineralization at the onset of the rainy season (although it must be admitted, that this suggestion is not easily put into action because of the uncertain progress of the rainy season). There is also a certain upward movement of nitrate from the subsoil by evaporation (formerly mistaken for a chemical N fixation at the soil surface by a hypothesis of Dhar in India).

The natural N supply may be sufficient for low yields, *e.g.*, of 1 to 3 t ha^{-1} of grain, but for medium yields additional N-sources like farm waste materials or even mineral N should be added (if there is sufficient moisture).

For adding organic material, depending on priority, there is the choice of mulching for soil protection or mixing it into the top soil as nutrient source, an increase of the very low soil organic matter level would be very desirable, but the possibilities are rather limited because of the high mineralization rate. The application of organic substances, however, is often limited by competitive use of crop residues, etc., for manuring, for animal feed or for fuel.

Another possibility to improve the natural nutrient supply (as well as of water) is the inclusion of a bare fallow period for storage of water and mobilized nutrients.

Besides N, also the phosphate supply is often insufficient, especially on sandy soils. Since P is specially required for (early) root growth and since deep rooting may be decisive for survival during dry spells, a good P supply (from fertiiization) is therefore important beyond the acute crop requirement. A good K supply is also essential for reducing the transpiration of crops, but for dryland farming on many arid soils (practically without leaching), there is often sufficient available K for at least low to medium yield levels. The same holds true for magnesium and sulfate.

As for micronutrients, due to immobilization at neutral soil reaction of arid soils, there is a frequent lack of available Fe or Zn. A certain improvement can be obtained by using strongly acidifying N fertilizers such as ammonium sulfate or (to a lower extent) urea. In addition, special fertilization may be required, more effective by leaf spray than *via* soil. In some cases the problem of micronutrient deficiency can be solved by using different crop varieties with high uptake efficiency.

Whereas many arid sols are rather coarse-textured, the vertisols represent the clay-type. Their natural supply of all nutrients is abundant even under intensive cropping with irrigation. The only exception is nitrogen because of the low soil organic matter content that therefore needs special nutrient management (Finck and Venkateswarlu, 1982; Dudal, 1989).

Although nutrient management on arid soils with many different crops includes a vast complex of problems in detail, only few can be mentioned in this overview.

Agrosystems in semi-arid regions with common agricultural practice may not be always sustainable, but can be made sustainable with the existing research knowledge and with producer's experience (Steward and Robinson, 1997; Ryan, 1997).

Saline soils

Since on parts of the arid lands the soil salinization adds even more problems, some comments may be added on the management of deleterious soil substances. If the excessive surplus of soluble salts (Na, Cal, SO_4, etc.) cannot be removed by amelioration, cropping must take into account a certain degree of soil salinization by adapting fertilization to this stress environment.

Whereas, the (salt-induced) water stress can hardly be reduced, at least the excessive uptake of Na may be lowered to a certain extent by (antagonistic) K fertilization with the additional advantage of an improved K status, which reduces transpiration losses. K fertilizers, however, should be chosen which cause the least increase of salinity stress, i.e., rather K sulfate than K chloride or even better, K nitrate (if N is required in corresponding amounts).

As for the micronutrient situation, in addition to deficiencies often occurring on neutral soils, at some sites boron toxicity may prove to be a special problem because it is difficult to ameliorate. Detailed information on nutrient management under conditions of salinity is given by Oertli (1992).

NUTRIENT MANAGEMENT IN HUMID TROPICS

Of this wide topic only some problems may be selected. Since strategies of nutrient management must be based on soil fertility properties, these will be discussed briefly. The widespread ferralsols (oxisols of tropical forest), in spite of their diversity in many respects, have some common properties due to the hot and moist enviroment.

As for soil acidity, in order to reach a normal pH-range of at least 5.5 to 6, considerable amounts of Ca-carbonate are required, which may, however, not always be available. The ash from burning the forest trees produces at lest some transitory effect of liming. Another source is fertilizers with an additional liming effect like rock phosphate.

Liming experiments, even if the pH is increased above the toxicity level of Al, sometimes give rather disappointing results due to some (not accounted for) yield limiting factor (whether major or micronutrient), which has to be added in order to get satisfactory yields.

A typical example of very acid soils are the acid sulfate soils with often very low yields, sometimes less than 1 t ha^{-1} of grain. However, even small amounts of lime in combination with rock phosphate may increase the yield level to 2 to 3 t ha^{-1}.

For compensation of the humus mineralized, crop residues should be left on the field. In farming systems with cash crops, there are often considerable amounts of residues from the processing factories that can be recycled. The nutrients of the added organic materials are rapidly mineralized (N- and P-source).

In order to reduce the losses by leaching, the period with bare soil between annual crops should therefore be kept as short as possible.

P fixation results in a strong P deficiency and an inefficiency of water-soluble P fertilizers because the phosphate is quickly fixed and thus rendered unavailable. To overcome the P fixation, large amounts must be applied, or rock phosphate maybe more effective.

Sustainability of highly productive farming systems can be obtained by using a nutrient management that takes care of these problems caused by production limiting soil properties and the humid hot climate.

The nutrient management of special annual or perennial crops on arable land or of tree plantations cannot be discussed here, except for a short comment on two topics.

Rice cropping on paddy soils

Irrigated rice presents special and large problems of nutrient management. A central and not yet really solved problem is the low efficiency of N fertilizers (urea being the main source used). A recent review (de Datta and Buresh, 1989) pointed out that usually only less than half of the N added is taken up by the crop (compared with about 70 per cent in intensive wheat cropping). Therefore, the losses by ammonia volatilization, denitrification as well as runoff and leaching should be reduced. However, in the paddy environment it is difficult to suggest a single superior method, but some progress seems to be possible by placement of urea, the use of nitrification inhibitors and top dressing at later stage.

The possibility of supplying N *via* the Azolla/Anabaena symbiosis appears to be very promising and could probably replace a large portion of mineral N fertilizer.

Agroforestry

For the nutrient management, the advantages of agroforestry are protection against nutrient leaching and soil erosion, nutrient mobilization and transfer from trees to annual crops and pumping nutrients from deeper soil layers (Buresh, 1995).

The potential of alley-cropping systems has been critically reviewed by Lai (1991). The advantage of alleys of shrubs or trees for erosion control is obvious, but obtained at the price of slightly lower yields from the annual crops (*e.g.*, 10% for maize under special conditions). The tree cuttings (as an organic nutrient source) are less effective than mineral N. The general failure of alley-cropping to give higher yields than conventional cropping results from shading effects, root competition for nutrient and water. N immobilization by the mulch, etc. Nutrients from deeper layers are only transferred to the surface soil if there are substantial nutrients in the subsoil.

In general, alley-cropping does not sustain production without substantial input in chemical fertilizer. Agroforestry has a potential to be a sustainable alternative to shifting cultivation, but its main advantage correlates with fertile soils.

INTEGRATED NUTRIENT MANAGEMENT

Integrated nutrient management (INM) aims at efficient and judicious use of all the major sources of plant nutrients in an integrated manner so as to get maximum economic yield without any deleterious effect on physico-chemical and biological properties of the soil. The basic concept underlying INM is maintenance and possible improvement in soil fertility for sustained productivity on a longterm basis. Major sources of plant nutrients are fertilizers, FYM/composts, green manures, bio-fertilizers and crop residues/recyclable waste. Proper integration of one or more sources will ensure optimum nutrient supply.

Fertilizer is the most important component in integrated nutrient supply system under intensive cropping. Use of balanced fertilization is required to boost the crop productivity. Chemical fertilizers are to be properly integrated with other sources.

Integration of fertilizers with bulky organics

Farmyard manure and compost are the traditional organic sources that have been used in crop production. About 50 per cent of the manurial potential of the livestock population is only utilized for crop production. Sizable amount of plant nutrients are lost because of improper storage, handling and incorporation techniques. Results of various field experiments have clearly indicated the importance of integrated use of FYM and fertilizers for overall improvement in soil fertility. Results also indicate that a part of fertilizer requirement of rainy season (kharif) crop can be met with the use of FYM in different cropping systems without any adverse effect on the total productivity. Based on a number of experiments on rice, it is concluded that 1 tonne of FYM supplying 12 kgs nutrients ($N+P_2O_5 + K_2O$) produces as much grain as 3.6 kg fertilizer nutrients (Singh and Dwivedi, 1996). In addition to supplying plant nutrients to the current crop, FYM leaves substantial residual effect on succeeding crops in the system. Meelu and Morris (1984) reported that 12 t FYM and 80 kg N/ha gave residual effect on the succeeding wheat equivalent to 30 kg/ha each of N and P_2O_5. There was also a build up in soil fertility with FYM application. Kulkarni *et al.* (1983) on the basis of 240 trials conducted in cultivators' fields in rice growing regions of the country concluded that application of 12 tonnes of FYM along with 90 kg N/ha to the kharif crop followed by 60 kg N/ha to rabi crop could produce an yield comparable to 120 kg N, 60 kg P_2O_5 and 60 kg $K/_2O$/ha in kharif and 60 kg N/ha to rabi crop in rice-rice cropping system.

Besides supplying plant nutrients, FYM application also improves the physico- chemical and biological properties of the soil. Application of FYM along with recommended level of fertilizers enables to maintain the organic matter in the soil compared to fertilizer application alone.

Green manuring with inorganic fertilizers

Before the introduction of inorganic fertilizers, green manuring was invariably practiced for crops like rice, wheat, sugarcane, etc. With the easy availability of fertilizers and adoption of highly intensive cropping, the practice was almost given up. In the recent years, there is a renewed interest on green manuring. Sunnhemp and dhaincha are the most common green manure crops in India. Green manures produce large amount of green biomass of narrow C:N ratio. When incorporated into the soil, green manures contribute sizable amount of plant nutrients, particularly N and also improve the soil physical conditions. Experiments carried out at several locations have distinctly established the advantage of introducing green manure crop as a supplement to fertilizers in cereal crop rotations. Green manuring along with the recommended level of fertilizers benefits the crops in the rotation and increase the total productivity of the system to the tune of 10-20 per cent. Incorporation of 10 tonnes / ha of green manure through *Sesbania* or *Crotolaria* supplement fertilizer N equivalent to 40-45 kg/ha. Integrating P with green manure in the first crop of rice produces higher yields of second season rice.

Green manuring in drylands is rare, but is practiced in small pockets in India. On vertisols receiving more than 1000 mm of rainfall in Khammam district of Andhra Pradesh, green manure is grown during the South-West monsoon season in June followed by its incorporation before sowing sorghum in September. Depending on sowing of green gram, it is either incorporated as green fodder or harvested as pods. This practice has been observed to supplement 50 per cent N. Inclusion of a grain legume has been found to be advantageous for sustained yields under rainfed situations, *e.g.* cowpea-fingermillet (Bangalore), green gram-finger millet (Bhubaneswar), sunnhemp-wheat and black gram-wheat (Rewa). The benefit of green manuring is felt only after continued applications for 3-5 years.

Wherever it is not possible to include green manure in the multiple cropping systems, there is a possibility of inclusion of legume in the system. Because of their shorter duration, small stature and erect growth habit, legumes could be easily accommodated as intercrops. Legumes of short (*Vigna* group) or long (pigeonpea) duration group offer greater advantage as intercrops in cereals by providing additional profit to the farmers. The *Vigna* group is harvested earlier and provides some nitrogen to the longer duration companion crop. Pigeonpea is of longer duration. It is least competitive during the early growth phase and starts using the space effectively by putting up additional growth after harvest of the early duration companion crop. These pulses provide N upto 50 kg/ha to the associated crops in vertisols. Higher benefits have been reported for crop combinations of cowpea (fodder) + sorghum, green gram/black gram + sunflower and pigeonpea + groundnut.

Green manure crops can be very well accommodated as intercrops in wide-spaced crops like sugarcane and maize. Since initial crop growth upto 100 days after planting of sugarcane is very slow, this period can be utilized for growing legumes in inter-row spaces as intercrops for grain or fodder purposes. Summer legume crops like black gram and green gram intercropped with spring planted sugarcane increased the cane yield markedly besides producing 0.4 - 0-5 tonne of pulse grain/ha (Yadav, 1980).

In addition to their capacity to fix atmospheric N, the legumes are capable of extracting less soluble form of P from the soil. They also extract the higher valency nutrient cations better.

Bio-fertilizers with inorganics

Various bio-fertilizers can be used according to needs of the crops. Bio-fertilizers act as complimentary and supplementary sources of plant nutrients. Bio-fertilizers help in increasing the biologically fixed atmospheric N and enhancing native P availability to the crops. Among the bio-fertilizers for increasing N supply, N fixing bacteria (*Rhizobium, Azotobacter* and *Azospirillum*), blue green algae (BGA) and *Azolla* are important. The availability of P is improved by P solubilizing microorganisms (PSM) and mycorrhizae.

Rhizobium is of vital importance to various pulses and some of the oilseeds and fodder legumes as 80 to 90 per cent of their N requirement and is met through biological nitrogen fixation (BNF). Inoculation of legumes with specific species of *Rhizobium* is widely used and is a successful practice throughout the world. Responses to *Rhizobium* under field conditions have been quite variable and depend on soil conditions, quality of inoculum and effectiveness of native Rhizobium. It fixes atmospheric N ranging from 50 to 60 kg/ha in groundnut and 100-300 kg/ha in alfalfa. Pulse crops fix 50-110 kg N/ha under optimum conditions.

It is generally accepted that the fixation is about 50 kg/ha in a season. Field studies have indicated an increase in pulse yields by 14-53 per cent due to *Rhizobium* inoculation.

Azospirillum and *Azotobacter* are the, other important groups of bacteria. *Azospirillum* fixes N in associative symbiosis with the plant roots and *Azotobacter* is a free-living N fixer. On an average, they contribute 15-20 kg N/ha to different crops when inoculated with efficient strains. Application of organic manure along with *Azospirillum* enhances N fixation to the tune of 20-40 kg/ha. Promising results have been obtained with the use of *Azospirillum* in crops like wheat, rice, maize, barley, sorghum and millets. *Azotobacter* has given promising results in rice, sugarcane, wheat and pearl millet. Response to the bacterial inoculant appears to be enhanced when applied along with N and P in rice and cotton and with P in sugarcane.

Blue green algae and *Azolla* are very well suited for rice ecosystems. In lowland rice, the average N contribution by these N fixers is equivalent to 25-40 kg/ha. Various field studies have shown positive influence of BGA on rice plants under different agro-climatic conditions. If this technology is popularized, nitrogen equivalent of 1.5-1.7 m.t. urea could be supplied to rice through BGA (Venkataraman and Tilak, 1990). Besides supplying N, BGA also synthesizes and liberates growth promoting substances such as auxin and amino compounds which stimulate the growth of rice plant. It also supplies additional humus to the soil. Results of the studies conducted by the International Network on Soil Fertility and Fertilizer Evaluation for Rice (INSFFER) have shown that incorporation of 10 tonnes of fresh azolla before or after transplanting is equivalent to split application of 30 kg fertilizer N/ha. It can be applied along with fertilizer N to step up rice yields. Based on field trials, an increase in rice yield by 13-54 per cent has been reported, besides building up organic carbon, total N and availability of P in the soil

In recent years, several strains of P solubilizing bacteria and fungi have been isolated. Phosphobacteria solubilize the residual and insoluble phosphates available in the soil-water solution very near to root surfaces. The phosphate solubilizing power is further enhanced by addition of organic matter. Studies reveal that integrated use of P solubilising cultures with low grade rock phosphate can add 30-35 kg P_2O_5/ha in neutral to mildly alkaline soils. Vesicular-arbuscular mycorrhizae (VAM) exploit the soil phosphate better, leading to more efficient use of added fertilizers, particularly of slowly mobile ions like NH_4^+, Cu^2+ and Zn^{2+}. VAM infected sorghum had significantly high P in roots and shoots and increased the dry matter production. Because of problems in isolation and multiplication of pure strains of VAM fungi, large-scale use on commercial basis is yet to be established.

Integrated Approach In Bio-fertilizer Use

It may be possible to integrate the use of more than one bio-fertilizer for increasing crop yields. *Rhizobium, Azotobacter,* mycorrhizae, phosphate solubilizers, etc. could be used together or separately. In India, where mixed cropping and double cropping is followed in many places, the combined application of more than one bio-fertilzer holds great promise. Integrated use of bio-fertilzers, organic manures and chemical fertilizers would not only give higher yields, however, help to maintain soil health by narrowing down the gap between nutrient removal and supply. It may be mentioned here that no single nutrient source, be it chemical fertilizer, organic manure or bio-fertilizer is in position to meet the increasing nutrient demand. Some possible fertilizer equivalents of diverse plant nutrient sources are given in the following table which may be helpful in adjusting fertilizer dose.

Low-Cost Technology For Enrichment of Compost

Recent experiments conducted at IARI. have shown that inoculation with *Azotobacter chroococcum* and phosphate solubilising micro-organisms *(Aspergillus awamori* or *Bacillus polymyxa)* improved the manorial value of compost (Gaur *et al.,* 1978, 1980). Inoculation of compost with nitrogen fixer and P solubiliser was done when the temperature had stabilized around 3O-35°C after one month of composting. Low-grade rock phosphate (10 kg/tonne of raw material) was applied at the initial steps of filling up of compost pits.

The results indicated that 31.5 per cent carbon was decomposed in control during the first month whereas the loss in different treatments ranged between 33.3 to 41.5 per cent. This was further increased during second month showing maximum loss of 52.4 per cent of organic carbon in rock phosphate. *Azotobacter* and P solubiliser inoculated series. In this treatment C/N ratio was reduced to 14.1 and 12.0 during 1st month and IInd month after inoculation respectively.

There was appreciable gain in nitrogen content per tonne of finished compost in control as well as inoculated series ranging from 60.5 to 111.6 per cent over the initial raw material. Addition of powdered rock phosphate alone resulted in an increase of 28.3 per cent over control. Inoculation with *A. chroococcum* and *A. awamori* amended with rock phosphate showed an increase of 32.0 per cent in nitrogen content over the control resulting in gain of 22 kg N/5 tonnes of finished compost. It was also noted that humus content increased in all the treatments including control. The best effect in humus content 9.3 per cent was observed in case of *A. chroococcum* + *A. awamori* after 1 month of inoculation.

In another study the number of *Azotobacter chroococcum* in compost was increased due to its inoculation and use of rock phosphate. The mean numbers of nitrogen fixers of nine weekly intervals per gram of dry compost in different treatments were as follows: Control 1,380, rock phosphate 3,590; *Azotobacter* 6,070; rock phosphate + *Azotobacter* 21,070. This also resulted in an increase in the nitrogen content of compost by 25 to 44 per cent over control. These findings clearly show that quality of compost can be improved by inoculation with *Azotobacter* and P solubilisers suitably amended with rock phosphate.

Sugarcane trash compost

Sugarcane trash left out after harvest re about 19-38 m. t. It is either burnt *in situ* or used as domestic fuel. It can be recycled after composting suitably. Technology has been developed for production of enriched compost from sugarcane trash at Pune (Bhavanase *et al.*, 1995). In the compost pit of lx lx 1 m³, chopped sugarcane trash is filled in layers. In the bottom of the pit, trash is filled to 30 cm thickness. A mixture of cellolytic fungi @ 500g / tonne of sugarcane trash and *Azotobacter* are added. These bio-fertilizers are mixed with cow dung. Sufficient quantity of water is applied on the surface of trash. A mixture of cellulolytic fungi is inoculated: *Trichoderma viride, Trichurus spiralis, Aspergillus awamori, Pencillium* spp. and *Paecilonmyces fusiparus.* These inoculants improve the rate of decomposition and mineralization of nutrients. Another layer of sugarcane trash is then added. Above this layer, urea (to supply 8.33 kg N /ha) and rock phosphate (5% of trash) are applied dissolving in sufficient quantity of water. Cow dung with bio-fertilizer mixture should not be applied simultaneously with the fertilizers. Thus the pit is filled with trash in layers. Water is regularly added on alternate days to maintain 60 per cent moisture in the compost pit. Adequate moisture is important for proper activities of the microbes. Turning of the material is to be done at regular intervals (at least once in a month) to improve aeration and maintain temperature at 50-60° C, which is optimum for composting.

Fresh sugarcane trash contains 0.36 per cent N with a wide C:N ratio of 122:1 Small bits of trash decompose earlier than big size trash. Addition of rock phosphate, urea, biofertilizer and moisture play significant role in early composting. The composted trash contains higher content of N (1.09%) with reduced C:N ratio (20:1).

Biogas slurry

Organic manures from animal wastes are very important nutrient sources in building up the soil fertility. In India, the estimated production of dung and urine from bovine population works out to 1002 and 658 million tonnes respectively. They contribute about 5.71 m. tonnes of N, P and K. Proper method of collection and preservation is required to fully utilize the manurial value of these materials. Cow dung is an input in biogas plants. The biogas route has the dual advantage of providing both fuel (gas) and fertilizer (slurry).

Table 10.1: Changes in Carbon (%), total Nitrogen (%), C/N ratio during enrichment of compost by *Azotobacter* and P solubilizing cultures

Treatment	1st month				IInd month			
	Carbon	Nitrogen	C/N ratio	Humus %	Carbon	Nitrogen	C/N ratio	Humus %
Control	31.4	1.36	23.0	7.8	28.5	1.38	20.6	4.85
Control + Rock Phosphate @ 10 kg P_2O_5/tonne	30.7	1.61	19.0	9.15	27.5	1.77	15.5	6.90
Azotobacter + P solubilizer	30.5	1.51	20.1	9.30	26.6	1.73	15.4	6.00
Rock phosphate + *Azotobacter* + *P* solubilizer	26.9	1.89	14.1	9.0	21.9	1.82	12.0	6.95

Initial sample: Organic carbon 46.0 per cent total nitrogen 0.86 per cent, C/N ratio 53.3.

The residual slurry that comes out of the digestion tank has a manurial value superior to that of FYM. The wet slurry should not be used as such, it should be dried for usage as manure. While drying, there is some loss of N and the dry manure contains about 1.8 %N, 1.10 per cent P_2O_5 and 1.50 % K_2O.

Vermicompost

Vermicompost is organic manure produced by the activity of earthworms. Vermicompost is a mixture of worm casts, which are rich in macro and micronutrients, vitamins, growth hormones and immobilized microflora. The average nutrient content of vermicompost is much higher than that of FYM. Vermicompost contains 1.60 per cent N, 5.04 per cent P_2O_5 and 0.80 per cent K_2O with small quantities of micronutrients. The C:N ratio of vermicompost is much lower (1:16) than that of FYM (1:30). Application of vermicompost facilitates easy availability of essential plant nutrients to crops. Numerous species of worms have been identified for vermicomposting.

Industrial wastes

Among the industrial by products, spent wash from distilleries and molasses and pressmud from sugar industry have good manurial value. It is important to use only well decomposed wastes, pressmud at 10 tonnes per ha. Addition of pressmud improves the soil fertility and enhances the activity of microbes. It is also used as an ameliorating agent in saline and sodic soils.

Coir waste is the byproduct from coir industry. Its production is about 1 million tonne in India. Coir waste can be used as manure after proper decomposition. Composted coir wastes (inoculated with *Pleurotus* spp. and 5 kg urea/tonne) is recommended for irrigated and dry crops. It has been reported that addition of 12.5 t/ha of composted coir waste with recommended fertilizers increased the yield of groundnut and maize.

Municipal and sewage wastes

Municipal and sewage wastes form an important component of organic wastes. In India, the total municipal refuse is about 12.m.t. per annum containing about 0.5 per cent N, 0.3 per cent P and 0.3 per cent K. Sewage sludge is available to an extent of 4 million tonne per annum containing 3 per cent N, 2 per cent P and 0.3 per cent K (Bharadwaj and Gaur, 1985). Sewage sludge, particularly from industrialized cities, is contaminated with heavy metals and thus pose hazard to plants, animals and human beings. Segregation of toxic wastes at the source will minimize the concentration of such elements in the sludge. High N input through excessive hydraulic loading of sewage can lead to ground water contamination. Further, survival of pathogens in soil and on crops causes health risk. This can be minimized by proper treatment, design of hydraulic loading selection of suitable crops and adoption of modified irrigation system.

MANAGEMENT OF MAJOR NUTRIENTS (N, P, K) WITH ORGANIC SOURCES

Organic farming system is based on the dynamic interaction between the soil, the plants, animals, humans, the ecosystem and the environment. The system is directed towards enhancing natural life cycles rather than suppressing nature. It relies largely on locally available resources and able to provide agricultural products of good quality while minimizing negative side-effects. Organic farming is gaining popularity not only among the farmers but also fast expanding market and it very useful for the readers to have knowledge of nutrient management in organic farming.

It is a difficult task to do well in conventional agriculture it is difficult to do well in sustainable agriculture, which is characterized by profitable farming while preserving the environment as much as possible. In fact, switching from conventional to sustainable agriculture is not a simple substitution, such as replacing insecticide with a predator insect or replacing commercial KCl fertilizer with green sand. It is reasonable to say that although more in tune with nature than conventional agriculture, sustainable agriculture is information intensive and requires strong management skills. For example, cultural and biological pest control requires detailed knowledge about a pest life cycle as well as economic threshold levels of the crop. Similarly, using chicken manure to replace urea as a N source for crop must take into account the release pattern of organic nitrogen from the manure and the nitrogen demand pattern of crop, so that the two can be synchronized. Soil fertility and plant nutrients are important to farming, whether it is conventional or sustainable. Although sustainable farming is much broader than organic farming, the two usually use the same standards for soil amendments. In the organic farming the use of non synthetic sources of nutrients is essential for certification point of view. It is also useful in terms of ecological and economical returns to use natural sources of nutrient. Nitrogen, Phosphorus and Potash are the nutrients required comparatively in large quantity. There management with organic sources is the gateway of organic or sustainable farming.

Nitrogen

Nitrogen is needed by all plants and usually in large quantities. In fact, nitrogen is so important to plant growth, and thus to food and fiber productions of the world.

Two German scientists who first invented the process of making NH_3 from atmospheric nitrogen gas (N_2) and natural gas-derived hydrogen (H_2) won Nobel prizes for their work in the early of this century. For example, average N concentrations needed for normal growth are about 3 per cent for corn and coffee, 4 per cent for tomato, and 2 per cent for macadamia. If plants do not have enough nitrogen, they are stunted. Their leaves are small and pale-colored, sometimes even yellow or reddish-tinted. The reason is that nitrogen is a component of chlorophyll, less nitrogen results in less chlorophyll, thus less green. Normal corn leaf is on the right side, N deficient leaf is on the left. Since proteins are continually being synthesized and degraded in the plant, meaning that nitrogen is quite mobile in the plant. Thus, N will move from older leaves to younger ones, trying to meet the N need of the most active growth regions. The consequence is that nitrogen deficiency will begin on older leaves then progress upward toward the growing points.

In soils, nitrogen must be present as either NH_4^+ or NO_3^- before plants can absorb and use it. That explains why urea [$(NH_2)_2CO + 2H_2O \rightarrow 2NH_4OH + CO_2$] and ammonium nitrate ($NH_4NO_3$) have been so popular as N fertilizers in conventional farming systems.

In organic farming systems, urea cannot be used nor NH_4NO_3, nor any synthetic chemicals for that matter. Alternatives must be sought (Table 10.2).

Table 10.2: Total N concentration in common organic sources as compared with urea (46% N).

Organic source	Total N (%)
Poultry manure	1.5-3.0
Pig, horse, cow manure	0.3-0.6
Green manure	1.5-5.0
Compost	0.5-2.0
Seaweed meal	2.0-3.0
Sewage sludge	1.0-5.0
Fish waste	4.0-10.0
Blood (slaughter house)	10.0-12.0
Human urine/night soil	1.0-1.5

(Adapted from Caplan, 1992; Hue, 1995; Tandon, 1992).

So on the basis of total N organic sources would have somewhere between ten and hundred times less N than urea. This means that in order to meet your crop N requirement, say 100kg N/acre for a crop of sweet corn, need:

Urea (46% N) → 100/0.46 = 217 kg/acre as urea or compost (1% N) → 100/0.01 = 10,000 kg/acre as compost.

This simple calculation shows that there is need of large amounts of compost (or most organic N sources) relative to urea in order to supply an equal amount of N.

Transportation cost might become a factor here. A close inspection, however, reveals that the assumption for the above calculation is incorrect. N from the compost is as readily available for plant uptake as N from urea, which is not true. Unlike urea, which can be hydrolized into NH_4 nearly instantaneously, nitrogen from compost, first must be released from its organic substrates, and this process may take from several days to several months to complete. In general, depending on types of organic materials and.

Environmental conditions, such as temperature and moisture, only 10 to 50 per cent of N from an organic source would be converted to NH_4 in a six-month period (Hue, 1995). Thus, in order to provide 100 kg N/acre that a crop of sweet corn needs over a growing season of approximately 3 months, it need to apply from 20 to 50 tons/acre of compost instead of 10 tons as the first calculation had indicated, if it is practical or economical to apply 50 tons of compost to each acre of land for a crop of sweet corn. Fortunately, this is more of a requirement only during the transition period (one or two years) from the conventional farming to sustainable farming systems. After about 2 years of using composts or green manures as a N source, N release from previous years applications would reduce the current application rates significantly. That explains why many sustainable farmers have seen their crop yields increase with time.

Synchronization

The need for N fertilizers would be reduced significantly if the crop's N requirement can be timed closely to the nitrogen release from organic sources. Using human as an example, it is know that babies and older folks require much less food intake than teenagers or young adults. The same principle applies to plants. Plants require different amounts of N at different stages of growth: seedlings and senescing plants definitely require much less N than flowering or fruiting plants. It is also established that different organic manures have different N releasing patterns. N release patterns of 10 organic sources; three of them are shown here as an illustration.

First, do not count on wood-based composts (blue line) as a source of N. In fact, adding such composts to soils may even cause N deficiency in fast growing crops such as tomato or lettuce as shown below.

Second, N from chicken manure and chicken manure-based composts (red line) was readily available right after application, then eclined gradually with time. The implication is that chicken manure can rovide quite large quantities of N the first 4 to 6 weeks after application. hus, its application should be timed closely to the fastest growing period f the crops.

Third, green manure took about two weeks for the N releasing eaction to start (green line). The green manure released most N between and 7 weeks after application. The release remained low and nearly onstant for another month (between 7 and 11 weeks) then started to crease again. This second phase came from the decomposition of icrobial more resistant substrates in the green manure. The main point that the N release patterns of organic manures depend on many factors nd require experience and knowledge to predict. Therefore, it can be oncluded that:

Successful use of organic manures (whether it is compost, green manure or animal waste) as a N source requires more experience and better knowledge about the manure, the crop, and environmental conditions than the use of chemical fertilizers (e.g., urea).

ENERAL PROPERTIES OF NITROGEN FROM RGANIC SOURCES

1. The availability of N declines as manures age or are composted.
2. Nitrogen from poultry manures (non-composted) is more quickly available than N in manure from cow, horses, and sheep. This is because poultry manure contains significant amounts of uric acid, which is readily decomposable. Also, roughage in cattle and horse diets results in manure that is less readily decomposed due to lignin and cellulose.
3. Presence of bedding or litter lowers N content by dilution, but its effect on N availability cannot be easily predicted.
4. Moist manure, when exposed to the air, undergoes significant loss of N as volatile NH_3. Nitrogen losses after spreading can be significantly reduced by incorporating the manure even shallow incorporation is adequate.
5. Nitrogen in composts is in a more stable form than N in manures. Thus, there is a decreased likelihood of losing compost N from the system. On the other hand, composts containing less than 1.5 per cent total N supply little or no N to crops during the first few weeks after application.
6. Green manures are fast growing catch crops like clovers, mustard, rye, and vetches that are incorporated into the soil while they are still green in order to improve the soil and to supply N to the associated/subsequent cash crop. A properly managed legume cover crop can fix up to 75 to 100 kg N/acre in 3 to 6 months.

7. Both manure and compost can improve soil tilth, but the **timing** and mechanisms may differ.

COVER CROPS AND RIDGE TILLAGE IN SUSTAINABLE FARMING

In practice, cover crops such as legumes (e.g., clover, vetch) and grasses are often grown either to supply N to subsequent cash crops or to reduce nitrate leaching and soil erosion. Crop rotation and intercropping have been used to achieve this goal. Work in tropical humid regions of India has shown that corn yields and N uptake increased by 15 to 20 per cent by intercropping with soybean or cowpea. Legume intercropping was equivalent to adding 80 kg N/ha of fertilizer N. A marked synchrony between plant growth stage and microbial population in the rhizosphere 60 days after seeding was observed in this study.

The N release from cover crops, however, depends on many factors, including the C to N ratio of the residue, its degree of incorporation into the soil and soil temperature and moisture regimes. It may take one to three Weeks after cover crop incorporation before N release exceeds N immobilization. The farmer may have to decide if additional fertilizer N is needed and, if so how much. On the other hand, when the soil is not cropped, cover crops, especially grass, can reduce the potential loss of N through leaching or denitrification. In the US mainland, rye is often used as a winter cover crop to control weeds through competition and allelopathy.

Along with crop rotation and intercropping, ridge tillage is often practiced in sustainable farming. This technique only tills a zone of soil 15 to 20 cm wide and 5 to 10 cm deep at planting time. The practice creates a desirable seedbed environment. It also covers crop residue and weeds in the area between rows with soil.

Subsequent between row cultivation a couple of weeks after planting promotes mineralization of soil organic residues, controls weeds and reforms the ridge with a raised bed for future crops.

Phosphorus

Along with nitrogen, phosphorus is a nutrient that plants need in relatively large quantities for normal growth. The two genetic entities that are essential for growth and reproduction of living organisms. Living organisms, whether plants or humans, also derive their internal energy from P containing compounds, mainly adenosine diphosphate (ADP) and adenosine triphosphate (ATP). This means that inadequate P supply will result in a decreased synthesis of RNA, the protein maker, leading to depressed growth.

Phosphorus-deficient plants, therefore, are stunted with a limited root system and thin stems. In many plants such as corn, guava, and tomato, seedlings look stunted, and older leaves may turn purple because of the accumulation of anthocyanins or purple pigments. Fruit trees deficient in P have few and short new shoots and malformed fruits and seeds. Thus not only low yields but also poor quality are the results of P deficiency.

Table 10.3. Sufficiency P levels in leaves of selected crops.

Crop	Plant P %
Cabbage	0.4-0.6
Coffee	0.2-0.3
Corn	0.3-0.5
Head lettuce	0.4-0.6
Macadamia	0.08-0.10
Soybean	0.3-0.5
Sugarcane	0.2-0.3
Tomato	0.3-0.8

Internally, most crops need from 0.2 per cent to 0.5 per cent P in the dry matter for normal growth. Macadamia is an exception, iron chlorosis may occur if P content is greater than 0.15 per cent in leaves.

Unlike animals and humans who can obtain P from various food sources, plants must extract P exclusively from the soil where they grow. Also unlike humans whose gastrointestinal enzymes can break up organic P in food, plant roots can absorb P only when P is in the soil solution and in either H_2PO_4 - or HPO_4 form. This fact is emphasized because not only do plants like H_2PO_4 - and HPO_4- but so do soils. There is a strong competition between plants and soils for P in the soil solution. And the winner usually is soils, especially highly weathered soils like those of tropics. Most of our soils here contain large amounts of iron and aluminum oxides or amorphous alumino-silicate clays, which tie up P firmly, making P virtually unavailable for plant uptake. For example, in order to provide enough P for many of our favorite vegetables, such as lettuce and tomato, first time growers must apply approximately: Of course, amounts of P required would vary, depending on how much P the soil has, to begin with. That s true, and that is why you need a soil test before trying to amend or fertilize your soils. In fact, by adding P to the soil year after year, you might build up soil P to a point that it becomes detrimental to your crops because of excess. The upside of this phenomenon is that once you have built your soil P to a good level, that level would remain for many years without any additional P input. The reason is that unlike nitrogen, P does not move easily with water. It virtually stays put. Leaching is minimal.

Table 10.4: Total P concentration in organically acceptable sources as compared with superphosphate (20% P)

Source	Total P %
Rock phosphate	17-26
Bone meal	20-30
Fish meal	5-10
Wood ash	2-5
Poultry manure	0.5-1.5
Green manure	0.2-0.5
Compost	0.2-0.5
Sewage sludge	0.4-2.5

In conventional farming you can use such fertilizers as superphosphate [$Ca(H_2PO_4)_2$] which contains about 20 per cent P or 46 per cent as P_2O_5 or diammonium phosphate (DAP) which has coincidently the same amount of P as in treble superphosphate. These fertilizers are highly soluble, dissolve quickly in water and can provide enough P to your crops before being tied up by the soil. These P fertilizers, however, are not acceptable in organic farming.

Table 10.4 shows P content of selected sources that are acceptable to organic farming community in most states. Among these, the first two, rock phosphate and bone meal, have reasonably high total P content: between 20 and 30 per cent. However, P in these two sources is very insoluble, thus much less plant available than P in superphosphate. More specifically, P in rock phosphate and bone meal has the formula: $Ca_5(OH)(PO_4)_3$ which is hydroxy apatite or apatite for short. A couple of things should be mentioned about rock phosphate. First, it is a source of P for long-term soil improvement, don't expect any noticeable effect from it within weeks or months, unless huge amounts of it used. Second, its solubility, and thus plant availability, depends strongly on soil pH and particle size. It is more effective in acid soils than in calcareous or alkaline soils; more effective when it is fine than coarse, and more effective in the presence of *mycorrhiza* than without.

Mycorrhiza

By contrast, P contents of chicken manure, compost, and sludge are relatively low, usually below 3 per cent. Thus, large amounts would be needed to meet P requirement of the crop. P from these organic sources is quite available to plants; sometimes even more effective than superphosphate. Organic matter from the manure interacts with clay minerals and reduces P sorption by the soil, thereby enhancing P availability to plants

Table 10.5: Sufficiency range of K in selected crops

Crop	Tissue K, %
Banana	3.0-5.0
Cabbage	4.5-7.5
Coffee	2.0-3.0
Corn	1.5-3.0
Lettuce	4.0-7.5
Papaya	3.0-5.0
Tomato	3.0-5.0

(Adapted from Tamimi *et al.*, 1994)

Potassium

Compared favorably with nitrogen, potassium is needed in large quantities by many crops. Table 10.6 lists the sufficiency range of K in selected crops.

In plants, potassium is required for maintaining osmotic potential of cell. That is, K makes plants look turgid. Since K regulates the osmotic potential of cells, and the close or open conditions of stomata, it plays an important role in water relations in the plant. Potassium is involved in water uptake from the soil, water retention in the plant tissue, and long distance transport of water in the xylem and of photosynthates in the phloem. Potassium affects cell extension. With adequate K, cell walls are thicker, thereby improving plant resistance to lodging, pests and disease. Fruits and vegetables grown with adequate K seem to have a longer shelf life in the grocery store.

Consequently, K deficient plants show low resistance to disease, their seeds and fruits are small and shriveled. In tomato, K deficiency results in smaller fruits whose flesh development is incomplete. In corn, the maturity is delayed and ears are smaller when K is deficient.

The stalks are weak and lodging is common. The most visual K deficiency symptom is the scorching or firing along leaf tips and margins as shown here for soybeans.

In alfalfa and clovers, the first sign of K deficiency shows up as small white or yellowish dots around the outer edges of leaves. As the deficiency intensifies, these edges turn yellow, then brown, and finally die.

In soils, potassium is quite mobile as compared to phosphate. It exists as K^+ in soil solution and is absorbed by roots in that form. Although K^+ can be retained to some extent by negative charges on clay surface, it can be displaced into the soil solution by Ca^{2+} or Mg^{2+}, when gypsum or dolomite is added. Thus if K is not taken up by plants, it might be lost by leaching. One way to reduce K leaching is to add organic matter such as compost or green manure to your soil. These organic materials usually have large cation exchange capacity, which can retain K effectively. Among soils, K deficiency occurs more often in sandy than in clayey soils, more often in highly weathered soils than in young soils, and more often in volcanic ash-derived soils If soil is low in K, in that case commercial KCl is an easy choice in conventional farming, but not acceptable in organic farming.

The first two sources are natural deposits of potassium minerals. Sul-Po-Mag as the name implies is a double salt of magnesium and potassium sulfates. It has about 22 per cent K. Polyhalite is a double salt of Ca and K sulfates. It has about 10 to 15 per cent K. Like Sul-Po-Mag , polyhalite is very soluble, not much different from KCl. In terms of plant response, this material is as good as or even better than KCl or gypsum Wood ash also contains considerable amount of potassium, and this source is also readily available (and alkaline).

Table 10. 6: Total K concentration in selected organically acceptable sources

Source	Total K %
Sul-Po-Mag [Mg, K, SO_4]	22.0
Polyhalite [Ca, K, SO_4] .	10-15
Wood ash	5-10
Green sand	5-7
Green manure	2-5
Seaweed meal	2-3
Compost	5-2.0

BIOLOGICAL APPROACH FOR SECONDARY AND MICRONUTRIENTS ACQUISITION

Secondary and micronutrients can be supplied through biological systems. Use of organic manures as a complete plant nutrient supply system is a time-tested practice. Vasicular Arbuscular *Mycorrhizae*, plant growth promoting rhizobacteria are some examples by which availability of secondary and micronutrients to the crop plants can be augmented.

Long term field expression show that no soil can support medium, high yields indefinitely without external nutrients input. The available nutrients gradually decline from optimum level to deficiency levels. A series of Long Term Field Experiments conducted during 1970s showed that application of a single nutrient did not support similar crop response over a period of time as deficiencies of other macro and micronutrients develop. Secondary (Mg, Ca, S) and micronutrients although needed in smaller quantities than N, P_2O_5 or K_2O are removed by every crop. There is ample data available to show that the nutrient reserves of Indian soils are being depleted. In India at present deficiencies of five nutrients (N, P, K, S, Zn) need the attention of agricultural scientists. The depletion of micronutrients particularly zinc in the soils is predicted due to the introduction of high yielding varieties (HYV), intensive cultivation practices and multiple cropping systems. Deficiency of secondary nutrient like S and micronutrient like Zn is widespread in rice growing areas. Acid tropical soil are generally deficient in molybdenum. The status of micronutrients in alkaline soils is poor because calcium carbonate renders many micronutrients, even if in good supply, insoluble.

Increased cropping intensity and decreased availability of organic matter leads to micronutrients deficiencies. A series of Long Term Field Experiments initiated during 1970's clearly showed that application of single nutrient die not support similar crop response over a period of time due to deficiency of macro and micronutrients, therefore, application of micronutrients in addition to the recommended NPK dose ensures significant improvement in crop yields and over all fertility status of the soil. It is also estimated that mineral fertilizer input accounts for 60 per cent and the rest is contributed by biological resources.

VAM

Most species of crop plants are normally colonized by mycorrhizal fungi. Numerous studies have indicated that VAM improves plant growth through assimilation of immobile soil nutrients (P, Cu, Zn) especially in soils which are poor in these micronutrients. Enhanced accumulation of plant nutrients like phosphorus, zinc, copper, manganese, iron through greatest exploration by mycorrhizal hyphae imported. Uptake all micro and secondary nutrients increase due to VAM inoculation when their efficiency exists in the soil. Improved plant uptake of potassium, present low concentration in the soil solution having low coefficient of diffusions increase in copper concentration *mycorrhizal Hevea braziliensis* root status was observed. However, a reduced in root colonization by arbuscion mycorrhizal fungi (AMF) under condition of heavy fertilization results in a decrease in the concentration of Ca and Zn in tissue. Thus AM fungi acts as a sensitive uptake system for various ions.

Table 10.7: Micronutrient uptake by crops following arbuscular mycorrhizal inoculation

Crop	Microorganisms (Arbuscular mycorrhizae)	Experimental conditions	Response
Sorghum	VAM fungi	Different temp. tested.	Root colonization by VAM fungi was temp. dependent. Higher phosphorus, potassium, zinc uptake by VAM plants than non-VAM plants observed.
Maize	*Glomus mosseae*		Phosphorus and zinc cotent of plants improved
Maize	*Glomus acrocarpum*	Soil having different concentration of zinc tested	Absorption of zinc by mycorrhizal maize was maximum in soils deficient in zinc
Wheat	*G. mosseae* and Phosphotase producing bacteria		Higher content of copper, manganese and zinc showing synergistic effect of both in inoculants on micronutrient translocation
Wheat	VAM + Phosphatase producing fungi		Enhanced shoot concentration of copper and zinc
Wheat Maize Potato	*Glomus macrocarpum*	Zinc deficient in soil	VAM infected plants significantly assimilated more zinc from soil than non-mycorrhizal plants
Barley	*Glomus Caledonium*		Increased dry matter production phosphorus, zinc, copper and bromium uptake
Groundnut			Significant gains observed in uptake of zinc, copper, iron and manganese
Field bean spring wheat	VAM fungi	Green house grown	Better uptake of micronutrients like Zn, Cu, Fe and Mn
Sorghum	VAM fungi		Higher amount of P, K, Mn, Mg, S, Ca, Fe Cu, Zn in mycorrhizal than non-mycorrhizal plants

Different mechanisms suggested for hanced micronutrient uptake mycorrhizal plants are greater physical ploration of soil, faster ion movement into mycorrhizal hyphae and modification of root environment. Increased transpiration rates of plants and hence greater transpiration pull for nutrients may also contribute to better micronutrient uptake.

Table 10.8: Microbial species known to produce siderphores

Bacteria	
Enteric sp.	Enterobactin, Aerobactin
Agrobacterium tumefaciens	Agrobactin
Pseudomonas sp.	Pyoverdine, Pseudobactin
Bacllus megaterium	Schizokinen
Arthobacter	Arthrobactin
Azotobacter vinelandii	2-3 dihydroxybenzayl Lycine
Acinomyces sp.	Ferrioxamines
Mycobacterium	Mycobactins
Penicillum, Aspergillus, Neurospora	Ferrichromes, Coprogen
Rhodotorula sps.	Rhodotorullic Acid

Plant Growth Promoting Rhizobacteria (PGPR)

Plant growth promoting rhizobacteria (PGPR) a heterogenous group of microorganisms are known to improve plant growth by their ability to colonize the rhizosphere besides their effect as bio-control agents and producers of plant hormones. PGPR also alter the plant physiological processes resulting in enhanced nutrient uptake. These organisms possess the ability to produce siderphores, a class of high affinity iron transport molecules which also act as a growth promoting factor. The ability of PGPR to produce siderophore or to affect the activity of siderophores produced by other organisms influences the uptake of iron by the plants when grown under Fe-deficient condition siderophore producing pseudomonads form a yellow, green fluorescent siderophore iron complex. A few microorganisms known to chelate iron through production of siderophores.

Organics

Large potential for the exploitation of manurial value of organic wastes exists in India. Efficient use of organic like biogas shurry, farm yard manure, vermicomposts, pressmud and poultry manure can provide a greater level of essential plant nutrients. Presented from sugar factories, exalic acid industry wastes, phosphogypsum and sulphur sludge from myon industry are an efficient source of nutrient sulphur.

Biogas slurry, poultry manure, compost, pressmud are reported to be better source of zinc compared to zinc sulphate under calcareous soil condition. Poultry manure is also known to improve iron availability to crop plants.

In a longterm rice-wheat cropping system based experiments conducted on a sodic soil (pH 8.8) application of organic manure along with mineral fertilizers increased the pH, electrical conductivity and improve micronutrient cation (Cu, Mn, Zn, Fe) status of the soil.

A significant increase in the uptake of 'S' and Fe was found over control following application of farm yard manure along with iron pyrites. Application of farm yard manure @ 20 t/ha increased the availability of hot water soluble boron in different the textured soils (clay, clay loam, sandy loam at sandy). The effect was found in the ordinary clay > clay loam > sandy loam > sand. Increase in the boron content over the control was of the tune of 21.05 per cent.

However, use of organics like sewa sludge, industrial wastes for crop show be done after proper treatment to avoid to entry of pathogens, toxins and heavy manuals into the food chain. In this direction optimization of organic manures in co-junction with mineral fertilizer without having negative environmental impact will the right approach.

Table 10.9: Micronutrient availability in some organics

Source	Fe	Zn	Mn	Cu
	Concentration (ppm)			
Farm yard manure	24.66	40.00	12.0	2.8
Sewage sludge	-	216.2	15.0	49.5
Biogas slurry	-	103	231.0	50.6
	-	237	-	112.4
Vermicomposts (mean	21.6	12.65	19.17	5.83
Pheritima elongata	27.28	18.00	16.40	7.64
Eisenia foetida	17.82	19.20	24.60	7.56
entration	19.80	O87	16.50	2.30

ORGANIC FARMING VS BIODYNAMIC FARMING

Biodynamic farming means biological dynamics. It is a method of organic agriculture, which considers farm as a living system and where one activity affects the other. Rudolf Steiner (1924) from Central Europe was founder of Biodynamic agriculture.

Agriculture has faced vast changes, challenges and difficulties in past years. Indiscriminate use of fertilizers, pesticides and herbicides has polluted our environment. Varied chemicals, which are applied to soil and plant systems were not completely degradable and further more appeared to have carcinogenic effects. Thus increase in the use of inorganic compounds has led to residual toxicity problem, which in turn poisoned our food chain. Pesticide residue of DDT and BHC in lactating women is a typical example of the deleterious effect of pesticides in agriculture. Moreover continuous use of insecticides in particular synthetic pyretheroids created the problem of pest resurgence and resistance against concerned chemicals. The continuous usage of inorganic nitrogenous fertilizers resulted in the excess vegetative growth, which is not accomplished with plant strength, structure and resistance. Thus the biodynamic farming will be great boon to the farmers, since the system reduces the pesticides and chemical fertilizers load to the soil eco-systems, which in turn reduce the cost of cultivation. This is a needful technology, which helps in the production of quality products, which will fetch special prize in future.

The bio-dynamic farming is more than just another organic method. It stands for a truly scientific way of producing humus. It does not involve in the application of organic matter in a more or less decomposed form but the use of completely digested from of crude organic matter known as stabilized and stable humus. In this aim, the method differs from organic farming. In the case of bio-dynamic farming the organic material to be used as basis for compost is transformed either by means of the bio-dynamic compost preparations or by means of the bio-dynamic compost starter.

PRINCIPLES OF BIODYNAMIC FARMING

1. Bio-dynamic farming aims to restore humus status of the soil eco-system to hold its fertility and productivity.
2. Also it helps to restore the soil for a balanced funtioning of flora and fauna. Because soil is a living system wherein the microbes can be fully established and maintained.
3. The bio-dynamic farming does not deny the role and importance of mineral nutrients of the soil like nitrogen, phosphate, potash, calcium, magnesium etc., and it considers the skilful use of organic matter as the factor for soil life.
4. It involves skilful application of all the factors contributing to soil life and health. Because a plant grows under the influence of abiotic factors like temperature, oxygen, CO_2 light, water etc. And these energies are transformed in the plant system into chemically active energies by way of photosynthesis.

5. Bio-dynamic farming considers a plant as living entity whih consists not only of mineral elements (like N, P, K, Ca, Mg, Mn, Cl, Fe, etc.,) but also of organic matter such as protein, carbohydrates, cellulose, starch.
6. Bio-dynamic farming gives importance to enzymes and growth substances.
7. To restore the soil fertility, bio-dynamic farming gives priority to proper crop rotation Soil exhausting crops should be cultivated alternatively with fertility restoring crops.
8. It also provides recognition to green manuring and cover ropping.
9. To restore the soil environmental conditions, forests, wind protection and water regulation are important.
10. Bio-dynamic farming also gives importance to maintain the soil structure (physical characters like bulk density, pore space, water holding capacity and texture).

RULES FOR USING BIODYNAMIC AGRICULTURE

1. Use of bio-dynamic sprays to stimulate and retain soil fertility.
2. Following crop rotation to combat pests and disease and to increase the beneficial micro flora.
3. Recycling on farm wastes.
4. Following prevention strategies against pest and disease by strengthening plant and animals in the farm.

The produce of this farming is guaranteed by presence of international certification trademark Demeter™ this assures for a buyer that produce is bio-dynamically grown. The Demeter™ appeared first in Germany around 1928. It is certification trademark of bio-dynamic farming.

FEW BIODYNAMIC PREPARATIONS

When a living organism/entity, leaves behind the dead mineral of some form that is subjected to laws of decay. The life force held the living creature from decay. To sustain and foster these forces bio-dynamic preparations were developed. The concept behind this is, these preparations/mediates influence the planets of the solar system and livings in the ethenic formative forces into the heap.

Table 10.10: Few bio-dynamic preparations

Preparation	Herb/material	Elements	Results
502	Yarrow Flower *Achillea millifolium*	Sulphur (S) Potassium (K)	Permits plants to attract trace elements in extremely dilute Quantities for their best nutrition.

Preparation	Herb/material	Elements	Results
503	Chamomile Flower	Calcium (Ca)	Stabilizes Nitrogen (N) within the compost and increase soil life so as to stimulate plant growth.
504	Stinging Nettle *Urtica dioca*	Sulphur (S) Potassium (K) Calcium (Ca) Iron (Fe)	Stimulate soil health, by Providing plants with the individual nutrition; enlives the earth (soil).
505	Oak Bark	Calcium(Ca)	Provides healing forces (or qualities) to combat harmful plant diseases.
506	Dandelion Flower *Taraxacum officinale*	Silicon (Si) or Siliclic Acid Potassium (K)	Stimulates relation between Si and K so that the Si can attract cosmic forces to the soil.
507	Valerian Flower *Valeriana officinalis*	Potassium (P)	Stimulates compost so that Phosphorous component is properly used by the soil.

:ONCLUSION

The natural nutrient supply, the flows and the nutrients added needs roper management for achieving as high crop yields as possible under ıe climatic circumstances without avoidable environmental pollution. In ıis contest the concept of fertilization need to be widened into a more omprehensive concept of nutrient management being integrated with ther production factors. This goal requires an optimum use of soil nutrient ources, a sustainable soil fertility, recycling of nutrients and a comprehen-ive fertilization in order to supply the crops with all nutrients in sufficient mounts. An improved nutrient management also includes the adaptation f crops to the nutrient supply available and better use of nutrients from revious crops in rotations. The heterogeneity of the nutrient supply in ırge fields, especially of N, should be compensated by precision ertilization.

Nutrient management should not only care for high yields, but also for good product quality, stress resistance and reduction of nutrient losses.

Different farming systems in different climatic regions require special nutrient management ranging from exploitation cropping to sustainable agriculture at low-medium or high yield level. The claim that the nutrient management of bio-farming produces better food is not justified.

Optimum nutrient management requires not only good expertise, but also knowledge and engagement of the farmers as well as an appreciation ofht: especial problems involved in primary production by the general public.

In the near future, several modifications of nutrient management are required for saving nutrients, at least those with a limited global supply, whereas, in a distant future the food production may have to be adapted to a sustainable nutrient use level.

11

Perspectives

The nitrogen fixing biological systems such as blue green algae, *Azolla, Axospirillum, Acetobacter,* and *Azorhizobium* are compatible to different cropping systems and could fix considerable amounts of nitrogen.

The biomass of biological systems decompose rapidly in soil and supply the nitrogen to various crops grown in the field. Besides nitrogen addition, these biofertilizers also contribute significant amounts of phosphorus, potassium, sulfur, zinc, iron, molybdenum and other micronutrients. The biological fertilizers were known to influence the total soil microbial population and soil enzymes activity, which directly reflect on soil fertility index.

The use of biological fertilizers would reduce the cost of chemical fertilizers involved in crop production. The effective utilization of these biological fertilizers for different cropping systems will not only provides economic benefits to rice farmers, but also improve and maintain the soil fertility and sustainability of the soil ecosystem.

Biological nitrogen fixation is an important process in rice farming systems because it is an inexpensive source of nitrogen for increasing the productivity of crops. The nitrogen fixing bio-systems such as *Azolla,* cyanobacteria and legume green manures were able to adopt well under wetland rice field ecological conditions and fixing considerable amounts of nitrogen. The biomass of these bio-systems decomposes rapidly in rice soil and supply the nitrogen to rice crop.

Besides nitrogen addition, these bio-fertilizers or bio-manures also contribute significant amounts of phosphorus, potassium, sulphur, zinc, iron, molybdenum and other micronutrients. The organic acids released during the mineralization process of the biomass of bio-manures would accelerate the phosphorus availability in rice soil.

These biological fertilizers or bio-manures were known to influence the total soil microbial population dynamics of nitrogen fixing free-living bacteria like, *Azotobacter, Azospirillum* and also the free-living symbiotic bacterium such as *Rhizobium.* It is evidently clear now that application of biological fertilizer enhanced the accumulation of soil enzymes, which directly reflected on soil fertility index. The use of bio-fertilizers would reduce the cost of chemical fertilizers involved in crop production. The effective utilization of bio-fertilizers for crops will not only provide economic benefits to the farmers but also improve and maintain the soil fertility and sustainability in natural soil ecosystem. Since these biosources represent a great diversity in chemical, physical and bio-logical characteristics, their ? efficient use depends upon the particular agro-ecological environment and local availability.

Therefore, it is very much essential to develop strong, workable and compatible package of nutrient management through organic sources for various crops based on scientific facts, local conditions and economic viability.

Bio-fertiilzers are environment friendly, low cost agricultural input playing a significant role in improving nutrient availability to the crop plants. It is wide term including a diverse category of bi-inoculants such as nitrogen fixers (symbiotic and asymbiotic) phosphate solubilises and plant growth promoting rhizobacteria etc. Performance of bio-fertilizers is highly unpredictable due to their biological nature and susceptibility to biotic and abiotic stresses. Future research should focus development of effective competitive and stress tolerant strains. The potential of bio-fertilizers to supply micronutrients is yet to *behamessed.* Lesser used bio-fertilizers, such as phosphate solubilizing bacteria and phosphate modilizers like VAM are promising in supplying phosphorus and other micronutrients. In this direction culture of obligate symbiont (VAM) under laboratory conditions will enable testing of their performance in field conditions. Genetic basis for competitive superiority needs to be worked out. Selection of an economical synthetic carrier capable of maintaining high viable count and improvement in inoculation techniques to ensure establishment and persistence in soil are areas needing further research.

CONSTRAINTS IN BIO-FERTILZER USE

Though the benefits derived from the use of bio-fertilizers are quite significant, they have not become popular due to various constraints at production, distribution, field and marketing level.

These constraints can be classified as:

(A) Production Constraints

(B) Marketing Constraints

(C) Resource Constraints

(D) Field Level Constraints

Production Constraints

Despite significant improvement/refinement in BF production technology over the years, the progress in the field of BF production is below satisfaction due to following constraints:

navailability of appropriate and efficient strains

Lack of region specific strains is one of the major constraints as o-fertilzers are not only crops specific but soil specific too. Moreover, e strains selected for production should have various qualities articularly competitive ability over other strains, N fixing ability over a nge of environmental conditions, ability to survive in adverse physical nditions; ability to multiply in broth and survive in inoculant carrier.

Strains having all these qualities are not available for various regions the country.

navailability of a suitable carrier

Unavailability of suitable carrier due to which shelf life of bio-fertilizers short, is a major constraint. Peat has been university recognized as e most suitable but its shelf life is about six months. Availability of od quality peat is major constraint. Being readily available, lignite is e most common carrier in the country, bio-fertilizer development cannot achieved to desired level unless a good carrier is evolved.

utation during fermentation

Bio-fertilizers tend to mutate during fermentation and thereby raising oduction and quality control cost. Presently there are no effective easures to eliminate mutation. Extensive research work on this aspect urgently needed.

ble 11.1: Number of Bio-fertilizer production units located in different ates/Union Territory

No.	Name of the State/Union Territory	Total No. of BFPU	Total BFP capacity (tonne/yr/state)	Distributed pattern of BFPU
	Andhra Pradesh	4	165	SG(1) + AU(1) +P(1) + FI(1)
	Assam	2	90	AI(1)+AU(1)
	Bihar	2	20	AU (2)
	Delhi	1	75	IARI
	Gujarat	3	300	FI(2) + MFD(1)
	Haryana	2	125	GI(1) + AU(1)
	Himachal Pradesh	1	10	SG(1)
	Karnataka	6	150	AU(2) + SG(1) + GI(1) + P(2)
).	Madhya Pradesh	4	450	GI(1)+AI(1) + MFD(1) + SG(1)

Sl No.	Name of the State/Union Territory	Total No. of BFPU	Total BFP capacity (tonne/yr/state)	Distributed pattern of BFPU
10.	Maharashtra	5	250	GI(1)+AI(2) + AU(1) + P(1)
11.	Manipur	1	50	GI(1)
12.	Orissa	2	125	GI(1) + AI(1)
13.	Punjab	1	75	GI(1) + (AI(1)
14.	Rajasthan	2	100	AI(1) + AU(1)
15.	Tamil Nadu	9	450	SG(4) + AU(1) + FI(3) + P(1)
16.	Uttar Pradesh	13	300	GI(1)+SG(10) +AU(2)
17.	West Bengal	4	150	AU(1) + P(3)
	Total	62	2885	

Abbreviations: AU = Agriculture University, AI = Agriculture Industries, BFP = Bio-fertilizer Production Unit, BFP = Bio-fertilizer Production, FI = Fertiliz Industries, GI = Government of India, MFD = Marketing Federation, P Private, SG = State Government. *Source:* Singh (1993).

The total estimated demand for various bio-fertilizers for different crop grown in India is as follows:

Rhizobium	35,730 tonnes
Azospirillum	4,82,000 tonnes
Azotobacter	1,62,610 tonnes
Blue Green Algae	2,67,720 tonnes
Azolla	20,380 tonnes
Phosphate solubilizers	2,75,500 tonnes

The demand is calculated based on the area under different crop and the dose of bio-fertilizer.

The present production capacities of different bio-fertilizers in Indi are as follows:

National Bio-fertilizer Development Centre (Central Sector)	375 tonnes
State Agricultural Universities	245 tonnes
State Agricultural Departments (Major Bio-fertilizer producing,	665 tonnes

States include Tamil Nadu, Uttar Pradesh and Maharashtra)	
Agro Industries Corporations	1130 tonnes
Private Sector	195 tonnes

The annual requirement and production of different bio-fertilizers have clearly shown tremendous gap in this area. Thus a strategy for judicious combination of chemical fertilizers and bio-fertilizers will be economically viable and ecologicall useful. It should also be remembered that bio-fertilizers are not a substitute, but a supplement to chemical fertilizers for maximizing not only yield but also agro system stability.

Table 11.2: Potential demand of Bio-fertilizers

Bio-fertilizer	Potential demand (based on area in 1992-93) (tonnes)	Estimated demand in 1999-2000 (tonnes)
Rhizobium	4950	12500
Azotobacter	1987	5850
Azospirillum	9264	18528
BGA	91050	205250
Total	107251	242128

Source: Biotech Consortium India Limited (1992).

Lack of standards in packaging

There are inadequate standards available with regard to type of package material to be used. Moreover, size of packs are also not standardized.

Market Level Constraints

Though use of bio-fertilizer in India started in late 50's, consumption has not picked up to desired level due to various marketing and market related constraints.

Lack of awareness of farmer

Inspite of considerable efforts in recent years, majority of farmers in India are not aware of bio-fertilizers, their usefulness in increasing crop yields and soil productivity.

Inadequate and inexperienced staff

Because of inadequate marketing staff and that too not technically qualified who can attend to technical problems, acceptance of bio-fertilzers has been very limited in the country. Farmers are not given proper instructions about the application aspects, particularly the typ and quantity of bio-fertilzers in different crops and cropping systems.

Lack of quality assurance

The sale of poor quality bio-innoculants through corrupt marketin practices results in loss of faith and as a result, product image is suffere It may mentioned here that to regain the faith once lost is very difficu and challenging.

Seasonal and unassured demand

A small scale production unit solely dependent on bio-fertilizer not economically viable because bio-fertilizer use is seasonal and bot production and distribution is done only in a few months of year. Moreove production units particularly in private sector are not sure of their deman During 1970s, many private sector units had to close their units becaus of their inability to book orders in those states where the governme was actively involved in production. The past experience have thus show that when state governments have their own production units and placin of indent depends on them, it is very difficult for other producers to mark their product in those states.

Limited scope for marketing

As bio-fertilzers are soil and crop specific, a large number o formulations of a microbial inoculant each having unique features ar required to be produced by a manufacturer. This limits the market siz for each type of bio-fertilizer by narrowly segmenting the markets.

Resource Constraints

In addition to technological and marketing constraints, resourc constraint is also one of the main constraints in production of bio-fertilizer on commercial scale.

Limited resources generation for BF production

The investment in bio-fertilizer production unit is considerably low But keeping in view of the risk involved largely because of short she life and no guarantee of off take of bio-fertilizers, the resource generatio particularly from private sector is very limited. Although Government o India is offering an aid of Rs. 13 lakh for setting up bio-fertilizer units the response is not that encouraging.

Limited risk taking capacity of farmers

Bio-fertilizer are considered as low cost input for the resourc poor farmers. But so long as the crop response to bio-fertilzer i inconsistent, poor farmers would find it difficult to take the risk of usin bio-fertilizers.

Field Level Constraints

Besides various production, marketing and resources constraints, there are a large number of field level constraints too in promoting Bio-fertilizer usage. There is low level of acceptance of bio-fertilizers at farmers level largely because the response is not immediately visible and many times it is erratic also.

Soil and climatic factors

Among soil and climatic conditions, high soil fertility status, unfavourable pH, high nitrate level, high temperature, drought, deficiency of P, Cu, Co, Mo or presence of certain elemens in toxic amounts affect the crop response.

Native microbial population

Antagonistic microorganisms already present in soil compete with microbial inoculants and many a times do not allow their effective establishment by out-competing the inoculated population.

Faulty inoculation techniques

What to talk of farmers, majority of marketing/sales personnel do not know proper inoculation techniques. Bio-fertilizers being living organisms required proper handling, transport and storage facilities otherwise these result in reduced shelf life and poor viability.

Crop management

Besides various soil and climatic factors, response to bio-fertilizer largely depends upon balanced use of other inputs and overall crop management. Poor crop management and use of poor agricultural practices make bio-fertilisers ineffective. It may be noted here that just making available bio-fertilizers to resources poor farmers is not going to benefit unless they are able to afford for other crop production inputs particularly improved seed, fertilizer and water.

Quality control

Quality control of bio-fertilizer is very important. Quality standards have been set up for *Rhizobium* and *Azotobacter.* But, its effectiveness is ensuring the supply of quality bio-fertilzers at field level is doubtful. Distribution of substandard inoculant particularly those whose shelf life is over, is also being practiced. This is eroding the farmer's belief in bio-fertilizers.

RESEARCH AND DEVELOPMENT NEEDS

Current annual use of bio-fertilizers at around 2200 tonnes (of which more than 1000 tonnes is of *Rhizobium* alone) is much below the projected requirement. Undoubtedly requirement calculated on the basis of crop acreage is not realistic. However, there is no difference of opinion that the country has potential to increase use of bio-fertilizers. To popularize bio-fertilizers' use, concerted efforts right from working out realistic demand estimates, delineation of areas which require inoculation on priority basis, development of suitable production technology, streamlining marketing and distribution channels and strengthening extension and training activities are needed. Some of the steps need urgent attention for successful production, promotion and distribution of biofertilizers.

Widening Research Base

The mechanism by which the introduced microorganisms benefit crop plants and soil is not fully understood. There is need to widen research base to understand the mechanism as these biological systems involve complex interactions among the host; rhizosphere micro fauna and flora; and other inputs used in crop production. Work on gene manipulation, which is necessary to bring desirable properties in strains should be done more extensively.

Screening New Efficient Strains

Identification of factors governing competitive ability and efficiency of strains is the prerequisite for screening more efficient and competitive strains which are capable of multiplication and fixing of N under varying agro-climatic conditions. Strains, which perform well under adverse conditions like soil acidity, salinity, moisture stress and insect resistance need to be selected, developed and tested for their performance. In order to harness potential benefits of biofertilizers, the survival and competitive ability of strains must be improved.

Improvement in Production Technology

At present the production of biofertilizers is being done by using septic conditions introducing acid producing contaminants, which are not inductive to the growth of *Rhizobium.* There is urgent need of improving the present system of mixing and packaging bio-fertilizers. Search for suitable synthetic carrier materials, which can be uniform, non-toxic, simple to use and sustain viability for longer period should be pursued vigorously.

Preparation of Bio-fertilizer Map

Like the soil maps for nutrient status, there is need to prepare bio-fertilizer map. Surveys should be conducted to quantify native soil microbial population, which will help in determining the priority areas and inoculation requirement for different kind of bio-fertilizers.

Quality Assurance

Strict quality control mandatory is a must for all bio-fertiliser producers. Quality control should not only be ensured at the production level but at the sales points also. Proper storage facilities should be provided at the production unit, sale points and during transportation to maintain required level of viable cells. Appropriate legislation should be enacted to prescribe the required standards for good quality inoculants.

Improving Distribution System

Distribution system, which is the key to supply quality products has not been effective in the past. Accessibility of farmers to bio-fertilizers needs to be ensured by expanding distribution network.

Improving Technical Support System

Technical support through skilled personnel should be provided to educate the farmers in storage and usage of bio-fertilizers. Intensive education of extension workers, dealers, farmers and exposition of policy makers through training, field demonstrations and *audio-visual* aids is needed to generate awareness about the importance of biofertilizers in sustainable agriculture.

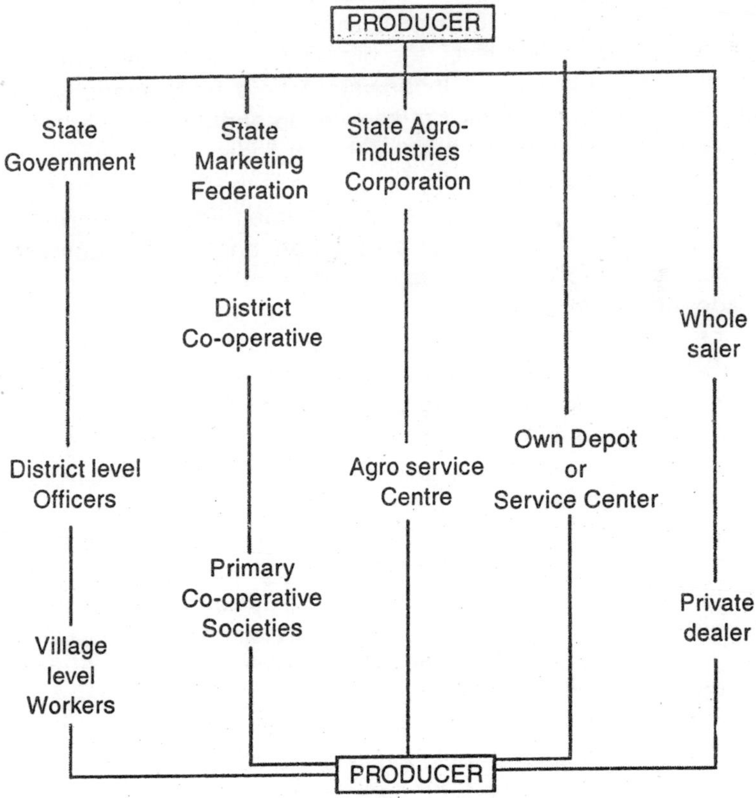

Fig. 11.1: Bio-fertilizer marketing channels in India.

Institutional Support for Research and Development

There has to be strong institutional support for ongoing research and development work. ICAR has AICRP on BNF with a few centers in different parts of the country. Ministry of Agriculture has sponsored the National Project on Bio-fertilizers with a few regional and sub-centres. Department of Biotechnology has established National Facility on Blue green algae and *Rhizobium* at IARI, New Delhi. Further, it is very much necessary that the Departments of Agricultural Microbiology in the State Agricultural Universities are strengthened to do more of fundamental research work. A few centers of excellence need to be prompted wherever some good work is being done. In each state, regional laboratories need to be established for isolation, testing and maintenance of cultures.

QUALITY CONTROL

Recently, the bio-fertilizer production technology has attracted much attention of the small and large producers because of its simple and cost effective nature. The current annual production of bio-fertilizers is in the range of 2000—2500 tonnes. Though there is lot of scope for scaling up the production level, the bio-fertilizer technology faces the problems of quality control, inconsistent field performances, poor transport and storage and lack of knowledge about these inputs. This has necessitated the implementation of better quality control mechanism to ensure the availability of quality inoculants to the farmers. The quality of biofertilizers depends on the use of specific and appropriate microbiological techniques for production and quality control of bio-fertilizers. The following points have to be taken into consideration while adopting quality control procedures for bio-fertilizers with the objectives of ensuring supply of quality inoculatns to the farmers.

1. Bio-fertilizer production unit should have adequate microbiological laboratory facilities to produce quality inoculum. The unit should be maintained by a qualified microbiologist. The production unit should have one quality control laboratory to check their own bio-fertilizer packets.
2. Each biofertilizer production unit should maintain crop specific and pretested efficient N_2 fixing microorganisms or phosphobacteria either collected from a reputed scientific organization or of their own. The maintenance of microorganisms should be as per the standard microbiological procedures and repeated sub-culturing should be avoided. If possible, lyophilized cultures should be used for each batch of biofertilizer production. The manufacturer should indicate the source of the culture in the bio-fertilizer packet produced.

3. A bio-fertilizer production unit should use fermentors so as to ensure high microbial counts at broth level itself.
4. The bio-fertilizer production unit should use good quality carrier material like peat or lignite or wood charcoal or any other suitable carrier and the bio-fertilizer products should indicate the name of the carrier.
5. The inoculum packet should contain 200 g carrier based culture packet in standard polythene or polyprophylene bags. The BGA biofertilizer packets should be in 1 kg, 4 kgs, 10 kgs pack size.
6. Recently the cost of 200 g pack size biofertilizer packet is fixed at Rs. 5 and therefore there is no need to enhance the cost at present.
7. The microbial inoculum must contain the specified population count at the time of packing and expiry. The packet should be crop specific and should give effective yield increase. The production centers and distribution centers should store the biofertilizer packets in cool temperature so as to ensure longer shelf life.

Table 11.3: Suggestions for Distribution Agencies

- Keep biofertilizer packets away from direct heat and sunlight. Store it in cool and dry palce.	- Don't store biofertilizer packets under heat and sunlight.
- Sell only biofertilizer packets which contain batch number, the name of the crop, the date of manufacture and expiry period.	- Don't sell biofertilizer packets after their expiry period is over.
- If the expiry period of the packet is over, discard it. It will not be effective.	- Don't prick holes into the packets or puncture them.
- Keep biofertilizer packets away from fertilizer or pesticide containers. packets.	- Don't store heavy items above biofertilizer.

1. Sample packets of bio-fertilizer should be drawn randomly for quality testing by the Central quality control authority appointed by the state, and out of 5 samples in a batch, at least 3 should pass the specified quality standards.
2. To ensure microbial inoculum quality control testing and quality assurance of the bio-fertilizers produced by different production units of the state, an exclusive Central Quality Control Laboratory with growth chambers and immunological laboratory facilities

should be established. A certification unit should be included in the Quality Control Laboratory for certification of the inoculants. An amount of Rs. 50 as certification charge should be collected for each batch of biofetilizer produced.

3. A central bio-fertilizer germplasm collections should be established with sub-centres at different agroclimatic zones so as to select efficient agriculturally useful microorganisms.
4. The government should make legislation for enforcement of quality standards for different biofertilizers produced in the state.

PROMOTIONAL STRATEGIES

1. The reason for inadequate popularity of biofertilizers is that biofertilizers cannot show instant and dramatic response like fertilizers.
2. In many cases, quality of culture supplied is poor.
3. Inadequate correct awareness among the farmers about inoculants.
4. Lack of strong promotion and extension work and insufficient publicity.
5. Lack of availability of the quality products in time in rural areas.

For successful launching of a bio-fertilizer programme it is necessary to equip the extension machinery at the grass-root level with the full technical back up of production as well as application technology. There is need to give emphasis to bio-fertilizers as supplementary, renewable and non-polluting sources of nutrients. Once the farmers are convinced that the bio-fertilizer are an inexpensive but effective way of keeping their soil fertility, they will accept them and this will lead to higher crop production and higher economic returns.

FUTURE THRUSTS

Developing strains of bacteria which can withstand high temperature and alkali, and are acid resistant and high pH tolerant; which produce antibiotics in the soil or any chemicals, which impart the strain competitive edge over other strain is the need of the hour. Some of the genes responsible for production of plant hormones have been characterized and cloned. These genes could be introduced into *Rhizobium* strains. Strains that can fix nitrogen in the presence of added nitrogen and those that can increase nitrogen-fixing efficiency should be selected.

Efforts to mass multiply mycorrhizae in a large quantity using lighter carrier material should be intensified. The PCR techniques should be standardized to identify mycorrhizal colonization within plant roots using different species specific primers.

12

List of Bio-fertilizers Units in India and Abroad

LIST OF BIO-FERTILIZER UNITS IN INDIA

1. Agriculture Bactroriology
   Section College of Agriculture
   Pune 411005
2. Acharya N.G. Ranga Agricultural University
   Agricultural Research Station
   Amaravathi 522020
   District Guntur
   Andhra Pradesh
3. Ajay Bio-Tech (India) Ltd.
   22658, Village Khalad
   District Pune 412301 (MS)
4. Assam Agro Industries Corpn.
   Agricultural Chemistry Research Stn., Guwahati, Assam
5. Azo Fertilizers (Pvt.) Ltd.
   1063/89, 1st Main, 7th Cross
   Vidyaranyapuram
   Mysore 570008, Karnataka
6. Arvee Biotech
   134, East Car Street
   Chidambaram 608001 District South Arcot Vallalar
   Tamil Nadu
7. BAIF Laboratories Ltd.
   Briahnagar
   Off Pune Nagar Road
   Wagholi 412207
   District Pune, Maharashtra
8. Balaji Biotech
   Village Sathanur Post Vazhuvur
   Vandhavas 604405, District T.S., Chennai
9. Bidhan Chandra Krishi Vishwa Vidyalaya
   Nodule Research Laboratory
   Mohanpur
   Nadia Dist. 741252
   West Bengal
10. Bio-fertilizer Production Unit
    Government. of Tamil Nadu
    Kukumiamalal
    District Pudukkottai
    Tamil Nadu 622104
11. Bio-fertilizer Plant
    The Madhya Pradesh State Agro Industries Development Corpn. Ltd.
    Agro Complex, C - Sector
    Indrapuri, Bhopal 462022, M.P.
12. Department of Agriculture
    Government of Himachal Pradesh
    Hawthomvilla, Shimla 4 (HP)
13. Bio-fertilizer Production Unit
    Department of Agriculture
    Government of Tamil Nadu
    83-E, Kannan Kurchi Main Road
    Salem 636007, Tamil Nadu

14. Department of Soil Science
and Agricultural Chemistry
Faculty of Agriculture
Birsa. Agricultural University
Ranchi 834006; Bihar

15. Esvin Bio-Systems Limited
Esvin House, Perungudi
Chennai 600096 (TN)

16. Farm Organics Indian Pvt. Ltd.
Khole Niwas
Gurudwara Road
Kopergaon 423601
Maharashtra

17. Godavari Fertilizers and
Chemicals Limited
Vaninilayam
50, Sebastian Road
Secunderabad 500003, A.P.

18. Gujarat State Co-operative
Marketing Federation Ltd.
Sahakar Bhavan 5351316
Relief Road
Ahmedabad 380001, Gujarat

19. Gujarat State Fertilizers &
Chemicals Limited
P.O. Fertilizernagar 391750
District Vadodara Gujarat

20. Hans Biogenics
14-146, Gandhipuram 2
Rajahmundry 533103
A.P.

21. Harayana Agricultural
University
Department of Microbiology
Hissar 125001
Haryana

22. Hindustan Fertilizer
Corporation
Ltd.
Fertilizer Promotion &
Agricultural
Research Division
52 A, Shakaspeare Sarani
Kolkata 700001

23. Hindustan Fertilizer Corporation
Ltd.
Fertilizer Promotion &
Agricultural Research Division
Durgapur 713212

24. Indian Agricultural Research
Institute
Division of Microbiology
New Delhi 110012

25. Indian Organic Chemicals Ltd.
Khopoli 410203
District Raigad Maharashtra
Regd. Office Chemtex House

26. 2nd Floor, Main Street Sector-12
Hiranandani Garden
Powai 400076 Mumbai

27. KadurAgro
R.V. Vidyaniketan P.O.
Mysore Road
Mylasandu Bangalore 560059

28. K. FertsLab.
25, First Floor
Gurunanak Market
Nanded431601
Maharashtra

29. Karnataka Department of
Agriculture
Rhizobium Culture Prodn.
Laboratories
Hebbal Bangalore 560024
Karnataka

30. Karnataka Department of
Agriculture
Soil Health Centre
Gulberga
Karnataka

31. Kerala Department of Agriculture
Vikas Bhawan
Thirurananthapuram 695035
Kerala

32. Kisan Agro Chem
Bhatia Complex
Behind Mundada Hospital
Near Gujrathi High School

Vazirabad
Nanded 431601 :

33. Krishak Bharati Co-op. Ltd.
Marketing Division
A-10, Sector-1 Noida 201301
District Ghaziabad

34. Kumar Krishi Mitra Bio-Products
(I) Pvt. Ltd.
12, Ganeshwadi Fergusson
College Rd.
Pune411004 Maharashtra

35. Lakshmj Bio-Techs
No. 32 Rajunaicken Street
West Mambalam
Chennai 600033

36. Nagam Associates
No. 11T.T.K. Road
Royapettah
Chennai 600014

37. Marthwada Agricultural University
Parbhani 431402
Maharashtra

38. M.P. State Agro Industries
Corporation Limited
Biofertilizer Plant
Agro Complex, C-Sector
Indrapuri
Bhopal 462022
M.P.

39. M.P. State Co-op. Oilseed
Growers 'Fedn. Ltd.
H.O.:
1, Arera Hills, Behind Govt. Press
Bhopal 462011
Madhya Pradesh
Factory:
Biotech Research Centre
Gulab Chokkar
Dhar 454001
Madhya Pradesh

40. Mahatma Phule Krishi Vidyapeeth
Deptt. of Agricultural
Bacteriology
College of Agriculture
Shivajinagar Pune 411005
Maharashtra

41. Madras Fertilizers Ltd.,
Post Box No. 2
Manali
Madras 600068
Tamil Nadu

42. Main Bio Control Research
Laboratory
26393 (A Unit of Tamil Nadu
Co-operative Sugar Fedn.)
2E/1, Rajeshwari Vedachalem
Street
Chegalpattu 603001
Tamil Nadu
H.O.:
Tamil Nadu Co-operative Sugar
Fedn. Ltd.
474, Anna Salai
Periyar EVR Building
5th Floor, Nandanam
Chennai 600035 Tamil Nadu

43. Micro Bac. India
OGG Road, Noapara
P.O. Shyamnagar 743127
Dist. 24 Parganas (N)
West Bangal

44. MLN Farmers Training Instt.
(Co-operative Rural Development
Trust)
IFFCO Bio-fertilizer Production
Unit
Ghiya Nagar, Phulpur
Allahabad 212404 U.P.

45. Monarch Bio-fertilizers
and Research Centre
Sidco Industrial Estate
Thirumazhisai
Chennai 602107
Tamil Nadu

46. Nafed Biofertilizer
(A Unit of National Agricultural In
Co-op. Mktg. Fedn. of India Ltd.)

Plot No. 5 I/A, Sector' F Sanwer Road Indore 452003 M.P.

47. National Biofertilizer Development Centre
Dept. of Agriculture & Co-operative
Ministry of Agriculture (GOI)
C.G.O. Complex 11, 204-B Wing
Kamla Nehru Nagar, Ghaziabad 201002 U.P.

48. National Fertilizers Limited
Area Office - Indore
First Floor, Vikas Tower Indira Complex Navlakha, Indore 452001 M.P.

49. Nitrofix Laboratories
25, Bansdroni Avenue
Calcutta 700070
West Bengal

50. Orissa State Oilseed Growers' Federation
95, Satya Nagar
Bhubaneswar751007
Orissa

51. Punjab Agricultural University
Ludhiana 141004
Punjab

52. Punjab Agro Industries Corpn.
2A, Sector 28-A, Madhya Marg
657398 Chandigarh 160002
Punjab

53. Pyrites, Phosphates & Chemicals Ltd.
4558893
12-A, Sector-24
Noida 201301 (U.P.)

54. Rajasthan State Agro Ind. Corpn. Ltd.
O-I, Subhash Nagar 71228
Jotwara Road
Jaipur 302016
Rajasthan

55. Rashtriya Chemicals & Fertilizers Ltd.
Priyadarshini Eastern Express Highway, Sion,
Mumbai 400022, Maharashtra

56. Regional Agricultural Testing Demonstration Centre
Azamgarh 276001, U.P.

57. Regional Agricultural Testing & Demonstration Centre
P.O. Industrial Estate
Varanasi221100, U.P.

58. Regional Biofertilizer Development Centre
CAU Campus, Iroisemba
P.B. No. 7
P.O. Lamphepat,
Imphal 795004

59. Regional Biofertilizer Development Centre
Deptt. of Agriculture & Co-operation
Ministry of Agriculture (GOI)
34, IInd Main Road Hebbal
Bangalore 560024 Karnataka

60. Regional Biofertilizer Development Centre
Deptt. of Agriculture & Co-operation
Ministry of Agriculture (GOI)
18, SirsaRoad
Near Sweak Sabha Hospital
Hissar 125001
Haryana

61. Regional Biofertilizer Development Centre
VCA Complex, Civil Lines
Nagpur440001
Maharashtra

62. Regional Biofertilizer Development Centre
Plot No. B, Industrial estate Near Shobhapur Railaway Crossing,
Adhartal Jabalpur 482004 M.P.

63. Regional Biofertilizer Development

A-158, Shahid Nagar
Bhubaneshwar751007
Orissa

64. Regional Research Station
(Rhizobium Culture Lab.)
Deptt. of Agriculture
Govt. of Rajasthan
Durgapura
Jaipur 302006
Rajasthan

65. Regional Soil Testing Laboratory
Department of Agriculture
Government of Andhra Pradesh
Rajendra Nagar
Hyderabad 500030 A.P.

66. Soil Testing Laboratory
Deptt. of Agriculture
P.O. Mele Pattambi
Dist. Palakkad
Kerala

67. Southern Petro Chemical
Industries
Corpn. Ltd.
8921SPICIn
Spic Bio-Products
Agro Industrial
Chettiar Agaram Road, Perur
Channai 600116
Tamil Nadu

68. T. Stanes and Company Ltd.
to213518
8/23-24, Race Course Road
TSCO In
Post Box No. 3709
Coimbatore 641018
Tamil Nadu

69. T. N. Department of Agriculture
Bacterial Culture Prodn. Unit
Post Box No. 3709
Coimbatore64IOI8
Tamil Nadu

70. Tamil Nadu Agricultural
University
Deptt. of Agricultural
Microbiology
Coimbatore 641003 Tamil Nadu

71. The Maharashtra Agro
Industries Development Corpn.
Ltd.
RCL Unit, Sugars Factory
Plot No. 52-2-D
MiDC Industrial Estate
Chinchwad
Pune 411019

72. Maharashtra
Regd. Office
Rajan House
3rd Floor, Prabhadevi
Mumbai 400025
Maharashtra

73. The Orissa Agro Industries
Corpn. Ltd.
(A Govt. of Orissa Undertaking)
95, Satya Nagar
Bhubaneswar 751207 Orissa

74. The SIMA Cotton Development
&
Research Association
'Shanmugha Manram'
P.O. Box No. 3871
Race Course
Coimbatore 641018

75. The University of Agricultural
Sciences
Department of Agril. Microbiology
Krishi Nagar
Dharwad 580005
Karnataka

76. University of Agricultural
Sciences
P. O. Bag No. 2477
Hebbal
Bangalore 560024 Karnataka

77. University of Agricultural
Sciences
Dept. of Agricultural
Microbiology
G.K.V.K. Campus
Bangalore 560065
Karnataka

78. U.P. Department of Agriculture
Soil Testing Laboratory
Badaun 243001
U.F.

79. U.P. Department of Agriculture
Regional Soil Testing Laboratory
Alambagh
Lucknow 226001
U.P.

80. U.P. Department of Agriculture
Regional Soil Testing and Demonstration Centre
Etawah 206001
U.P.

81. U.P. Department of Agriculture
Regional Soil Testing Laboratory
Civil Lines
Jhansi 284001
U.P.

82. U.P. Department of Agriculture
Regional Agricultural Testing and Demonstration Centre
B-2, Adarsh Nagar
Meerut 250001
U.P.

83. U.P. Department of Agriculture
Regional Agricultural Testing and Demonstration Centre
Collectri Farm
Varanasi 221001 U.P.

84. U.P. Department of Agriculture
Soil Testing Laboratory
Civil Lines
Banda210001
U.P.

85. U.P. Department of Agriculture.
Soil Testing Laboratory
Malladiya Nala Sultanpur 228001
U.P.

86. U.P. Department of Agriculture
Soil Testing Laboratory
Ramghat Road Aligarh 202001
U.P.

87. Green Fibldo Agrotech Vivek V-Gangwar 20/1, Vrmila Society Dhankawadi Pune 411043

88. Niku Bio-Research Lab. 613, Nanapeth Pune 411002 89. Inora
Division of Know-Row Foundation
c/o Resoon 43/1, Karve Road
Pune 411038

90. 3, ACE Bio-Tech 43/2, randawana Off. Karve Road Behind Resoon Pune411038

91. Bio-E,a Technologies B-15, Corporation on Building 1st Floor, Link Road, Sadar Nagpur 440001

92. Biodynamic Products 4, Oriental Apartment Lane No. 2 Dahanukar Colony Kothrud
Pune 411029

93. A.V.S. Agro Products At. Post Nimgaon Jali Tal, Sangamner Dist. Ahmednagar413714

94. Nooscute Labe (I) Pvt. Ltd.
11/B, Tiwari Industries Estate Ram Mandir Road Goragaon (W.) Mumbai-400104

95. Tajasvi Bio-fert. At - Dhumewadi Pune - Saswad Road Dist. Pune

96. Bharat Laboratories & Technologies for Agriculture Jambhale Complex Near Rajkamal Theatre Distt. Dhule

97. Nav Maharashtra Chakan Oil Mills Ltd.
Nav Maharashtra House 43, Shaniwar Peth Post Box 571 Opp. Shaniwarwada Pune 411030

98. Nomin Agro Bio Pvt. Ltd.,
K-3, Flat No. 267/D/I Pt.
Jawaharlal Nehru Industrial Estate Tal. Mulahi Dist. Pune

9. Nirantan Biotech 45, Vinak Girija Society NIT College Road Pune 411030

00. Nirmal Seeds Ltd. / Bhadgaon Road At Post Tal. Pachora Dist. Jalgaon 424201

01. Krishival Biofertilizers
NIDC lalampur
Flat No. D-14 Tal. Walva Dist. Sangli

02. ECOTekAgro
3 Prashanti 7th
Lane Prabhat road Pune 411004

03. Maharashtra Biotech Industries
171, Kisan Kunj
Wanwadigaon
Pune411040

04. Associate Director (Research)
College of Agriculture
Latur
Marathwada Agriculture University
Parbhani

05. Innovative Pest Control Laboratory
No. 2552, Yashashaswini
13th Main, Kumaraswamy Layout
II Stage Bangalore 560078

06. Green Field Organics Pvt. Ltd.
1257, Dalai Street
Nipani 591237

07. HMG Biotech Pvt. Ltd. 197,
II Cross, 7th Main I Block,
Koramangala
Bangalore 560034

08. T. Stanes & Co. Ltd.
13/2, 4th Cross
Nagappa Street
Palace Nagar
Bangalore 560003

109. Zuari Industries Ltd.
Jubilee Building IIIrd Floor
45, Museum Road
P.B. No. 5151 Bangalore 560001

110. KadurAgro
R.V.V. Post
Mylasandra
Bangalore 560059

111. Madras Fertiiizers Ltd.
3/1, Deewan N. Madhav Rao Road
Basavanagudi
Bangalore 560004

112. Fertilizer and Chemicals Travancore Ltd.
28/1, Ulsoor Road Bangalore 560042

113. Southern Petro Chemicals Industries Corporation Ltd.
67, Ulsoor Road
Bangalore 560042

114. Karnataka Antibiotics and Pharmaceuticals Ltd. 3321350
Dr. Rajkumar Road, I Block
Rajaji Nagar Bangalore 560010

115. Rashtriya Chemicals & Fertilizers Ltd.
17/7, AliAsker Road Bangalore 560052

116. Samarth Bio Tech Industries
D-302 & B-500, Industrial Estate
Airport Road
Hubli 580030

117. Vimpex Agencies
No. 7, Balaji Nilaya
I Cross, Swamming Pool Extension (Pipe Line)
Malleswaram, Bangalore 560003

118. West Coast Hebochem Pvt. Ltd.,
105/B Industrial Suburb, II Stage
III Cross
Goruguntepalay, Tumkur Road
Bangalore 560022

119. Terra Firma Biotechnologies Ltd., 104, Ranka Pert 5, Lalbagh Road, Bangalore 560027

120. Mardia Chemicals Ltd., (GNV FEL) No. 3698 9th Cross Service Road, HAL IInd Stage 13th D Main Bangalore 560008

121. Krishak Bharati Co-op. Ltd. 101/102, Swiss Complex 35, Race Course Road Bangalore 560001

122. Associate Professor Popularization of Bio-fertilizer Scheme, Dept. of Agriculture, Microbiology, UAS, GKVK, Bangalore 560065

123. Hubli Biotechnology Pvt. Ltd., Sumangala Complex, Lamington Road, Hubli, Karnataka

124. Karnataka Bio-fertilizers Kiran Cottage Compound Near Railway Bridge Sindagi Road Bijapur 586104

125. Eugenic Bio-Derviatives Off. 12/2 & 12/3 Bellad Building Vidyapeeth Road Fort, Dharwad-8 Karnataka

126. Micro-Tech D. No. 1208/77, 6th Cross Taralabalu Extn. Davangere 577005

127. Regional Director Regional Bio-fertilizer Develpt. Centre Hebbal, Bangalore 560024

128. Professor & Head Dept. of Agricultural Microbiology University of Agril. Sciences Krishinagar, Dharwad 580005

129. Senior Scientist Agri. Research Station (UAS) Kotnur, Gulbarga

130. Biofertilizer Production Unit Motilal Nehru Farmers Training Institute Cordet Phulpur Allahabad (UP)

FOREIGN

1. Agrproyectos Rivadavia y Obispo Gelabert3000 Sante Fe Argentina Contact: Ing. Oscar Alloatti

2. Dra. Haydee Lackner Crawford, Keen y Cia. S.A. Florida 681, 3er, Piso CEP 1375, Buenos Aires Argentina

3. INTA Departmento de Microbiologia C.C. 25-1712 Castelar Argentina Contact: Ing. Agr. Rosa Dieguez

4. Centro de Investigacion y Desarrollo de Fermentaciones Industriaies (CINDEFI) Calles47y 115(1900) La Plata Argentina Contact: Dr. Gabriel Favelukes

5. Fac. De Ciencias Exactas y Naturales Avda. Uruguay No. 151 6300 Santa Rosa La Pampa Argentina Contact: Dr. Antonio Pedro Balatti

6. Bio-Care Technology.. Pty. Ltd 95-99 Carlingsford Road Sefton

New South Wales P.O. Box 8
Regents Park 2143 Australia

7. Inoculant Services
Teangi
Bethanga
Victoria 3691
Contact:
Principal: Mr. Sandy Montague
Lab Manager: Dr. Greg Bender

8. Bio-Care Technology Pty. Ltd.
84 Rawson Road P.O. Box 367
Woy Woy
New South Wales 2256
Australia
Contacts:
Director: Garry K. Bullard
Director: David J. Pulsford

9. Queensland Inoculants
P.O.Box 1052
Toowoomba QLD 4350
Australia

10. University of Queensland
Dept. of Agriculture
Queensland 4072
Australia
Contact: Dr. Peter Dart

11. Verband der Landwirtschaftlicher
Genossenschaften
Sailergasse - A - 1010
Vienna
Austria
Importer of Inoculant from:
Hellebiogri Gaiba, Italy

12. Biolink
c/o Department of Soil Science
Bangladesh Ag Univ. (BAU)
Mymensingh 2202
Bangladesh
Contact: Executive Director
Mr. Mahurul Haque

13. Soil Microbiology Laboratory
Bangladesh Institute of Nuclear
Agriculture P. O. Box 4,
Mymensingh 2200 Bangladesh

14. Centro de Investigation Agricola
Tropical (CIAT)
Av. Ejercito Nacional No. 131
Casilla 247
Santa Cruz de la Sierra
Bolivia
Contact: Ing. Renato Valenzuela

15. Agro-Quimic Planlto Ltda
R. Carlos Alberto Beninica 294 P.
Fun'do - RS CEP: 99100 Brazil

16. Bio-SojaLTDA
Caixa Postal 87
Rua Soa Joaquim da Barra
SP 14600
Brazil
Contact: Carlos Alberto
Mantovani

17. Centro de Energia Nuclear en
Agricultura (CENA)
Av. Martins Francisco 119
Caixa Postal 96 CEP 13400
Piracicaba, Sao Paulo
Brazil
Contact: Dra. Alaides Puppin
Rushchel

18. Empresa Brasilera de Pesquisa
Agropecuaria (Embrapa)
Rodovia Carlos Joao Strass
Acesso Orlando Amaral
Caixa Postal 1061,
86001, Londrina, Parana
Brazil
Contact: Dra. Mariangela Hungria

19. IRFA
Av. Hulio de Castilhos 342
15qAndar Porto Alegre,
RS9003O0 Brazil '

20. Nitral Ltda
Rua Rio Piquiri, 650
Pinhais, Piraquara
PR 83340
Brazil
Contact: Sonia Donadelo

21. Nitroar, Ind. Com. Prod. Agric.
Caixa Postal 70.008
Planaltina, DF 73300

Brazil
Contact: Samuel Rumor

22. Cento de Reciirsos Microbiologicos en Rhizobium MIRCEN
Fac. De Agronomia, UFRGS Av. Bento Gonzalves 7712 91500 Porto Alegre, R.G.S. Brazil 83420
Contact: Jardim Freire

23. Facotrigo Central-Sul-Cruz alta Brazil
Industria Bio-Soja de Inoculantes LTDA
Via Anhaguera Km 383 Marginal esquerda, n! 1.000
Caixa Postal n! 87
CEP: 14.600
Sao Joquim da Barra - SP
Brazil

24. Leivas Leite S/A
Rua Benjamin Constant 1637
Pelotas, RS 96010
Brazil
Contact: Paulo Leite

25. Nitral S.A. Industria Comercio de Inoculantes Products Agropecuarios
Rua Luiza Verone Picolli, 594 - Bacacheri
Caixa Postal, 4.162
80.00 Curitiba PR
Brazil

26. Solo-Fix
Av. Candido Abreu. 526
Conj. 407-A
Centro Civico
Curitiba, PR 80530
Brazil
Contact: Solon C. Araujo

27. Turfal
Caixa Postal 7410 CEP: 80.000
Curitiba PR Brazil

28. Turfal, Ind. Com. Prod. Quim. LTDA
Rodovia BR 116 km 79
Quatro Barass, PR
Brazil
Contact: Rubens Buschmann

29. Agricultural Research Institute
Plant Pathology Division
Yezin
Burma
Contact: Deputy General Manager Dr. H la Than

30. ISABU (Burundian Institute of Agronomic Sciences)
Bujumbura, Burundi
Contacts: A. Moudiongui .
S. Ntihabose
C. Ruraduma

31. Candian Seed Coaters, Ltd.
P.O. Box 219 Brampton, Ontario L6V 2L2 Canada

32. First Line Seeds Ltd. , RR # 2
Gueip, Ontario
N1H6H8
Canada

33. Lamorna Enterprises Ltd,
2896 West 38th Avenue
Vancouver, B.C.
V6N2X1
Canada

34. ESSO Chemical Canada, Ag Biologicals # 402-15 Innovation Bl vd. Saskatoon, SK Canada S7N 2X8 Contact: R. J. Rennie

35. Institut Rosell, INC. 8480 Boulevard St. Laurent Montreal, Quebec H2P 2M6 Canada

36. Mclver Scientific, INC.
343 A Elgin St.
Cambridge, Ontario
NIR 7H9
Canada

37. Microbio Khizogen Corporation 818 48th St. East Saskatoon, Sask STK3R3 Canada

38. Rhizogen Corp.
Bay 5, 116

103rd Street East
Sask, Saskatchewan S7N 1Y7
Canada
Contacts: Dir. of Tech Trans Div:
Peter Innes, Ph.D
CEO: Dr. Roger H. Gilmour
Dir of R & D: Paul G. Boseley, Ph.D

39. Philom Bios, INC.
Mall 2, # 104-110 Research Dr.
Innovation Place
Sask, Saskatchewan S7N 3R3
Canada

40. University of British Colombia
Dept. of Plant Science
Suite 248, 2357 Main Mall
Vancouver B.C. V6T
Canada
Contact: Dr. F.B. Holl (Speciality Inoculants)

41. Campax
Casilla 87
Temuco
Chile
Contact: Erik van Baer

42. Probical Ltda.
Alcalde Pedro Alarcon 754
Santiago
Chile
Contact: Martha Granger M

43. Microagro Ltda.
Transversal 22 No. 61 - 17
Bogota
Colombia
Contact: Dr. Fernando Munevar

44. Universidad de Costa Rica
Centra de inestigaciones Agron'micas
San Pedro, Montes de Oca
San Jose
Costa Rica
Contact: Ing. Oscar Acusa

45. Estaclon Experimental la Renee
Quivican
Ministerio de Agricultura
La Habana
Cuba
Contact: Ing. German Hernandez

46. Soils and Water Research Inst.
Department of Agricultural Microbiology
Agricultural Research Centre
Giza
Egypt
Contacts: Dr. Samil M. Abdel-Wahab
Dr. Mohamed E. Hassan

47. International Livestock Centre for Africa (ILCA)
P.O. Box 5687
Addis Ababa
Ethiopia
Contact: Director: Dr. I. Hague

48. Bioprox
6, Rue Barbes
B.P. 177
F - 92305 Levallois-Perret Cedex
France

49. INRA
F - 86600 Lusignan
France
Contact: Jean Gondrau

50. Lipha
34 rue St. Romain
B.P. 8481
F-69539 Lyon Cedex 08
France

51. GEP
P.O. Box 63
F-41004 Bloiz Cedex
France
Contact: Muriel Lasneau

52. Laboratoire de Microbilogie des Sols
INRA, BP 1540
21034 Dijon Cedrex
France
Contact Gerard Catroux

53. Liphatech
10 Avenue de Lattre de Tassigny
69330 Meyzieu
France
Contact: P. Wadoux

54. Elomestari Ltd.
Partala
51900 Juva
Finland
Contact: Petri elnonen

55. Nat. Ag. Research Inst. (NARI) Soil Microbiology Laboratory Mon Repos East Coast Demerara Guyana Contact: Dr. J. Octive

56. Biotecnologia de Honduras P.O. Box 1881 San Pedro Sula Honduras

57. Esuela Agricola Penamericana
P.O. Box 93
Tegucigalpa
Honduras

58. Rhizogin Indonesia
Ventura Building
Third Floor Suite 303
Jl. Jagorwi-Cilandak
Outer Ring Road No. 26
Jakarta Selatan, 12430
Indonesia
Contact: Owner/Director Mr. N. Pesik

59. Agricultural Research Institute
Tokachi Federation of Agricultural Cooperatves (Tokachi Nokyoren)
KITA - 1 NISHI - 24
Hokkaido
Japan

60. Mircen Laboratory
c/o Head
Dept. Soil Sci/Fac. of Ag.
Box No. 30197
Nairobi
Kenya
Contact: Mr. S. Wangaruro

61. Chitedze Agricultural Research Station
P.O. Box 158
Lilongwe
Malawi
Contact: Soil Microbiologist
Dr. D. J. Khonj

62. Empresa Nitragin S.A.
RioTizapan 1716
Colonia Atlas
Guadalajara, Jalisco
Mexico
Contact: Biol. Alvaro Nathal Sanchez

63. Institute of Agronomy & Veterinary
Hassan II
BP 6202
Rabat
Morocco
Contact: Dr. Ali Hilali

64. PTG
Postbus 8
2670 AA Naaldwijk The Netherlands Contact: Mr. J.S. Paternotte

65. IPO
Postbus 9060
6700 GW Wageningen
The Netherlands
Contact: Mrs. C.E. Winterswijk

66. Mintech (NZ) Ltd.
Agricultural Division
P.O. Box 440
Nelson
New Zealand

67. Rhizocoat Coated Seed Ltd.
P.O. Box 11 - 007
Christchurch
New Zealand

68. University of Lfe
Dept. of Plant Science
He - Ife Oyo State
Contact: Chief Tech.: Mr. S.O. Sagay

69. Klonar, Paraquay S.R.L. :
Biotechnolgia Aplicada

Yegros 437 - Edificio
San Rafael - Piso 19
Asuncion
Paraquay
Contact: Sci. Dir. Jorge Peisajovich

70. Universidad Nacional de Cajamarca
Laboratorio de Rhizobiologia
Giudad Universitaria
Cajamarca
Peru
Contact: Ing. Oscar Amoros

71. Universidad de San Cristobal de Huamanga
Laboratori de Rhizobiologia
Portal Independencia 57
Ayacucho
Peru
Contact: Biol. Freddy Mackie Martinez

72. Universidad Nacional de San Aqustin de Arequipa
Departmento de Microbiologia
Av. Alcides Carrison s/n,
La Pampilla, Arequipa
Peru
Contact: Dra. Gloria Cornejo de Zvietcovch

73. Los Banos Biotechnology Corporation
Suite 504, F&M Building
Legaspi St.
Legaspi Village, Makati
Metro Manila
Philippines

74. Republic of the Philippines
Department of Agriculture
Regional Soils Laboratory Region
San Fernando
La Union 2500
Philippines
Contact: Dr. Josefina O. Bautista Chief

75. University of the Philippines Los Banos
Department of Soil Science
College Laguna
The Philippines Contact: Dr. Erlinda Paterno

76. Zaklad Przemyslu Rolnego
Bydgoska 41
78. 600 Walcz Poland

77. Oil and Protein Seed Centre
Private Bag XI251
Potchefstroom
South Africa
Contacts: Mr. A.J. Liebenberg
Mr. Jeff Seutloali

78. Stimuplant
Republic of South Africa Contact:
Owner: Peitar L. Steyrt

79. Project Engrais FAO
GCPE/RWA/006/DEN
BP 337 Butare
Rwanda
Contact: J.A. Scaglia

80. Centro Inv. y Des. Agrario "Las Torres"
CTRA, Rinconada - Alcald
Apartado Official
41.200 - Alcola del Rio (Sevilla)
Spain
Contact: Rafel Orive Ecuejarrieta

81. Central Laboratory for Biological Nitrogen Fixation
Institute of Environmental and Natural Resources Research The National Centre for Research P.O. Box 6096 Peoples' Hall Khartoum, Sudan

82. National Taiwan University
Dept. of Agricultural Chemistry
Taipei
Taiwan
Contact: Dr. Liang - Ping Lin

83. Bangkok Seeds Industry Co.
36 Soil Yeshit, Chan Road
Yannava
Bangkok 10120 Thailand

84. Entite, Industrial & Commercial Enterprises, Inc.
Burkres Sokak 19/6
Cankaya - Ankara
Turkey
Contact: Consultant Dr. Velettin Gurgun
Ziraat Facultesi (Microbiology)
Ankara, University,
Diskapi/Ankara
Turkey

85. Makerere University
Inoculum Production Unit
Soil Science Department
P.O. Box 7062
Kampala
Uganda
Contacts: Director Dr. M.A. Bekunda
Supervisor: Charles Nkwine

86. Agricultural Genetics Company Ldt.
154 Science Park Milton Road
Cambridge, Cambs CB4 4G6
United Kingdom

87. Agricultural Genetics Co. Ltd.
Micro Bio Division
Church Street (0763) 208881
Thriplow, Nr Royston Heris SG 877RE United Kingdom Contact: Mr. J.H. Stephens

88. Biotal Ltd. & Biotechnica Ltd.
United Kingdom
Institute of Arable Crops Research
Crop Management Department
Rothamsed Exper. Station
Harpenden, Herts
AL5 2 JQ
United Kingdom
Contact: J.M. Day

89. Abbott Laboratories
1 Abbott Park Road
Abbot Park Ilinois 60064
USA
Contacts: CEO: Duane Burham
Public Relations J. Weiner

90. Agbiochem Inc.
3 Fleetwood Court Orinda, California 94563 USA

91. Agracetus
8520 University Green
Middletown, Wisconsin 53562
USA
Contacts: CEO: Robert Walton, Ph.D
Project Coordinator: Kenneth A. Barton, Ph.D
Purchasing: Michael Henderson

92. Bentech Laboratories Inc.
14424 S.E. Industrial Way
Clackamas, Oregon 97015
USA

93. Clagene
1920 Fifth Street Davis, California 95616-4918 USA . Contact: CEO: Roger Salquist

94. Liphatech Inc.
3103 West Custer Avenue
Milwauke, WI53209
USA
Contacts: CEO: Thomas H. Winkofske
VP R&D: Arthur Nethery, Ph.D.
Dir. of Ag.: wart Smith, Ph.D
Foreign Affiliate: Nitragin, S.A.

95. NifTAL Center
1000 Holomua Road
Paia, HI 96779
USA
Contact: Joe Rourke

96. Hi-Bred International Inc.
P.O. Box 38
7300 Northwest 62nd Ave
Johnston, Iowa 50131 USA

97. Bentech Laboratories Inc.
14424 S.E. Industrial Way
Clackamas, Oregon 97015
USA

98. Celpril Industries
251 Oak Street
Manteca, California 95336-1937
USA
Contact: CEO Maximilian Clara

99. Microlife Technics
Box 3917/1833
57th Street
Sarasota, Florida 33578 USA

100. Pioneer Hi-Bred Intl., Inc.
700 Capital Square
400 Locust Street
Des Moines, Iowa 50309
USA
Contact: CEO: Thomas N. Urban
Dept. of Biotech Res.

101. Trace Chemicals
839 Brenkman Drive
Pekin.IL 61554
USA

102. Urbana Laboratories
P.O. Box 1393
3105 Third St.
St. Joseph, Missouri 64502
USA
Contact:
Res Micro: Thomas Wacek, Ph.D.

103. Yellowstone Valley Chemical
361 Rothiemay Rd.
Ryegate, Montana 59074
USA
Contact: Andy Lulum

104, Laboratorio de Microbiologia de Suelos y
Latinamerican Society of Rhizobiology Control de Inoculantes del Plan Agropecuario Bulevar Artigas 3802 Montevideo Uruguay
Contact: Dr. Carlos Labandera

105. Miguel Castiglioni
ENZUR, S.A.
Azara 3787, Montevideo Uruguay

106. Instituto Venezolano de Investigaciones Cientificas (IVIC)
Aptdo 21827
Caracas 1020 A
Venezuela
Contact: Margarita Sicardi de Mallorca

107. Venezolano de Inoculantes C.A.
Av. La Anunciaciou Residencias Grinoco
Piso8
Apto 8-A
San Antonio de Los altos 1204
Edo Miranda
Venezuela
Contact: President - Peter Ladera

108. Universidad de Los Andes
Facultad de Ciencias
Dept de Biologia
Merida edo Merida
Venezuela
Contact: Dr. Roberto Skwierinski

109. Mt. Makulu Cen Res. Sta.
Soil Micro/noculum Prod
Private Bag No. 7
Chilanga
Zambia
Contact: Supervisor - Gilbert Tembo

110. Grasslands Research Inst.
Soil Productivity Laboratory
Private Bag No. 3757
Marondera
Zimbabwe
Contact:
Director: Ms. Mary Ryder

13

Plant Economics of Agrofertilizer from Leaves

Capacity = 5 Ton/Day

LAND & BUILDING (Land Area 3000 sq.mt.) = Rs. 83,00,000.00

PLANT & MACHINERY

1. Mixer
2. Pulverizer
3. Screens (Vibratory)
4. Packaging Machine
5. Laboratory Testing Equpments

FIXED CAPITAL

1. LAND & BUILDING	Rs.	83,00,000.00
2. PLANT & MACHINERY	Rs.	39,00,000.00
3. OTHER FIXED ASSETS	Rs.	7,25,000.00
TOTAL	Rs.	1,29,25,000.00

RAW MATERIALS

1. Leaves
2. Hydrolytate Enzymes
3. Packaging Material

TOTAL WORKING CAPITAL/MONTH

1. RAW MATERIAL	Rs.	17,05,000.00
2. SALARY & WAGES	Rs.	1,54,929.00
3. UTILITIES & OVERHEADS	Rs.	1,32,300.00
TOTAL	Rs.	19,92,229.00

TOTAL CAPITAL INVESTMENT

TOTAL FIXED CAPITAL	Rs.	1,29,25,000.00
TOTAL WORKING CAPITAL FOR 3 MONTHS	Rs.	59,76,688.00
TOTAL	Rs.	1,89,01,688.00

TURN OVER/ANNUM

Receipt By sale of Agrofertilizer from Leaves 1500 MT	Rs.	3,37,50,000.00

PROFIT SALES RATIO = Profit / Sales x 100 = 18%

RATE OF RETURN = Operating profit / T.C.I x 100 = 32%

BREAK EVEN POINT (B.E.P) = 46%

14

Plant Economics of Biofertilizers from Chicken Refuges, Oil Cakes, Bone Mills

Capacity = 50 MT/Day

LAND & BUILDING (Land 10 Acres) = Rs. 1,57,00,000.00

PLANT & MACHINERY

1. BUCKET ELEVATOR
2. Screw type mixing unit
3. Pulverizer
4. Conveyor belt
5. Magnetic Drum
6. Hammer mill
7. Pasteurisation Chamber
8. Air Blower
9. Boiler
10. Chimney
11. Composting chamber
12. Granulation tower
13. Scrubber for air cleaning
14. Laboratory testing eqpts
15. Transformer
16. Genset

FIXED CAPITAL

1.	LAND & BUILDING	Rs.	1,57,00,000.00
2.	PLANT & MACHINERY	Rs.	2,34,70,000.00
3.	OTHER FIXED ASSETS	Rs.	1,05,00,000.00
	TOTAL	Rs.	4,96,70,000.00

RAW MATERIALS

1. Chicken refuges, oil cake, bone
2. Laboratory Chemicals
3. Chemical additives

TOTAL WORKING CAPITAL/MONTH

1.	RAW MATERIAL	Rs.	48,45,000.00
2.	SALARY & WAGES	Rs.	4,52,655.00
3.	UTILITIES & OVERHEADS	Rs.	8,01,000.00
	TOTAL	Rs.	60,98,655.00

TOTAL CAPITAL INVESTMENT

TOTAL FIXED CAPITAL	Rs.	4,96,70,000.00
TOTAL WORKING CAPITAL FOR 2 MONTHS	Rs.	1,21,97,310.00
TOTAL	Rs.	6,18,67,310.00

TURN OVER/ANNUM

By sale of 15000 MT. Organic Fertiliser in 50 kgs bags, (3,00,000 Nos)	Rs.	12,00,00,000.00

PROFIT SALES RATIO = Profit / Sales x 100 = 25%

RATE OF RETURN = Operating profit / T.C.I x 100 = 49%

BREAK EVEN POINT (B.E.P) = 42%

15

Plant Economics of Biofertilizers from Cowdung & other Wastage

Capacity = 5 TONS/Day

LAND & BUILDING (Land 5 acres) = Rs. 13,50,000.00

PLANT & MACHINERY

1. Mixing machine (S.S. lined)
2. Bucket elevator & conveyor
3. Granulating machine (SS Lined)
4. Vibrating screen with 3 H.P motor
5. Fluidized bed dryer with air heating & blowing arrangement
6. Semi automatic bags filling, weighing & stiching machine
7. Weighing balance platform type
8. Storage silo (s.s. lined)
9. Laboratory equipments
10. Miscellaneous tools, jigs, fixture

FIXED CAPITAL

1.	LAND & BUILDING	Rs.	13,50,000.00
2.	PLANT & MACHINERY	Rs.	23,75,000.00
3.	OTHER FIXED ASSETS	Rs.	5,00,000.00
	TOTAL	Rs.	42,25,000.00

RAW MATERIALS

1. Cowdung
2. Urine
3. Paddy husk
4. Diammmonium Phosphate
5. Potassium nitrate
6. Packaging bags

TOTAL WORKING CAPITAL/MONTH

1.	RAW MATERIAL	Rs.	13,81,450.00
2.	SALARY & WAGES	Rs.	94,000.00
3.	UTILITIES & OVERHEADS	Rs.	1,28,500.00
	TOTAL	Rs.	16,03,950.00

TOTAL CAPITAL INVESTMENT

TOTAL FIXED CAPITAL	Rs.	42,25,000.00
TOTAL WORKING CAPITAL FOR 1 MONTH	Rs.	16,03,950.00
TOTAL	Rs.	58,28,950.00

TURN OVER/ANNUM

By sale of 1500 tons fertilizer Rs. 2,40,00,000.00

PROFIT SALES RATIO = Profit / Sales x 100 = 14%

RATE OF RETURN = Operating profit / T.C.I x 100 = 57%

BREAK EVEN POINT (B.E.P) = 43%

16

Plant Economics of Biofertilizers (Organic Fertilizers) from Garbage (MSW)

Capacity = 13500 MT./Annum

LAND & BUILDING (Land Area 7.5 Acres) = Rs. 50,25,000.00

PLANT & MACHINERY

1. BUCKET ELEVATOR (Gosse neck type) made up of mild steel with 3HPmotor starter, accessories
2. Sieving Machine M.S. baby with stainless steel sieves (Reciprocation) with 3 HP motor
3. Conveyor belt with accessories and 5 HP motor
4. Magnetic Drum
5. Hammer mill
6. Pasteurisation Chamber
7. Air Blower
8. Boiler
9. Chimney
10. Composting Rotary kiln
11. Conical type mixing mill
12. Granulation tower
13. Scrubber
14. Bags filling, sealing and weighing system
15. Conveyor belt
16. Pipes, fittings, structures, pumps, valves & Misc. Attachments electrical eqpts. accessories
17. Laboratory testing eqpts. and instruments, process control - equipments.
18. Tools, jigs, fixturs etc.

19. Installation,Erection,Commissioning charges
20. Transformer
21. Genset

FIXED CAPITAL

1.	LAND & BUILDING	Rs.	50,25,000.00
2.	PLANT & MACHINERY	Rs.	1,17,30,000.00
3.	OTHER FIXED ASSETS	Rs.	29,50,000.00
	TOTAL	Rs.	1,97,05,000.00

RAW MATERIALS

1. Municipalty Garbage solid - cellulosic waste
2. Laboratory Chemicals
3. Chemical additives as lime, Ammonium Compound
4. Bags

TOTAL WORKING CAPITAL/MONTH

1.	RAW MATERIAL	Rs.	3,75,000.00
2.	SALARY & WAGES	Rs.	3,87,500.00
3.	UTILITIES & OVERHEADS	Rs.	6,24,000.00
	TOTAL	Rs.	13,86,500.00

TOTAL CAPITAL INVESTMENT

TOTAL FIXED CAPITAL	Rs.	1,97,05,000.00
TOTAL WORKING CAPITAL FOR 1 MONTH	Rs.	13,86,500.00
TOTAL	Rs.	2,10,91,500.00

TURN OVER/ANNUM

By sale of 13500 MT. Organic Fertiliser in 50 kgs bags	Rs.	3,24,00,000.00

PROFIT SALES RATIO = Profit / Sales x 100 = 31%

RATE OF RETURN = Operating profit / T.C.I x 100 = 47%

BREAK EVEN POINT (B.E.P) = 52%

17

Plant Economics of Organic Manure

Capacity = 20 TON/Day

LAND & BUILDING (Land Area 3000 sq. mt.) = Rs. 21,30,000.00

PLANT & MACHINERY

1. Cement storage tank
2. Mixing tank
3. Separator & Cooling tank
4. Plate & frame filter press
5. Cabinet Dryer
6. Pulverizer
7. High Pressure vessel
8. Grinding Mill
9. Boiler
10. Miscellaneous Accessories & fitting
11. Packaging Machine

FIXED CAPITAL

1.	LAND & BUILDING	Rs.	21,30,000.00
2.	PLANT & MACHINERY	Rs.	13,95,000.00
3.	OTHER FIXED ASSETS	Rs.	2,60,000.00
	TOTAL	Rs.	37,85,000.00

RAW MATERIALS

1. Sewage sludge, Night soil, animal & human waste
2. Sulphuric acid & other chemists

TOTAL WORKING CAPITAL/MONTH

1.	RAW MATERIAL	Rs.	1,95,000.00
2.	SALARY & WAGES	Rs.	81,600.00
3.	UTILITIES & OVERHEADS	Rs.	1,08,500.00
	TOTAL	Rs.	3,85,100.00

TOTAL CAPITAL INVESTMENT

TOTAL FIXED CAPITAL	Rs.	37,85,000.00
TOTAL WORKING CAPITAL FOR 3 MONTHS	Rs.	11,55,300.00
TOTAL	Rs.	49,40,300.00

TURN OVER/ANNUM

By sale of 6000 Tonne/annum	Rs.	1,20,00,000.00

PROFIT SALES RATIO = Profit / Sales x 100 = 50%

RATE OF RETURN = Operating profit / T.C.I x 100 = 122%

BREAK EVEN POINT (B.E.P) = 27%

18

Plant Economics of Sea Weed Liquid Fertilizer

Capacity = 25 MT/Day

LAND & BUILDING (Land Area 2 Acres) = Rs. 1,41,20,000.00

PLANT & MACHINERY

1. Extractor(ss)
2. Mixing Vessel
3. Storage Tanks
4. Boiler
5. D.G. Set
6. Laboratory Equipments
7. Instrumentation & Process control equipments
8. Filling machine
9. Miscellaneous equipments viz. pipe fittings, pumps, motors etc.

FIXED CAPITAL

1.	LAND & BUILDING	Rs.	1,41,20,000.00
2.	PLANT & MACHINERY	Rs.	2,76,50,000.00
3.	OTHER FIXED ASSETS	Rs.	87,25,000.00
	TOTAL	Rs.	5,04,95,000.00

RAW MATERIALS

1. Seedweed/Rockweed
2. Non-Ionic Emulsifier
3. Aromax Solvent
4. Distilled Water
5. Benzene
6. Packing Materials

TOTAL WORKING CAPITAL/MONTH

1.	RAW MATERIAL	Rs.	1,91,05,000.00
2.	SALARY & WAGES	Rs.	4,78,800.00
3.	UTILITIES & OVERHEADS	Rs.	5,35,000.00
	TOTAL	Rs.	2,01,18,800.00

TOTAL CAPITAL INVESTMENT

TOTAL FIXED CAPITAL	Rs.	5,04,95,000.00
TOTAL WORKING CAPITAL FOR 1 MONTH	Rs.	2,01,18,800.00
TOTAL	Rs.	7,06,13,800.00

TURN OVER/ANNUM

Receipts from sale of 7500 MT. of Seaweed Liquid Fertilizer	Rs.	30,00,00,000.00

PROFIT SALES RATIO = Profit / Sales x 100 = 14%

RATE OF RETURN = Operating profit / T.C.I x 100 = 59%

BREAK EVEN POINT (B.E.P) = 34%

19

Plant Economics of Vermi-Composting

Capacity = 30 MT./Day

LAND & BUILDING (Land Area 20000 Sq.mt.) = Rs. 2,03,62,500.00

PLANT & MACHINERY

1. Special Bins, Water Sprinklers, Pumps, Piping Structure, Cooling Equipments, Technical Know-how etc.

FIXED CAPITAL

1.	LAND & BUILDING	Rs.	2,03,62,500.00
2.	PLANT & MACHINERY	Rs.	75,00,000.00
3.	OTHER FIXED ASSETS	Rs.	19,89,000.00
	TOTAL	Rs.	2,98,51,500.00

RAW MATERIALS

1. Garbage/municipal waste/cowdung/ rotten vegetables etc.
2. Packaging Material.

TOTAL WORKING CAPITAL/MONTH

1.	RAW MATERIAL	Rs.	6,50,000.00
2.	SALARY & WAGES	Rs.	1,89,000.00
3.	UTILITIES & OVERHEADS	Rs.	2,13,500.00
	TOTAL	Rs.	10,52,500.00

TOTAL CAPITAL INVESTMENT

TOTAL FIXED CAPITAL	Rs.	2,98,51,500.00
TOTAL WORKING CAPITAL FOR 2 MONTHS	Rs.	21,05,000.00
TOTAL	Rs.	3,19,56,500.00

TURN OVER/ANNUM

By sale of 10950 MT Per annum of Vermi Composting	Rs.	3,72,30,000.00

PROFIT SALES RATIO = Profit / Sales x 100 = 46%

RATE OF RETURN = Operating profit / T.C.I x 100 = 54%

BREAK EVEN POINT (B.E.P) = 35%

117. MANUFACTURE OF TIN CONTAINERS
118. MANUFACTURE OF STORAGE TANKS, PRESSURE VESSELS, HEAT EXCHANGERS
119. MARK II HAND PUMPS
120. MARUTI WORKSHOP CUM - SERVICE STATION
121. MECHANICAL JACKS
122. METAL CUTTING DIE DESIGN
123. METAL CUTTING OF AND GRINDING WHEELS (ABRASIVE CUTTING WHEELS)
124. METAL HOOKS & CLIPS
125. METAL SEPARATION (COPPER, TIN, LEAD) FROM SPENT WASH ACID
126. METALLIC RING JOINTS
127. METALLIC GASKET (SPIRAL WOUND)
128. MICROVEE & ABSOLUTE FILTER
129. MICROWAVE OVEN
130. MILD STEEL INGOTS
131. MINI STEEL PLANT
132. MODERN VEHICLE WORKSHOP
133. MOPED
134. M.S.HINGES
135. M.S.INGOT AND HR. STEEL STRUCTURALS
136. M.S.INGOT BY INDUCTION FURNACES
137. M.S.PIPES
138. M.S. WELDING ELECTRODE
139. MUFFLERS & SILENCERS FOR THREE WHEELERS
140. NAIL CUTTER WITH FILER & MANICURE
141. NICHROME WIRE
142. NICKEL LINED SCREENS
143. NON-FERROUS ALLOY ROLLING
144. NON-FERROUS FORGING
145. NON-FERROUS FOUNDRY
146. NON PRESSURE
147. INCANDESCENT LAMP
148. NUMBER COMBINATION LOCKS FOR LUGGAGES
149. NUTS & BOLTS
150. PAPER COATED ALUMINIUM AND COPPER WIRE
151. PETROMAX CONTAINER
152. PHOTO ETCHING OF STAINLESS STEEL PLATES
153. PIPE GALVANIZING PLANT
154. PISTON RING-AUTOMOBILE
155. PLANT PROTECTION EQUIPMENTS
156. PLATINUM LABORATORY APPARATUS
157. PRESSURE COOKER & ALUMINIUM UTENSILS
158. PRESSURE COOKER (ALUMINIUM)
159. PRESSURE DIE CASTING
160. PRINTED ALUMINIUM COLLAPSIBLE TUBES
161. PRINTED TIN CONTAINERS
162. PRINTING PRESS (CYLINDER MACHINE)
163. PUMPS FOR CHEMICAL INDUSTRY (SPECIAL)
164. RAILWAY SLEEPERS (M.S.)
165. RAZOR TWIN BLADE
166. R.C.C SPUN PIPES
167. RECONDITIONING OF M.S. DRUMS/BARRELS
168. RE-ROLLING COPPER AND BRASS SHEET AND RODS
169. RE-ROLLING MILLS
170. RESIN COATED SAND
171. RESIN CORED SOFT SOLDER WIRES
172. ROLLING MILL (BY INDUCTION FURNACE) & MANUFACTURE OF BARS, ANGLES, SQUARES, TUBES AND OTHERS
173. ROLLER BEARING & FORGING
174. ROLLING OF STAINLESS STEEL PATTA
175. RUBBER INSULATED PLIERS (HAND TOOLS)
176. RUBBING COMPOUND FOR AUTOMOBILES
177. SCIENTIFIC LABORATORY EQUIPMENTS
178. SCOOTER ASSEMBLING
179. SECONDARY LEAD EXTRACTION BY SCRAP BATTERY PLATES,PIPES & SHEET
180. SEAMLESS M.S. TUBES & PIPES
181. SELF TAPPING STEEL SCREW
182. SEWING NEEDLES
183. S.G. IRON & ALLOY STEEL
184. SHEET METAL PRODUCTS, (FERROUS/NON-FERROUS)
185. SHIP/MARINE CONTAINER
186. SHOCK ABSORBERS
187. SHOE EYELETS
188. SHOT AND GRITS BY AUTOMIZATION PROCESS
189. SHOVELS
190. SILICO MANGANESE ALLOYS
191. SILENCERS (MUFFLERS) EXHAUST & TAIL PIPE FOR ALL TYPES OF VEHICLES
192. SINTERED BEARING
193. SINTERED BUSHES
194. SINTERED METAL PRODUCTS
195. SOFT AND HARD FERRITES
196. SPANNERS
197. SPARK PLUGS
198. STEEL PLANT (ELECTRIC ARC FURNACE BASED- EAF)
199. SPHERIODAL GRAPHITE CAST IRON
200. SPRAY DRYER
201. STAINLESS STEEL HINGES
202. STAINLESS STEEL SHEET ROLLING TO PRODUCE STAINLESS STEEL UTENSILS
203. STAINLESS STEEL UTENSILS
204. STAPLE PINS,PAPER PIN, GEM CLIPS ETC.
205. STEEL CASTINGS
206. STEEL CHAIN
207. STEEL FOUNDRY
208. STEEL FURNITURES AND ELECTRICAL APPLIANCES
209. STEEL PLANT (MINI)
210. STEEL RODS AND COILS FROM SCRAPS
211. STEEL ROLLING MILL
212. STEEL STRIPS (COLD ROLLED) SILICON WITH GRAIN RIENTED FOR ELECTRIC USE
213. STEEL TRANSMISSION LINE TOWERS & ROLLING MILL TO PRODUCE STEEL SECTION
214. STEEL FURNITURES AND ELECTRICAL APPLIANCES
215. STEEL WIRE DRAWING AND GALVANIZING
216. STEEL WOOL
217. SUBMERGED ARC WELDED PIPES
218. SUBMERSIBLE PUMP MANUFACTURING
219. SUPER ENAMELLED COPPER WIRE
220. THREE WHEELERS
221. TIE-ROD ENDS
222. TIN CONTAINERS
223. TOOLROOM AND SHEET METAL PRODUCTS
224. TRACTOR TRAILERS
225. TRANSMISSION POWER FITTING
226. TUBULAR POLES
227. SUPER ENAMELLED COPPER WIRES
228. TUBULAR POLES FOR ELECTRICAL TRANSMISSION (BY FABRICATION PROCESS)
229. TUBULAR POLES OF M.S. & HIGH TENSILE STEEL
230. VACUUM CLEANERS
231. VACUUM FLASK (STAINLESS STEEL)
232. VALVES FOR REFRIGERATION AND AIR-CONDITION
233. VEHICLE WELDING & PAINTING
234. VENETION BLIND
235. WASHING MACHINES (AUTOMATIC & COMPUTERISED)
236. WATER CONTROLLER (AUTOMATIC)
237. WATCH STRAPS/CHAINS/ BRACELETS/BELT BRASS & STAINLESS STEEL
238. WATER COOLERS
239. WELDED WIRE MESH
240. WELDING ELECTRODES
241. WICK STOVES
242. WIND MILL WINDOW FRAME (FERROUS & NON-FERROUS)
243. WRIST WATCH

359. DI ETHYL OXALATE
360. DI METHYL ORTHOPHTHALATE
361. DI-METHYL PHTHALATE
362. DICLOFENAC GEL
363. DIOCTYL PHTHALATE (DOP)
364. DI PHENYL GLYCERINE
365. DI PHENYL OXIDE
366. DINITRO-CHLORO BENZENE
367. DISTILLED WATER
368. DODECYL BENZENE SULPHONATE
369. DUSTLESS CHALK
370. EDTA & ITS SALTS
371. ELECTROLESS NICKEL PLATING ON PLASTICS
372. ENDOSULFAN
373. EPOXY RESIN BASED COMPOUND
374. ETHYL ACETATE
375. EHTYL ETHER
376. ETHYL ALCOHOL (POTABLE LIQUOR)
377. ETHYL HEXANOL
378. EXTRACTION OF ESSENTIAL OILS BY SUGAR CRITICAL FLUID (CARBON DIOXIDE) METHOD FROM FLOWERS, HERBAL & SPICES
379. FERRIC ALUM
380. FERRO CHROME LIGNO SULPHONATE
381. FERRO MANGANESE
382. FERRO SILICONE
383. FERRO VANADIUM FROM VANADIUM SLUDGE
384. FERROUS SILICATE
385. FERROUS SULPHATE
386. FERTILIZER FROM ANIMAL BLOOD & LEATHER WASTE
387. FLUORESCENT TUBE LIGHT POWDER
388. FOAMED PVC COMPOUNDING & ITS PRODUCTS
389. FORMALDEHYDE
390. FRACTIONAL DISTILLATION OF D.M.O (DEMENTHOLIZED OIL)
391. FRACTIONAL DISTILLATION OF ESSENTIAL OIL & MEDICINAL PLANT EXTRACT
392. FRICTION DUST (LIQUID & POWDER) FROM CNSL
393. FRUIT FLAVOURS
394. FURFURAL FROM RICE HUSK
395. GARLIC ACID
396. GASKET SHELLAC COMPOUND
397. GEAR OIL
398. GIBBERELLIC ACID
399. GLASS PUTTY
400. GLYCERINE
401. GOSSYPOL (POLY PHENOL) FROM COTTON SEED OIL
402. GUAR GUM POWDER
403. HAIR FIXER (HAIR GEL TYPE)
404. H - ACID
405. HENNA PASTE MAKING
406. HEPTAL DEHYDE
407. HIGH CARBON FERRO CHROME
408. HYDRATED CALCIUM SILICATE BRICK
409. HYDRATED LIME FROM SEA SHELL
410. HYDROCHLORIC ACID
411. HYDRO FLUORIC ACID
412. HYDROGEN PEROXIDE (BY AUTO-OXIDATION PROCESS)
413. ICE PACKS (SOLUTIONS TYPE, WHITE GEL TYPE, VIOLET SEMI SOLID POLYMER TYPE)
414. IMPROVING DROP POINT PARAFFIN WAX FROM 45-50°C TO 75-80°C
415. INDUSTRIAL ALCOHOL
416. INTEGERATED COMPLEX OF EASTER & ALLIED PRODUCTS (D.O.P, D.B.P, ETHYL ACETATE WIRE ENAMEL & CABLE JELLY)
417. IMFL (WHISKY) & COUNTRY LIQUOR
418. IRON OXIDE FOR MAKING FERITTE
419. IRON SULPHIDE
420. JUTE BATCHING OIL
421. KESH KALA TEL (HAIR DYE LOTION) (VASMOL 33, BLACK NITE TYPE)
422. L-LYSINE MONOHYDROCHLORIDE
423. LACTIC ACID FROM WHITE SUGAR BY FERMENTATION PROCESS
424. LDPE GRANULES FROM VIRGIN (LDPE RESIN)
425. LEAD EXTRACTION FROM BATTERY SCRAP
426. LEAD OXIDE (A) LEAD MONOXIDE
(B) LEAD TETRA OXIDE
(C) GREYLEAD OXIDE
427. LIQUID GLUCOSE & ITS BY PRODUCTS
428. LIQUID OXYGEN BOTTLING PLANT
429. LIQUID SHOE POLISH
430. LIQUID FLOOR POLISH
431. LUBE OIL VISCOSITY IMPROVED FOR P.P.G/P.E.G.
432. LUBRICANTS ASHLESS 100% COMBUSTION
433. MAGNESIUM CARBONATE AND MAGNESIUM BICARMONATE
434. MAGNESIUM HYDROXIDE POWDER
435. MAGNESIUM SILICATE
436. MAGNESIUM SULPHATE
437. MALACHITE GREEN
438. MALEIC ANHYDRIDE
439. MANGANESE SULPHATE
440. MANUFACTURING OF CARBON MONO-OXIDE WATER GAS
441. MENTHOL BOLD CRYSTALS FROM FLAKES
442. MENTHOL CRYSTAL & MENTHA OIL
443. MERCURIC OXIDE
444. METAL PRE-TREATMENT CHEMICALS
445. METHANE GAS BY SODIUM ACETATE & SODA LIME
446. METHYL ACETYL RICINOLATE
447. METOL
448. METOL FROM HYDROQUINONE & METHYLAMINE
449. MICANITE
450. MICRO NUTRIENT MIXTURE
451. MINERAL WATER
452. MINERAL WATER AND PET BOTTILNG PLANT
453. MINERAL WATER IN BOTTLES, GLASS AND POUCHES
454. MINI CEMENT PLANT (BY ROTARY KILN PROCESS)
455. MIXED FERTILIZER
456. MOSQUITO & FLIES REPELLENT AGARBATTI (INCENSE STICKS)
457. MONO CHLORO ACETIC ACID
458. MONOCROTOPHOS (TECHNICAL)
459. MOSQUITO COIL
460. MOSQUITO COIL & MAT
461. MOSQUITO MAT
462. MOTHER TINCTURE & BIO CHEMIC MEDICINES
463. NAPHTHALENE & PHENYL (INTEGRATED UNIT)
464. NATURAL MINERAL WATER BY REVERSE OSMOSIS PROCESS
465. NICKEL PLATING BRIGHTNER (PRIMARY OR CARRIER BRIGHTNER & SECONDARY BRIGHTNER)
466. NICKEL SULPHATE
467. NICOTINE FROM TOBACCO WASTE
468. NICOTINE SULPHATE FROM TOBACCO WASTE
469. NITRO BENZENE
470. NITRO CELLULOSE SANDING SEALER/LACQUER
471. NITRO MUSK
472. NITROGEN & OXYGEN GAS PLANT
473. NON-IONIC SURFACTANT (WETTING AGENT)
474. NO-CARB PASTE
475. OCTANOL
476. ORTHO NITRO PHENOL
477. OXALIC ACID FROM MOLASSES
478. OXALIC ACID FROMRICE HUSK
479. OXALIC ACID FROM TREE BARK
470. OXALIC ACID FROM WASTE VEGETABLES
471. OXYGEN GAS PLANT
472. OXYGEN GAS PLANT (AIR SEPERATION METHOD)
473. PARA-AMINO BENZOIC ACID
474. PARA-AMINO PHENOL
475. PARA TOLUENE SULPHONIC ACID
476. PECTIN FROM RAW PAPAYA
477. PERFUME (LEMON & OTHERS)

CRUDE NAPHTHA
570. TRIMETHYL AMMONIUM CHLORIDE
571. TRIPHENYL PHOSPHITE (T.P.P)
572. ULTRAMARINE BLUE (LIQUID)
573. UREA FORMALDEHYDE & MELAMINE FORMALDEHYDE POWDER
574. UNDECYLINIC ACID
575. VINYL ACETATE MONOMER
576. VITAMIN C
577. VITAMIN E
578. WASTE WATER TREATMENT PLANT FOR INDUSTRIAL SECTOR IN INDIA (ONLY MARKER SURVEY)
579. WIRE DRAWING LUBRICANT
580. WIRE ENAMEL
581. XANTHATES
582. YELLOW DEXTRIN
583. ZINC CHLORIDE
584. ZINC OXIDE
585. ZINC PHOSPHATING BY COLD PROCESS
586. ZINC SILICATE
587. ZINC STEARATE
588. ZINC SULPHATE
589. ZINC SULPHATE MONOHYDRATE
590. ACID BLACK
591. AURAMINE 'O'
592. AZO DYES STUFF
593. DYE & DYE INTERMEDIATE
594. DYE INTERMEDIATES
595. MALACHITE GREEN
596. METHYLENE BLUE
597. PHTHALOCYANINE BLUE
598. PHTHALOCYANINE BLUE & GREEN
599. REACTIVE DYES
600. SULPHUR BLACK DYE
601. VAT DYES
602. WATER CHILLING PLANT
603. WADDING OIL (100%) FOR WADDING OF COTTON HOSIERY CLOTH IN THE DYEING PROCESS
604. WHITE OIL
605. WAX FLOOR POLISH

ELECTRICAL, ELECTONICS, COMPUTERS AND INFOTECH/IT PROJECTS

606. AIR CONDITIONING
607. ALUMINIUM ALLOY CONDUCTOR
608. ALUMINIUM CABLE
609. ALUMINIUM ELECTROYTIC CAPACITORS
610. AUDIO CASSETTE ASSEMBLING & RECORDING
611. AUDIO CASSETTES DUPLICATING RECORDING
612. AUDIO CASSETTES & AUDIO STUDIO
613. AUDIO CASSETTES PLANE & RECORDED
614. AUDIO MAGNETIC HEADS
615. AUDIO MAGNETIC TAPE
616. AUDIO/VIDEO CASSETTES
617. AUTO BULB/LAMPS
618. AUTOMATIC VOLTAGE STABILIZER
619. BATTERY PLATES
620. BACK OFFICE (Rs. 5000/-)
621. B/W TV & COMPUTER MONITOR PICTURE TUBE
622. BREAD BOARDS
623. CALL CENTRE
624. CAMERA (35 MM)
625. CAPACITORS
626. CARBON ELECTRODE USED FOR BATTERY CELL
627. CARBON POTETIOMETERS
628. CEILING FAN
629. CERAMIC INSULATOR
630. CHILDREN INFOTECH TRAINING INSTITUTE (Rs. 5000/-)
631. CHOKE AND PATTI
632. CHOKE AND STARTER
633. CHOKE USED FOR FLUORESCENT LAMPS
634. COLOUR TELEVISION
635. COLOUR AND BLACK & WHITE TELEVISION
636. COMPACT DISC
637. COMPACT DISC PLAYER (AUDIO/VIDEO)
638. COMPUTER EDUCATION INSTITUTE
639. COMPUTER ASSEMBLY
640. COMPUTER HARDWARE
641. COMPUTER KEYBOARD
642. COMPUTER PERIPHERALS
643. COMPUTER PRINTERS
644. COMPUTER RIBBON
645. COMPUTER RIBBON REINKING OR REFILLING
646. COMPUTER STATIONERY
647. COMPUTER STATIONERY &

IMPORTED HARDWARE PARTS
648. COMPUTER TERMINALS
649. COMPUTERISED WASHING MACHINE (AUTOMATIC)
650. COMPUTER SOFTWARE
651. CONDENSER FOR MOTOR USING MPP FILM
652. CONTENT DEVELOPMENT CENTRE (EOU) (Rs. 5000/-)
653. CONTROL PANEL BOARD
654. COOLING COIL FOR AIR CONDITIONERS
655. COPPER STRIP COIL FROM SCRAP
656. CORDLESS TELEPHONES
657. CYBER CAFE
658. CYBERKIOSK (Rs. 5000/-)
659. DATA PROCESSING CENTRE (Rs. 5000/-)
660. D.C. MICRO MOTORS
661. D.G.SETS
662. DISH ANTENNA AND CABLE T.V. NETWORK EQUIPMENT
663. DISTRIBUTION TRANSFORMERS & REPAIRS
664. DOMESTIC ELECTRICAL APPLIANCES- ROOM COOLER, WASHING MACHINE, WATER HEATER, ELECTRIC ROOM HEATER
665. E-SCHOOL
666. E-COMMERCE/BUSINESS
667. ELECTRIC ENERGY METER
668. ELECTRIC FANS
669. ELECTRIC HORN FOR AUTOMOBILE
670. ELECTRIC LAMP/GLS (INCANDESCENT LAMP)
671. ELECTRIC MIXER
672. ELECTRIC MOTORS UP TO 10 HP. REWINDING OF ALL TYPES OF MOTORS WATER PUMPS
673. ELECTRIC MOTOR WINDING (FOR FAN, MIXIES, ETC.)
674. ELECTRIC STEAM IRON
675. ELECTRICAL APPLIANCES
676. ELECTRICAL FIXTURES
677. ELECTRICAL STAMPING
678. ELECTROLYTIC CAPACITORS
679. ELECTROMAGNETIC RELAY
680. ELECTRONIC BALAST/CHOK
681. ELECTRICAL CHOKE
682. ELECTRONIC DIGITAL WATCHES
683. ELECTRONIC DIGITAL WEIGHING MACHINE
684. ELECTRONIC FIRE ALARM
685. ELECTRONIC GAS STOVE LIGHTERS
686. ELECTRONIC PRESSURE INDICATORS, ELECTRICALS, ELECTRONIC LIQUID LEVEL INDICATORS, ELECTRONIC TEMPERATURE INDICATOR, DIGITAL TACHOMETER
687. ELECTRONIC TELEPHONE INSTRUMENTS
688. ELECTRONIC TOYS
689. ELECTRONIC WATCHES & CLOCKS
690. FAX MACHINES
691. F.H.P MOTORS
692. FLOPPY DISKETTES
693. FLUORESCENT LAMP STARTER
694. FLUORESCENT TUBULAR

Above all the "Detailed Project Reports" are available at *"ENGINEERS INDIA RESEARCH INSTITUTE"*. 4449, Nai Sarak (D), Main Road Delhi - 110 006 (India) ● Ph : 91-11-23918117, 2391 6431, 2384 0361 ● Fax : 91-11- 2391 6431 ●E-Mail : eirisidi@bol.net.in ● WebSite : www.eiriindia.org

LAMPS WITH INTRODUCTION TO MERCURY VAPOUR LAMP
695. FRANCHISEE COMPUTER EDUCATION CENTRE (Rs. 5000)
696. GAS DETECTOR (L.P.G)
697. GENERATOR SET & PUMP SETS
698. GENERATOR (BATTERY OPERATED)
699. GIS SERVICE CENTRE (GEOGRAPHICAL INFORMATION SYSTEMS)
700. HARDWARE FITTING FOR TRANSMISSION LINE OVERHEAD LINE MATERIAL
701. HEADERS FOR TRANSISTOR ICS SEMI CONDUCTOR
702. H.T & L.T INSULATORS
703. H.T & M.V INDUSTRIAL CUBICAL SWITCH BOARD
704. INFORMATION MOVING DISPLAY (L.E.D TYPE)
705. INSURANCE CLAIM PROCESSING CENTRE (EOU) (Rs. 5000/-)
706. INTEGRATED CIRCUITS
707. INTERNET BASED STOCK TRADING (Rs. 5000/-)
708. INTERNET SERVICE PROVIDER (I.S.P.)
709. JELLY FILLED TELEPHONE CABLES
710. LAP TOP COMPUTERS
711. LEAD ACID BATTERIES
712. LEAD ACID BATTERY PLATES AND ASSEMBLING OF BATTERY
713. LEGAL TRANSCRIPTION & SECRETARIAL SERVICES CENTER (EOU)(Rs. 5000/-)
714. LIGHT EMITTING DIODES (L.E.D)
715. LINEAR ICS TRAINER KIT
716. LOUD SPEAKER
717. L.T TRANSFORMER REPAIRING
718. MEDICAL TRANSCRIPTION CENTRE
719. METAL FILM RESISTORS
720. METALLISED POLYPROPYLENE, POLYESTER FILM CAPACITOR
721. MICA BASE ELECTRONIC COMPONENTS
722. MICA PAPER WASTE PAPER FROM MICA WASTE
723. MICRO PROCESSORS TRAINER KITS BASED ON MICRO PROCESSORS
724. MINI COMPUTER (PERSONAL COMPUTER)
725. MINIATURE CIRCUIT BREAKER (M.C.B)
726. MINIATURE WATCH BATTERIES (BUTTON CELL)
727. MIXER/GRINDER (MIXI)
728. MONO CHROME COMPUTER MONITOR
729. MOTOR START ELECTROLYTIC CAPACITOR
730. MULTI LAYER P.C.B
731. MULTIPLE RELAY FOR LOW VOLTAGE
732. NEON INDICATOR
733. NEON SIGN MANUFACTURE
734. OPTICAL FIBRE CABLES
735. ON LINE SHOPPING MALL (Rs. 5000/-)
736. OPTO MECHANICAL & ELECTRICAL EQUIPMENTS
737. PHOTO COLOUR LAB
738. PICTURE TUBE (B/W)
739. PLAIN PAPER COPIER
740. PLASTIC FILM CAPACITORS
741. POLYESTER CAPACITORS
742. PORTABLE GENERATOR SET
743. PORTAL
744. PORTABLE TELEVISION(TV)
745. POWER CAPACITORS
746. POWER INVERTERS
747. POWER PLANT
748. POWER TRANSFORMERS UP TO 600 KVA
749. PRINTED CIRCUIT BOARD
750. PVC WIRES & CABLES
751. RE-CONDITIONING OF PICTURE TUBE
752. RESIN CAST CT & PT (1 KV)
753. SEMI CONDUCTOR DEVICE
754. SEMI CONDUCTORS FOR TRANSISTORS & DIODES
755. SETTING UP OF A VIDEO STUDIO
756. SMOKE DETECTORS
757. SOLAR CELLS
758. SOLAR MODULES
759. SOLAR PHOTO VOLTAIC SYSTEM
760. SOLDER FLUXES
761. SOLAR WATER HEATING PANELS
762. STEEL FURNITURE & ELECTRICAL APPLIANCES
763. STEREO AMPLIFIERS
764. STEREO CASSETTE RECORDERS/PLAYERS
765. STREET LIGHT FITTINGS SURGE SUPPRESSOR
766. TANTALUM CAPACITORS
767. TEFLON COATED ELECTRIC CABLE
768. TELEMEDICINE (DISTANCE HEALTH CARE) (Rs. 5000/-)
769. TELEPHONE CORD/CABLE
770. TELEPHONE (PUSH BUTTON TYPE)
771. TELEPHONE (PUSH BUTTON & CORDLESS)
772. TELEVISION (CTV & B/W)
773. TELEVISION (3-D)
774. TELEVISION DEFLECTION COMPONENTS
775. TELEVISION SIGNAL BOOSTERS
776. TELEVISION TUNERS
777. TRACTION BATTERIES
778. TRAINING INSTITUTE OF MEDICAL TRANSCRIPTION
779. TRANSFORMER FOR B/W TV
780. TRANSFORMER FOR VOLTAGE STABILIZER & E.H.T
781. TRANSMISSION POWER LINE FITTING
782. TRANSMISSION TOWER FITTING
783. TV AUDIO EQUIPMENT CABINETS & THEIR ASSEMBLING UNIT
784. UN-INTERRUPTED POWER SUPPLY (U.P.S)
785. VARIABLE FREQUENCY
786. VARIABLE VOLTAGE A.C. DRIVE
787. VIDEO CASSETTES (COMPLETE MANUFACTURING & ASSEMBLING)
788. VIDEO CASSETTES RECORDER (V.C.R)
789. VIDEO FILM STUDIO
790. VOLTAGE REGULATOR FOR AUTOMOBILES
791. VOLTAGE STABILIZERS
792. VOLTAGE STABLIZER & T.V. GAIN BOOSTER
793. WAX AND CHEMICAL COATED, BRAIDED TINSEL WIRE
794. WEBSITE DESIGN & E-MAIL REGISTERING
795. WELDING ELECTRODES
796. WIND ENERGY POWER PROJECT (10 MW) WIRE WOUND POTENTIOMETERS

FOOD, AGRO FOOD, PROCESSED FOOD, AGRO PLANTATION, CULTIVATION, FARMING, DAIRY/MILK, TOBACCO/PAN MASALA, BREWERY & DISTILLERY, EDIBLE OILS, EOU FOOD PRODUCTS AND ALLIED PRODUCTS

797. ALCOHOLIC BEVERAGES & VENEGAR FROM COCONUT WATER
798. ALCOHOL DRINKS FROM ETHYL ALCOHOL BY MIXING OF VARIOUS FLAVOURS
799. ANTI SCALE COMPOUND FOR ADDING INTO SUGAR JUICE BOILING
800. APPLE JUICE CONCENTRATED & DEHYDRATED FRUIT & VEGETABLES
801. ARTIFICIAL FISH MEAL FOR POULTRY FEED
802. AUTOMATIC BISCUIT PLANT
803. BABY CEREAL FOOD AND MILK POWDER
804. BACTERIA FOR CANE JUICE
805. BAKER'S YEAST
806. BAKERY INDUSTRY
807. BANANA PUREE
808. BEER & WINE
809. BEER PLANT (BREWERY)
810. BIDI
811. BIDI & CIGARETTE
812. BISCUIT PLANT

813. BREAD (AUTOMATIC PLANT)
814. BLACK PEPPER (SPICES)
815. BREAD AND BISCUITS
816. BREEDING FARM
817. BROILER CHICKEN
819. BUTTON MUSHROOM CULTIVATION & PROCESSING
820. CANNING OF RASAGULLAS IN METAL CANS
821. CAFFEIN FROM TEA WASTE
822. CANNING OF FRUITS & VEGETABLES
823. CASEIN AND BY-PRODUCTS
824. CASHEW FRUIT JUICE FROM CASHEW FRUIT APPLE
825. CASHEWNUT KERNEL EXTRACTION FROM CASHEWNUT FRUIT
826. CASHEWNUT SHELL LIQUID & KERNEL PROCESSING
827. CASHEW FENI
828. CATECHEU (BY CHEMICAL PROCESS)
829. CATTLE FEED FROM TAPIOCA
830. CHEWING & BUBBLE GUM
831. CHICKEN/SHEEP MEAT PROCESSING
832. CHOCOLATE (MILK)
833. CIGARETTE AND BEEDIES
834. COCOA BUTTER FROM COCOA MASS
835. COCONUT PRODUCTS & BY PRODUCTS PROCESS COMPLEX
836. COLD/SOFT DRINKS
837. COLLECTION OF MILK AND MILK MAKING POWDER
838. COLLECTION OF MILK AND PACKING IN POLYTHENE POUCH (1/2 KG.1 KG. & 2 KG.)
839. CONDENSED MILK (SWEETNED)
840. CONFECTIONERY INDUSTRY (TOFFEE & CANDY, SEMI-AUTOMATIC PLANT)
841. COUNTRY LIQUOR FROM MOLASSES
842. CIGARETTE
843. DAIRY FARM AND DAIRY (MILK) PRODUCTS (PASTEURISED MILK, BUTTER, GHEE, PANEER)
844. DAIRY FARM TO PRODUCE MILK & PACKING IN POUCHES (50%) & CAN(50%)
845. DAIRY FOR MILK PROCESSING
846. DAIRY FARM (BUFALO)
847. DAL (PULSE) MILL UNIT
848. DEHYDRATION OF CARROT & GARLIC
849. DEHYDRATION & CANNING OF FRUITS & VEGETABLES
850. DEHYDRATION OF FIGS
851. DEHYDRATION OF FRUITS AND VEGETABLES
852. DEHYDRATED ONIONS AND ONION POWDER
853. DRY ICE BY BREAKING OF AIR
854. DRYING OF RED CHILLIES, HALDI, DHANIA, AND GREEN PEAS
855. EGG POWDER (40,000 EGGS PROCESSING PER DAY)
856. EXPORT OF PROCESSED FOODS AND MARINE PRODUCTS
857. FISH CANNING & POUCHING
859. FISH FARMING (PRAWN & OTHER MARINE PRODUCTS)
860. FISH MEAL
861. FLOUR MILL AND MUSTARD OIL
862. FOOD COLOUR & ORASTED GROUNDNUT GRAM PEAS, ETC IN POUCHES
863. FROG LEGS PROCESSING
864. FROZEN MEATS PROCESSING
865. FOOD FLAVOURS (WHISKY). VODKA, GRAPE, BUTTER SCOTCH)
866. FOOD PRODUCTS COMPLEX (DEHYDRATED ONIONS, GARLIC POWDER & FLAKES, CATTLE FEED, TOMATO POWDER, TOMATO PRODUCTS, CANNED FRUITS & VEGETABLES, TOMATO PURE, GROUN NUT OIL, REFIND OIL, DEHYDRATED GRAPES, BANANA POWDER & WAFFERS)
867 FRUIT JUICE, JAM, JELLIES & ALLIED PRODUCTS
868. FRUIT JUICE, PICKLES PROCESSING AND CANNING
869. FRUIT JUICE MAKING & PACKING IN PLASTIC CONTAINER/POUCHES
870. FRUIT PROCESSING (JAM & JELLIES)
871. FRUIT PULP & JUICE CONCENTRATES
872. FRUIT & VEGETABLE DRYING (FREEZE DRYING METHOD)
873. GOAT & SHEEP FARMING
874. GRAM DALL/PULSE MILL
875. GRAPE DEHYDRATION
876. HARD BOILED CANDY (TOFFEE & CANDY)
877. HERBAL CIGARETTES
878. HONEY PROCESSING & PACKAGING
879. ICE CREAM OF DIFFERENT FLAVOURS
880. ICE CREAM STABILIZER
881. ICE MAKING PLANT
882. INDIAN MADE FOREIGN LIQUOR (I.M.F.L)
883. INSTANT FOOD (IDLI MIX, DOSA MIX, GULAB JAMUN MIX)
884. INSTANT FOOD (INSTANT FOOD & FAST FOOD PARLOUR)
885. INSTANT NOODLES
886. INSTANT TEA
887. INSTANT TEA FROM BLACK TEA
888. INTEGERATED STARCH BAKING POWDER/YEAST INDUSTRY
889. IODIZED SALT
890. IODIZED SALT (ORDINARY MOISTURE-LESS/FREE FLOWING IN PLASTIC BAGS AND CONTAINERS)
891. JAM, JELLIES, FRUIT JUICE & ALLIED PRODUCTS
892. KATHA AND CUTCH
893. KHANDSARI SUGAR
894. KHANDSARI SUGAR & IMFL
895. LACTIC ACID FROM WHITE SUGAR BY FERMENTATION PROCESS
896. LACTOSE & BY PRODUCTS PROCESSING FROM MILK
897. LIQUID GLUCOSE AND ITS BYE PRODUCTS
898. MACRONI AND VERMICILLI
899. MALT EXTRACTION FROM BARLEY
900. MANGO PROCESSING (MANGO PULP, JUICE & SLICES)
901. MAYUR BRAND TYPE CHEWING TOBACCO
902. MINERAL WATER
903. MILK PRESERVATION & MARKETING TO WHOLE SELLERS (INPOUCH PACKING BY UHT TECHNOLOGY)
904. MILK PROCESSING AND PACKAGING OF MILK PRODUCTS
905. MILK PRODUCTS (CASEIN, LACTOSE, GHEE & WHEY POWDER)
906. MILK TOFFEE
907. MINI FLOUR MILL
908. MINI SUGAR PLANT
909. MISRI (PEARL SUGAR CANDIES)
910. MODERN RICE MILL
911. MURABBA
912. MUSTARD OIL EXTRACTION & REFINING
913. MUTTON TALLOW
914. NAMKEEN INDUSTRY (BHUJIA, CHANA CHUR ETC.)
915. NAMKEEN & SWEETS
916. NON-BASMATI RICE FROM PADDY
917. OLEORESIN, ESSENTIAL OIL, DYES & POWDER OF SPICES
918. OLEORESIN EXTRACTION FROM DIPTERO-CARPUT TURMINATUS AND PINUS KHASYANA
919. OLEORESIN EXTRACTION FROM CHILLI
920. PAN MASALA AND POUCH

1059. BUFFALO HORN TIP, HOOF
1060. BANQUET HALL
1061. BUTTON
1062. CALCINED PETROLEUM (C.P) COKE
1063. CANVAS SHOES
1064. CANVAS SHOES, JUNGLE BOOTS
1065. CARBON BRUSH, BRUSH HOLDER & SLIP RING
1066. CEMENT SHEETS WITH COIR FIBRE & OTHER SEGMENTS
1067. CERAMIC TILES (GLAZED) BY DOUBLE FIRING/HEATING
1068. CHILDREN RECREATION CENTRE
1069. COAL BRIQUETTES
1070. COLD STORAGE & ICE
1071. COLD STORAGE FOR FRUITS AND VEGETABLES
1072. COMPRESSOR (HERMETIC) FOR AIR CONDITIONER
1073. COSTUME JEWELLERY/ IMITATION JEWELLERY
1074. DECORATIVE LAMINATED SHEET (SUNMICA)
1075. DIAMOND CUTTING & EXPORTS
1076. DRINKING STRAW FROM PROPYLENE
1077. ENGINEERING COLLEGE
1078. ENTERTAINMENT CLUB
1079. FASHION TECHNOLOGY INSTITUTE
1080. FAST FOOD PARLOUR
1081. FAST FOOD (INSTANT FOOD & FAST FOOD PARLOUR)
1082. FIRE EXTINGUISHERS (SODA ACID TYPE)
1083. FISH NET
1084. FLORICULTURE (CUT FLOWER ROSE) WITH GREEN HOUSE
1085. FLOOR COVERING SHEET
1086. FILM STUDIO (VIDEO)
1087. FLUSH DOOR, CHIP BOARD, WOOD WOOL & OTHER INSULATING BOARDS
1088. GAS DETECTORS OF L.P.G
1089. GEMS MANUFACTURING
1090. GLASS BOTTLE BY SCRAP
1092. GOAT & SHEEP FARMING
1093. GOLD ELECTROPLATING
1094. GOLD JEWELLERY (E.O.U)
1095. GOLD PLATED SILVER JEWELLERY & CUTLERY
1096. GRANITE SLAB AND TILES
1097. GREEN HOUSE
1098. HARD CHROMIUM PLATING
1099. HEALTH CLUB AND BEAUTY PARLOUR CUM HAIR SALOON WITH SONA BATH
1100. HEALTH CLUB CUM BEAUTY PARLOUR TRAININGINSTITUTE
1101. HORN TIP,HOOVE BUTTON
1102. HOSPITAL
1103. HOSPITAL (100 BEDS)
1104. HOSPITAL (200 BEDS)
1105. ICE MAKING PLANT
1106. IMITATION AND COSTUME
1107. JEWELLERY (NECKLACE, EARRINGS EAR TOP ETC.)
1108. INITMATE SCENT CHEMICALS FROM ALL TYPES OF FLAVOUR
1109. INVESTMENT CASTING
1110. JUTE, COIR, GLASS ROPE/ SUTLI
1111. JUTE TWINE
1112. L.P.G BOTTLING PLANT
1113. L.P.G REGULATOR (DOMESTIC PURPOSE)
1114. LAMINATED PARTICLE BOARD & HARD BOARD
1115. LAMINATED SAFETY AND TOUGHENED GLASS
1116. LEASING & HIRE PURCHASE
1117. LICHEN (CHARILA)
1118. MANILA ROPES
1119. MEDICAL COLLEGE
1120. MATCH UNIT FROM WAXED PAPER
1121. MEDIUM DENSITY FIBRE BOARD
1122. MELAMINE CROCKERY
1123. MINERAL WATER
1124. MINI CEMENT PLANT
1125. MIRROR SILVER, GOLDEN, PINK, BLACK & SMOKES
1126. MODERN ADVERTISING AGENCY WITH DTP & FILM STUDIO
1127. MOTEL/SMALL HOTEL
1128. MULTI COLOUR PRINTING
1129. MULTI STOREY COMMERCIAL COMPLEX ALONGWITH RESIDENTIALAND DELUX FLATS FOR FOREIGN TOURISTS & REVOLVING RESTAURENT AT THE TOP
1130. MULTIPLE LAMINATION INDUSTRY
1131. MUSHROOM GROWING AND PROCESSING (BY DEEP FREEZING METHOD)
1132. NEWS PAPER PRINTING
1133. NICKEL LINED INDUSTRIAL SCREEN
1134. OFFSET COLOUR PRINTING PRESS (SIX COLOUR)
1135. OFFSET PRINTING PRESS
1136. P.C.C ELECTRIC POLES
1137. PHOTOGRAPHIC DEVELOPER & FIXER
1138. PVC EXTRUSION PROFILE (DOOR & WINDOWS)
1139. POP-CORN
1140. PHOTO ETCHING OF S.S.
1141. PRE STRESSED CEMENT CONCRETE PIPES
1142. PILFER PROOF CAPS
1143. PILFER PROOF CAPS AND CROWN CAP
1144. POUCH MAKING & GRAVURE PRINTING (ROTO PRINTING)
1145. POULTRY & FISH FARMING (INTEGERATED UNIT)
1146. PRINTING OF TIN SHEETS
1147. READYMADE GARMENTS
1148. RESTAURANT
1149. ROSE PLANTATION AND ROSE OIL EXTRACTION
1150. ROTOGRAVURE PRINTING
1151. SAFETY BELTS
1152. SAFETY MATCHES
1153. SHOE LACES
1154. SILK COCOON CULTIVATION (GROWING OF SILK COCOON WARM)
1155. SILK SCREEN PRINTING FORMULATIONS FOR PLASTIC, PAPER & CLOTH
1156. SPIKENARD (JATAMANSI)
1157. STENCIL COATING SOLUTION
1158. SUGAR CANDY (MISRI)
1159. SUGAR CANE PLANTATION
1160. SUGAR CANE JUICE PRESERVATION
1161. SURAT ZARI
1162. SYNTHETIC SHOES & SOLES
1163. TEA PACKAGING INDUSTRY
1164. TENNIS BALLS
1165. THREE STAR HOTEL
1166. TRAVELLING AGENCY
1167. TRAYS, TROLLEYS FOR HOSPITAL WITH SCRATCHLESS COATING
1168. WAX EXTRACTS (TANNING POWDER)
1169. WIRE ROPE SLINGS
1170. WOOD WOOL SLAB
1171. WOODEN CANE FURNITURE WITH EXPORT POTENTIAL
1172. WOODEN FURNITURE
1173. WOODEN PANEL INCLUDING KILN SEASONING
1174. WOODEN FURNITURE
1175. WATCH CASE BUFFING
1176. WATCH DIAL
1177. WRIST WATCHES
1178. WATCHES (ELECTRONIC)
1179. ZEDOARY (KACHUR)

EDIBLE OILS, ESSENTIAL OILS LURICATIING OILS, GREASES, VEGETABLE OILS, WAXES, CAMPHOR, PERFUMES & PERFUMERY COMPOUNDS AND REFINED OILS ETC.

1180. AROMATIC PERFUMERY COMPOUND
1181. AEROSOL
1182. AGARBATTI PERFUMERY COMPOUND
1183. BEES WAX MANUFACTURE
1184. CAMPHOR
1185. CARDANOL FROM CASHEW NUT SHELL LIQUID
1186. CASTOR OIL
1187. CASTOR OIL DERIVATIVE OLEORESINS
1188. CHILLI OIL
1189. CITRONELLA OILS
1190. CLOVE OIL
1191. CONCENTRATE OF ROSE JASMINE & LILY ETC.
1192. COLOURED FLAME CANDLE

1193. CANDLES (SEMI-AUTOMATIC)
1194. CORN OIL (MAIZE OIL)
1195. DEHYDRATED CASTOR OIL
1196. EUGENOL FROM CINNAMON LEAF OIL
1197. EXTRACTION OF ESSENTIAL OIL (CARDAMON, JEERA, AJOWAN, GINGER OILS ETC. & PACKAGING OF GROUND SPICES)
1198. EXTRACTION OF JASMINE ESSENCE
1199. EXTRACTION OF ESSENTIAL OILS BY SUPER CRITICAL FLUID METHOD FROM FLOWERS, HERBS & SPICES
1200. EUCALYPTUS OIL
1201. EXTRACTION OF OIL FROM OIL SEED EXPANDEREXTRUSION TECHNOLOGY)
1202. FAT LIQUOR SULPHATED OIL
1203. FLAVOURS FOR FOOD
1204. GARLIC OIL & POWDER
1205. GINGER OIL, SANDALWOOD OIL AND NAGARMOTHA OIL
1206. GINGER OIL
1207. GINGER OIL & GINGER DUST
1208. INTEGERATED WAX COMPLEX
1209. IONONE FROM LEMON GRASS OIL
1210. JASMINE & LILLY FLOWER OIL
1211. LEMON GRASS OIL
1212. LIQUID PARAFFIN
1213. LUBE OIL & GREASE
1214. LUBRICATING OIL
1215. MENTHOL CRYSTALS
1216. MENTHOL OIL & CRYSTAL
1217. MICRO CRYSTALLINE WAX
1218. MUSTARD OIL (EDIBLE OIL)
1219. OIL FROM ARTEMISIA HERBS
1220. PALM OIL CRUSHING UNIT
1221. PAN MASALA
1222. PARAFFIN WAX
1223. PARAFFIN WAX FROM SLACK WAX
1224. REFINED OIL-SUN FLOWER OIL, GROUNDNUT OIL, STAFF FLOWER OIL & COTTON SEED OIL
1225. REFINED VEGETABLE OIL
1226. RECLAMATION OF USED ENGINE OIL
1227. RICE BRAN OIL (R.B.O)
1228. ROSE OIL EXTRACTION
1229. SMOKE LESS CANDLE
1230. SPICE OIL & OLEORESINS
1231. SOLVENT EXTRACTION PLANT (OIL CAKE BASED)
1232. SYNTHETIC ALMOND OIL
1233. SYNTHETIC TALLOW
1234. SYNTHETIC GHEE
1235. VEGETABLE OIL EXTRACTION & REFINING
1236. WADDING OIL (100%) FOR WADDING OF COTTON HOSIERY CLOTH IN DYEING PROCESS
1237. WAX EMULSION FOR TEXTILE
1238. WAX FLOOR POLISH

PAINT, ENAMEL, SOLVENTS, THINNERS, INKS & VARNISH

1239. ACRYLIC EMULSION PAINTS
1240. ALUMINIUM PAINT
1241. AUTOMOBILE PAINTS
1242. BALL POINT PEN REFILL INK
1243. BITUMINIOUS ROAD EMULSION
1244. BITUMEN
1245. BITUMINIOUS FELTS FOR WATER & DAMP PROOFING
1246. BITUMINIOUS ROAD EMULSION RAPID MEDIUM & SLOW SETTING
1247. BUFFING & POLISHING
1248. CEMENT PAINT FOR WHITE & GREY CEMENT

1249. DISPERSANT
1250. DRY DISTEMPER
1251. DRY DISTEMPER & CEMENT PAINT
1252. DUPLICATING INK BLACK FOR GESTNER DUPLICATOR
1255. EMULSION PAINTS (WATER BASED)
1256. HAMMERTONE PAINT
1257. INSULATING VARNISH & WIRE ENAMEL
1258. IRON OXIDE PIGMENTS
1259. INSULATING VARNISH (POLY VINYL BUTYRAL BASED, FFC GRADE)
1260. LIME COLOUR (CEMENT COLOUR)
1261. SYNTHETIC RED OXIDE FOR FLOORINGS
1262. SOLVENT & THINNERS
1263. MARKING INKS (WATER PROOF)
1264. METAL NAPHTHANATE (AS DRIER FOR PAINTS)
1265. N.C.PUTTY
1266. OFFSET PRINTING INK
1267. OIL BOUND DISTEMPER PAINT
1268. PAINT BRUSHES
1269. PAINT REMOVERS
1270. PAINT INDUSTRY
1271. PAINT & VARNISH
1272. PICTURE VARNISH
1273. POWDER COATING PAINT
1274. PRINTING INKS (OFFSET, FLEXO & ROTO GRAVURE)
1275. PRIMER PAINT & ENAMEL PAINT
1276. PUTTY & WATER PROOFING PAINT
1277. PRINTING INKS (FLEXO-GRAPH'C INK)
1278. PUTTY (METAL CASEMENT)
1279. RED OXIDE PRIMER (ANTI CORROSIVE)
1280. REFRECTORY PAINT (GRAPHITE BASED)
1281. SCREEN PRINTING INKS
1282. SILK SCREEN PRINTING INK FORMULATION FOR PLASTIC, PAPER, CLOTH
1283. STAMP & PAD INK
1284. STOVING PAINT
1285. SPIRIT SOLUBLE MALEIC RESIN
1286. TEXTURE PAINT
1287. THINNERS AND ITS ALLIED PRODUCTS
1288. TONER INK
1289. VARNISH THINNER (SOLVENT)
1290. VACUUM METALLIZING LACQUERS
1291. WOOD PRIMER

PHARMACEUTICAL, DRUGS, AYURVEDIC/HERBAL COSMETICS & MEDICINES, HOMOEOPATHIC MEDICINES, DISPOSABLE SYRINGE, DENTA COLLEGE & FINE CHEMICALS ETC.

1292. AROMATIC PILLS
1293. ASPIRIN
1294. AYURVEDIC PAIN BALM OINTMENTS
1295. AYURVEDIC CHURAN AND TABLETS
1296. AYURVEDIC TABLETS (HAJMOLA TYPE)
1297. AYURVEDIC/HERBAL PHARMACY
1298. AYURVEDIC SHERBATS
1299. AYURVEDIC PRODUCTS
1300. BULK DRUGS (E.O.U)
1301. BLOOD BAGS
1302. CALCIUM GLUCONATE
1303. CAPSULE, TABLET & INJECTION WITH MODERN INSTRUMENTS
1304. CASHEW FENI
1305. CHLOROQUINONE PHOSPHATE (BULK DRUGS)
1306. CLINICAL THERMOMETER
1307. DENTAL CLINIC

Above all the "Detailed Project Reports" are available at *"ENGINEERS INDIA RESEARCH INSTITUTE"*. 4449, Nai Sarak (D), Main Road Delhi - 110 006 (India) ● Ph : 91-11-23918117, 2391 6431, 2384 0361 ● Fax : 91-11- 2391 6431 ●E-Mail : eirisidi@bol.net.in ● WebSite : www.eiriindia.org

1308. DENTAL COLLEGE
1309. DENTAL GRADE EUGENOL
1310. DEXTROSE MONOHYDRATE, LIQUID GLUCOSE
1311. DEHYDRATED ONION & ONION POWDER
1312. DEXTROSE POWDER (ANHYDROUS FROM STARCH)
1314. DEXTROSE SALINE SOLUTION
1315. DISTILLERY (I.M.F.L)
1316. DISPOSABLE NEEDLES FOR SYRINGES
1317. DISPRIN
1318. DISTILLED WATER
1319. EMPTY HARD GELATINE CAPSULES
1320. FILLING & PACKING OF CAPSULES
1321. GLUCOSE - D - POWDER
1322. GLYCERINE
1323. HERBAL COSMETICS
1324. HERBAL SHAMPOO
1325. HERBAL HAIR OILS (AYURVEDIC)
1326. HOMOE & BIO-MEDICINES WITH MOTHER TINCTURE
1327. HOMOEPATHIC MEDICINES
1328. HYPODERMIC NEEDLES
1329. I.V. FLUIDS
1330. IBUPROFEN
1331. INFUSION & TRANSFUSION SETS (I.V. SET)
1332. INJECTABLE FOR PHARMACEUTICALS
1333. INJECTION AMPOULES PACKAGING BOX
1334. INTEGERATED SURGICAL COTTON
1335. ICE MAKING PLANT
1336. ICE & COLD STORAGE
1337. LACTOSE & BY PRODUCTS PROCESSING FROM MILK
1338. LICHEN (JATAMANSI CHARILA)
1339. LIQUID GLUCOSE AND ITS BY-PRODUCTS
1340. L-LYSINE MONOHYDRO CHLORIDE
1341. LIQUID GLUCOSE FROM POTATOES
1342 MEDICAL COLLEGE
1343 NICOTINE FROM TOBACCO WASTE
1344. OINTMENT-AYURVEDIC (YELLOW & WHITE)
1345. PHARMACEUTICAL AND FOOD GRADE GELATINE
1346. PHARMACEUTICAL INDUSTRY (TABLETS, CAPSULES, LIQUID, GEL, OINTMENT POWDER INJECTABLE)
1347. PHARMACEUTICAL UNIT (EOU) WITH FORMULA TIONS, INJECTABLES, ETC. PYRIDINE & DERIVATIVES
1348. SALT (IODIZED SALT)
1349. SALINE & INJECTION WATER
1350. SALINE WATER & DEXTROSE SOLUTION (I.V.FLUID IN PLASTIC BOTTLES)
1351. SORBITOL
1352. STARCH (MAIZE)
1353. SURGICAL ADHESIVE PLASTER
1354. SURGICAL BANDAGES
1355. SURGICAL GLOVES
1357. SURGICAL COTTON
1358. SURGICAL COTTON AND BANDAGE
1359. SYNTHETIC CAMPHOR POWDER
1360. TABLETS & CAPSULES
1361. TISSUE CULTURE
1362. TINCTURE FROM RECTIFIED SPIRIT
1363. TRIMETHOPIME
1364. VETERENARY MEDICINES (ONLY FORMULATIONS)
1365. VITAMIN 'C', SORBITOL' ANHYDROUS DEXTROSE, STARCH

PULP, PAPER, STRAW/GREY BOARD, KRAFT PAPER, PACKAGING, PAPER CARRY BAGE, PAPER FROM AGRO WASTE & STATIONERY ETC.

1366. AMMONIA PAPER
1367. AUTOMATIC BOOK BINDING
1368. ADHESIVE (FEVICOL TYPE)
1369. ALL PIN & GEM CLIPS
1370. CARBON PAPER
1371. CARD BOARD
1372. CARBON LESS PAPER
1373. CELLPHANE PAPER
1374. COMPUTER FORMS & SECURITY PRINTING PRESS
1375. CORRUGATED BOARD & BOX (PRINTED & LAMINATED)
1376. CORRUGATED BOARD AND BOXES FROM FROM CARD BOARDS
1377. CORRUGATED CARTONS FROM PLAIN PAPERS
1378. CORRUGATRED PACKING & MATERIAL (BULB & TUBES PACKING)
1379. DESK TOP PUBLISHING
1380. DEFOAMING AGENT FOR PAPER PLANT
1381. DRINKING STRAW PAPER
1382. D.T.P CUM OFFSET PRESS
1383. EGG TRAYS
1384. EXERCISE NOTE BOOK, REGISTER AND PAD
1385. FLEXOGRAPHIC INK
1386. GREETING CARD BY OFFSET PRESS
1387. HAND MADE PAPER FILTER PAPER
1388. HARD BOARD
1389. INJECTION AMPOULES PACKAGING BOXES
1390. INSULATIING PAPER
1391. KRAFT PAPER
1392. KRAFT PAPER FROM BAGASSE
1393. LAMINATED PACKAGING PAPER WITH PRINTING
1394. LAMINATION & COATING ON PAPER
1395. M.G. PAPER FROM WASTE PAPER
1396. MILL PAPER FROM WASTE PAPER
1397. MILL BOARD FROM RICE & WHEAT STRAWS
1398. MILL BOARD FROM WASTE PAPER
1399. MINI PAPER PLANT FROM SISAL
1400. MINI PAPER PLANT
1401. MULTI WALL PAPER SACKS
1402. NEWS PAPER FOR CHILDREN
1403. NEWS PRINT PAPER FROM RICE STRAW BAGASSE
1404. NEWS PAPER CHILDRENS
1405. NEWS PRINT PAPER
1406. OFFSET AND TREADLE TYPE PRINTING PRESS
1407. MILL BOARD BASED ON RICE STRAW
1408. PAPER AND BOARD FROM STRAW
1409. PAPER & PAPER PRODUCTS
1410. PAPER ENVELOPES
1411. PAPER CARRY BAGS
1412. PAPER BOARD CARTON
1413. PAPER CONES FOR LOUD SPEAKERS
1414. PAPER FROM AKRA
1415. PAPER FROM BAGASSE WITH CORRUGATED BOARD & BOXES
1416. PAPER FROM BAMBOO
1417. PAPER GLASSES FOR BEVERAGES
1418. PAPER FROM RICE HUSK & WHEAT HUSK
1419. PAPER FROM TREE BARK, EUCALYPRUS WOOD
1420. PAPER PRODUCTS
1421. PAPER PLANT (WHITE WRITING & NEWS PAPER FOR PULP & WASTE PAPER)
1422. PAPER PLATES, PAPER GLASS
1423. PAPER CONES & TUBES
1425. PAPER PLANT WITH DTP & PRINTING & PUBLISHING UNIT
1426. PAPER BASED PHENOLIC SHEET
1427. PAPER CUP FOR ICE CREAM
1428. PAPER TUBES SPIRAL WINDING COMPOSIT CONTAINER
1429. PAPER LABLE FOR BEER BOTTLES
1430. PARTICLE BOARD & BLACK BOARD WITH SANDING & LAMINATION OF PARTICLE BOARD
1431. PARTICLE BOARD FROM RICE HUSK
1432. POUCH FILLING & MAKING FOR TOMATO SAUCE
1433. POUCH MAKING &

GRAVURE PRINTING
1434. PROCESSING OF PAPER FOR FEEDING IN COMPUTER
1435. PULP FROM BAMBOO & WOOD
1436. PAPER FILES
1437. PLAYING CARDS
1438. ROSIN SIZING AGENT (FOR PAPER PLANT)
1439. SAND PAPER
1440. SANITRY NAPKINS
1441. SILICON COATED PAPER
1442. STENCIL PAPER
1443. STRAW BOARD AND GREY BOARD
1444. STRAW BOARD & MILL BOARD
1445. STRAW BOARD AND PAPER BOARD
1446. TISSUE PAPER FACIAL
1447. TISSUE MOIST TOILETERY CLEANSING TISSUE AND RELATED PRODUCTS
1448. TISSUE PAPER ROLLS
1449. TETRA PACK FOR MILK PACKAGING, GHEE & OTHER LIQUIDS
1450. TOILET PAPER ROLLS
1451. TOILET PAPER & NAPKINS
1452. WAX COATED PRINTED PAPER
1453. WET FACE FRESHNER TISSUE
1454. WHITE WRITING & PRINTING PAPER
1455. WRITING & PRINTING PAPER (PAPER MILLS)

PLASTIC, B.O.P.P, ACRYLIC, DISPOSABLE PLASTIC PRODUCTS, PET PRODUCTS, P.V.C, H.D.P.E, P.P, L.D.P.E., P.U, A.B.S, THERMOFOARMING, MASTER BATCHES, & POLYMER AND RUBBER PRODUCTS, TYRE, TUBE, ADHESIVE, SHEET, COIR & MANY OTHERS

1456. ABS GRANULES FROM ABS SCRAPS FROM OLD T.V. CABINETS, WHITE GOODS ETC.
1457. ACRYLIC BEADS
1458. ACRYLIC COPOLYMER EMULSION
1459. ACRYLIC LATEX
1460. ACRYLIC SHEET
1461. ACRYLIC SHEET & MOULDED PRODUCTS
1462. ACRYLIC TEETH
1463. AUTO TUBES
1464. AUTO FLAPS FOR TRUCKS & BUSES
1465. AUTO TYRES & TUBES
1466. BABY BOTTLES (PLASTIC) WITH WHITESILICON RUBBER NIPPLES
1467. B.O.P.P. FILM
1468. B.O.P.P. PRESSURE SENSITIVE SELF ADHESIVE TAPE
1469. BABY NIPPLE (SILICON)
1470. BABY NIPPLE (BIG SIZE)
1471. BALLOON PLASTIC ADVERTISING
1472. BLISTER FILM PVC
1473. BLISTER PACKAGING & POUCH PAKAGING
1474. BLOW MOULDING PLASTIC CONTAINER
1475. COATING ON METALIZED POLYESTER FILM/METALISED PAPER/ ALIMINIUM FOIL
1476. COATING ON PLASTIC (ELECTROLYSIS) & GLASS
1477. COIR FOAM (RUBBERISED)
1478. COLOUR COATING ON PLASTICS
1479. COLOUR MASTER BATCHES FOR VARIOUS PLASTICS
1480. CYCLE TYRES AND TUBES
1481. DISPOSABLE PLASTIC CUPS GLASSES, ETC.
1482. DISPOSABLE PLASTIC SYRINGES & NEEDLES
1483. DISPOSABLE PLASTIC SYRINGES
1484. DOUGH MOULDING COMPOUND (D.M.C)
1485. EPOXY RESIN
1486. EXPANDED POLYESTRENE MOULDING (THERMOCOLE)
1487. F.R.P AUTO,SCOOTER ROOFS & CEILINGS
1488. F.R.P PRODUCTS (HELMET, WASHBASIN SHEETS, ROOFING SHEETS)
1489. FIBRE REINFORCED PLASTIC (HIGH PRESSURE MOULDING WITH SMC BMC AND DMC)
1490. FIELD RUBBER CONVERTED TO THE 60% LATEX RUBBER
1491. FLEXIBLE P.U. FOAM
1492. FORMALDEHYDE CROCKERY & OTHER ITEMS
1493. FORMALDEHYDE RESIN (UREA, PHENOL,MELEMINE)
1494. GASKET SHEET
1495. GUM BOTTLE (PVC)
1496. GLASS BEADS
1497. HDPE COATED PAPER SACK
1498. H.D.P.E. BAGS
1499. H.D.P.E. CONTAINERS (BLOW MOULDING)
1500. H.D.P.E. CONTAINER, POLY JARS BY INJECTION MOULDING (FOOD GRADE)
1501. H.D.P.E. JERRY CANS
1502. HDPE MANUFACTURING FROM ETHYLALCOHOL
1503. H.D.P.E PIPE AND FITTINGS
1504. H.D.P.E. PIPES
1505. H.D.P.E PRINTED BAGS
1506. H.D.P.E TWINES AND ROPES
1507. H.D.P.E. & L.D.P.E PIPES AND FITTINGS
1508. H.D.P.E/PP BOX STRAPPING
1509. H.D.P.E/PP WOVEN SACKS USING PLAIN LOOMS
1510. HOLOGRAM STICKERS-3D
1511. H.M BAG PLANT WITH PRINTING UNIT
1512. HAWAI CHAPPALS (RUBBER)
1513. I.V PLASTIC BOTTLE
1514. ICE CREAM CUP (PLASTIC)
1515. INJECTION MOULDED AUTO COMPONENTS
1516. INJECTION & BLOW MOULDED PLASTIC PRODUCTS
1517. INJECTION MOULDED PLASTIC PRODUCTS
1518. INTEGERATED COMPLEX ESTER'S & ALLIED PRODUCTS (D.O.P,D.B.P, & ETHYL ACETATE, BUYTL ACETATE, WIRE ENAMELS, JELLY CABLE COMPOUND)
1519. L.D.P.E. (LOW DENSITY POLY ETHYLENE) GRANULES FROM VIRGIN (L.D.P.E. RESIN)
1520. INTEGERATED SURGICAL RUBBER GOODS INDUSTRY
1521. INJECTION MOULDED PLASTIC BALLS
1522. L.D.P.E FROM ETHYL ALCOHOL
1523. LDPE MOULDED PRODUCTS
1524. LAMINATION OF COEXTRUSION MULTILAYER FILM IN ROLL FORM
1525. LATEX RUBBER
1526. LATEX RUBBER CONDOM
1527. MASTER BATCHES (COLOURED, P.V.C, L.D.P.E, H.D.P.E, ETC.)
1528. MELAMINE FORMALHYDE RESIN
1529. MOULDED LUGGAGE
1530. MULTI-LAYER (3 LAYER BAGS)
1531. MULTI-LAYER (3 LAYER) FILM WITH LAMINATION & PRINTING
1532. OIL SEAL
1533. PET BOTTLE/CONTAINERS
1534. PET BOTTLES FROM PRE FORM
1535. PET BOTTLE & MINERAL WATER
1536. PET PRE-FORM FROM PET RESIN
1537. PET PRE-FORM CUM PET BOTTLES
1538. PET PRE-FORM PET BOTTLES CUM MINERAL WATERS
1539. POLY CARBONATE RESIN
1540. PTFE COMPONENTS
1541. PU/PVC SOLE FOR SPORT SHOE BY IMPORTED M/C.
1542. PVC BATTERY SEPARATOR
1543. P.V.C COMPOUNDS (FRESH)
1544. P.V.C COMPOUNDS (SCRAP)
1545. P.V.C ELECTRICAL INSULATING TAPE
1546. P.V.C. EXTRUSION PROFILES
1547. P.V.C FITTINGS
1548. P.V.C FLEXIBLE FUSIBLE POWDER HEAT FUSIBLE POWDER
1549. P.V.C GRANULES (FOR

Above all the "Detailed Project Reports" are available at *"ENGINEERS INDIA RESEARCH INSTITUTE"*. 4449, Nai Sarak (D), Main Road Delhi - 110 006 (India) • Ph : 91-11-23918117, 2391 6431, 2384 0361 • Fax : 91-11- 2391 6431 •E-Mail : eirisidi@bol.net.in • WebSite : www.eiriindia.org

INSULATION & SHEETS GRADES)
1550. P.V.C GRANULES FROM PVC SCRAPS (WITH POLLUTION CONTROL)
1551. P.V.C HOSES
1552. P.V.C LEATHER CLOTH
1553. P.V.C FLEXIBLE PIPES
1554. P.V.C PIPES AND FITTINGS
1555. POLYTHENE BAGS (PRINTED)
1556. PVC PLASTICS FILM SHEET SOFT/RIGID
1557. PVC RESIN AND COMPOUND
1558. PVC RULAR
1559. PVC STABLIZERS (SINGLE PACK SYSTEM)
1560. PVC WIRE AND CABLES
1561. PAPER BASED PHENOLIC SHEET FOR ELECTRICAL
1562. PHENOL FORMALDEHYDE RESIN
1563. PHENOLIC RESIN
1564. PLASTIC BEADS FROM PLASTIC SCRAPS
1565. PLASTIC BUTTONS
1566. PLASTIC CANS
1567. PLASTIC COLLAPSIBLE TUBE
1568. PLASTIC CORRUGATED SHEET & BOXES
1569. PLASTIC FILM AND SHEETS WITH PRINTING FLEXO & ROTO/LDPE/HDPE/PP/HM/PVC
1570. PLASTIC FILTER MASTER BATCH & OTHER MASTER BATCHES FOR VARIOUS PLASTICS
1571. PLASTIC JERRY CANS
1572. PLASTIC GRANULES OR POWDER FROM PLASTIC SCRAP
1573. PLASTIC INJECTION MOULDED T.V. CABINETS
1574. PLASTIC ITEMS MANUFAC TURE FROM POWDER MELAMINE
1575. PLASTIC GOODS
1576. PLASTIC PIPES & TARPAULINES
1577. PLASTIC SHEET FROM SCRAP
1578. PLASTIC PLANT (BLOW MOULDING & INJECTION MOULDING)
1579. PLASTIC PRODUCTS (GOLD, SILVER, NICKEL)
1580. PLASTIC TOYS
1581. POLYESTER BEADING
1582. POLYESTER FILM
1583. POLYTHENE BAGS & AUTOMATIC PRINTING
1584. POLYTHENE PRINTED BAGS
1585. POLYURETHANE FOAM AND ITS PRODUCTS
1586. PROPYLENE FILM (PRINTED) & BAG MANUFACTURING
1587. PLASTIC MATS
1588. RAINBOW COLOUR ON PVC FILM & SHEET
1589. RED MUD PVC PIPES AND FITTINGS
1590. RE-RUBBERISED OF SOLID TYPE
1591. RESIN COATED SAND REXINE
1592. REXINE CLOTH & ALLIED PRODUCTS
1593. RUBBER ADHESIVE
1594. RUBBER AUTO PARTS
1595. RUBBER BELTING
1596. RUBBER MOULDING UNIT INCLUDING LINING RUBBER SHEETING
1597. RUBBER RECLAIMING
1598. RUBBER ROLLERS FOR TEXTILE MILLS & PAPER INDUSTRIES
1599. RUBBER & PLASTIC SHEETS, MATS & FLAPS
1600. RUBBER SHEET AND ALLIED HOSPITAL RUBBER GOODS
1601. RUBBERIZED PVC GASKET
1602. RUBBERISED COIR
1603. RUBBER COMPOUND FOR AUTOMOBILES
1604. SAFETY BELTS
1605. SILVER AND GOLD PLATING ON PVC AND NYLON-6
1606. SILICONE RUBBER NIPPLES/ TEATS
1607. SPECTACLE FRAMES (PLASTIC)
1608. SPUNGE RUBBER
1609. SURGICAL EXAMINATION GLOVES
1610. SYNTHETIC PEARL COATING ON POLYSTYRENE BEADS
1611. SYNTHETIC RUBBER ADHESIVE
1612. TEFLON MANUFACTURING
1613. TEFLON TAPE
1614. TEFLON TAPES & CABLES
1615. THERMOCOLE SHEET AND MOULDED PRODUCTS EXPANDED POLYESTERENE EXTRUSION PROFILES
1616. THERMOFORMED PACKAGING (BLISTER PACKAGING & POUCH PACKAGING)
1617. THERMOPLASTIC POLYURETHANE
1618. THERMOFORMED CUPS, PLATES & GLASS WITH HIPS SHEET
1619. THERMOCOLE
1620. THERMOCOLE BASED DISPOSABLE GLASS, CUPS & PLATES
1621. TOOTH BRUSHES
1622. TOY BALLOON, DECORA TIVE & INDUSTRIAL BALLOONS
1623. TREAD RUBBER
1624. TYRE RETREADING (HOT)
1625. TYRE RETREADING BY COLD PROCESS
1626. TYRE TUBES & FLAPS
1627. TYRE & TUBES
1628. UNSATURATED POLYESTER FOR REXINE
1629. V-BELT AND FAN BELT
1630. VINYL ASBESTOS AND PVC WALL PAPER
1631. VITON (FLUORO ELASTOMER)

SOAP, COSMETICS & PERFUMS

1632. ACID SLURRY, SYNTHETIC DETERGENT POWDER
1632. ACID SLURRY
1633. AGARBATTI SYNTHETIC, PERFUMERY COMPOUND
1634. AFTER SHAVE LOTION
1635. ANTISEPTIC CREAM
1636. BETA IONONE
1637. BLEACHING POWDER
1638. BLUE DETERGENT POWDER
1639. CLEANING POWDER (VIMTYPE)
1640. COLD CREAM
1641. COLOURED FLAME & PERFUMED CANDLES (RED, BLUE, GREEN FLAME)
1642. COSMETIC INDUSTRY (MODERN)
1643. COSMETIC INDUSTRY (SHAMPOO, SPRAY PERFUME, TALCUM POWDER
1644. DETERGENT POWDER (ARIEL TYPE)
1645. DETERGENT POWDER (NIRMA TYPE) FULLY AUTOMATIC PLANT
1646. DETERGENT WASHING POWDER
1647. FISH OIL SOAP
1648. GLYCERINE TRANSPARENT SOAP
1649. HAIR REMOVING CREAM
1650. HERBAL COSMETICS
1651. HERBAL SHAMPO & CREAM
1652. HERBAL/AYURVEDIC COSMETICS
1653. INCENSE POWDER,INCENSE STICKS & INCENSE CAKE
1654. OPTICAL WHITENERS
1655. ROSE OIL EXTRACTION
1656. SHAMPOOS (COCONUT OIL BASED COLD PROCESS)
1657. SHAVING CREAM
1658. SINDUR (KUMKUM)
1659. SOAP COATED PAPER
1660. SPRAY DRIED DETERGENT POWDER
1661. STAIN REMOVER
1662. TALCUM POWDER (FACE & TOILET POWDER)
1663. TOILET AND HERBAL SOAP
1664. TOOTH PASTE & POWDER
1365. WASHING DETERGENT POWDER AND WASHING SOAP
1666. WASHING POWDER LIQUID DETERGENTS,LOTION & SHAMPOO

TEXTILE INDUSTRIES, READYMADE GARMENTS, COTTON, DYEING, BLEACHING, CLOTH, HOSIERY, POWER LOOM, HAND LOOM, WOOLLEN, SILK, SOCKS, SURGICAL COTTON & MANY OTHERS

1667. ANGORA RABBIT WOOL
1668. BUCKRAM
1669. CANVAS SHOES, JUNGLE BOOT, BOOT RUBBER KNEES & BOOT COMBAT
1670. CARPET FROM COTTON WASTE
1671. CERAMIC THREAD GUIDE
1672. COTTON BUDS/SWABS
1673. COTTON FROM WASTE YARN
1674. COTTON ROLLS
1675. COTTON SPIDERS FOR LOUD SPEAKERS
1676. DENIM CLOTH
1677. DENIM CLOTH (INTEGERATED UNIT WITH BLEACHING, DYEING AND PRINTING)
1678. DISPERSENT FOR TEXTILE
1679. DYEING & BLEACHING
1680. DYEING OF HANK YARN
1681. EMULSIFIER FOR WOOL BATCHING OIL
1682. EMBROIDERY ON FABRICS
1683. GARMENT DYEING, WASHING & STITCHING (JEANS, JACKETS, SKIRTS & SHIRTS)
1684. GOVES KNITTING
1685. GUNNY BAGS
1687. HDPE WOVEN SACKS
1688. HDPE TARPAULINS USING PLAIN LOOM WITH LAMINATION
1689. HDPE/PP WOVEN SACKS USING CIRCULAR LOOMS
1690. HOSIERY CLOTH (COTTON) PROCESSING (BLEACHING, DYEING, FINISHING OF CLOTH)
1691. HOSIERY INDUSTRY
1692. HOSIERY MERCERISING
1693. HOSIERY PRODUCTS LIKE VEST, BRIEF, T-SHIRTS & SOCKS
1694. JACQUARD FABRICS
1695. JUTE COIR, GRASS ROPE/ SUTLI MAKING
1696. JUTE FELT
1697. JUTE TWINES
1698. KNITTED FABRICS
1699. LAMINATED JUTE BAGS
1700. LAMINATION OF HDPE WOVEN CLOTH (JUTE,COTTON, PAPER)
1701. NYLON YARN CRIMPING, DOUBLING AND BLEACHING
1702. PIGMENT BINDER FOR TEXTILE PRINTING
1704. POLYESTER RESIN FOR WIRE ENAMEL
1705. POLYESTER RESIN
1706. POLYESTER YARN FROM WASTE POLYESTER ZIP FASTENERS
1707. POWER LOOM
1708. READYMADE GARMENTS & HOSIERY
1709. READYMADE GARMENTS MERCHANDISE
1710. READYMADE GARMENTS & COVERS
1711. READYMADE GARMENTS & EMBROIDERY OF GOWNS, SHIRTS, BLOUSES, T-SHIRTS ETC. (ONLY LADIES)
1712. READYMADE SALWAR SUIT
1713. RECOVERY OF NYLON FROM NYLON WASTE
1714. ROTARY PRINTING AND DYEING ON COTTON, SYNTHETIC TEXTILE
1715. SANITARY NAPKINS
1716. SCREEN PRINTING ON COTTON CLOTH
1717. SEWING THREAD REELS & BALLS MAKING INDUSTRIES
1718. SCREEN PRINTING ON COTTON, POLYESTER & ACRYLIC
1719. SHAWLS (WOOLLEN)
1720. SHOE LACES
1721. SILK FABRICS ON HANDLOOM
1722. SOCKS KNITTING
1723. SPINNING, DOUBLING DYEING MERCERISING & BLEACHING OF COTTON YARN
1724. SPINNING & CARDING OF WOOL INTO YARNS
1725. STARCH BOOK BINDING CLOTH
1726. SURAT JARI
1727. SURGICAL COTTON & BANDAGE
1728. SYNTHETIC TEXTILE INDUSTRY(SUITING, SHIRTING, SAREES) TERRY CLOTH
1729. T-SHIRTS
1730. TOWELS, BED SHEET COVERS
1731. TERRY TOWEL
1732. TERRY FABRICS WEAVING UNIT
1733. TEXTILE AUXILLIARIES & CHEMICALS
1734. TEXTILE BLEACHING, DYEING & FINISHING & PRINTING OF COTTON FABRICS
1735. TEXTILE (HOSIERY)
1736. TEXTILE MILL
1737. TEXTILE DYEING & PRINTING
1738. TEXTILE PRINTING (JOB WORK)
1739. TEXTILE PIGMENT PRINTING BINDER
1740. TOWEL (TERRY)
1741. VELVET CLOTH BY FLOCKING PROCESS
1742. VISCOSE STAPLE FIBRE
1743. WADDING OIL (100%) FOR WADDING OF COTTON HOSIERY CLOTH IN THE DYEING PROCESS
1744. WEAVING OF DASUTI CLOTH WITH PRINTING, DYEING, EMBROIDERY & FINISHING
1745. WASHING OF JEANS & OTHER GARMENTS
1746. WORSTED WOOLLEN YARN CLOTH
1747. ZARI GLITTER SALMA SITARA OF PLASTIC FILM

INFOTECH/IT, HOSPITALITY, HOSPITAL, COLLEGE, SCHOOL, MEDICAL, ENTERTAINMENT CLUB, WARE HOUSING & REAL ESTATE, PROJECTS

1748. AMUSEMENT PARK
1749. AMUSEMENT PARK CUM WATER PARK
1750. BANQUET HALL
1751. CALL CENTER (DOMESTIC)
1752. CALL CENTER (INTERNATIONAL)
1753. CHILDREN RECREATION CENTRE
1754. COLD STORAGE
1755. COMMUNITY HALL
1756. COMPUTER EDUCATION INSTITUTE
1757. COMPUTER SOFTWARE
1758. COLLEGE
1759. CYBER CAFE
1760. DENTAL CLINIC
1761. DENTAL COLLEGE
1762. DIAGONOSTIC CENTRE
1763. E-COMMERCE/BUSINESS
1764. E-SCHOOL (Rs. 5000/-)
1765. ENGINEERING COLLEGE
1766. ENTERTAINMENT CLUB
1767. ENTERTAINMENT CLUB, HOLIDAY RESORT, 4 STAR HOTEL, AMUSEMENT PARK CUM WATER PARK, MUSHROOM & ITS PRODUCTS, FISH FARMING, LAKE FOR BOATING, DEER PARK
1768. FASHION TECHNOLOGY INSTITUTE
1769. FAST FOOD PARLOUR
1770. FIVE STAR HOTEL
1771. FOOD PARLOUR
1772. FRANCHISE TRAINING PROGRAMME FOR IIT & ENGINEERING ENTRANCE EXAMS.
1773. GOLF COURSE
1774. HEALTH CLUB, BEAUTY PARLOUR
1775. HEALTH CLUB AND FITNESS CENTER
1776. HEALTH RESORTS
1777. HOLIDAY RESORTS
1778. HOLIDAY RESORT CUM

ENTERTAINMENT CLUB WITH 4 STAR HOTEL
1779. HOSPITALS
1780. ICE CREAM PARLOUR
1781. INTERNET SERVICE PROVIDER (I.S.P.)
1782. MEDICAL COLLEGE
1783. MEDICAL COLLEGE, HOSPITAL & RESEARCH INSTITUTE
1784. MEDICAL TRANSCRIPTION CENTRE
1785. MENTAL RETARDATION HOSPITAL & CEREBRAL PALSY
1786. MOTEL/SMALL HOTEL
1787. MULTISTOREY COMMERCIAL COMPLEX
1788. MULTISTOREY RESIDENTIAL COMPLEX
1789. NURSERY SCHOOL
1790. NATURE CARE CENTRE
1791. NURSING HOME
1792. ONLINE SHOPPING MALL (RS. 5000/- REPORT)
1793. PORTAL
1794. REHABILITATION CENTRE FOR AGED & NEEDY PERSONS
1795. RESIDENTIAL CUM COMMERCIAL COMPLEX
1796. RESTAURANT
1797. RESTAURANT WITH PUB
1798. SCHOOL (PRIMARY)
1799. SCHOOL (HIGHER SECONDARY)
1800. THREE STAR HOTEL
1801. TOURIST CLUB
1802. TRAINING INSTITUTE FOR MEDICAL TRANSCRIPTION
1803. VIDEO FILM STUDIO
1804. WARE HOUSE
1805. WEBSITE DESIGN & E-MAIL REGISTERING

AGRO BASED INDUSTRIES

1806. COAL BRIQUETTES FROM AGROWASTE
1807. FURFURALFROM RICEHULL
1808. MUSHROOM CULTIVATION & PROCESSING (BUTTON)
1809. MUSHROOM GROWING & PROCESSING WITH AIR CONDITIONING
1810. MUSHROOM CULTIVATION & PROCESSING UNIT DEHYDRATION & PACKAGING OF OYSTER & PADDY STRAW MUSHROOMS
1811. ORGANIC MANURE
1812. PAPAYA CULTIVATION
1813. PAPAYA & TOMATO CULTIVATION
1814. PROCESSING & UTILISATION OF COCONUT
1815. PROCESSING OF SHEEP HAIR TO PRODUCE WOOL

BAKERY, CONFECTIONERY & FOOD PRODUCTS

1816. AGROLACTOR SOYA MILK
1817. APPLE FRUIT JUICE WITH CANNING BOTTLING
1818. AYURVEDIC SHARBAT
1819. BAKERY UNIT (PASTRIES, BREAD, BUNS, CAKE, TOFFEE ETC.)
1820. BAKING POWDER
1821. BANANA & ITS BY PRODUCTS
1822. BANANA POWDER
1823. BANANA WAFERS
1824. BANANA CULTIVATION
1825. BEER INDUSTRY
1826. DEHULLING OF JAUN FOR BEER
1827. BEER & WINE
1828. BEER, ALCOHOL, IMFL
1829. BESEN PLANT
1830. BISCUIT PLANT
1831. BREAD & BISCUIT PLANT
1832. BOTTLING PLANT COUNTRY LIQUOR FROM RECTIFIED SPIRIT
1833. BRANDY
1834. BREAD RUSKS
1835. CANNED FRUITS & VEGETABLES
1836. CANNING & PRESERVATION OF MEAT
1837. CANNING & PRESERVATION OF VEGETABLES
1838. CANNING OF MANGO PULP & MANGO SLICES
1839. CARBONATED BEVERAGS
1840. CASHEW FENI
1841. CASHEW NUT (DRIED & FRIED)
1842. CATTLE BREEDING
1843. CATTLE BREEDING & DAIRY FARM TO PRODUCE MILK
1844. CATTLE FEED FROM TAPIOCA
1845. CHEWING GINGER & AMLOKI
1846. CHEWING GUM
1847. CHILLI SAUCE
1848. CHILLI POWDER
1849. CHOCOLATE
1850. CIDER PLANT
1851. COCOA POWDER
1852. COCOA BUTTER & COCOA POWDER
1853. COCONUT SHELL POWDER
1854. COCONUT WATER
1855. COCONUT SWEET (WATERY)
1656. COCONUT MILK POWDER (DEHYDRATED)
1857. COCONUT PRODUCTS & BY PRODUCTS (INTEGRATED PLANT)
1858. COLD DRINK
1859. CURRY POWDER
1860. DAIRY FOR MILK PROCESSING (GHEE, BUTTER & PANEER)
1861. DAIRY PRODUCTS
1862. DAIRY PRODUCTS MILK PACKAGING IN POUCH (GHEE, BUTTER, ETC.
1863. DAIRY FARM TO PRDUCE MILK WITH PACKAGING (COW)
1864. DAIRY FARM TO PRDUCE MILK WITH PACKAGING (BUFALLOE)
1865. DAIRY FARM & MILK PRODUCTS
1866. DAL MOTH, CHANACHUR & BHUJIYA
1867. DEHYDRATION OF FRUITS & VEGETABLE
1868. DESICCATED COCONUT POWDER FROM COCONUTS
1869. DEHYDRATION & CANNING OF FRUITS & VEGETABLES
1870. DRY FRUIT ROASTING & PACKAGING
1871. DRYING OF RED CHILLIES, HALDI, DHANIYA, PEAS & GROUND NUT
1872. EGG POWDER
1873. FISH CANNING IN TIN & POUCHES
1874. FISH DEHYRATION (DRYING OF FISH)
1875. FISH MEAL
1876. FISH PROCESSING (BEAST FREEZING PROCESSES)
1877. FLAVOURS FOR FOOD INDUSTRIES
1878. FLOUR MILL (ROLLER)
1879. FROZEN MEAT
1880. FOOD DEHYDRATION (FRUITS & VEGETABLES)
1881. FRIED & ROASTED GROUND NUT, GRAMS, PEAR ETC.
1882. FRUIT JUICE MAKING & PACKAGING IN PLASTIC CONTAINER
1883. FRUIT JUICE IN TETRA PACK (DRINKS)
1884. FRUIT JUICE, SQUASHES, SAUCE & KETCHUP, JAM, JELLY, VINEGAR ETC.
1885. GARLIC FLAKES
1886. GARLIC POWDER
1887. GHEE & BUTTER
1888. GINGER (PULVERISED)
1889. GINGER GLAZING & PRESERVATION
1890. GINGER STORAGE
1891. GINGER PROCESSING
1892. GINGER OIL & GINGER DUST
1893. GINGER POWDER (DRY) & OLEORESIN
1894. GRAPE DEHYDRATION
1895. GRAPE CULTIVATION
1896. GRAPE JUICE
1897. HONEY PROCESSING & PACKAGING
1898. ICE CREAM & ICE CANDY
1899. ICE CUBE
1900. INVERT SUGAR
1901. IDLI MIX, DOSA MIX SAMBHAR MIX, VADA MIX, GULAB JAMUN MIX
1902. INSTANT COFFEE & INSTANT TEA

1903. INSTANT NOODLES
1904. INSTANT SOUPS
1905. IODIZED SALT FROM CRUDE SALT
1906. JAM CHUTNEY PICKLES & SQUASHES
1907. KATHA MANUFACTURING
1908. LECITHIN (SOYA BASED)
1909. LEMON & ITS PRODUCTS
1910. MACARONI MANUFACTURING
1911. MACARONI, SPAGHETTI, VERMICELLI & NOODLES
1912. MAIZE & ITS BY PRODUCTS MALTING PLANT
1913. MANGO PAPPAD (AAM PAPPAD)
1914. MANGO POWDER RIPE
1915. MANGO POWDER
1916. MANGO PROCESSING & CANNING (MANGO PULP)
1917. MEAT PROCESSING (CHICKEN MUTTON)
1918. MEAT PROCESSING (BUFFALO)
1919. MENTHOL BOLD FROM MENTHOL FLAKES
1020. MILK POWDER
1921. MILK POWDER & GHEE
1922. MILK POWDER, GHEE & SPICES
1923. MILK PRESERVATION & MARKETING TO WHOLE SELLERS
1924. MILK PRESERVATION & MARKETING TO WHOLE SELLERS (IN POUCHES)
1925. MILK TOFFEE MANUFACTURES
1926. MINERAL WATER
1927. MINERAL WATER IN POUCHES
1928. MINI FLOUR MILL ATTA MAIDA, SUJI & WHEAT BRAN
1929. MITHAI/HALWAI (SWEET & NAMKEEN)
1930. MUTTON PROCESSING
1931. PAN MASALA (MEETHA, SADA, ZARDA) MAKING & PACKING
1932. PAN MASALA AND POUCH MAKING
1933. PANEER (CHEESE)
1934. PAPAD & BARIYAN
1935. PAPAD PLANT
1936. PEPSICOLA IN POLYTUBES
1937. PETHA PACKAGING
1938. PICKLES
1939. PIGGERY/MEAT/CHICKEN PROCESSING
1940. PINE APPLE JUICE CANNING
1941. POTATO & ONION POWDER
1942. POTATO & ONION FLAKES
1943. POTATO CHIPS
1944. POTATO GRANULES
1945. POUCH FILLING FOR SAUNF SUPARI ILAICHI ETC.
1946. PRESERVATION OF RAWS MANGO JUICE
1947. PROCESSED CHEESE & MARINE PDTS.
1948. PULP FROM TARMARIND
1949. READYMATE PROCESSED FOOD
1950. RICE & CORN FLAKES
1951. RICE BASMATI (TRADING)
1952. RICE POLISHING & PACKAGING IN POUCH
1953. ROASTED/SALTED/MASALA/ CASHEW NUTS ALMONDS & PEA NUT
1954. ROLLER FLOUR MILL

INFOTECH/IT PROJECTS

1955. MEDICAL TRANSCRIPTION
1956. E-COMMERCE
1957. CYBERCAFE
1958. INTERNET SERVICE PROVIDER (ISP)
1959. COMPUTER EDUCATION CENTRE
1960. PORTAL (WEBSITE DESIGN)
1961. CALL CENTRE

TERMS AND CONDITIONS

FOR INDIA

1. Please ask for Quotations/ Proforma Invoice for Each *"Market Survey Cum Detailed Techno Economic Feasibility Report"*. Payable in advance through Draft/M.O./Cash in favour of 'ENGINEERS INDIA RESEARCH INSTITUTE', Delhi. Delivery by Regd. Post within 2 Days. (Postage Free)

2. Ask for a Hi Tech Projects, monthly magazine. Each issue covers approx. 75 project profiles.

FOR OVERSEAS

1. Please ask for Quotations/ Proforma Invoice in US $ for Each *"Market Survey Cum Detailed Techno Economic Feasibility Report"*. Payable in advance through Draft in favour of 'ENGINEERS INDIA RESEARCH INSTITUTE', Delhi (Payable in India). Delivery by Regd. Air Mail Post within 3 Days. (Postage Free).

2. Ask for a Hi Tech Projects, monthly magazine. Each issue covers approx. 75 project profiles.

ENGINEERS INDIA RESEARCH INSTITUTE

4449, Nai Sarak (D), Main Road, Delhi - 110 006 (India)
Ph:. 91-11-23918117, 23916431, 23840361, 9312282370
Fax: 91-11-23916431 E-Mail : eirisidi@bol.net.in
Website:www.eiriindia.org
Also at : 4/27, Roop Nagar, Near Roop Nagar No. 1 School, Delhi - 110 007 (India) Ph:. 91-11-2384 0361

PAINTS, VARNISH, COATINGS, POLYMERS & PLASTICS, RESINS, FIBER GLASS, PVC COMPOUNDING, RUBBER CHEMICALS & GOODS

PAINT PIGMENT VARNISH & LACQUER MANUFACTURING

ISBN. 81-86732-16-0 # Rs. 450/-

The Book covers Process, Formulations, Technology, Project Profiles on various Paint, Varnish, Lacquer manufacturing industries. Suppliers of Plant, Equipments and Machinery with Raw Materials have also been incorporated.

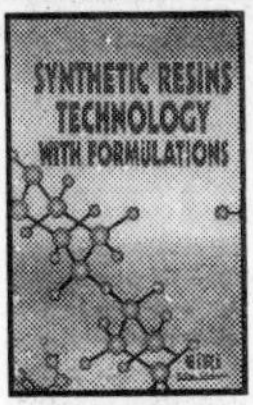

SYNTHETIC RESINS TECHNOLOGY WITH FORMULATIONS

ISBN. 81-86732-40-3 * Rs. 800/-

Book covers latest technology to manufacture various Synthetic Resins with formulae including epoxy resin, alkyd resins, acrylics, ion-exchange resin, melamine formaldehyde resin, phenol formaldehyde resin, polyester resin, polyvinyl acetate, polyvinyl alcohol, pvc resin & plastisol, silicones, etc. Suppliers of Machinery and Raw Materials.

PAINT VARNISH SOLVENTS & COATING TECHNOLOGY

ISBN. 81-86732-44-6 * Rs. 750/-

Introduction, General Pigments Physical Properties, Pigments Processing, Plasticizers and Solvents, Synthetic Resins, Cellulose Ester and Ether Products, Varnishes, Coatings, Industrial Paints & Coatings, Testing & Evaluation, Miscellaneous Formulae, Project Profiles, Suppliers of Raw Materials, Suppliers of Plant and Machinery, Present Manufacturers, Packaging Material Addresses etc.

PLASTIC COMPOUNDING MASTERBATCHES, PET AND OTHER PLASTIC PROCESSING INDUSTRIES

ISBN. 81-86732-49-7 * Rs. 750/-

Book covers Polyethylene, Extrusion, Injection Moulding, Blowmoulding, PET, Rotational Moulding, Post Extrusion Process, Vacuum Metallizing, Identification of Plastic Materials, Thermosetting Plastics, Recycling, PVC Compounding with Formulations, Colour Master Batch, Co-Extruded Multilayer Film, Egg Trays, Suppliers of Plant, Equipments & Machineries, Suppliers of Raw Materials etc.

TECHNOLOGY OF COATINGS, RESINS, PIGMENTS & INKS INDUSTRIES

ISBN. 81-86732-64-0 ★ Rs. 975/-

Introduction, Coating Properties, Polyurethane Coatings, Powder Coatings, UV Curable Powder Coatings, Polyurethane Coating, Pigments Dispersions, Colour of Pigments, Caprolactone Acrylic, Additives in Paints, Development in Resin for Powder Coatings, etc.

HAND BOOK OF FIBRE GLASS MOULDING

ISBN 81-86732-94-2 # Rs. 450/-

Reinforced Plastics & Composites, Product Introduction, Designing in Fibre Reinforced Plastics, Details of Moulds, Processes of Moulding, Polyester Resins, Catalysts, Accelerators and Inhibitors for Unsaturated Polyester Resins, Epoxy Resins, Fibre Glass, Fibre Glass Wire etc.

MOULDS DESIGN & PROCESSING HANDBOOK

ISBN. 81-86732-23-3 * Rs. 495/-

Covers Classification of Moulds, Vent in The Mould, Ejection Mechanism, Production Schedule of Plastic Injection Mould, Steel for Injection Mould, Trouble Shooting Tips, Properties of Plastics, Injection Mould Design, Compression and Transfer Mould - Pot Calculations, Blow Mould Design Aspects, Standard Mould Parts, Conversion Table etc.

HAND BOOK OF POLYMER & PLASTIC TECHNOLOGY

ISBN 81-86732-92-6 # Rs. 950/-

Basic concept of high polymer systems, Raw materials, Polyesters,Thermoplastics, Plasticisers, Stabilisers, Fillers, Colourants, & Special additives, Extrusion, Injection & blow Moulding, Thermoforming, Miscellaneous Processing Techniques etc.

PLASTIC PROCESSING AND PACKAGING INDUSTRIES

ISBN. 81-86732-11-X # Rs. 450/-

Introduction, Plastic Processing, Injection & Blow Moulding, Compounding & Processing of PVC, PU, Project profiles and directory section. The book is covering with the 54 fully detailed chapters.

TECHNOLOGY OF PVC COMPOUNDING AND ITS APPLICATIONS

ISBN 81-86732-88-8 # Rs. 900/-

The book cover PVC Resins Manufacture & Properties, Processing of PVC, Additives for PVC, Compounding, Compounding of PVC Pastes, Speciality Plastic Compounds & Masterbatches, PVC compounds, Xlpe cable compound, jelly filled tele communication cable compound & sheating compound etc.

RUBBER CHEMICALS & PROCESSING INDUSTRIES

ISBN. 81-86732-15-2 * Rs. 400/-

The book covers Technology of Rubber Chemicals and Manufacturing of Rubber Products/Goods.Various Project Profiles are given, Suppliers of Raw Materials and Machinery are also provided plus much more other details are provided.

TECHNOLOGY OF RUBBER & RUBBER GOODS INDUSTRIES

ISBN. 81-86732-59-4 ★ Rs. 900/-

Natural rubber, Classification, Properties, Uses and Manufacture, Latex processing and applications, Chemical aspects of rubber technology, Physical aspects of rubber technology, Styrene Butadiene Rubber (SBR), Processing and curing of Polybutadiene and Polyisoprene, Manufacture and Processing of EPDM etc.

ENGINEERS INDIA RESEARCH INSTITUTE Mobile : 9811437895

4449, Nai Sarak, Main Road, Delhi - 110 006 (INDIA) Ph./Fax : 91-11- 23918117, 23916431, 23840361

BAKERY, CONFECTIONERY, DAIRY FARM, MILK PROCESSING, SOAPS & DETERGENT, MEDICINAL & AROMATIC PLANTS AND HERBS CULTIVATION

HAND BOOK OF MODERN BAKERY PRODUCTS

 # ISBN. 81-86732-61-6 # Rs. 750/-

Baking, Biscuits, Breads & Rolls, Cakes, Cookies and Pastries, Bread Making, Cake-Making, Cookies, Pastry, Cookies, Biscuits, Cakes, Buns Pies, Icings Breads & Pizzas, Health Breads, Chicken Patties, Noodles, Fried Snack Foods: Sev, Bhujia, Bombay Mix, Fried Nuts and Dal, Packaging for biscuits, Chapati Making Unit, Details of Plant & Machinery, Bakery Machinery etc.

MILK PROCESSING & DAIRY PRODUCTS INDUSTRIES

ISBN. 81-86732-47-0 * Rs. 750/-

Book covers Milk Products, Cheese, Butter, Yoghurt, Evaporated and Condensed Milks, Dried Milk/Milk Powder, Ice-Cream, Some Dried Dairy Products, Dahi, Packaging of Milk and Milk Products, Fermented Milk Products, Dairy Products, Coffee, Paneer, Cheese, Yoghurt, Tea, Casein, Suppliers of Machineries.

HAND BOOK OF BAKERY INDUSTRIES

ISBN. 81-86732-8-7 * Rs. 350/-

Bakery Raw Materials, Bread Making Processes, Biscuits, Cookies & Crackers, Sponge Cakes, Pies & Puff Pastries, Sweet Yeast Dough Products, Bakery Machinery, Confectionery, Process, Packaging for Biscuits, Project Profile of Bakery, Cofectionery, Bubble Gum Plant etc., Manufacturers & Suppliers of Machineries, Manufacturers & Suppliers of Raw Materials etc.

HAND BOOK OF ICE CREAM TECHNOLOGY & FORMULAE

ISBN. 81-86732-70-5 ★ Rs. 525/-

Introduction, Nutritional Value and Classification of Ice cream, Composition and Properties of Ice Cream Mixes, Raw Material used to Produce Ice Cream, Manufacturing Process, Ice Cream Freezing, Ice

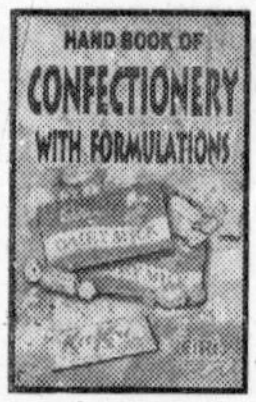

HAND BOOK OF CONFECTIONERY WITH FORMULATIONS

ISBN. 81-86732-35-7 * Rs. 600/-

The book is covering Confectionery Processes & formulations, Caramels Toffees, Butterscotch Fudge, Chocolates, Supari, Nougat, Soft Nougat, Milk Toffee, Chocolate & Confectionery Spreads Chocolates Syrups, Multiple Confectionery Bars, Project Profiles, Details of Plant & Machinery, Addresses etc.

HAND BOOK OF DAIRY FARMING

ISBN. 81-86732-66-7 ★ Rs. 375/-

Dairy Farming, Ration for cattles, Housing for dairy animals, Livestock Management, Care for dry cows, Livestock records maintenance, Manufacturing Process, Clean milk production, Dairy cattle economics, Diseases of Animals, Milk Storage, Distribution of Milk, Suppliers of Equipments, Seeds, Drugs, etc., Packaging of Milk, Plant Economics of Dairy Farm.

HAND BOOK OF DAIRY FORMULATIONS PROCESSES & MILK PROCESSING INDUSTRIES

ISBN. 81-86732-10-1 ★ Rs. 375/-

Book covers Introduction, Manufacturing, Technologies, Packaging, Formulations of various Milk & Milk Based Products, Project Profiles on Dairy & Milk Products including Baby Cerial Food & Milk Powder, Casein from Milk, Confectionery Industry, Dairy Farm, Dairy Products, Flavoured Milk, Ice Cream, Milk Powder, Milk Preservation, and Suppliers of Raw Materials and Machineries with Technologies etc.

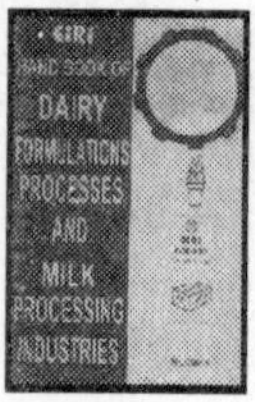

HAND BOOK OF SYNTHETIC DETERGENTS WITH FORMULATIONS

ISBN. 81-86732-43-8 # Rs. 900/-

Group of Synthetic Detergents, Synthesis of Detergents, Manufacture of Synthetic Detergents with Formulae, Testing of Detergents and Soaps, Project Profiles, Suppliers of Machinery and Raw Materials, Acid Slurry, Sirf Excel Type Detergent, Ariel Type Detergent, Dry Mix Process etc.

HAND BOOK OF MEDICINAL & AROMATIC PLANTS

CULTIVATION, UTILISATION& EXTRACTION PROCESSES

ISBN 81-86732-68-3 * Rs. 875/- or US $ 100/-

Book covers Cultivation of Dioscorea, Production of Ergot Alkaloids, Nomenclatural Ambiguity of Medicinal Plants, Biotechnology & Genetic Improvement of Medicinal Plants, Improvement on Medicinal Plants Cultivation, Safed Musli, Lavender, Lemon Grass, Palmarosa, Patchouli, etc.

MANUFACTURE OF HOUSEHOLD SOAPS, TOILET SOAPS & OTHER SOAPS WITH FORMULATIONS

ISBN. 81-86732-53-5 # Rs. 750/-

Soap base manufacture, Solid, household and toilet soaps manufacture, Production of soap base, Perfuming, Manufacturing process & formulations, Miscellaneous formulae, Scourig bar, Detergent cake & powder, Toilet & herbal soap, Laundry soap, Liquid soap, Complete plant Suppliers, Suppliers of chemicals etc.

HAND BOOK OF HERBS, MEDICINAL & AROMATIC PLANTS CULTIVATION

ISBN. 81-86732-36-5 + Rs. 650/-

Aloe Vera, Ashwagandha, Belladonna, Buckwheat, Datura, Digitalis, Discorea, Duboisa, Foxglove, Geranium, Guggal, Hop, Henna, Isabgol, Liquorice, Lemon Grass, Long Pepper, Neem, Parrot Tree, Perivinkle, Primrose, Pyrethrum, Rauvolfia, Roselle, Roselle, Rutin Bearing Eucalyptus, Rose, Senna, Steroid Bearing Solanum etc.

PROFITABLE SMALL SCALE MANUFACTURE OF SOAPS & DETERGENTS

ISBN. 81-86732-25-X # Rs. 375/-

Raw materials, soap manufacture, soap from non edible oil, soap from soap stock, Medicated soap, Shaving soap, shaving creams, synthetic detergent powder, detergent cake and powder, Enzyme detergent powder, Project Profiles on various Soap and Detergent projects, Suppliers of Plant and Machinery and raw materials etc.

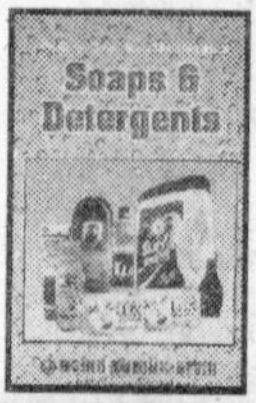

ENGINEERS INDIA RESEARCH INSTITUTE Mobile : 9811437895

4449, Nai Sarak, Main Road, Delhi - 110 006 (INDIA) Ph./Fax : 91-11- 23918117, 23916431, 23840361